Documents in World History,
1945-1967

Documents in World History, 1945-1967

*

W. Bruce Lincoln
Northern Illinois University

 CHANDLER PUBLISHING COMPANY
124 Spear Street • San Francisco, California 94105

 Science Research Associates, Inc., 259 East Erie Street, Chicago, Illinois 60611
A Subsidiary of IBM   Distributors

Designed by Joseph M. Roter

****

To my father

****

Contents

Preface

This collection of documents is designed to be used as a supplementary source book by undergraduate college students studying the history of the post-World War II world. Since texts on this period, by virtue of the vast amount of material to be covered, often can touch only briefly upon important issues in the history of the modern world, an effort has been made here to offer the student materials which will permit him a deeper insight into the nature of major world problems.

It has been my experience that students are often not clearly aware of the stand taken by non-western nations on important international issues. Therefore, I have tried to juxtapose, where possible, the views of the communist East and the non-communist West to illustrate the positions of both sides in the Cold War. In addition, considerable space has been devoted to materials on the so-called Third World—the emerging nations of Africa and Asia—which is less familiar than the West to the average college student.

Because space is at a premium in a collection of this nature, and the number of documents available is so vast, I have avoided the practice of using brief introductions for each document in order to devote all possible space to source materials. For those who are just beginning a study of the post-1945 world, sufficient material about the background and significance of the documents in this collection can be obtained from any good text on the post-war period.

Because the choice of source materials in an area as broad as the one under consideration is virtually limitless, some basic criteria in the selection of documents for a book such as this had to be clearly established. My choice of materials was guided to a large extent by the documents discussed in Stewart C. Easton's new book, *World History since 1945*, which this collection was originally designed to supplement.

My thanks go especially to Stewart C. Easton, and to Memphis State University Professor Dalvan M. Coger for their advice on portions of this book; to Miss Virginia L. Redrow of The Brookings Institution, Washington, D.C., who gave me invaluable aid in obtaining copies of much needed documents when I had difficulty obtaining them elsewhere; and finally to my wife, who helped with the physical preparation of the final portions of the manuscript.

May 19, 1967   W. Bruce Lincoln

Excisions in Documents

Excisions in documents are indicated in three ways. Brackets ([ ]) at the beginning and the end of a document indicate that material has been omitted. Brackets within the body of a document indicate either that the material omitted is lengthy or that its absence affects the structure of the document. Ellipses (. . .) within the body of a document indicate that material has been excised which does not alter the physical organization of the document itself.

Part I

*

The New Postwar World

··{*I*}·· *The Last Year of the War*

THE ATLANTIC CHARTER[1]
Joint Declaration by the President of the United States and the Prime Minister of Great Britain

[ ]
Joint declaration of the President of the United States of America and the Prime Minister, Mr. Churchill, representing His Majesty's Government in the United Kingdom, being met together, deem it right to make known certain common principles in the national policies of their respective countries on which they base their hopes for a better future for the world.

First, their countries seek no aggrandizement, territorial or other;

Second, they desire to see no territorial changes that do not accord with the freely expressed wishes of the peoples concerned;

Third, they respect the right of all peoples to choose the form of government under which they will live; and they wish to see sovereign rights and self-government restored to those who have been forcibly deprived of them;

Fourth, they will endeavor, with due respect for their existing obligations, to further the enjoyment by all States, great or small, victor or vanquished, of access, on equal terms, to the trade and to the raw materials of the world which are needed for their economic prosperity;

Fifth, they desire to bring about the fullest collaboration between all nations in the economic field with the object of securing, for all, improved labor standards, economic advancement, and social security;

Sixth, after the final destruction of the Nazi tyranny, they hope to see established a peace which will afford to all nations the means of dwelling in safety within their own boundaries, and which will afford assurance that all the men in all the lands may live out their lives in freedom from fear and want;

---

[1] This statement, subsequently referred to as the "Atlantic Charter," was made public on August 14, 1941. Reprinted from *The Department of State Bulletin*, V, No. 122 (August 16, 1941), pp. 125–126.

Seventh, such a peace should enable all men to traverse the high seas and oceans without hindrance;

Eighth, they believe that all of the nations of the world, for realistic as well as spiritual reasons, must come to the abandonment of the use of force. Since no future peace can be maintained if land, sea, or air armaments continue to be employed by nations which threaten, or may threaten, aggression outside of their frontiers, they believe, pending the establishment of a wider and permanent system of general security, that the disarmament of such nations is essential. They will likewise aid and encourage all other practicable measures which will lighten for peace-loving peoples the crushing burden of armaments.

FRANKLIN D ROOSEVELT
WINSTON S CHURCHILL

A DECLARATION ON LIBERATED EUROPE[1]
Issued by the Premier of the U.S.S.R., the Prime Minister of the United Kingdom, and the President of the United States at the Crimea Conference

The Premier of the Union of Soviet Socialist Republics, the Prime Minister of the United Kingdom, and the President of the United States of America have consulted with each other in the common interests of the peoples of their countries and those of liberated Europe. They jointly declare their mutual agreement to concert during the temporary period of instability in liberated Europe the policies of their three governments in assisting the peoples liberated from the domination of Nazi Germany and the peoples of the former Axis satellite states of Europe to solve by democratic means their pressing political and economic problems.

The establishment of order in Europe and the rebuilding of national economic life must be achieved by processes which will enable the liberated peoples to destroy the last vestiges of Nazism and Fascism and to create democratic institutions of their own choice. This is a principle of the Atlantic Charter—the right of all peoples to choose the form of government under which they will live—the restoration of sovereign rights and self-government to those peoples who have been forcibly deprived of them by the aggressor nations.

To foster the conditions in which the liberated peoples may exercise these rights, the three governments will jointly assist the people in any European liberated state or former Axis satellite state in Europe where in their judgment conditions require (A) to establish conditions of internal peace; (B) to carry out emergency measures for the relief of distressed

---

[1] Reprinted from *The Department of State Bulletin*, XII, No. 295 (February 18, 1945), p. 215.

peoples; (C) to form interim governmental authorities broadly representative of all democratic elements in the population and pledged to the earliest possible establishment through free elections of governments responsive to the will of the people; and (D) to facilitate where necessary the holding of such elections.

The three governments will consult the other United Nations and provisional authorities or other governments in Europe when matters of direct interest to them are under consideration.

When, in the opinion of the three governments, conditions in any European liberated state or any former Axis satellite state in Europe make such action necessary, they will immediately consult together on the measures necessary to discharge the joint responsibilities set forth in this declaration.

By this declaration we reaffirm our faith in the principles of the Atlantic Charter, our pledge in the declaration by the United Nations, and our determination to build in cooperation with other peace-loving nations world order under law, dedicated to peace, security, freedom and general well-being of all mankind.

In issuing this declaration, the three powers express the hope that the Provisional Government of the French Republic may be associated with them in the procedure suggested.

Signed: WINSTON S. CHURCHILL
FRANKLIN D. ROOSEVELT
J. STALIN

February 11, 1945.

A REPORT TO THE SECRETARY OF WAR[1]

[ ]
The consequences of nuclear warfare, and the type of measures which would have to be taken to protect a country from total destruction by nuclear bombing, must be as abhorrent to other nations as to the United States. England, France, and the smaller nations of the European continent, with their congeries of people and industries, would be in a particularly desperate situation in the face of such a threat. Russia and China are the only great nations at present which could survive a nuclear attack. However, even though these countries may value human life less than the peoples of Western Europe and America, and even though Russia, in particular, has an

---

[1] This report, produced by the committee on the social and political implications of atomic energy in Chicago, Illinois, was presented to the War Department in June, 1945, by James Franck, chairman of the committee. Reprinted from *The Bulletin of the Atomic Scientists*, I, No. 10 (May 1, 1946), pp. 2–4, 16.

immense space over which its vital industries could be dispersed and a government which can order this dispersion the day it is convinced that such a measure is necessary—there is no doubt that Russia, too, will shudder at the possibility of a sudden disintegration of Moscow and Leningrad, almost miraculously preserved in the present war, and of its new industrial cities in the Urals and Siberia. Therefore, only lack of mutual trust, and not lack of desire for agreement, can stand in the path of an efficient agreement for the prevention of nuclear warfare. The achievement of such an agreement will thus essentially depend on the integrity of intentions and readiness to sacrifice the necessary fraction of one's own sovereignty, by all the parties to the agreement.

One possible way to introduce nuclear weapons to one world—which may particularly appeal to those who consider nuclear bombs primarily as a secret weapon developed to help win the present war—is to use them without warning on appropriately selected objects in Japan.

Although important tactical results undoubtedly can be achieved by a sudden introduction of nuclear weapons, we nevertheless think that the question of the use of the very first available atomic bombs in the Japanese war should be weighed very carefully, not only by military authorities, but by the highest political leadership of this country.

Russia, and even allied countries which bear less mistrust of our ways and intentions, as well as neutral countries may be deeply shocked by this step. It may be very difficult to persuade the world that a nation which was capable of secretly preparing and suddenly releasing a new weapon, as indiscriminate as the rocket bomb and a thousand times more destructive, is to be trusted in its proclaimed desire of having such weapons abolished by international agreement. We have large accumulations of poison gas, but do not use them, and recent polls have shown that public opinion in this country would disapprove of such a use even if it would accelerate the winning of the Far Eastern war. It is true that some irrational element in mass psychology makes gas poisoning more revolting than blasting by explosives, even though gas warfare is in no way more "inhuman" than the war of bombs and bullets. Nevertheless, it is not at all certain that American public opinion, if it could be enlightened as to the effect of atomic explosives, would approve of our own country being the first to introduce such an indiscriminate method of wholesale destruction of civilian life.

Thus, from the "optimistic" point of view—looking forward to an international agreement on the prevention of nuclear warfare—the military advantages and the saving of American lives achieved by the sudden use of atomic bombs against Japan may be outweighed by the ensuing loss of confidence and by a wave of horror and repulsion sweeping over the rest of the world and perhaps even dividing public opinion at home.

From this point of view, a demonstration of the new weapon might best be made, before the eyes of representatives of all the United Nations, on the desert or a barren island. The best possible atmosphere for the achievement of an international agreement could be achieved if America could say to the world, "You see what sort of a weapon we had but did not use. We are ready to renounce its use in the future if other nations join us in this renunciation and agree to the establishment of an efficient international control."

After such a demonstration the weapon might perhaps be used against Japan if the sanction of the United Nations (and of public opinion at home) were obtained, perhaps after a preliminary ultimatum to Japan to surrender or at least to evacuate certain regions as an alternative to their total destruction. This may sound fantastic, but in nuclear weapons we have something entirely new in order of magnitude of destructive power, and if we want to capitalize fully on the advantage their possession gives us, we must use new and imaginative methods.

It must be stressed that if one takes the pessimistic point of view and discounts the possibility of an effective international control over nuclear weapons at the present time, then the advisability of an early use of nuclear bombs against Japan becomes even more doubtful—quite independently of any humanitarian considerations. If an international agreement is not concluded immediately after the first demonstration, this will mean a flying start toward an unlimited armaments race. If this race is inevitable, we have every reason to delay its beginning as long as possible in order to increase our head start still further.

[ ]

Thus, if the prospects of an agreement will be considered poor in the immediate future, the pros and cons of an early revelation of our possession of nuclear weapons to the world—not only by their actual use against Japan, but also by a prearranged demonstration—must be carefully weighed by the supreme political and military leadership of the country, and the decision should not be left to the considerations of military tactics alone. . . .

METHODS OF INTERNATIONAL CONTROL

We now consider the question of how an effective international control of nuclear armaments can be achieved. This is a difficult problem, but we think it soluble. It requires study by statesmen and international lawyers, and we can offer only some preliminary suggestions for such a study. . . .

One thing is clear: any international agreement on prevention of nuclear armaments must be backed by actual and efficient controls. No paper agreement can be sufficient since neither this or any other nation can stake its whole existence on trust in other nations' signatures. Every attempt to impede the international control agencies would have to be considered equivalent to denunciation of the agreement. . . .

SUMMARY

[ ]
Nuclear bombs cannot possibly remain a "secret weapon" at the exclusive disposal of this country for more than a few years. The scientific facts on which their construction is based are well known to scientists of other countries. Unless an effective international control of nuclear explosives is instituted, a race for nuclear armaments is certain to ensue following the first revelation of our possession of nuclear weapons to the world. Within ten years other countries may have nuclear bombs, each of which, weighing less than a ton, could destroy an urban area of more than ten square miles. In the war to which such an armaments race is likely to lead, the United States, with its agglomeration of population and industry in comparatively few metropolitan districts, will be at a disadvantage compared to nations whose population and industry are scattered over large areas.

We believe that these considerations make the use of nuclear bombs for an early unannounced attack against Japan inadvisable. If the United States were to be the first to release this new means of indiscriminate destruction upon mankind, she would sacrifice public support throughout the world, precipitate the race for armaments, and prejudice the possibility of reaching an international agreement on the future control of such weapons.

THE EFFECTS OF THE ATOMIC BOMB ON HIROSHIMA AND NAGASAKI[1]

[ ]
On 6 August and 9 August 1945, the first two atomic bombs to be used for military purposes were dropped on Hiroshima and Nagasaki respectively. One hundred thousand people were killed, 6 square miles or over 50 percent of the built-up areas of the two cities were destroyed. . . .

Eyewitness accounts of the explosion all describe similar pictures. The bombs exploded with a tremendous flash of blue-white light, like a giant magnesium flare. The flash was of short duration and accompanied by intense glare and heat. It was followed by a tremendous pressure wave and the rumbling sound of the explosion. This sound is not clearly recollected by those who survived near the center of the explosion, although it was clearly heard by others as much as fifteen miles away. A huge snow-white cloud shot

---

[1] Reprinted from the United States Strategic Bombing Survey, *Summary Report* (*Pacific War*) (Washington: G.P.O., 1946), pp. 22–25.

rapidly into the sky and the scene on the ground was obscured first by a bluish haze and then by a purple-brown cloud of dust and smoke.

Such eyewitness accounts reveal the sequence of events. At the time of the explosion, energy was given off in the forms of light, heat, radiation, and pressure. The complete band of radiations, from X- and gamma-rays, through ultraviolet and light rays to the radiant heat of infra-red rays, travelled with the speed of light. The shock wave created by the enormous pressures built up almost instantaneously at the point of explosion but moved out more slowly, that is at about the speed of sound. The superheated gases constituting the original fire ball expanded outward and upward at a slower rate.

The light and radiant heat rays accompanying the flash travelled in a straight line and any opaque object, even a single leaf of a vine, shielded objects lying behind it. The duration of the flash was only a fraction of a second, but it was sufficiently intense to cause third degree burns to exposed human skin up to a distance of a mile. Clothing ignited, though it could be quickly beaten out, telephone poles charred, thatchroofed houses caught fire. Black or other dark-colored surfaces of combustible material absorbed the heat and immediately charred or burst into flames; white or light-colored surfaces reflected a substantial portion of the rays and were not consumed. The heavy black clay tiles which are an almost universal feature of the roofs of Japanese houses bubbled at distances up to a mile. Test of samples of this tile by the National Bureau of Standards in Washington indicates that temperatures in excess of 1,800°C. must have been generated in the surface of the tile to produce such an effect. The surfaces of granite blocks exposed to the flash scarred and spalled at distances up to almost a mile. In the immediate area of ground zero (the point on the ground immediately below the explosion), the heat charred corpses beyond recognition.

Penetrating rays such as gamma-rays exposed X-ray films stored in the basement of a concrete hospital almost a mile from ground zero. Symptoms of their effect on human beings close to the center of the explosion, who survived other effects thereof, were generally delayed for two or three days. The bone marrow and as a result the process of blood formation were affected. The white corpuscle count went down and the human processes of resisting infection were destroyed. Death generally followed shortly thereafter.

The majority of radiation cases who were at greater distances did not show severe symptoms until 1 to 4 weeks after the explosion. The first symptoms were loss of appetite, lassitude and general discomfort. Within 12 to 48 hours, fever became evident in many cases, going as high as 104° to 105°F., which in fatal cases continued until death. If the fever subsided, the patient usually showed a rapid disappearance of other symptoms and soon regained his feeling of good health. Other symptoms were loss of white blood corpuscles, loss of hair, and decrease in sperm count.

Even though rays of this nature have great powers of penetration, intervening substances filter out portions of them. As the weight of the intervening material increases the percentage of the rays penetrating goes down. It appears that a few feet of concrete, or a somewhat greater thickness of earth, furnished sufficient protection to humans, even those close to ground zero, to prevent serious after effects from radiation.

The blast wave which followed the flash was of sufficient force to press in the roofs of reinforced-concrete structures and to flatten completely all less sturdy structures. Due to the height of the explosion, the peak pressure of the wave at ground zero was no higher than that produced by a near-miss of a high-explosive bomb, and decreased at greater distances from ground zero. Reflection and shielding by intervening hills and structures produced some unevenness in the pattern. The blast wave, however, was of far greater extent and duration than that of a high-explosive bomb and most reinforced-concrete structures suffered structural damage or collapse up to 700 feet at Hiroshima and 2,000 feet at Nagasaki. Brick buildings were flattened up to 7,300 feet at Hiroshima and 8,500 feet at Nagasaki. Typical Japanese houses of wood construction suffered total collapse up to approximately 7,300 feet at Hiroshima and 8,200 feet at Nagasaki. Beyond these distances structures received less serious damage to roofs, wall partitions, and the like. Glass windows were blown out at distances up to 5 miles. The blast wave, being of longer duration than that caused by high-explosive detonations, was accompanied by more flying debris. Window frames, doors, and partitions which would have been shaken down by a near-miss of a high-explosive bomb were hurled at high velocity through those buildings which did not collapse. Machine tools and most other production equipment in industrial plants were not directly damaged by the blast wave, but were damaged by collapsing buildings or ensuing general fires. . . .

The Survey has estimated that the damage and casualties caused at Hiroshima by the one atomic bomb dropped from a single plane would have required 220 B-29s carrying 1,200 tons of incendiary bombs, 400 tons of high-explosive bombs, and 500 tons of anti-personnel fragmentation bombs, if conventional weapons, rather than an atomic bomb, had been used. One hunderd and twenty-five B-29s carrying 1,200 tons of bombs would have been required to approximate the damage and casualties at Nagasaki. . . .

As might be expected, the primary reaction of the populace to the bomb was fear, uncontrolled terror, strengthened by the sheer horror of the destruction and suffering witnessed and experienced by the survivors. . . .

The effect of the atomic bomb on the confidence of the Japanese civilian population outside the two cities was more restricted. This was in part due to the effect of distance, lack of understanding of the nature of atomic energy, and the impact of other demoralizing experiences. The role of the atomic bomb in the surrender must be considered along with all the other forces which bore upon that question with Japan.   [ ]

UNITED STATES POLICY ON THE CONTROL OF ATOMIC ENERGY[1]

Statement by Bernard M. Baruch to the United Nations Atomic Energy Commission, June 14, 1946

My fellow members of the United Nations Atomic Energy Commission, and My Fellow Citizens of the World:

We are here to make a choice between the quick and the dead.

That is our business.

Behind the black portent of the new atomic age lies a hope which, seized upon with faith, can work our salvation. If we fail, then we have damned every man to be the slave of Fear. Let us not deceive ourselves: We must elect World Peace or World Destruction. . . .

The United States proposes the creation of an International Atomic Development Authority, to which should be entrusted all phases of the development and use of atomic energy, starting with the raw material and including—

1. Managerial control or ownership of all atomic-energy activities potentially dangerous to world security.

2. Power to control, inspect, and license all other atomic activities.

3. The duty of fostering the beneficial uses of atomic energy.

4. Research and development responsibilities of an affirmative character intended to put the Authority in the forefront of atomic knowledge and thus to enable it to comprehend, and therefor to detect, misuse of atomic energy. To be effective, the Authority must itself be the world's leader in the field of atomic knowledge and development and thus supplement its legal authority with the great power inherent in possession of leadership in knowledge.

I offer this as a basis for beginning our discussion.

But I think the peoples we serve would not believe—and without faith nothing counts—that a treaty, merely outlawing possession or use of the atomic bomb, constitutes effective fulfilment of the instructions to this Commission. Previous failures have been recorded in trying the method of simple renunciation, unsupported by effective guaranties of security and armament limitation. No one would have faith in that approach alone.

Now, if ever, is the time to act for the common good. Public opinion supports a world movement toward security. If I read the signs aright, the peoples want a program not composed merely of pious thoughts but of enforceable sanctions—an international law with teeth in it. . . .

When an adequate system for control of atomic energy, including the renunciation of the bomb as a weapon, has been agreed upon and put into

---

[1] Reprinted from *The United States and the United Nations Report Series*, No. 2, Department of State Publication No. 2560, pp. 1–12.

effective operation and condign punishments set up for violations of the rules of control which are to be stigmatized as international crimes, we propose that—

1. Manufacture of atomic bombs shall stop;
2. Existing bombs shall be disposed of pursuant to the terms of the treaty; and
3. The Authority shall be in possession of full information as to the know-how for the production of atomic energy.

Let me repeat, so as to avoid misunderstanding: My country is ready to make its full contribution toward the end we seek, subject of course to our constitutional processes and to an adequate system of control becoming fully effective, as we finally work it out.

Now as to violations: In the agreement, penalties of as serious a nature as the nations may wish and as immediate and certain in their execution as possible should be fixed for—

1. Illegal possession or use of an atomic bomb;
2. Illegal possession, or separation, of atomic material suitable for use in an atomic bomb;
3. Seizure of any plant or other property belonging to or licensed by the Authority;
4. Wilful interference with the activities of the Authority;
5. Creation or operation of dangerous projects in a manner contrary to, or in the absence of, a license granted by the international control body.

It would be a deception, to which I am unwilling to lend myself, were I not to say to you and to our peoples that the matter of punishment lies at the very heart of our present security system. It might as well be admitted, here and now, that the subject goes straight to the veto power contained in the Charter of the United Nations so far as it relates to the field of atomic energy. The Charter permits penalization only by concurrence of each of the five great powers—the Union of Soviet Socialist Republics, the United Kingdom, China, France, and the United States.

I want to make very plain that I am concerned here with the veto power only as it affects this particular problem. There must be no veto to protect those who violate their solemn agreements not to develop or use atomic energy for destructive purposes. . . .

I now submit the following measures as representing the fundamental features of a plan which would give effect to certain of the conclusions which I have epitomized.

1. *General.* The Authority should set up a thorough plan for control of the field of atomic energy, through various forms of ownership, dominion, licenses, operation, inspection, research, and management by competent per-

sonnel. After this is provided for, there should be as little interference as may be with the economic plans and the present private, corporate, and state relationships in the several countries involved.

2. *Raw Materials.* The Authority should have as one of its earliest purposes to obtain and maintain complete and accurate information on world supplies of uranium and thorium and to bring them under its dominion. . . .

. . . Only after all current information on world sources of uranium and thorium is known to us all can equitable plans be made for their production, refining, and distribution.

3. *Primary Production Plants.* The Authority should exercise complete managerial control of the production of fissionable materials. . . .

4. *Atomic Explosives.* The Authority should be given sole and exclusive right to conduct research in the field of atomic explosives. . . . Only by maintaining its position as the best-informed agency will the Authority be able to determine the line between intrinsically dangerous and non-dangerous activities.

5. *Strategic Distribution of Activities and Materials.* The activities entrusted exclusively to the Authority because they are intrinsically dangerous to security should be distributed throughout the world. Similarly, stockpiles of raw materials and fissionable materials should not be centralized.

6. *Non-Dangerous Activities.* A function of the Authority should be promotion of the peacetime benefits of atomic energy.

Atomic research (except in explosives), the use of research reactors, the production of radioactive tracers by means of non-dangerous reactors, the use of such tracers, and to some extent the production of power should be open to nations and their citizens under reasonable licensing arrangements from the Authority. . . .

7. *Definition of Dangerous and Non-Dangerous Activities.* Although a reasonable dividing line can be drawn between dangerous and non-dangerous activities, it is not hard and fast. Provision should, therefore, be made to assure constant reexamination of the questions and to permit revision of the dividing line as changing conditions and new discoveries may require.

8. *Operations of Dangerous Activities.* Any plant dealing with uranium or thorium after it once reaches the potential of dangerous use must be not only subject to the most rigorous and competent inspection by the Authority, but its actual operation shall be under the management, supervision, and control of the Authority.

9. *Inspection.* . . . If the Authority is the only agency which may lawfully conduct dangerous activities, then visible operation by others than the Authority will constitute an unambiguous danger signal. Inspection will also occur in connection with the licensing functions of the Authority.

10. *Freedom of Access.* Adequate ingress and egress for all qualified representatives of the Authority must be assured. . . . Important measures of inspection will be associated with the tight control of raw materials, for this is a keystone of the plan. . . .

11. *Personnel.* The personnel of the Authority should be recruited on a basis of proven competence but also so far as possible on an international basis.

12. *Progress by Stages.* . . . Once a charter for the Authority has been adopted, the Authority and the system of control for which it will be responsible will require time to become fully organized and effective. The plan of control will, therefore, have to come into effect in successive stages. These should be specifically fixed in the charter or means should be otherwise set forth in the charter for transitions from one stage to another, as contemplated in the resolution of the United Nations Assembly which created this Commission.

13. *Disclosures.* In the deliberations of the United Nations Commission on Atomic Energy, the United States is prepared to make available the information essential to a reasonable understanding of the proposals which it advocates. . . . When the Authority is actually created, the United States will join the other nations in making available the further information essential to that organization for the performance of its functions. As the successive stages of international control are reached, the United States will be prepared to yield, to the extent required by each stage, national control of activities in this field to the Authority.

14. *International Control.* . . . Purely national authorities for control and development of atomic energy should to the extent necessary for the effective operation of the Authority be subordinate to it. This is neither an endorsement nor a disapproval of the creation of national authorities. The Commission should evolve a clear demarcation of the scope of duties and responsibilities of such national authorities.

And now I end. I have submitted an outline for present discussion. Our consideration will be broadened by the criticism of the United States proposals and by the plans of the other nations, which, it is to be hoped, will be submitted at their early convenience. . . .

Let us keep in mind the exhortation of Abraham Lincoln, whose words, uttered at a moment of shattering national peril, form a complete text for our deliberation. I quote, paraphrasing slightly:

We cannot escape history. We of this meeting will be remembered in spite of ourselves. No personal significance or insignificance can spare one or another of us. The fiery trial through which we are passing will light us down in honor or dishonor to the latest generation.

We say we are for Peace. The world will not forget that we say this. We know how to save Peace. The world knows that we do. We, even we here, hold the power and have the responsibility.

We shall nobly save, or meanly lose, the last, best hope of earth. The way is plain, peaceful, generous, just—a way which, if followed, the world will forever applaud.

My thanks for your attention.

··{2}·· *The Establishment of Soviet Hegemony in Eastern Europe*

THE SINEWS OF PEACE[1]
Speech Delivered by Sir Winston Churchill at Westminster College on March 5, 1946

[ ]
Ladies and gentlemen, the United States stands at this time at the pinnacle of world power. It is a solemn moment for the American democracy. . . . Opportunity is here now, clear and shining, for both our countries. To reject it or ignore it or fritter it away will bring upon us all the long reproaches of the after-time. It is necessary that constancy of mind, persistency of purpose and the grand simplicity of decision shall guide and rule the conduct of the English-speaking peoples in peace as they did in war. We must and I believe we shall prove ourselves equal to this severe requirement.

President McCluer, when American military men approach some serious situation they are wont to write at the head of their directive the words, "Overall Strategic Concept." There is wisdom in this as it lends to clarity of thought. What, then, is the Overall Strategic Concept which we should inscribe today? It is nothing less than the safety and welfare, the freedom and progress of all the homes and families of all the men and women in all the lands. . . .

To give security of these countless homes they must be shielded from the two gaunt marauders—War and Tyranny. . . .

. . . Our supreme task and duty is to guard the homes of the common people from the horrors and miseries of another war. We are all agreed upon that.

Our American military colleagues, after having proclaimed the "Overall Strategic Concept" and computed all available resources, always proceed to the next step, namely The Method. Here again there is widespread agree-

---

[1] The text of this speech, delivered at Westminster College, Fulton, Missouri, under the auspices of the John Findley Green Foundation, is reprinted with the permission of Westminster College.

ment. A World Organization has already been erected for the prime purpose of preventing war. UNO, the successor of the League of Nations, with the decisive addition of the United States and all that that means, is already at work. . . .

Now, I come to the second of the two marauders, to the second danger which threatens the cottage home and ordinary people, namely Tyranny. We cannot be blind to the fact that the liberties enjoyed by individual citizens throughout the United States and throughout the British Empire are not valid in a considerable number of countries, some of which are very powerful. In these States, control is enforced upon the common people by various kinds of all-embracing police governments, to a degree which is overwhelming and contrary to every principle of democracy. The power of the State is exercised without restraint, either by dictators or by compact oligarchies operating through a privileged party and a political police. It is not our duty at this time, when difficulties are so numerous, to interfere forcibly in the internal affairs of countries which we have not conquered in war. But we must never cease to proclaim in fearless tones the great principles of freedom and the rights of men, which are the joint inheritance of the English-speaking world and which, through Magna Carta, the Bill of Rights, the Habeas Corpus, Trial by Jury and the English Common Law, find their most famous expression in the American Declaration of Independence. . . .

I have now stated the two great dangers which menace the homes of the people—War and Tyranny. I have not yet spoken of poverty and privation which are in many cases the prevailing anxiety. But if the dangers of War and Tyranny are removed, there is no doubt that science and co-operation can bring in the next few years—certainly in the next few decades—to the world, newly taught in the sharpening school of war, an expansion of material well-being beyond anything that has yet occurred in human experience. . . . Now, while still pursuing the method of realizing our overall strategic concept, I come to the crux of what I have traveled here to say.

Neither the sure prevention of war, nor the continuous rise of world organization will be gained without what I have called the fraternal association of the English-speaking peoples. This means a special relationship between the British Commonwealth and Empire and the United States of America. . . .

There is, however, an important question we must ask ourselves. Would a special relationship between the United States and the British Commonwealth be inconsistent with our overriding loyalties to the World Organization? I reply that, on the contrary, it is probably the only means by which that organization will achieve its full stature and strength. . . .

A shadow has fallen upon the scene so lately lighted by the Allied victory. Nobody knows what Soviet Russia and its Communist international organization intends to do in the immediate future, or what are the limits, if any, to their expansive and proselytizing tendencies. . . .

From Stettin in the Baltic to Trieste in the Adriatic, an iron curtain has descended across the continent. Behind that line lie all the capitals of the ancient states of Central and Eastern Europe. Warsaw, Berlin, Prague, Vienna, Budapest, Belgrade, Bucharest and Sofia, all those famous cities and the populations around them, lie in what I must call the Soviet sphere and all are subject in one form or another, not only to Soviet influence but to a very high and increasing measure of control from Moscow. Athens alone, with its immortal glories, is free to decide its future at an election under British, American and French observation. The Russian-dominated Polish Government has been encouraged to make enormous and wrongful inroads upon Germany, and mass expulsions of millions of Germans on a scale grievous and undreamed of are now taking place. The Communist parties which were very small in all these Eastern States of Europe, have been raised to pre-eminence and power far beyond their numbers and are seeking everywhere to obtain totalitarian control. Police governments are prevailing in nearly every case and, so far, except in Czechoslovakia, there is no true democracy. Turkey and Persia are both profoundly alarmed and disturbed at the claims which are made upon them and at the pressure being exerted by the Moscow Government. An attempt is being made by the Russians in Berlin to build up a quasi-Communist party in their zone of Occupied Germany by showing special favors to groups of left-wing German leaders. . . . If now the Soviet Government tries, by separate action, to build up a pro-Communist Germany in their areas, this will cause new serious difficulties in the British and American Zones, and will give the defeated Germans the power of putting themselves up to auction between the Soviets and the Western Democracies. Whatever conclusions may be drawn from these facts, and facts they are, this is certainly not the liberated Europe we fought to build up. Nor is it one which contains the essentials of permanent peace. . . .

Except in the British Commonwealth and in the United States, where Communism is in its infancy, the Communist parties or fifth columns constitute a growing challenge and peril to Christian civilization. These are sombre facts for anyone to have to recite on the morrow of a victory gained by so much splendid comradeship in arms and in the cause of freedom and democracy, but we should be most unwise not to face them squarely while time remains. . . .

From what I have seen of our Russian friends and allies during the war, I am convinced that there is nothing they admire so much as strength, and there is nothing for which they have less respect than for weakness, especially military weakness. For that reason the old doctrine of a balance of power is unsound. We cannot afford, if we can help it, to work on narrow margins, offering temptations to a trial of strength.

If the western democracies stand together in strict adherence to the principles of the United Nations Charter, their influence for furthering those principles will be immense and no one is likely to molest them. If, however, they become divided or falter in their duty, and if these all important years are allowed to slip away then indeed a catastrophe may overwhelm us all. . . .

There never was a war in all history easier to prevent by timely action than the one which has just desolated such great areas of the globe. It could have been prevented in my belief without the firing of a single shot, and Germany might be powerful, prosperous and honored today, but no one would listen and one by one we were all sucked into the awful whirlpool.

We surely must not let that happen again. This can only be achieved by reaching now, in 1946, a good understanding on all points with Russia under the general authority of the United Nations Organization and by the maintenance of that good understanding through many peaceful years, by the world instrument supported by the whole strength of the English-speaking world and all its connections. There is the solution which I would offer to you in this address to which I have given the title, "Sinews of Peace.". . .

If the population of the English-speaking Commonwealth be added to that of the United States, with all that such cooperation implies in the air, on the sea and in science and industry, and in moral laws, there will be no quivering, precarious balance of power to offer its temptation to ambition or adventure. On the contrary, there will be an overwhelming assurance of security.

If we adhere faithfully to the Charter of the United Nations and walk forward in sedate and sober strength, seeking no one's land or treasure, seeking to lay no arbitrary control upon the thoughts of men, if all British moral and material forces and convictions are joined with your own in fraternal association, the high roads of the future will be clear, not only for us but for all, not only for our time, but for the century to come.

THE TRUMAN DOCTRINE[1]
Speech Delivered by President Truman to Congress on March 12, 1947

MR. PRESIDENT, MR. SPEAKER, MEMBERS OF THE CONGRESS OF THE UNITED STATES:

The gravity of the situation which confronts the world today necessitates my appearance before a joint session of the Congress. . . .

The United States has received from the Greek Government an urgent appeal for financial and economic assistance. Preliminary reports from the American Economic Mission now in Greece and reports from the American

---

[1] Reprinted from *The Department of State Bulletin*, XVI, No. 403 (March 23, 1947), pp. 534–537.

Ambassador in Greece corroborate the statement of the Greek Government that assistance is imperative if Greece is to survive as a free nation.

I do not believe that the American people and the Congress wish to turn a deaf ear to the appeal of the Greek Government. . . .

Greece is today without funds to finance the importation of those goods which are essential to bare subsistence. Under these circumstances the people of Greece cannot make progress in solving their problems of reconstruction. Greece is in desperate need of financial and economic assistance to enable it to resume purchases of food, clothing, fuel, and seeds. These are indispensable for the subsistence of its people and are obtainable only from abroad. Greece must have help to import the goods necessary to restore internal order and security so essential for economic and political recovery.

The Greek Government has also asked for the assistance of experienced American administrators, economists, and technicians to insure that the financial and other aid given to Greece shall be used effectively in creating a stable and self-sustaining economy and in improving its public administration.

The very existence of the Greek state is today threatened by the terrorist activities of several thousand armed men, led by Communists, who defy the Government's authority at a number of points, particularly along the northern boundaries. A commission appointed by the United Nations Security Council is at present investigating disturbed conditions in northern Greece and alleged border violations along the frontier between Greece on the one hand and Albania, Bulgaria, and Yugoslavia on the other.

Meanwhile, the Greek Government is unable to cope with the situation. The Greek Army is small and poorly equipped. It needs supplies and equipment if it is to restore authority to the Government throughout Greek territory.

Greece must have assistance if it is to become a self-supporting and self-respecting democracy.

The United States must supply that assistance. We have already extended to Greece certain types of relief and economic aid, but these are inadequate.

There is no other country to which democratic Greece can turn.

No other nation is willing and able to provide the necessary support for a democratic Greek Government. . . .

Greece's neighbor, Turkey, also deserves our attention.

The future of Turkey as an independent and economically sound state is clearly no less important to the freedom-loving peoples of the world than the future of Greece. The circumstances in which Turkey finds itself today are considerably different from those of Greece. Turkey has been spared the disasters that have beset Greece. And during the war the United States and Great Britain furnished Turkey with material aid.

Nevertheless, Turkey now needs our support.

Since the war Turkey has sought additional financial assistance from

Great Britain and the United States for the purpose of effecting that modernization necessary for the maintenance of its national integrity.

That integrity is essential to the preservation of order in the Middle East. . . .

I am fully aware of the broad implications involved if the United States extends assistance to Greece and Turkey, and I shall discuss these implications with you at this time.

One of the primary objectives of the foreign policy of the United States is the creation of conditions in which we and other nations will be able to work out a way of life free from coercion. This was a fundamental issue in the war with Germany and Japan. Our victory was won over countries which sought to impose their will, and their way of life, upon other nations.

To insure the peaceful development of nations, free from coercion, the United States has taken a leading part in establishing the United Nations. The United Nations is designed to make possible lasting freedom and independence for all its members. We shall not realize our objectives, however, unless we are willing to help free peoples to maintain their free institutions and their national integrity against aggressive movements that seek to impose upon them totalitarian regimes. This is no more than a frank recognition that totalitarian regimes imposed upon free peoples, by direct or indirect aggression, undermine the foundations of international peace and hence the security of the United States. . . .

At the present moment in world history nearly every nation must choose between alternative ways of life. The choice is too often not a free one.

One way of life is based upon the will of the majority, and is distinguished by free institutions, representative government, free elections, guaranties of individual liberty, freedom of speech and religion, and freedom from political oppression.

The second way of life is based upon the will of a minority forcibly imposed upon the majority. It relies upon terror and oppression, a controlled press and radio, fixed elections, and the suppression of personal freedoms.

I believe that it must be the policy of the United States to support free peoples who are resisting attempted subjugation by armed minorities or by outside pressures.

I believe that we must assist free peoples to work out their own destinies in their own way.

I believe that our help should be primarily through economic and financial aid which is essential to economic stability and orderly political processes.

The world is not static, and the *status quo* is not sacred. But we cannot allow changes in the *status quo* in violation of the Charter of the United Nations by such methods as coercion, or by such subterfuges as political infiltration. In helping free and independent nations to maintain their freedom, the United States will be giving effect to the principles of the Charter of the United Nations. . . .

This is a serious course upon which we embark.

I would not recommend it except that the alternative is much more serious.

The United States contributed $341,000,000,000 toward winning World War II. This is an investment in world freedom and world peace.

The assistance that I am recommending for Greece and Turkey amounts to little more than one tenth of one percent of this investment. It is only common sense that we should safeguard this investment and make sure that it was not in vain.

The seeds of totalitarian regimes are nurtured by misery and want. They spread and grow in the evil soil of poverty and strife. They reach their full growth when the hope of a people for a better life has died.

We must keep that hope alive.

The free peoples of the world look to us for support in maintaining their freedoms.

If we falter in our leadership, we may endanger the peace of the world— and we shall surely endanger the welfare of our own Nation.

Great responsibilities have been placed upon us by the swift movement of events.

I am confident that the Congress will face these responsibilities squarely.

DOOMED TO FAILURE[1]
Soviet Commentary on the Truman Doctrine

[ ]
The pathetic appeal of the Tsaldaris Government to the U.S.A. is clear evidence of the bankruptcy of the political regime in Greece. But the matter does not lie solely with the Greek Monarchists and their friends, now cracked up to American Congressmen as the direct descendants of the heroes of Thermopylae: it is well known that the real masters of Greece have been and are the British military authorities.

British troops have been on Greek territory since 1944. On Churchill's initiative, Britain took on herself the responsibility for "stabilising" political conditions in Greece. The British authorities did not confine themselves to perpetuating the rule of the reactionary, anti-democratic forces in Greece, making no scruple in supporting ex-collaborators with the Germans. The entire political and economic activities under a number of short-lived Greek Governments have been carried on under close British control and direction.

To-day we can see the results of this policy—complete bankruptcy. British troops failed to bring peace and tranquility to tormented Greece. The

---

[1] Appeared originally in *Izvestia* on March 13, 1947; reprinted with permission from the *Soviet News*, March 15, 1947, p. 3.

Greek people have been plunged into the abyss of new sufferings, of hunger and poverty. Civil war takes on ever fiercer forms.

Was not the presence of foreign troops on Greek territory instrumental in bringing about this state of affairs? Does not Britain, who proclaimed herself the guardian of Greece, bear responsibility for the bankruptcy of her charge?

The American President's message completely glosses over these questions. The U.S.A. does not wish to criticise Britain, since she herself intends to follow the British example. Truman's statement makes it clear that the U.S.A. does not intend to deviate from the course of British policy in Greece. So one cannot expect better results.

The U.S. Government has no intention of acting in the Greek question as one might have expected a member of UNO, concerned about the fate of another member, to act. It is obvious that in Washington they do not wish to take into account the obligations assumed by the U.S. Government regarding UNO. Truman did not even consider it necessary to wait for the findings of the Security Council Commission specially sent to Greece to investigate the situation on the spot.

Truman, indeed, failed to reckon either with the international organisation or with the sovereignty of Greece. What will be left of Greek sovereignty when the "American military and civilian personnel" gets to work in Greece by means of the 250 million dollars brought into that country? The sovereignty and independence of Greece will be the first victims of such singular "defence."

The American arguments for assisting Turkey base themselves on the existence of a threat to the integrity of Turkish territory—though no-one and nothing actually threatens Turkey's integrity. This "assistance" is evidently aimed at putting this country also under U.S. control.

Some American commentators admit this quite openly. Walter Lippman, for example, frankly points out in the *Herald Tribune* that an American alliance with Turkey would give the U.S.A. a strategic position, incomparably more advantageous than any other, from which power could be wielded over the Middle East. . . .

We are now witnessing a fresh intrusion of the U.S.A. into the affairs of other states. American claims to leadership in international affairs grow parallel with the growing appetite of the American quarters concerned. But the American leaders, in the new historical circumstances, fail to reckon with the fact that the old methods of the colonisers and die-hard politicians have out-lived their time and are doomed to failure. In this lies the chief weakness of Truman's message.

··{*3*}·· *Postwar Reconstruction in Western Europe*

THE MARSHALL PLAN[1]
Speech Delivered by General George Marshall at Harvard University on June 5, 1947

I need not tell you gentlemen that the world situation is very serious. That must be apparent to all intelligent people. I think one difficulty is that the problem is one of such enormous complexity that the very mass of facts presented to the public by press and radio make it exceedingly difficult for the man in the street to reach a clear appraisement of the situation. Furthermore, the people of this country are distant from the troubled areas of the earth and it is hard for them to comprehend the plight and consequent reactions of the long-suffering peoples, and the effect of those reactions on their governments in connection with our efforts to promote peace in the world.

In considering the requirements for the rehabilitation of Europe, the physical loss of life, the visible destruction of cities, factories, mines, and railroads was correctly estimated, but it has become obvious during recent months that this visible destruction was probably less serious than the dislocation of the entire fabric of European economy. For the past 10 years conditions have been highly abnormal. The feverish preparation for war and the more feverish maintenance of the war effort engulfed all aspects of national economies. Machinery has fallen into disrepair or is entirely obsolete. Under the arbitrary and destructive Nazi rule, virtually every possible enterprise was geared into the German war machine. Long-standing commercial ties, private institutions, banks, insurance companies, and shipping companies disappeared, through loss of capital, absorption through nationalization, or by simple destruction. In many countries, confidence in the local currency has been severely shaken. The breakdown of the business structure of Europe during the war was complete. Recovery has been seriously retarded by the fact that two years after the close of hostilities a peace settlement with Germany and Austria has not been agreed upon. But even given a more prompt solution of these difficult problems, the rehabilitation of the economic struc-

---

[1] Reprinted from *The Department of State Bulletin*, XVI, No. 415 (June 15, 1947), pp. 1159–1160.

22

ture of Europe quite evidently will require a much longer time and greater effort than had been foreseen.

There is a phase of this matter which is both interesting and serious. The farmer has always produced the foodstuffs to exchange with the city dweller for the other necessities of life. This division of labor is the basis of modern civilization. At the present time it is threatened with breakdown. The town and city industries are not producing adequate goods to exchange with the food-producing farmer. Raw materials and fuel are in short supply. Machinery is lacking or worn out. The farmer or the peasant cannot find the goods for sale which he desires to purchase. So the sale of his farm produce for money which he cannot use seems to him an unprofitable transaction. He, therefore, has withdrawn many fields from crop cultivation and is using them for grazing. He feeds more grain to stock and finds for himself and his family an ample supply of food, however short he may be on clothing and the other ordinary gadgets of civilization. Meanwhile people in the cities are short of food and fuel. So the governments are forced to use their foreign money and credits to procure these necessities abroad. This process exhausts funds which are urgently needed for reconstruction. Thus a very serious situation is rapidly developing which bodes no good for the world. The modern system of the division of labor upon which the exchange of products is based is in danger of breaking down.

The truth of the matter is that Europe's requirements for the next three or four years of foreign food and other essential products—principally from America—are so much greater than her present ability to pay that she must have substantial additional help or face economic, social, and political deterioration of a very grave character.

The remedy lies in breaking the vicious circle and restoring the confidence of the European people in the economic future of their own countries and of Europe as a whole. The manufacturer and the farmer throughout wide areas must be able and willing to exchange their products for currencies the continuing value of which is not open to question.

Aside from the demoralizing effect on the world at large and the possibilities of disturbances arising as a result of the desperation of the people concerned, the consequences to the economy of the United States should be apparent to all. It is logical that the United States should do whatever it is able to do to assist in the return of normal economic health in the world, without which there can be no political stability and no assured peace. Our policy is directed not against any country or doctrine but against hunger, poverty, desperation, and chaos. Its purpose should be the revival of a working economy in the world so as to permit the emergence of political and social conditions in which free institutions can exist. Such assistance, I am convinced, must not be on a piecemeal basis as various crises develop. Any assistance that this Government may render in the future should provide a cure rather than a mere palliative. Any government that is willing to assist in the task of recovery will find full cooperation, I am sure, on the part of the United States Government. Any government which maneuvers to block the recovery of other countries cannot expect help from us. Furthermore, governments, political parties, or groups which seek to perpetuate human misery in order to profit therefrom politically or otherwise will encounter the opposition of the United States.

It is already evident that, before the United States Government can proceed much further in its efforts to alleviate the situation and help start the European world on its way to recovery, there must be some agreement among the countries of Europe as to the requirements of the situation and the part those countries themselves will take in order to give proper effect to whatever action might be undertaken by this Government. It would be neither fitting nor efficacious for this Government to undertake to draw up unilaterally a program designed to place Europe on its feet economically. This is the business of the Europeans. The initiative, I think, must come from Europe. The role of this country should consist of friendly aid in the drafting of a European program and of later support of such a program so far as it may be practical for us to do so. The program should be a joint one, agreed to by a number, if not all, European nations.

An essential part of any successful action on the part of the United States is an understanding on the part of the people of America of the character of the problem and the remedies to be applied. Political passion and prejudice should have no part. With foresight, and a willingness on the part of our people to face up to the vast responsibility which history has clearly placed upon our country, the difficulties I have outlined can and will be overcome.

NORTH ATLANTIC TREATY[1]
Proposed for Signature during First Week in April, 1949

PREAMBLE

The Parties to this Treaty reaffirm their faith in the purposes and principles of the Charter of the United Nations and their desire to live in peace with all peoples and all governments.

They are determined to safeguard the freedom, common heritage and civilization of their peoples, founded on the principles of democracy, individual liberty and the rule of law.

They seek to promote stability and well-being in the North Atlantic area.

They are resolved to unite their efforts for collective defense and for the preservation of peace and security.

They therefore agree to this North Atlantic Treaty:

---

[1] Reprinted from *The Department of State Bulletin*, XX, No. 507 (March 20, 1949), pp. 339–342.

Article 1. The Parties undertake, as set forth in the Charter of the United Nations, to settle any international disputes in which they may be involved by peaceful means in such a manner that international peace and security, and justice, are not endangered, and to refrain in their international relations from the threat or use of force in any manner inconsistent with the purposes of the United Nations.

Article 2. The Parties will contribute toward the further development of peaceful and friendly international relations by strengthening their free institutions, by bringing about a better understanding of the principles upon which these institutions are founded, and by promoting conditions of stability and well-being. They will seek to eliminate conflict in their international economic policies and will encourage economic collaboration between any or all of them.

Article 3. In order more effectively to achieve the objectives of this Treaty, the Parties, separately and jointly, by means of continuous and effective self-help and mutual aid, will maintain and develop their individual and collective capacity to resist armed attack.

Article 4. The Parties will consult together whenever, in the opinion of any of them, the territorial integrity, political independence or security of any of the Parties is threatened.

Article 5. The Parties agreed that an armed attack against one or more of them in Europe or North America shall be considered an attack against them all; and consequently they agree that, if such an armed attack occurs, each of them, in exercise of the right of individual or collective self-defense recognized by Article 51 of the Charter of the United Nations, will assist the Party or Parties so attacked by taking forthwith, individually and in concert with the other Parties, such action as it deems necessary, including the use of armed force, to restore and maintain the security of the North Atlantic area.

Any such armed attack and all measures taken as a result thereof shall immediately be reported to the Security Council. Such measures shall be terminated when the Security Council has taken the measures necessary to restore and maintain international peace and security.

Article 6. For the purpose of Article 5 an armed attack on one or more of the Parties is deemed to include an armed attack on the territory of any of the Parties in Europe or North America, on the Algerian departments of France, on the occupation forces of any Party in Europe, on the islands under the jurisdiction of any Party in the North Atlantic area north of the Tropic of Cancer or on the vessels or aircraft in this area of any of the Parties.

Article 7. This Treaty does not affect, and shall not be interpreted as affecting, in any way the rights and obligations under the Charter of the Parties which are members of the United Nations, or the primary responsibility of the Security Council for the maintenance of international peace and security.

Article 8. Each Party declares that none of the international engagements now in force between it and any other of the Parties or any third state is in conflict with the provisions of this Treaty, and undertakes not to enter into any international engagement in conflict with this Treaty.

Article 9. The Parties hereby establish a council, on which each of them shall be represented, to consider matters concerning the implementation of this Treaty. The council shall be so organized as to be able to meet promptly at any time. The council shall set up such subsidiary bodies as may be necessary; in particular it shall establish immediately a defense committee which shall recommend measures for the implementation of Articles 3 and 5.

Article 10. The Parties may, by unanimous agreement, invite any other European state in a position to further the principles of this Treaty and to contribute to the security of the North Atlantic area to accede to this Treaty. Any state so invited may become a party to the Treaty by depositing its instrument of accession with the Government of the United States of America. The Government of the United States of America will inform each of the Parties of the deposit of each such instrument of accession.

Article 11. This Treaty shall be ratified and its provisions carried out by the Parties in accordance with their respective constitutional processes. The instruments of ratification shall be deposited as soon as possible with the Government of the United States of America, which will notify all the other signatories of each deposit. The Treaty shall enter into force between the states which have ratified it as soon as the ratifications of the majority of the signatories, including the ratifications of Belgium, Canada, France, Luxembourg, the Netherlands, the United Kingdom and the United States, have been deposited and shall come into effect with respect to other states on the date of the deposit of their ratifications.

Article 12. After the Treaty has been in force for ten years, or at any time thereafter, the Parties shall, if any of them so requests, consult together for the purpose of reviewing the Treaty, having regard for the factors then affecting peace and security in the North Atlantic area, including the development of universal as well as regional arrangements under the Charter of the United Nations for the maintenance of international peace and security.

Article 13. After the Treaty has been in force for twenty years, any Party may cease to be a party one year after its notice of denunciation has been given to the Government of the United States of America, which will inform the Governments of the other Parties of the deposit of each notice of denunciation.

Article 14. This Treaty, of which the English and French texts are equally authentic, shall be deposited in the archives of the Government of the United States of America. Duly certified copies thereof will be transmitted by that Government to the Governments of the other signatories.

In witness whereof, the undersigned plenipotentiaries have signed this Treaty.

Done at Washington, the   day of April, 1949.

··{4}·· The Communist Takeover of China, 1945–1949

THE SITUATION IN CHINA[1]
Statement by General Marshall, January 7, 1947

[ ]
In this intricate and confused situation, I shall merely endeavor here to touch on some of the more important considerations—as they appeared to me —during my connection with the negotiations to bring about peace in China and a stable democratic form of government.

In the first place, the greatest obstacle to peace has been the complete, almost overwhelming suspicion with which the Chinese Communist Party and the Kuomintang regard each other.

On the one hand, the leaders of the Government are strongly opposed to a communistic form of government. On the other, the Communists frankly state that they are Marxists and intend to work toward establishing a communistic form of government in China, though first advancing through the medium of a democratic form of government of the American or British type. . . .

I think the most important factors involved in the recent break-down of negotiations are these: On the side of the National Government, which is in effect the Kuomintang, there is a dominant group of reactionaries who have been opposed, in my opinion, to almost every effort I have made to influence the formation of a genuine coalition government. . . . This group includes military as well as political leaders.

On the side of the Chinese Communist Party there are, I believe, liberals as well as radicals, though this view is vigorously opposed by many who believe that the Chinese Communist Party discipline is too rigidly enforced to admit of such differences of viewpoint. Nevertheless, it has appeared to me that there is a definite liberal group among the Communists, especially of young men who have turned to the Communists in disgust at the corruption evident in the local governments—men who would put the interest of the Chinese people above ruthless measures to establish a Communist ideology in

---

[1] Reprinted from *The Department of State Bulletin*, XVI, No. 394 (January 19, 1947), pp. 83–85.

the immediate future. The dyed-in-the-wool Communists do not hesitate at the most drastic measures to gain their end . . . They completely distrust the leaders of the Kuomintang and appear convinced that every Government proposal is designed to crush the Chinese Communist Party. I must say that the quite evidently inspired mob actions of last February and March, some within a few blocks of where I was then engaged in completing negotiations, gave the Communists good excuse for such suspicions. . . .

Sincere efforts to achieve settlement have been frustrated time and again by extremist elements of both sides. The agreements reached by the Political Consultative Conference a year ago were a liberal and forward-looking charter which then offered China a basis for peace and reconstruction. However, irreconcilable groups within the Kuomintang, interested in the preservation of their own feudal control of China, evidently had no real intention of implementing them. . . .

Between this dominant reactionary group in the Government and the irreconcilable Communists who, I must state, did not so appear last February, lies the problem of how peace and well-being are to be brought to the long-suffering and presently inarticulate mass of the people of China. The reactionaries in the Government have evidently counted on substantial American support regardless of their actions. The Communists by their unwillingness to compromise in the national interest are evidently counting on an economic collapse to bring about the fall of the Government, accelerated by extensive guerrilla action against the long lines of rail communications—regardless of the cost in suffering to the Chinese people.

The salvation of the situation, as I see it, would be the assumption of leadership by the liberals in the Government and in the minority parties, a splendid group of men, but who as yet lack the political power to exercise a controlling influence. Successful action on their part under the leadership of Generalissimo Chiang Kai-shek would, I believe, lead to unity through good government. . . .

I have spoken very frankly because in no other way can I hope to bring the people of the United States to even a partial understanding of this complex problem. I have expressed all these views privately in the course of negotiations; they are well known, I think, to most of the individuals concerned. I express them now publicly, as it is my duty, to present my estimate of the situation and its possibilities to the American people who have a deep interest in the development of conditions in the Far East promising an enduring peace in the Pacific.

STATEMENT OF THE CENTRAL COMMITTEE OF THE CHINESE COMMUNIST PARTY[1]
February 1, 1947

The Political Consultative Conference, comprising all major political parties, groups and prominent social figures, convened on January 10, 1946 in accordance with stipulations of the summary of Kuomintang-Communist talks in Chungking on October 10, 1945, is universally recognized by the people of the entire country and world powers as the highest political body in China. Until China has a really democratic national parliament, all important internal and diplomatic affairs which would be passed by a parliament in democratic countries should pass through this Conference or obtain agreement of major political parties and groups before they can be regarded as effective.

Since January 10, 1946, however, Chinese Kuomintang government has not only enacted many arbitrary domestic measures but has also many times singly conducted diplomatic negotiations of a serious nature with certain foreign governments. . . . These diplomatic negotiations include loans from foreign governments, continuation of Lend-Lease, buying and accepting of munitions and surplus war materials, forming of treaties regarding special rights in commerce, navigation, aviation and other economic and legal special rights.

These negotiations and agreements request or permit foreign land, sea and naval forces to be stationed in or operate on the seas, waterways, territories, and in the air of the country, and to enter or occupy and jointly construct or make use of military bases and points strategic to the national defense. They furthermore request or permit foreign military and other personnel to participate in organization, training, transportation and military operations of land, air and naval forces of the country, and to become conversant with military and other state secrets of the country. They also permit such serious matters as foreign intervention in internal affairs.

Those measures of the Chinese Kuomintang government are completely contrary to the will of the Chinese people and they have plunged and will continue to plunge China into civil war, reaction, national disgrace, loss of national rights, colonization and crises of chaos and collapse. In order to rescue the motherland from this calamity, to protect national rights and interests and the dignity of the Political Consultative Conference, the Chinese Communist Party solemnly states: this party will not either now nor in the future recognize any foreign loans, any treaties which disgrace the

---

[1] Reprinted from *U.S. Relations with China with Special Reference to the Period 1944–1949*, Department of State Publication No. 3573 (Washington: G.P.O., 1949), pp. 719–720.

country and strip away its rights, and any of the above-mentioned agreements and understandings established by the Kuomintang government after January 10, 1946, nor will it recognize any future diplomatic negotiation of the same character which have not been passed by Political Consultative Conference or which have not obtained agreement of this party and other parties and groups participating in the Political Consultative Conference.   [ ]

UNITED STATES POSITION ON CHINA[1]
Statement by Secretary of State Dean Acheson, August 5, 1949

[ ]
The reasons for the failures of the Chinese National Government . . . do not stem from any inadequacy of American aid. Our military observers on the spot have reported that the Nationalist armies did not lose a single battle during the crucial year of 1948 through lack of arms or ammunition. The fact was that the decay which our observers had detected in Chungking early in the war had fatally sapped the powers of resistance of the Kuomintang. Its leaders had proved incapable of meeting the crisis confronting them, its troops had lost the will to fight, and its Government had lost popular support. The Communists, on the other hand, through a ruthless discipline and fanatical zeal, attempted to sell themselves as guardians and liberators of the people. The Nationalist armies did not have to be defeated; they disintegrated. History has proved again and again that a regime without faith in itself and an army without morale cannot survive the test of battle. . . .

The historic policy of the United States of friendship and aid toward the people of China was, however, maintained in both peace and war. Since V–J Day, the United States Government has authorized aid to Nationalist China in the form of grants and credits totaling approximately 2 billion dollars, an amount equivalent in value to more than 50 percent of the monetary expenditures of the Chinese Government and of proportionately greater magnitude in relation to the budget of that Government than the United States has provided to any nation of Western Europe since the end of the war. In addition to these grants and credits, the United States Government has sold the Chinese Government large quantities of military and civilian war surplus property with a total procurement cost of over 1 billion dollars, for which the agreed realization to the United States was 232 million dollars. A large proportion of the military supplies furnished the Chinese armies by the United States since V–J Day has, however, fallen into the hands of the Chinese Communists through the military ineptitude of the Nationalist

---

[1] Reprinted from *U.S. Relations with China with Special Reference to the Period 1944–1949*, Department of State Publication No. 3573 (Washington: G.P.O., 1949), pp. xiv–xvii.

leaders, their defections and surrenders, and the absence among their forces of the will to fight.

It has been urged that relatively small amounts of additional aid—military and economic—to the National Government would have enabled it to destroy communism in China. The most trustworthy military, economic, and political information available to our Government does not bear out this view.

A realistic appraisal of conditions in China, past and present, leads to the conclusion that the only alternative open to the United States was full-scale intervention in behalf of a Government which had lost the confidence of its own troops and its own people. Such intervention would have required the expenditure of even greater sums than have been fruitlessly spent thus far, the command of Nationalist armies by American officers, and the probable participation of American armed forces—land, sea, and air—in the resulting war. Intervention of such a scope and magnitude would have been resented by the mass of the Chinese people, would have diametrically reversed our historic policy, and would have been condemned by the American people. . . .

The unfortunate but inescapable fact is that the ominous result of the civil war in China was beyond the control of the government of the United States. Nothing that this country did or could have done within the reasonable limits of its capabilities could have changed that result; nothing that was left undone by this country has contributed to it. It was the product of internal Chinese forces, forces which this country tried to influence but could not. A decision was arrived at within China, if only a decision by default.

And now it is abundantly clear that we must face the situation as it exists in fact. We will not help the Chinese or ourselves by basing our policy on wishful thinking. We continue to believe that, however tragic may be the immediate future of China and however ruthlessly a major portion of this great people may be exploited by a party in the interest of a foreign imperialism, ultimately the profound civilization and the democratic individualism of China will reassert themselves and she will throw off the foreign yoke. I consider that we should encourage all developments in China which now and in the future work toward this end.

In the immediate future, however, the implementation of our historic policy of friendship for China must be profoundly affected by current developments. It will necessarily be influenced by the degree to which the Chinese people come to recognize that the Communist regime serves not their interests but those of Soviet Russia and the manner in which, having become aware of the facts, they react to this foreign domination. One point, however, is clear. Should the Communist regime lend itself to the aims of Soviet Russian imperialism and attempt to engage in aggression against China's neighbors, we and the other members of the United Nations would be confronted by a situation violative of the principles of the United Nations Charter and threatening international peace and security.

Meanwhile our policy will continue to be based upon our own respect for the Charter, our friendship for China, and our traditional support for the Open Door and for China's independence and administrative and territorial integrity.

THE COMMON PROGRAM OF THE CHINESE PEOPLE'S POLITICAL CONSULTATIVE CONFERENCE[1]
Adopted by the First Plenary Session of the Chinese People's PCC on September 29th, 1949 in Peking

PREAMBLE

[ ]
The Chinese People's Political Consultative Conference, representing the will of the people of the whole country, proclaims the establishment of the People's Republic of China and is organizing the people's own central government. The Chinese People's Political Consultative Conference unanimously agrees that New Democracy, or the People's Democracy, shall be the political foundation for the national construction of the People's Republic of China. It has also adopted the following Common Program which should be jointly observed by all units participating in the Conference, by the people's government of all levels, and by the people of the whole country.

Article 1. The People's Republic of China is a New Democratic or a People's Democratic state. It carries out the people's democratic dictatorship led by the working class, based on the alliance of workers and peasants, and uniting all democratic classes and all nationalities in China. It opposes imperialism, feudalism and bureaucratic capitalism and strives for independence, democracy, peace, unity, prosperity and strength of China.

Article 2. The Central People's Government of the People's Republic of China must undertake to wage the people's war of liberation to the very end, to liberate all the territory of China, and to achieve the unification of China.

Article 3. The People's Republic of China must abolish all the prerogatives of imperialist countries in China. It must confiscate bureaucratic capital and put it into the possession of the people's state. It must systematically transform the feudal and semi-feudal land ownership system into a system of peasant land ownership; it must protect the public property of the state and of the cooperatives and must protect the economic interests and private property of workers, peasants, the petty bourgeoisie and the national bourgeoisie. It must develop the people's economy of New Democracy and steadily transform the country from an agricultural into an industrial one.

---

[1] Reprinted from *The Important Documents of the First Plenary Session of the Chinese People's Political Consultative Conference* (Peking: Foreign Languages Press, 1949), pp. 1–20.

Article 4. The people of the People's Republic of China shall have the right to elect and to be elected according to law.

Article 5. The people of the People's Republic of China shall have freedom of thought, speech, publication, assembly, association, correspondence, person, domicile, change of domicile, religious belief and the freedom of holding processions and demonstrations.

Article 6. The People's Republic of China shall abolish the feudal system which holds women in bondage. Women shall enjoy equal rights with men in political, economic, cultural, educational and social life. Freedom of marriage for men and women shall be put into effect.

Article 7. The People's Republic of China shall suppress all counter-revolutionary activities, severely punish all Kuomintang counter-revolutionary war criminals and other leading incorrigible counter-revolutionary elements who collaborate with imperialism, commit treason against the fatherland and oppose the cause of people's democracy. Feudal landlords, bureaucratic capitalists and reactionary elements in general, after they have been disarmed and have had their special powers abolished, shall, in addition, be deprived of their political rights in accordance with law for a necessary period. But, at the same time, they shall be given some means of livelihood and shall be compelled to reform themselves through labour so as to become new men. If they continue their counter-revolutionary activities, they will be severely punished.

Article 8. It is the duty of every national of the People's Republic of China to defend the fatherland, to abide by the law, to observe labour discipline, to protect public property, to perform public and military service, and to pay taxes.

Article 9. All nationalities in the People's Republic of China shall have equal rights and duties.

Article 10. The armed forces of the People's Republic of China, namely, the People's Liberation Army, the people's public security forces and the people's police belong to the people. It is the task of these armed forces to defend the independence, territorial integrity and sovereignty of China, and to defend the revolutionary gains and all legitimate rights and interests of the Chinese people. The Central People's Government of the People's Republic of China shall endeavour to consolidate and strengthen the people's armed forces, so as to enable them to accomplish their tasks effectively.

Article 11. The People's Republic of China shall unite with all peace-loving and freedom-loving countries and peoples throughout the world, first of all, with the U.S.S.R., all Peoples' Democracies and all oppressed nations. It shall take its stand in the camp of international peace and democracy, to oppose imperialist aggression to defend lasting world peace.

[ ]

Article 27. Agrarian reform is the necessary condition for the development of the nation's productive power and for its industrialization. In all areas where agrarian reform has been carried out, the ownership of the land acquired by the peasants shall be protected. In areas where agrarian reform has not been carried out, the peasant masses must be set in motion to establish peasant organisations and to put into effect the policy of "land to the tiller" through such measures as the elimination of local bandits and despots, the reduction of rent and interest and the distribution of land.

Article 28. State-owned economy is of a Socialist nature. All enterprises relating to the economic life of the country and exercising a dominant influence over the people's livelihood shall be under the unified operation of the state. All state-owned resources and enterprises are the public property of all the people and are the main material basis on which the People's Republic will develop production and bring about a prosperous economy. They are the leading force of the entire social economy.

Article 29. Co-operative economy is of a semi-Socialist nature and is an important component of the people's economy as a whole. The People's Government shall foster its development and accord it preferential treatment.

Article 30. The People's Government shall encourage the active operation of all private economic enterprises beneficial to the national welfare and to the people's livelihood and shall assist in their development.

Article 31. The economy jointly operated by state and private capital is of a state-capitalist nature. Whenever necessary and possible, private capital shall be encouraged to develop in the direction of state-capitalism, in such ways as processing for state-owned enterprises and exploiting state-owned resources in the form of concessions.

Article 32. The system of worker's participation in the administration of production shall, for the present period, be established in state-owned enterprises. This means that factory administrative committees shall be set up under the leadership of the factory managers. In privately-owned enterprises, in order to carry out the principle of benefitting both labour and capital, collective contracts shall be signed by the trade union, representing the workers and employees, and the employer. For the present period, an eight to ten-hour day should in general be enforced in publicly and privately operated enterprises, but under special circumstances this matter may be dealt with at discretion. The people's governments shall fix minimum wages according to the conditions prevailing in various localities and trades. Labour insurance shall be gradually established. The special interests of juvenile and women workers shall be safeguarded. Inspection of industries and mines shall be carried out in order to improve their safety devices and sanitary facilities.

[ ]

Article 37. Commerce: All legitimate public and private trade shall be protected. Control shall be exercised over foreign trade and the policy of protecting trade shall be adopted. Freedom of domestic trade shall be established under a unified economic state plan, but commercial speculation disturbing the market shall be strictly prohibited. State-owned trading organizations shall assume the responsibility of adjusting supply and demand, stabilizing commodity prices and assisting the people's co-operatives. The people's government shall adopt the measures necessary to encourage the people in saving, to facilitate remittances from overseas Chinese, and to channel into industry and other productive enterprises, all socially idle capital and commercial capital which is not beneficial to the national welfare and/or to the people's livelihood.

Article 38. Co-operatives: The broad masses of working people shall be encouraged and assisted to develop co-operatives according to the principle of willingness. Supply and marketing co-operatives, as well as consumers', credit, producers', and transport co-operatives shall be organized in towns and villages. Consumers' co-operatives shall first be organised in factories, institutions and schools.

[ ]

Article 41. The culture and education of the People's Republic of China shall be New Democratic—national, scientific and popular. The main tasks of the People's Government in cultural and educational work shall be the raising of the cultural level of the people, the training of personnel for national construction work, the eradicating of feudal, compradore and fascist ideology and the developing of the ideology of service to the people.

[ ]

Article 49. Freedom of reporting truthful news shall be safeguarded. The utilization of the press for slander, for undermining the interests of the state and the people and for provoking world war shall be prohibited. The people's radio and publication work shall be developed. Attention shall be paid to publishing popular books and journals beneficial to the people.

Article 50. All nationalities within the boundaries of the People's Republic of China are equal. They shall establish unity and mutual aid among themselves, and shall oppose imperialism and their own public enemies, so that the People's Republic of China will become a big fraternal and co-operative family composed of all its nationalities. Greater Nationalism and chauvinism shall be opposed. Acts involving discrimination, oppression and splitting of the unity of the various nationalities shall be prohibited.

Article 51. Regional autonomy shall be exercised in areas where national minorities are concentrated and various kinds of autonomy organizations of the different nationalities shall be set up according to the size of the respective populations and regions. In places where different nationalities live together and in the autonomous areas of the national minorities, the different nationalities shall each have an appropriate number of representatives in the local organs of political power.

[ ]

Article 53. All national minorities shall have freedom to develop their dialects and languages, to preserve or reform their traditions, customs and religious beliefs. The People's Government shall assist the masses of the people of all national minorities to develop their political, economic, cultural and educational construction work.

Article 54. The principle of the foreign policy of the People's Republic of China is protection of the independence, freedom, integrity of territory and sovereignty of the country, upholding of lasting international peace and friendly co-operation between the peoples of all countries, and opposition to the imperialist policy of aggression and war.

Article 55. The Central People's Government of the People's Republic of China shall examine the treaties and agreements concluded between the Kuomintang and foreign governments, and shall recognize, abrogate, revise, or re-negotiate them according to their respective contents.

Article 56. The Central People's Government of the People's Republic of China may, on the basis of equality, mutual benefit and mutual respect for territory and sovereignty, negotiate with foreign governments which have severed relations with the Kuomintang reactionary clique and which adopt a friendly attitude towards the People's Republic of China, and may establish diplomatic relations with them.

Article 57. The People's Republic of China may restore and develop commercial relations with foreign governments and peoples on a basis of equality and mutual benefit.

Article 58. The Central People's Government of the People's Republic of China shall do its utmost to protect the proper rights and interests of Chinese residing abroad.

Article 59. The People's Government of the People's Republic of China protects law-abiding foreign nationals in China.

Article 60. The People's Republic of China shall accord the right of asylum to foreign nationals who seek refuge in China because they have been oppressed by their own governments for supporting the people's interests and taking part in the struggle for peace and democracy.

··{**5**}·· *The Retreat from Colonialism in the Far East, 1945–1954*

POLICY IN BURMA[1]
British Government's Statement, May, 1945

[ ]
The considered policy of His Majesty's Government of promoting full self-government in Burma has frequently been declared. It is and has consistently been our aim to assist her political development till she can sustain the responsibilities of complete self-government within the British Commonwealth and consequently attain a status equal to that of the Dominions and of this country.

2. Inevitably Burma's progress towards full self-government has been interrupted and set back by the Japanese invasion and the long interval of enemy occupation and active warfare in her territories, during which she has suffered grave damage not only in the form of material destruction but in a shattering of the foundations of her economic and social life. It is, of course, upon these foundations that a political structure rests, and until the foundations are once again firm the political institutions which were in operation before the Japanese invasion cannot be restored. . . .

3. Until these foundations are restored sufficiently to enable the first essential political process to be undertaken, that is for a General Election to be held, it is not possible to re-establish a Burmese Government as it existed in 1941. It is accordingly necessary, so long as the government of the country cannot be carried on in accordance with the provisions of the 1935 Act, that recourse should continue to be had to the provisions of Section 139, under which the administration is carried on by the Governor in direct responsibility to His Majesty's Government. . . . But though this initial period of controlled government is necessary, His Majesty's Government are anxious that all the functions of government should not in fact be concentrated in the

---

[1] Reprinted from *Burma: Statement of Policy by His Majesty's Government, May, 1945*, Cmd. 6635 (London: H.M.S.O., 1945), pp. 9–11.

Governor, but that he should be provided with definite means of obtaining Burmese assistance and advice in the discharge of them and have power to associate with himself representatives of Burmese opinion in executive and legislative capacities. It is proposed, therefore, to take power to introduce by Orders in Council modifications to enable the system of administration authorised by Section 139 as it now stands to be liberalised. It is contemplated that early opportunity will be taken under these proposed powers to establish an Executive Council which, though it might at the outset be a small and mainly official body, could be expanded as opportunity offers by the inclusion in it of non-official Burmese. Such a Council would, pending the revival of normal constitutional methods, give Burmans a share in the administrative task of restoring the economy of their country, subject to the retention of the Governor's powers of supervision and control. . . .

4. . . . It is the intention of His Majesty's Government that when conditions are sufficiently restored to make it possible to hold an election and terminate the operation of Section 139, the normal provisions of the Act (unless amended by the incorporation of temporary provisions which had been found to commend themselves to Burmans) will re-enter into force. A General Election could then be held, and a Legislature formed with the same degree of authority over the same range of matters as it enjoyed before the Japanese invasion.

5. Government in accordance with the provisions of the Act of 1935 having thus been restored, as soon as the conditions in the country permit, a second phase in constitutional development will begin, during which the ground will be prepared for the attainment of full self-government. At the same time the necessary measures for the restoration of Burma's economy beyond the point which must be attained before even the first General Election can be held, would continue and her financial position would progressively develop towards a standard of self-sufficiency.

6. The ultimate objective of His Majesty's Government will be that representatives of the Burmese people, after reaching a sufficient measure of agreement between the various parties and sections, should draw up a Constitution of a type which they themselves consider most suitable for Burma, taking into account not only the British but the other various types of constitution in democratically governed countries. What the machinery for this should be will be a matter for discussion and agreement with representative Burmans. A simultaneous process would be discussion of the content of the agreements to be made with His Majesty's Government on matters on which the latter would have continuing obligations after the establishment of full self-government in Burma.

7. When once the duly appointed representatives of the Burmese people have agreed, in the light of preparatory study of the subject, on the type of constitution most suitable for Burma, and it is clear that the proposed constitution has a sufficient measure of support in Burma to justify endorse-

ment by Parliament, His Majesty's Government will enter into discussions with representatives of Burma with a view to satisfactory agreements being made to enable them to fulfil their continuing obligations and to safeguard any outstanding financial advances made by His Majesty's Government, so that, when the necessary administrative organisation is in existence, and the other arrangements have been completed, full self-government within the British Commonwealth can thereupon be established in Burma proper. The administration of the Scheduled Areas, that is the Shan States and the tribal areas in the mountainous fringes of the country, inhabited by peoples differing in language, social customs and degree of political development from the Burmans inhabitating the central areas, would for the time being be subject to a special regime under the Governor until such time as their inhabitants signify their desire for some suitable form of amalgamation of their territories with Burma proper.

POLICY IN INDIA[1]
British Government's Statement, 1946

1. On the 15th March last, just before the despatch of the Cabinet Mission to India, Mr. Attlee, the British Prime Minister, used these words:

My colleagues are going to India with the intention of using their utmost endeavours to help her to attain her freedom as speedily and fully as possible. What form of Government is to replace the present régime is for India to decide; but our desire is to help her to set up forthwith the machinery for making that decision . . . .

I hope that the Indian people may elect to remain within the British Commonwealth. I am certain that she will find great advantages in doing so . . . .

But if she does so elect, it must be by her own free will. The British Commonwealth and Empire is not bound together by chains of external compulsion. It is a free association of free peoples. If, on the other hand, she elects for independence, in our view she has a right to do so. It will be for us to help to make the transition as smooth and easy as possible.

2. Charged in these historic words, we—the Cabinet Ministers and the Viceroy—have done our utmost to assist the two main political parties to reach agreement upon the fundamental issue of the unity or division of India. After prolonged discussions in New Delhi we succeeded in bringing the Congress and the Muslim League together in conference at Simla. There was a full exchange of views and both parties were prepared to make considerable concessions in order to try to reach a settlement, but it ultimately proved impossible to close the remainder of the gap between the parties and

---

[1] Reprinted from *India (Cabinet Mission): Statement by the Cabinet Mission and His Excellency the Viceroy*, Cmd. 6821 (London: H.M.S.O., 1946), pp. 2–9.

so no agreement could be concluded. Since no agreement has been reached, we feel that it is our duty to put forward what we consider are the best arrangements possible to ensure a speedy setting up of the new constitution. This statement is made with the full approval of His Majesty's Government in the United Kingdom.

3. We have accordingly decided that immediate arrangements should be made whereby Indians may decide the future constitution of India, and an interim Government may be set up at once to carry on the administration of British India until such time as a new constitution can be brought into being. We have endeavoured to be just to the smaller as well as to the larger sections of the people; and to recommend a solution which will lead to a practicable way of governing the India of the future, and will give a sound basis for defence and a good opportunity for progress in the social, political and economic field.

4. It is not intended in this statement to review the voluminous evidence which has been submitted to the Mission; but it is right that we should state that it has shown an almost universal desire, outside the supporters of the Muslim League, for the unity of India.

5. This consideration did not, however, deter us from examining closely and impartially the possibility of a partition of India; since we were greatly impressed by the very genuine and acute anxiety of the Muslims lest they should find themselves subjected to a perpetual Hindu-majority rule. This feeling has become so strong and widespread amongst the Muslims that it cannot be allayed by mere paper safeguards. If there is to be internal peace in India it must be secured by measures which will assure to the Muslims a control in all matters vital to their culture, religion, and economic or other interests.

6. We therefore examined in the first instance the question of a separate and fully independent sovereign state of Pakistan as claimed by the Muslim League. Such a Pakistan would comprise two areas: one in the North-West consisting of the provinces of the Punjab, Sind, North-West Frontier, and British Baluchistan; the other in the North-East consisting of the provinces of Bengal and Assam. The League were prepared to consider adjustment of boundaries at a later stage, but insisted that the principle of Pakistan should first be acknowledged. The argument for a separate state of Pakistan was based, first, upon the right of the Muslim majority to decide their method of government according to their wishes, and, secondly, upon the necessity to include substantial areas in which Muslims are in a minority, in order to make Pakistan administratively and economically workable.

. . . the setting up of a separate sovereign state of Pakistan on the lines claimed by the Muslim League would not solve the communal minority problem; nor can we see any justification for including within a sovereign Pakistan those districts of the Punjab and of Bengal and Assam in which the population is predominantly non-Muslim. Every argument that can be used in favour of Pakistan can equally, in our view, be used in favour of the exclusion of the non-Muslim areas from Pakistan. This point would particularly affect the position of the Sikhs.

7. We, therefore, considered whether a smaller sovereign Pakistan confined to the Muslim majority areas alone might be a possible basis of compromise. Such a Pakistan is regarded by the Muslim League as quite impracticable because it would entail the exclusion from Pakistan of (*a*) the whole of the Ambala and Jullundur divisions in the Punjab; (*b*) the whole of Assam except the district of Sylhet; and (*c*) a large part of Western Bengal, including Calcutta, in which city the percentage of the Muslim population is 23.6 per cent. We ourselves are also convinced that any solution which involves a radical partition of the Punjab and Bengal, as this would do, would be contrary to the wishes and interests of a very large proportion of the inhabitants of these provinces. Bengal and the Punjab each has its own common language and a long history and tradition. Moreover, any division of the Punjab would of necessity divide the Sikhs, leaving substantial bodies of Sikhs on both sides of the boundary. We have therefore been forced to the conclusion that neither a larger nor a smaller sovereign state of Pakistan would provide an acceptable solution for the communal problem.

8. Apart from the great force of the foregoing arguments there are weighty administrative, economic and military considerations. . . .

10. Finally, there is the geographical fact that the two halves of the proposed Pakistan state are separated by some seven hundred miles and the communications between them both in war and peace would be dependent on the goodwill of Hindustan.

11. We are therefore unable to advise the British Government that the power which at present resides in British hands should be handed over to two entirely separate sovereign states.

12. This decision does not, however, blind us to the very real Muslim apprehensions that their culture and political and social life might become submerged in a purely unitary India, in which the Hindus with their greatly superior numbers must be a dominating element. To meet this the Congress have put forward a scheme under which provinces would have full autonomy subject only to a minimum of central subjects, such as foreign affairs, defence and communications.

Under this scheme provinces, if they wished to take part in economic and administrative planning on a large scale, could cede to the centre optional subjects in addition to the compulsory ones mentioned above.

13. Such a scheme would, in our view, present considerable constitutional disadvantages and anomalies. It would be very difficult to work a central executive and legislature in which some ministers, who dealt with compulsory subjects, were responsible to the whole of India while other ministers, who dealt with optional subjects, would be responsible only to those provinces who had elected to act together in respect of such subjects.

This difficulty would be accentuated in the central legislature, where it would be necessary to exclude certain members from speaking and voting when subjects with which their provinces were not concerned were under discussion. Apart from the difficulty of working such a scheme, we do not consider that it would be fair to deny to other provinces, which did not desire to take the optional subjects at the centre, the right to form themselves into a group for a similar purpose. This would indeed be no more than the exercise of their autonomous powers in a particular way.

14. Before putting forward our recommendations we turn to deal with the relationship of the Indian States to British India. It is quite clear that with the attainment of independence by British India, whether inside or outside the British Commonwealth, the relationship which has hitherto existed between the Rulers of the States and the British Crown will no longer be possible. Paramountcy can neither be retained by the British Crown nor transferred to the new government. This fact has been fully recognised by those whom we interviewed from the States. They have at the same time assured us that the States are ready and willing to co-operate in the new development of India. The precise form which their co-operation will take must be a matter for negotiation during the building up of the new constitutional structure and it by no means follows that it will be identical for all the States. . . .

15. We now indicate the nature of a solution which in our view would be just to the essential claims of all parties and would at the same time be most likely to bring about a stable and practicable form of constitution for All-India.

We recommend that the constitution should take the following basic form:

(1) There should be a Union of India, embracing both British India and the States, which should deal with the following subjects: foreign affairs, defence, and communications; and should have the powers necessary to raise the finances required for the above subjects.

(2) The Union should have an executive and a legislature constituted from British Indian and States representatives. Any question raising a major communal issue in the legislature should require for its decision a majority of the representatives present and voting of each of the two major communities as well as a majority of all the members present and voting.

(3) All subjects other than the Union subjects and all residuary powers should vest in the provinces.

(4) The States will retain all subjects and powers other than those ceded to the Union.

(5) Provinces should be free to form groups with executives and legislatures, and each group could determine the provincial subjects to be taken in common.

(6) The constitutions of the Union and of the groups should contain a provision whereby any province could by a majority vote of its legislative assembly call for a reconsideration of the terms of the constitution after an initial period of ten years and at ten-yearly intervals thereafter.

[ ]

23. While the constitution-making proceeds the administration of India has to be carried on. We attach the greatest importance therefore to the setting up at once of an interim Government having the support of the major political parties. It is essential during the interim period that there should be the maximum of co-operation in carrying through the difficult tasks that face the Government of India. Besides the heavy tasks of day-to-day administration, there is the grave danger of famine to be countered, there are decisions to be taken in many matters of post-war development which will have a far-reaching effect on India's future and there are important international conferences in which India has to be represented. For all these purposes a government having popular support is necessary. The Viceroy has already started discussions to this end and hopes soon to form an interim government in which all the portfolios, including that of War Member, will be held by Indian leaders having the full confidence of the people. The British Government, recognising the significance of the changes, will give the fullest measure of co-operation to the Government so formed in the accomplishment of its tasks of administration and in bringing about as rapid and smooth a transition as possible. . . .

We hope that the new independent India may choose to be a member of the British Commonwealth. We hope, in any event, that you will remain in close and friendly association with our people. But these are matters for your own free choice. Whatever that choice may be, we look forward with you to your ever-increasing prosperity among the greatest nations of the world and to a future even more glorious than your past.

REPORT OF THE UNITED NATIONS COMMISSION ON KOREA[1]
Covering the Period from December 15, 1949 to September 4, 1950

ANALYSIS AND CONCLUSIONS

A. *Responsibility for the aggression.* The invasion of the territory of the Republic of Korea by the armed forces of the North Korean authorities, which began on June 25, 1950, was an act of aggression initiated without warning and without provocation, in execution of a carefully prepared plan.

This plan of aggression, it is now clear, was an essential part of the policy

---

[1] Reprinted from U.S. *Policy in the Korean Conflict, July 1950–February 1951*, U.S. Department of State Publication No. 4263 (Washington: U.S.G.P.O., 1951), pp. 14–16.

of the North Korean authorities, the object of which was to secure control over the whole of Korea. If control could not be gained by peaceful means, it would be achieved by overthrowing the Republic of Korea, either by undermining it from within or, should that prove ineffective, by resorting to direct aggression. As the methods used for undermining the Republic from within proved unsuccessful, the North Korean authorities launched an invasion of the territory of the Republic of Korea.

B. *Origin and nature of the conflict.* The origin of the conflict is to be found in the artificial division of Korea and in the failure, in 1945, of the occupying Powers to reach agreement on the method to be used for giving independence to Korea. This failure was not due to anything inherent in the attitude of the people of Korea themselves, but was a reflection of those wider and more fundamental differences of outlook and policy which have become so marked a feature of the international scene.

This artificial division was consolidated by the exclusion from North Korea of the United Nations Temporary Commission, which had been charged by the General Assembly to observe the holding of elections on a democratic basis in the whole of Korea. In the circumstances, it was decided to hold such elections in South Korea alone.

Had internationally supervised elections been allowed to take place in the whole of Korea, and had a unified and independent Korea thereby come into existence, the present conflict could never have arisen.

C. *Prospects of unification.* The Korean people, one in race, language and culture, fervently desire to live in a unified and independent Korea. Unification can be the only aim regarding Korea. It did, however, appear to the Commission, before the aggression took place, that unification through negotiation was unlikely to be achieved if such negotiation involved the holding of internationally-supervised elections on a democratic basis in the whole of Korea. Experience suggested that the North Korean authorities would never agree to such elections.

It was hoped that, at some stage, it might be possible to break down the economic and social barriers between the two political entities as a step toward unification. That too proved illusory, as the North Korean authorities persisted in their policy of aiming at the overthrow of the Republic of Korea.

After the consolidation of the division of Korea, propaganda and hostile activities on the part of the North Korean authorities accentuated tension which, in turn, stiffened the attitude of the Government and people of the Republic of Korea, and even further prejudiced such possibility of unification by negotiation as might have remained. Notwithstanding the continued efforts of the Commission, it appeared on the eve of the aggression that the Korean peninsula would remain divided indefinitely, or at least until international tension had slackened.

D. *Development of representative government in the Republic of Korea.* The necessity to safeguard the stability and security of the Republic of Korea from the threat from the North gradually became a controlling factor in all the major activities of the administration of the Republic, and absorbed energies and resources which were needed to develop the new form of representative government and to carry out the economic and social recon-struction programme.

The first two years of the new National Assembly reflected clearly the difficulties which it would be normal to expect in a body dealing with a new and unfamiliar political structure. It had become clear, long before the act of aggression occurred, that the Legislature was making good progress in its efforts to exert parliamentary control over all departments of government, and would not rest content until its relations with the Executive had been satisfactorily adjusted. The growing civic responsibility shown by the Legisla-ture augured well for the future of representative government in Korea.

At the elections of May 30, 1950, the people showed very considerable enthusiasm, and the electoral machinery functioned well. Among the cases of interference with candidates which occurred, some were explainable in the light of the stringent precautions which the Government found it necessary to take in order to safeguard the stability and security of the State against the threat from the North. Although there appeared to be little justification for interference in some other cases, the results of the elections, in which many candidates critical of the Administration were returned, showed that the voters were in fact able to exercise their democratic freedom of choice among candidates, and had cast their votes accordingly. The results also showed popular support of the Republic, and a determination to improve the Admin-istration by constitutional means.

The division of Korea added to the economic difficulties that had arisen at the end of the Japanese domination, and made it most difficult for the Republic of Korea to become self-supporting. Funds which might have been expended for the execution of the social and economic programme of the Republic were consumed by heavy defence expenditures. Nevertheless, when the aggression occurred, substantial progress was being made with that pro-gramme.

E. Korean needs and aspirations. Serious problems of reconstruction and rehabilitation, particularly the grave refugee problem, already confront the country. To these problems will be added problems of yet greater magnitude when the military conflict comes to an end. It will be quite beyond the capacity of the country to provide from its own resources means for rehabilita-tion. A healthy and viable democracy in Korea cannot come into being unless very considerable aid and assistance are provided from outside Korea.

Finally, as the division of the country and the resulting antagonisms were artificial, the Commission believes that, when the conditions under which they arose disappear, it will be possible for the Korean people of both North and South to come again together, to live in peace and to build the strong foundations of a free, democratic Korea.

Done in a single copy in the English language at House No. 328 at Camp Hialeah, Pusan, Korea, this fourth day of September in the year nineteen hundred and fifty.

AMERICAN INTERVENTION IN KOREA[1]
Statement by A. A. Gromyko, Deputy Minister of Foreign Affairs of the U.S.S.R., July 4, 1950

The events now taking place in Korea broke out on June 25 as the result of a provocative attack by the troops of the South Korean authorities on the frontier areas of the Korean People's Democratic Republic. This attack was the outcome of a premeditated plan.

From time to time Syngman Rhee himself and other representatives of the South Korean authorities had blurted out the fact that the South Korean Syngman Rhee clique had such a plan.

As long ago as October 7, 1949, Syngman Rhee, boasting of success in training his army, stated outright, in an interview given to an American *United Press* correspondent, that the South Korean Army could capture Pyongyang in the course of three days.

On October 31, 1949, Sin Sen Mo, Defence Minister of the Syngman Rhee Government, also told newspaper correspondents that the South Korean troops were strong enough to act and take Pyongyang within a few days. Only one week before the provocative attack of the South Korean troops on the frontier areas of the Korean People's Democratic Republic, Syngman Rhee said, in a speech on June 19 in the so-called "National Assembly" where Mr. Dulles, adviser to the U.S. State Department, was present: "If we cannot protect democracy in the cold war, we shall win in a hot war."

It is not difficult to understand that representatives of the South Korean authorities could only make such statements because they felt that they had American support behind them. One month before the present developments in Korea, on May 19, 1950, Mr. Johnson, chief American administrator of aid to Korea, told the American Congress House of Representatives' Appropriations Committee that 100,000 officers and men of the South Korean Army, equipped with American weapons and trained by the American Military Mission, had completed their preparations and could begin war at any time.

It is known that only a few days before the Korean events, the United States Defence Secretary, Mr. Johnson, the Chief of the General Staff of the United States Armed Forces, General Bradley, and the State Department adviser, Mr. Dulles, arrived in Japan and had special conferences with General MacArthur, and that afterwards Mr. Dulles visited South Korea and went to frontier areas on the 38th Parallel.

Only one week before the events—on June 19—Mr. Dulles, adviser to

---

[1] Reprinted with permission from the *Soviet News*, No. 2393 (July 5, 1950), pp. 1–2.

the State Department, declared in the above-mentioned "National Assembly" of South Korea that the United States was ready to give all necessary moral and material support to South Korea which was fighting against Communism.

These facts speak for themselves and need no comment. . . .

The United States Government tries to justify armed intervention against Korea by alleging that it was undertaken on the authorisation of the Security Council. The falsity of such an allegation strikes the eye.

What really happened? It is known that the United States Government had started armed intervention in Korea before the Security Council was summoned to meet on June 27, without taking into consideration what decision the Security Council might take. Thus the United States Government confronted the United Nations Organisation with a *fait accompli*, with a violation of peace.

The Security Council merely rubber-stamped and back-dated the resolution proposed by the United States Government, approving the aggressive actions which this Government had undertaken. . . .

The illegal resolution of June 27, adopted by the Security Council under pressure from the United States Government, shows that the Security Council is acting, not as a body which is charged with the main responsibility for the maintenance of peace, but as a tool utilised by the ruling circles of the United States for unleashing war. This resolution of the Security Council constitutes a hostile act against peace.

If the Security Council valued the cause of peace, it should have attempted to reconcile the fighting sides in Korea before it adopted such a scandalous resolution. Only the Security Council and the United Nations Secretary-General could have done this. However, they did not make such an attempt, evidently knowing that such peaceful action contradicts the aggressors' plans. [ ]

THE MANIFESTO OF THE LAODONG PARTY[1]
February, 1951

[ ]

The main task of the Viet Nam Laodong Party now is:

To unite and lead the working class, the working masses and the entire people of Viet Nam in their struggle to wipe out the French colonialists and defeat the American interventionists; to bring the liberation war of the Viet Nam people to complete victory, thereby making Viet Nam a genuinely independent and united country.

The Viet Nam Laodong Party fully supports the Government of the Viet Nam Democratic Republic, unites and co-operates closely with other

---

[1] New China News Agency, April 6, 1951.

parties and organisations in the Lien Viet Front in order to realise fully the peoples democratic regime—politically, economically, socially and culturally.

The Viet Nam Laodong Party stands for guaranteeing the legitimate interests of all strata of the people.

It recommends that special care should be taken to raise the material and moral standards of living of the army, which fights for the defence of the country against the enemy, and which had been enduring the greatest hardships.

The workers, who are fighters in production, must have the opportunity continually to improve their living conditions and to take part in running their own enterprises.

The peasants, who are production combatants in the rural areas, must benefit from the reduction of land rent and interest and from appropriate agrarian reforms.

The intellectual workers must be encouraged and assisted in developing their abilities.

Small tradespeople and small employers must be assisted in developing trade and handicrafts.

The national bourgeoisie must be encouraged, helped and guided in their undertakings to contribute to the development of the national economy.

The right of the patriotic landlords to collect land rent in accordance with the law must be guaranteed.

The national minorities must be given every assistance and must enjoy absolute equality in rights and duties.

Effective help must be rendered to the women so as to bring about equality between men and women.

Believers in all religions must enjoy freedom of worship. Overseas Vietnamese in foreign countries must be protected.

The lives and properties of foreign residents in Viet Nam must be protected. Chinese nationals in particular, if they so desire, will be allowed to enjoy the same rights and perform the same duties as Vietnamese citizens.

In the field of external affairs, the Viet Nam Laodong Party recommends: 'The Viet Nam people must unite closely with and help the peoples of Cambodia and Laos in their struggle for independence and, with them, liberate jointly the whole of Indo-China; actively support the national liberation movements of oppressed peoples; unite closely with the Soviet Union, China and other people's democracies; form close alliances with the peoples of France and the French colonies so as to contribute to the anti-imperialist struggle to defend world peace and democracy.'

Confident in the efforts of all its members, in the support of working men and women and in the sympathy of the entire people, the Viet Nam Laodong is sure to fulfil its tasks of:

Bringing the liberation war to complete victory.

Developing the people's democratic regime.

Contributing to the defence of world peace and democracy.
Leading the Viet Nam people toward Socialism.

THE FINAL DECLARATION OF THE GENEVA CONFERENCE[1]
On Restoring Peace in Indochina, July 21, 1954

Final declaration, dated July 21, 1954, of the Geneva Conference on the problem of restoring peace in Indochina, in which the representatives of Cambodia, the Democratic Republic of Viet-Nam, France, Laos, the People's Republic of China, the State of Viet-Nam, the Union of Soviet Socialist Republics, the United Kingdom and the United States of America took part.

1. The Conference takes note of the agreements ending hostilities in Cambodia, Laos, and Viet-Nam and organizing international control and the supervision of the execution of the provisions of these agreements.

2. The Conference expresses satisfaction at the ending of hostilities in Cambodia, Laos, and Viet-Nam. The Conference expresses its conviction that the execution of the provisions set out in the present declaration and in the agreements on the cessation of hostilities will permit Cambodia, Laos, and Viet-Nam henceforth to play their part, in full independence and sovereignty, in the peaceful community of nations.

3. The Conference takes note of the declarations made by the Governments of Cambodia and of Laos of their intention to adopt measures permitting all citizens to take their place in the national community, in particular by participating in the next general elections, which, in conformity with the constitution of each of these countries, shall take place in the course of the year 1955, by secret ballot and in conditions of respect for fundamental freedoms.

4. The Conference takes note of the clauses in the agreement on the cessation of hostilities in Viet-Nam prohibiting the introduction into Viet-Nam of foreign troops and military personnel as well as of all kinds of arms and munitions. The Conference also takes note of the declarations made by the Governments of Cambodia and Laos of their resolution not to request foreign aid, whether in war material, in personnel, or in instructors except for the purpose of effective defense of their territory and, in the case of Laos, to the extent defined by the agreements on the cessation of hostilities in Laos.

5. The Conference takes note of the clauses in the agreement on the cessation of hostilities in Viet-Nam to the effect that no military base at the disposition of a foreign state may be established in the regrouping zones of the two parties, the latter having the obligation to see that the zones allotted to them shall not constitute part of any military alliance and shall not be utilized for the resumption of hostilities or in the service of an aggressive

---

[1] Reprinted from *The Department of State Bulletin*, XXXI, No. 788 (August 2, 1954), p. 164.

policy. The Conference also takes note of the declarations of the Governments of Cambodia and Laos to the effect that they will not join in any agreement with other states if this agreement includes the obligation to participate in a military alliance not in conformity with the principles of the charter of the United Nations or, in the case of Laos, with the principles of the agreement on the cessation of hostilities in Laos or, so long as their security is not threatened, the obligation to establish bases on Cambodian or Laotian territory for the military forces of foreign powers.

6. The Conference recognizes that the essential purpose of the agreement relating to Viet-Nam is to settle military questions with a view to ending hostilities and that the military demarcation line should not in any way be interpreted as constituting a political or territorial boundary. The Conference expresses its conviction that the execution of the provisions set out in the present declaration and in the agreement on the cessation of hostilities creates the necessary basis for the achievement in the near future of a political settlement in Viet-Nam.

7. The Conference declares that, so far as Viet-Nam is concerned, the settlement of political problems, effected on the basis of respect for the principles of independence, unity, and territorial integrity, shall permit the Vietnamese people to enjoy the fundamental freedoms, guaranteed by democratic institutions established as a result of free general elections by secret ballot.

In order to insure that sufficient progress in the restoration of peace has been made, and that all the necessary conditions obtain for free expression of the national will, general elections shall be held in July 1956, under the supervision of an international commission composed of representatives of the member states of the International Supervisory Commission referred to in the agreement on the cessation of hostilities. Consultations will be held on this subject between the competent representative authorities of the two zones from April 20, 1955, onwards.

8. The provisions of the agreements on the cessation of hostilities intended to insure the protection of individuals and of property must be most strictly applied and must, in particular, allow every one in Viet-Nam to decide freely in which zone he wishes to live.

9. The competent representative authorities of the northern and southern zones of Viet-Nam, as well as the authorities of Laos and Cambodia, must not permit any individual or collective reprisals against persons who have collaborated in any way with one of the parties during the war, or against members of such persons' families.

10. The Conference takes note of the declaration of the French Government to the effect that it is ready to withdraw its troops from the territory of Cambodia, Laos, and Viet-Nam, at the request of the governments concerned and within a period which shall be fixed by agreement between the parties except in the cases where, by agreement between the two parties, a certain number of French troops shall remain at specified points and for a specified time.

11. The Conference takes note of the declaration of the French Government to the effect that for the settlement of all the problems connected with the reestablishment and consolidation of peace in Cambodia, Laos, and Viet-Nam, the French Government will proceed from the principle of respect for the independence and sovereignty, unity, and territorial integrity of Cambodia, Laos, and Viet-Nam.

12. In their relations with Cambodia, Laos, and Viet-Nam, each member of the Geneva Conference undertakes to respect the sovereignty, the independence, the unity, and the territorial integrity of the above-mentioned states, and to refrain from any interference in their internal affairs.

13. The members of the Conference agree to consult one another on any question which may be referred to them by the International Supervisory Commission, in order to study such measures as may prove necessary to insure that the agreements on the cessation of hostilities in Cambodia, Loas, and Viet-Nam are respected.

SPEECH BY PRESIDENT SUKARNO OF INDONESIA AT THE OPENING OF THE BANDUNG CONFERENCE[1]
April 18, 1955

[ ]

This twentieth century has been a period of terrific dynamism. Perhaps the last fifty years have seen more developments and more material progress than the previous five hundred years. Man has learned to control many of the scourges which once threatened him. He has learned to consume distance. He has learned to project his voice and his picture across oceans and continents. He has probed deep into the secrets of nature and learned how to make the desert bloom and the plants of the earth increase their bounty. He has learned how to release the immense forces locked in the smallest particles of matter.

But has man's political skill marched hand-in-hand with his technical and scientific skill? Man can chain lightning to his command—can he control the society in which he lives? The answer is No! The political skill of man has been far outstripped by technical skill, and what he has made he cannot be sure of controlling.

The result of this is fear. And man gasps for safety and morality.

Perhaps now more than at any other moment in the history of the world, society, government and statesmanship need to be based upon the highest code of morality and ethics. And in political terms, what is the highest code of morality? It is the subordination of everything to the well-being of mankind. But today we are faced with a situation where the well-being of mankind is not always the primary consideration. Many who are in places of high power think, rather, of controlling the world.

---

[1] Reprinted from *Asia-Africa Speaks from Bandung* (Djakarta: Indonesian Ministry of Foreign Affairs, 1955), pp. 19–29.

Yes, we are living in a world of fear. The life of man today is corroded and made bitter by fear. Fear of the future, fear of the hydrogen bomb, fear of ideologies. Perhaps this fear is a greater danger than the danger itself, because it is fear which drives men to act foolishly, to act thoughtlessly, to act dangerously. . . .

All of us, I am certain, are united by more important things than those which superficially divide us. We are united, for instance, by a common detestation of colonialism in whatever form it appears. We are united by a common detestation of racialism. And we are united by a common determination to preserve and stabilise peace in the world. . . .

We are often told "Colonialism is dead." Let us not be deceived or even soothed by that. I say to you, colonialism is not yet dead. How can we say it is dead, so long as vast areas of Asia and Africa are unfree.

And, I beg of you do not think of colonialism only in the classic form which we of Indonesia, and our brothers in different parts of Asia and Africa, knew. Colonialism has also its modern dress, in the form of economic control, intellectual control, actual physical control by a small but alien community within a nation. It is a skilful and determined enemy, and it appears in many guises. It does not give up its loot easily. Wherever, whenever and however it appears, colonialism is an evil thing, and one which must be eradicated from the earth. . . .

Not so very long ago we argued that peace was necessary for us because an outbreak of fighting in our part of the world would imperil our precious independence, so recently won at such great cost.

Today, the picture is more black. War would not only mean a threat to our independence, it may mean the end of civilisation and even of human life. There is a force loose in the world whose potentiality for evil no man truly knows. Even in practice and rehearsal for war the effects may well be building up into something of unknown horror.

Not so long ago it was possible to take some little comfort from the idea that the clash, if it came, could perhaps be settled by what were called "conventional weapons"—bombs, tanks, cannon and men. Today that little grain of comfort is denied us for it has been made clear that the weapons of ultimate horror will certainly be used, and the military planning of nations is on that basis. The unconventional has become the conventional, and who knows what other examples of misguided and diabolical scientific skill have been discovered as a plague on humanity.

And do not think that the oceans and the seas will protect us. The food that we eat, the water that we drink, yes, even the very air that we breathe can be contaminated by poisons originating from thousands of miles away. And it could be that, even if we ourselves escaped lightly, the unborn generations of our children would bear on their distorted bodies the marks of our failure to control the forces which have been released on the world.

No task is more urgent than that of preserving peace. Without peace our independence means little. The rehabilitation and upbuilding of our countries will have little meaning. Our revolutions will not be allowed to run their course. . . .

What can we do? We can do much! We can inject the voice of reason into world affairs. We can mobilise all the spiritual, all the moral, all the political strength of Asia and Africa on the side of peace. Yes, we! We, the peoples of Asia and Africa, 1,400,000,000 strong, far more than half the human population of the world, we can mobilise what I have called the Moral Violence of Nations in favour of peace. We can demonstrate to the minority of the world which lives on the other continents that we, the majority, are for peace, not for war, and that whatever strength we have will always be thrown on to the side of peace.

In this struggle, some success has already been scored. I think it is generally recognised that the activity of the Prime Ministers of the Sponsoring Countries which invited you here had a not unimportant role to play in ending the fighting in Indo-China.

Look, the peoples of Asia raised their voices, and the world listened. It was no small victory and no negligible precedent! The five Prime Ministers did not make threats. They issued no ultimatum, they mobilised no troops. Instead they consulted together, discussed the issues, pooled their ideas, added together their individual political skills and came forward with sound and reasoned suggestions which formed the basis for a settlement of the long struggle in Indo-China.

I have often since then asked myself why these five were successful when others, with long records of diplomacy, were unsuccessful, and, in fact, had allowed a bad situation to get worse, so that there was a danger of the conflict spreading. . . . I think that the answer really lies in the fact that those five Prime Ministers brought a fresh approach to bear on the problem. They were not seeking advantage for their own countries. They had no axe of power-politics to grind. They had but one interest—how to end the fighting in such a way that the chances of continuing peace and stability were enhanced. . . .

So, let this Asian-African Conference be a great success! Make the "Live and let live" principle and the "Unity in Diversity" motto the unifying force which brings us all together—to seek in friendly, uninhibited discussion, ways and means by which each of us can live his own life, and let others live their own lives, in their own way, in harmony, and in peace.

If we succeed in doing so, the effect of it for the freedom, independence and the welfare of man will be great on the world at large. The Light of Understanding has again been lit, the Pillar of Cooperation again erected. The likelihood of success of this Conference is proved already by the very presence of you all here today. It is for us to give it strength, to give it the power of inspiration—to spread its message all over the World.   [ ]

PART II

*

Domestic Developments in Non-Communist Europe

··{6}·· Great Britain and the Commonwealth

LET US FACE THE FUTURE[1]
A Declaration of Labour Policy for the Consideration of the Nation

I

Victory is assured for us and our allies in the European war. The war in the East goes the same way. The British Labour Party is firmly resolved that Japanese barbarism shall be defeated just as decisively as Nazi aggression and tyranny. The people will have won both struggles. The gallant men and women in the Fighting Services, in the Merchant Navy, Home Guard and Civil Defence, in the factories and in the bombed areas—they deserve and must be assured a happier future than faced so many of them after the last war. Labour regards their welfare as a sacred trust. . . .

II

Britain's coming Election will be the greatest test in our history of the judgment and common sense of our people.

The nation wants food, work and homes. It wants more than that—it wants good food in plenty, useful work for all, and comfortable, labour-saving homes that take full advantage of the resources of modern science and productive industry. It wants a high and rising standard of living, security for all against a rainy day, an educational system that will give every boy and girl a chance to develop the best that is in them. . . .

The Labour Party stands for freedom—for freedom of worship, freedom of speech, freedom of the Press. The Labour Party will see to it that we keep and enlarge these freedoms, and that we enjoy again the personal civil liberties we have, of our own free will, sacrificed to win the war. The freedom of the Trade Unions, denied by the Trade Disputes and Trade Unions Act, 1927, must also be restored. But there are certain so-called freedoms that Labour will not tolerate: freedom to exploit other people; freedom to pay

---

[1] This Declaration of Policy was issued by the National Executive Committee of the British Labour Party in April, 1945. It was later approved by the Annual Conference of the Party. Reprinted by permission of the British Labour Party.

poor wages and to push up prices for selfish profit; freedom to deprive the people of the means of living full, happy, healthy lives. . . .

III

All parties pay lip service to the idea of jobs for all. All parties are ready to promise to achieve that end by keeping up the national purchasing power and controlling changes in the national expenditure through Government action. Where agreement ceases is in the degree of control of private industry that is necessary to achieve the desired end. . . .

What will the Labour Party do?

First, the whole of the national resources, in land, material and labour must be fully employed. Production must be raised to the highest level and related to purchasing power. Over-production is not the cause of depression and unemployment; it is under-consumption that is responsible. It is doubtful whether we have ever, except in war, used the whole of our productive capacity. This must be corrected because, upon our ability to produce and organise a fair and generous distribution of the product, the standard of living of our people depends.

Secondly, a high and constant purchasing power can be maintained through good wages, social services and insurance, and taxation which bears less heavily on the lower-income groups. But everybody knows that money and savings lose their value if prices rise, so rents and the prices of the necessities of life will be controlled.

Thirdly, planned investment in essential industries and on houses, schools, hospitals and civic centres will occupy a large field of capital expenditure. A National Investment Board will determine social priorities and promote better timing in private investment. In suitable cases we would transfer the use of efficient Government factories from war production to meet the needs of peace. The location of new factories will be suitably controlled, and where necessary the Government will itself build factories. There must be no depressed areas in the New Britain.

Fourthly, the Bank of England with its financial powers must be brought under public ownership, and the operations of the other banks harmonised with industrial needs. . . .

IV

By the test of war some industries have shown themselves capable of rising to new heights of efficiency and expansion. Others, including some of our older industries fundamental to our economic structure, have wholly or partly failed. . . .

The Labour Party is a Socialist Party, and proud of it. Its ultimate purpose at home is the establishment of the Socialist Commonwealth of Great Britain—free, democratic, efficient, progressive, public-spirited, its material resources organised in the service of the British people.

But Socialism cannot come overnight, as the product of a week-end revolution. The members of the Labour Party, like the British people, are practical-minded men and women.

There are basic industries ripe and over-ripe for public ownership and management in the direct service of the nation. There are many smaller businesses rendering good service which can be left to go on with their useful work.

There are big industries not yet ripe for public ownership which must nevertheless be required by constructive supervision to further the nation's needs and not to prejudice national interests by restrictive anti-social monopoly or cartel agreements—caring for their own capital structures and profits at the cost of a lower standard of living for all.

In the light of these considerations, the Labour Party submits to the nation the following industrial programme:

1. *Public ownership of the fuel and power industries.* . . .

2. *Public ownership of inland transport.* . . .

3. *Public ownership of iron and steel.* . . .

4. *Public supervision of monopolies and cartels* with the aim of advancing industrial efficiency in the service of the nation. . . .

5. *A firm and clear-cut programme for the export trade.* . . .

6. *The shaping of suitable economic and price controls* to secure that first things shall come first in the transition from war to peace and that every citizen (including the demobilised Service men and women) shall get fair play. . . .

7. *The better organisation of Government departments* and the Civil Service for work in relation to these ends. The economic purpose of government must be to spur industry forward and not to choke it with red tape.

V

Agriculture is not only a job for the farmers; it is also a way of feeding the people. So we need a prosperous and efficient agricultural industry ensuring a fair return for the farmer and farm worker without excessive prices to the consumer. Our agriculture should be planned to give us the food we can best produce at home, and large enough to give us as much of those foods as possible. . . .

Our good farm lands are part of the wealth of the nation and that wealth should not be wasted. The land must be farmed, not starved. If a landlord cannot or will not provide proper facilities for his tenant farmers, the State should take over his land at a fair valuation. The people need food at prices they can afford to pay. This means that our food supplies will have to be planned. Never again should they be left at the mercy of the city financier or speculator. Instead there must be stable markets, to the great gain of both producer and consumer. . . .

VI

Everybody says that we must have houses. Only the Labour Party is ready to take the necessary steps—a full programme of land planning and drastic action to ensure an efficient building industry that will neither burden the community with a crippling financial load nor impose bad conditions and heavy unemployment on its workpeople. There must be no restrictive price rings to keep up prices and bleed the taxpayer, the owner-occupier and the tenant alike. Modern methods, modern materials will have to be the order of the day. . . .

VII

In the interests of agriculture, housing and town and country planning alike, we declare for a radical solution for the crippling problems of land acquisition and use in the service of the national plan.

Labour believes in land nationalisation and will work towards it, but as a first step the State and the local authorities must have wider and speedier powers to acquire land for public purposes wherever the public interest so requires. In this regard and for the purposes of controlling land use under town and country planning, we will provide for fair compensation; but we will also provide for a revenue for public funds from "betterment."

VIII

An important step forward has been taken by the passing of the recent Education Act. Labour will put that Act not merely into legal force but into practical effect, including the raising of the school leaving age to 16 at the earliest possible moment, "further" or adult education, and free secondary education for all. . . .

IX

By good food and good homes, much avoidable ill-health can be prevented. In addition the best health services should be available for all. Money must no longer be the passport to the best treatment.

In the new National Health Service there should be health centres where the people may get the best that modern science can offer, more and better hospitals, and proper conditions for our doctors and nurses. More research is required into the causes of disease and the ways to prevent and cure it.

Labour will work specially for the care of Britain's mothers and their children—children's allowances and school medical and feeding services, better maternity and child welfare services. A healthy family life must be fully ensured and parenthood must not be penalised if the population of Britain is to be prevented from dwindling.

X

The Labour Party has played a leading part in the long campaign for proper social security for all—social provision against rainy days, coupled with economic policies calculated to reduce rainy days to a minimum. Labour led the fight against the mean and shabby treatment which was the lot of millions while Conservative Governments were in power over long years. A Labour Government will press on rapidly with legislation extending social insurance over the necessary wide field to all. . . .

XI

No domestic policy, however wisely framed and courageously applied, can succeed in a world still threatened by war. Economic strife and political and military insecurity are enemies of peace. We cannot cut ourselves off from the rest of the world—and we ought not to try.

Now that victory has been won, at so great a cost of life and material destruction, we must make sure that Germany and Japan are deprived of all power to make war again. We must consolidate in peace the great war-time association of the British Commonwealth with the U.S.A. and the U.S.S.R. Let it not be forgotten that in the years leading up to the war the Tories were so scared of Russia that they missed the chance to establish a partnership which might well have prevented the war. . . .

If peace is to be protected we must plan and act. Peace must not be regarded as a thing of passive inactivity: it must be a thing of life and action and work. . . .

The British, while putting their own house in order, must play the part of brave and constructive leaders in international affairs. The British Labour Movement comes to the tasks of international organisation with one great asset: it has a common bond with the working peoples of all countries, who have achieved a new dignity and influence through their long struggles against Nazi tyranny.

And in all this worth-while work—whether political, military or economic—the Labour Party will seek to promote mutual understanding and cordial co-operation between the Dominions of the British Commonwealth, the advancement of India to responsible self-government, and the planned progress of our Colonial Dependencies.

XII

[ ]
In these circumstances we appeal to all men and women of progressive outlook, and who believe in constructive change, to support the Labour Party. We respect the views of those progressive Liberals and others who would wish to support one or other of the smaller parties of their choice. But by so doing

they may help the Conservatives, or they may contribute to a situation in which there is no parliamentary majority for any major issue of policy.

In the interests of the nation and of the world, we earnestly urge all progressives to see to it—as they certainly can—that the next Government is not a Conservative Government but a Labour Government which will act on the principles of policy set out in the present Declaration.

IRON AND STEEL BILL[1]
Speech Delivered by the Minister of Supply, G. R. Strauss, on Nationalizing the Iron and Steel Industry, November 15, 1948

[ ]

It is a platitude, perhaps, to talk of the importance of the steel industry. All parties agree upon that. Without steel the life of Britain would collapse. So far as I can see there is not one trade of importance that could be carried on without it. All our capital equipment depends on steel. Steel, and steel-using industries, account for nearly half the value of our exports. This proportion has grown considerably since the war and may well grow further. Our future dependence on these industries in achieving solvency and prosperity will then become even greater. Not only our prosperity, but our security and influence on world affairs will depend largely upon our iron and steel industry; on whether it is efficient enough over a long period to produce cheap steel in ample quantities, and responsive enough to national requirements. It is because we believe that it cannot become either of these things as long as it remains in its present private ownership that we have introduced this Bill. We should have been failing in our duty if we had not done so.

There are, as far as I know, only three ways in which this industry can operate. Its ownership and control can be left in the hands of the steel masters as in the early pre-war years; or ownership can remain with the steel masters subject to a certain amount of State supervision through a body such as the Import Duties Advisory Committee or the Steel Board. Alternatively, and this is the only solution which appears to us satisfactory, ownership and control can be combined in the hands of the State. . . .

In our view it would be madness for a Government determined to build the nation's future prosperity on sound economic foundations to perpetuate in this basic industry a system in which serious clashes on matters of major policy between private and public interests are bound sooner or later to arise, possibly with the gravest consequences. To take such a risk would be to fly in the face of common sense and experience. We are not prepared to endanger the welfare and security of the country in this way. We say in short that the iron and steel industry shall no longer be distracted by two loyalties. Schiz-

---

[1] Reprinted from Hansard, *Parliamentary Debates* (House of Commons, Official Report, 5th Series), Vol. 458 (London: H.M.S.O., 1948), Columns 53–78.

ophrenia is a malady as dangerous in an industry as in an individual. And if
it is said that this malady has not yet reached a harmful stage, I reply that it is
far better, and far easier, to cure it before it becomes chronic. . . .

I now want to say a word about efficiency. Some spokesmen of the steel
industry claim that it is already efficient, and in support of that they say that
British steel prices compare very favourably with those of any other country in
the world except Australia. This argument can only be accepted with serious
qualifications. It does not take into account the effect of our Government
subsidies and price controls. I am not sure if those controls are among those
which hon. Gentlemen opposite want to abolish, but I hope they will tell us if
that is so during the Debate. The fact is, however, that if we withdrew the
subsidies on imported ore and scrap—and I may say in parenthesis that the
question of subsidies to this industry is now under review—and if we also
withdrew the control price on scrap, and the British steel industry had to buy
its material at the same prices as the Americans do, then our steel prices
would in the main be above American prices, despite the fact that American
wages are much higher. . . .

I come now to the question of the industry's capacity. It is naturally
more advantageous for private owners of the steel industry to have a total
productive capacity below potential demand. They would rather be reasonably certain of being able to sell limited quantities of products at good prices
than risk heavy expenditure on new plants which might from time to time
prove redundant. On the other hand, it is in the interests of the country and
of consumers of steel that productive capacity should be capable of meeting
industrial requirements in peace, and military requirements in war. I am far
from saying that the steel industry should be expanded, regardless of economics, to meet the peak demand which the most optimistic can foresee in the
next decade or so.

But in estimating the steel demand for which we should cater, we cannot
—we dare not—be conservative and cautious as the steel industry has been
and is bound to be, as soon as the present boom conditions fall off. Moreover
security against possible aggression is, unfortunately, still a problem for us,
and iron and steel capacity is still the best single index of the war potential of
a modern state. For all these reasons it must be for the nation and not for
private owners to decide what the capacity of the British iron and steel
industry should be, and this again can only be done effectively if the nation
becomes the owner. . . .

We, therefore, propose in the Bill that there shall be an Iron and Steel
Corporation of Great Britain owning all the securities of the major concerns
at the core of the industry—that is, the sections of the industry responsible for
the production of iron ore, pig iron, ingot steel or the hot rolling of steel.
These are the activities defined in the Second Schedule. The Corporation is
empowered to enter the business of steel production and its ancillary activities, but it is intended that it shall normally operate through the companies it

will own. The Corporation will inherit all the powers the companies possess in their memoranda of association, but none of the companies can alter its own memorandum without the consent of the Minister.

The Minister can give the Corporation directions of a general character which appear to him to affect the national interest. It is, of course, essential that there shall be the closest co-operation between the Minister and the Corporation on all matters of general concern. The Corporation must have the national interests, as seen by the Government of the day, constantly before it. The Minister is able to order that any of the activities of the Corporation or any of its companies be stopped or restricted. . . .

The Corporation will be the sole shareholder of every company that on the average of the years 1946 and 1947 produced more than 50,000 tons of iron ore, produced more than 20,000 tons of pig iron, or 20,000 tons of ingot steel, including alloy steel, and shaped more than 20,000 tons of steel by hot rolling. . . .

It is also because of our desire to avoid dislocation, and our anxiety to preserve the most valuable fruits of this industry's past activities and successes, that we propose to keep intact the identity of the individual concerns. Their personnel and internal organisations, and such *esprit de corps* as they may have achieved, will be unaffected. Indeed, on the morning after vesting day the only difference for them will be that the ownership of the securities has changed hands. The companies will continue to win ore, produce iron and steel and sell their products as before. . . .

Let no one suppose because we are here building for the future rather than the present, and proceeding by evolutionary rather than revolutionary steps, that the proposals in this Bill are devoid of historic significance. This great reform removes from the private sector of our economy to the public the industry which is the citadel of British capitalism. It transfers to Parliament and the community that power to dominate the economic life of this country which now resides with the steelmasters in Steel House.

It will enable our steel industry, which through its key position could do so much to lessen the severity of trade depressions, to become an effective national instrument for planning full employment. It will offer greater security to those who work in it. It will enable our home consumers to get the steel they require at low cost. It will enable the Colonies to get the steel called for by their development plans. It will enable us to co-operate the better with the peoples of Europe in the revival of the industrial prosperity of that continent and the strengthening of its democratic foundations. It is for these great ends that we are asking Parliament to make Britain's iron and steel monopoly the servant rather than the master of the British people.

··{ *7* }·· *France and West Germany*

SPEECH DELIVERED BY PREMIER DE GAULLE AT
CONSTANTINE, ALGERIA[1]
October 3, 1958

Last Sunday, three and a half million men and women of Algeria, without distinction of community, in complete equality, gave France and myself their vote of confidence. They did this quite simply without any constraint and in spite of the threats that certain fanatics brought to bear against them, their families and their property. This is a fact, as clear as the bright light of day. And this fact is fundamental not only because it mutually and forever pledges, one to the other, Algeria and France, but also because it ties in with what happened that same day in Metropolitan France, in the Overseas Departments, in the Territories of the Community.

The least that can be said of this great demonstration is that the French people proved to themselves and to the entire world their determination for renovation, and that, at the same time, a hundred million men decided to build their future together in Liberty, Equality and Fraternity.

With regard to Algeria, what is the future to which France is calling her? Women and men of Algeria, I have come here to tell you what it is.

What must be achieved is the basic transformation of this country, so brave, so alive, but also so full of difficulties and suffering. This means that it is necessary for the living conditions of each man and woman to improve from day to day. This means that, for the benefit of the inhabitants, the resources of the earth and the ability of the elites must be brought to light and developed. This means that children must be taught. This means that all Algeria must have her share in what modern civilization can and must bring to men in terms of well-being and dignity.

But the loftiest plans call for practical measures. Here are the measures that my Government intends to take in the near future covering the next five years by virtue of the full powers that the new Constitution has just conferred upon it.

During these five years, of the young people in Metropolitan France—

---

[1] The text of Premier de Gaulle's speech was made available in translation through the courtesy of the Information Service of the French Embassy in New York.

yes, I say in Metropolitan France—that enter the service of the State, in the Administration, in the Army, in education and in the public services, at least a tenth of these young people must be recruited from the Arab, the Kabyle and Mozabite communities, and that without prejudice to an increased proportion of Algerians serving in Algeria.

In the course of these five years, salaries and wages in Algeria will be raised to a level comparable to what they are in Metropolitan France.

Before the end of these five years, 250,000 hectares [617,500 acres] of new land will be allotted to Moslem farmers.

Before the end of these five years, the first phase of the plan for the agricultural and industrial development of Algeria will be brought to its conclusion. This phase includes, in particular, the delivery and the distribution of the oil and gas of the Sahara, the setting up, on this soil, of great metallurgical and chemical complexes, the construction of housing for a million people, the corresponding development of health services, of roads, ports, means of communication—in short, the regular employment of 400,000 new workers.

Gradually in the course of these five years, two-thirds of the girls and boys will be enrolled in school and, during the three years after that, complete school enrollment of all Algerian youth will be achieved.

During these five years, the human contact that has been made especially by the French Army—by its career officers, its reserve officers, its fighting men, its young conscripts—will be continued and developed and, in Metropolitan France, the same must be true, in Paris and in our provinces.

What will be the political consequences of this evolution which calls for very extensive and prolonged efforts? I believe it is quite useless to freeze in advance, in words, that which, in any event, is going to take shape, little by little, as it is undertaken. But, in any case, two things are certain as of now: the first concerns the present.

In two months, Algeria will elect her representatives under the same conditions as will Metropolitan France. But at least two thirds of her representatives will have to be Moslem citizens.

The other refers to the future. The future of Algeria will in any event—because that is the nature of things—be built on a double foundation: her personality and her close solidarity with Metropolitan France.

In any case, it is absolutely essential that this fruitful transformation be accomplished. This is necessary for the good of the men of Algeria, for the good of the women, for the good of the children who live here; but it is also necessary for the honor of mankind. It is necessary for the peace of the world. For no one has any interest in the stagnation of a people, except the kind of people, who, to serve their ambitions, gamble on the spirit of revolt and the poverty of others.

This transformation, this immense political, economic, social and cultural task—who could effect this transformation, if not France?

Now it happens that France has the will and the means to do so. It also happens that the vote of the Algerians has just proved that they desire this transformation and that it should be carried out with France.

Therefore, turning toward those who are prolonging a fratricidal conflict, who are organizing lamentable attacks in Metropolitan France, or who are spreading—through the chancelleries, through underground dens, by means of the radios and the newspapers of certain foreign capitals—vilifications of France, to those I say: Why kill? We must enable people to live. Why destroy? Our duty is to build. Why hate? We must cooperate.

Stop this absurd fighting and you will at once see a new blossoming of hope over all the land of Algeria. You will see the prisons emptying; you will see the opening up of a future big enough for everybody, and for you yourselves in particular. And then, speaking to those States which are throwing oil on the fire here while their unhappy peoples writhe under dictatorships, I say: Could you do what France is in a position to do here, what only France is capable of doing? Could you people do it? No. Then let France carry on, unless you deliberately decide to envenom the conflict in order to distract attention from your own difficulties. But in the present state of the world, where can these bitter incitements lead if not to a universal cataclysm? Only two paths lie open to the human race today: war or brotherhood. In Algeria as everywhere, France, for her part, has chosen brotherhood.

Long live the Republic! Long live Algeria and long live France!

DE GAULLE'S VIEW OF EUROPE AND ITS ROLE IN WORLD AFFAIRS[1]

In discussing Europe and in trying to distinguish what it should be, it is always necessary to ascertain what the world is. At the end of the last World War, the distribution of forces in the world was as simple, as brutal as possible. It appeared suddenly at Yalta. Only America and Russia had remained powers and all the more considerable powers in that all the rest found themselves dislocated, the vanquished engulfed in their unconditional defeat and the European victors destroyed to their foundations. For the countries of the free world, threatened by the Soviets' ambition, American leadership could then seem inevitable. The New World was, of all of them, the great victor of the war. Under the command of the United States, owner of atomic bombs—the Atlantic Alliance ensured their security. Thanks to the Marshall Plan their economies were being revived. Wherever the colonial powers were effecting, under more or less violent conditions, the transfer of their sovereignty to self-governing regimes, there pressure was felt, openly or not, from Washington. At the same time, America was seen to assume the conduct of

---

[1] The text of President de Gaulle's speech, delivered at his tenth press conference on July 23, 1964, was made available in translation through the courtesy of the Information Service of the French Embassy, New York.

political and strategic affairs in all the regions where the free world found itself in contact with the direct or indirect action of the Soviets.

It did this either unilaterally or through the channels of regional international bodies which in practice were at its disposal: in Europe, NATO; in Western Asia, CENTO; in Southeast Asia, SEATO; in America, the OAS; or, thanks to its supremacy in the North Pacific, or, finally, through military or diplomatic intervention, in Korea, in the Congo, or during the Suez crisis through the offices of the United Nations Organization which it dominated by its preponderance.

It is clear that things have changed. The Western States of our old continent have rebuilt their economies. They are rebuilding their military forces. One of them—France—is becoming a nuclear power. Above all they have become aware of their natural ties. In short, Western Europe appears likely to constitute a major entity full of merit and resources, capable of living its own life, indeed, not in opposition to the New World, but right alongside it.

On the other hand, the monolithic nature of the totalitarian world is in the process of dislocation. China, separated from Moscow, enters on the world scene by its mass, its needs and its resources, avid for progress and consideration. The Soviet Empire, the last and the largest colonial power of this time, is seeing first the Chinese contest the domination it exercises over vast regions of Asia and second is seeing the European satellites which it had subjugated by force moving further and further away. At the same time the Communist regime, despite the enormous effort it has been making in Russia for a half a century and despite the results it has achieved in certain massive undertakings, is meeting with failure with respect to the standard of living, the satisfaction and the dignity of men in comparison with the system applied in Western Europe which combines "dirigisme" with freedom. Lastly, great aspirations and great difficulties are deeply agitating the developing countries.

The result of all these new factors, complicated, and interrelated, is that the division of the world into two camps lead by Washington and Moscow respectively corresponds less and less to the real situation. With respect to the gradually splitting totalitarian world or the problems posed by China, the conduct to be adopted toward many countries of Asia, Africa and Latin America, or the remodeling of the United Nations Organization that necessarily ensues, or the adjustment of world exchanges of all kinds, etc., it appears that Europe, provided that it wishes it is henceforth called upon to play a role which is its own. Undoubtedly it should maintain an alliance with America, in which, in the North Atlantic, both are interested so long as the Soviet threat remains. But, the reasons which, for Europe, made this alliance a form of subordination are fading away day by day. Europe must assume its share of the responsibilities. Everything indicates, moreover, that this event would be in accordance with the interest of the United States, whatever may be its merit, its power and its good intentions, for the multiplicity and complexity of the tasks henceforth go beyond and perhaps dangerously, its means and its capacity. That is why the United States declares that it wishes to see the old continent unite and organize itself while many among the Gallic, Germanic and Latin peoples cry out "Let us build Europe!"

But which Europe? That is the question. Indeed, the established conveniences, the accepted renunciations, the deep-rooted reservations do not fade away easily. According to us French, it is a question of Europe's being made in order for it to be European. A European Europe means that it exists by itself for itself, in other words in the midst of the world it has its own policy. But that is precisely what is rejected consciously or unconsciously by some who claim, however, to want it to be established. In reality, the fact that Europe, not having a policy, would be subject to the policy that came to it from the other side of the Atlantic appears to them, even today, normal and satisfactory. We have seen many people, quite often, what is more, worthy and sincere, advocate for Europe not an independent policy, which in reality they do not visualize, but an organization unsuited to have one, linked in this field as in that of defense and of the economy, an Atlantic system, in other words, American, and consequently subordinate to what the United States calls its leadership. This organization, entitled federal, would have had as its bases: on the one hand, a council of experts withdrawn from the affiliation to the States, and which would have been dubbed "executive," and on the other hand a Parliament without national qualifications and which would have been called "legislative." Doubtless each of these two elements would have supplied that for which it would have been fitted, that is to say, studies for the council and debates for the Parliament. But, without a doubt, neither of the two would have made what indeed no one wanted them to make, that is a policy, for if the policy must take the debates and studies into account, it is another thing entirely than studies and debates.

A policy is an action, that is to say a body of decisions taken, of things done, of risks assumed, all this with the support of a people. The governments of nations alone can be capable of and responsible for making policy. It is of course not forbidden to imagine that a day will come when all the peoples of our continent will become one and that then there could be a Government of Europe, but it would be ridiculous to act as if that day had come.

That is why France—refusing to let Europe get bogged down, becoming bogged down herself in a guileful undertaking that would have stripped States, misled peoples and prevented the independence of our continent—took the initiative of proposing to her five partners of the Rome Treaty a beginning for the organization of their cooperation. Thus, we would begin to live in common, pending the time when habit and evolution would gradually draw the ties closer together. We know that the German Government adhered in principle to this project. We know that a meeting of the six States in Paris, then another one in Bonn, seemed at first on the road to success, but that Rome refused to call the decisive meeting, its objections, joined with those of The Hague and Brussels, being powerful enough to halt everything. Finally, we know that the opponents invoked two arguments, moreover contradictory. The first argument: the French plan, which maintains the sovereignty of the States, does not conform to our conception of a Europe having as its Executive a commission of experts, and as its Legislative a Parliament cut off from national realities. The second argument: although Britain does not agree to lose its sovereignty, we will not enter into any European political organization to which it would not belong.

The French plan for European organization not being adopted by Italy and by the Benelux countries; moreover, integration not being able to lead to anything other than an American protectorate; finally, Great Britain having shown throughout the interminable Brussels negotiations that it was not in a position to accept the common economic rules and, by the Nassau agreement, that its defense force, particularly in the nuclear domain, would not be European for lack of being autonomous in relation to the United States—it seemed to the Government of the Federal Republic of Germany and to the Government of the French Republic that their bilateral cooperation could have some value. ˙

It was then that, on the proposal of the German Government, the French-German Treaty of January 22, 1963 was concluded, which I had the honor of signing right here with Chancellor Adenauer. However, it must be noted that, if the French-German Treaty made possible limited results in some areas, also if it led the two Governments and their services to establish contacts which, for our part, and altogether, we judge can be useful and which are, in any case, very pleasant, up to now a common line of conduct has not emerged. Assuredly there is not, and there could not be any opposition, strictly speaking, between Bonn and Paris. But, whether it is a matter of the effective solidarity of France and Germany concerning their defense, or even of the stand to take and the action to pursue toward the East, above all the Moscow satellites, or correlatively of the question of boundaries and nationalities in Central and Eastern Europe, or of the recognition of China and of the diplomatic and economic mission which can be opened to Europe in relation to that great people, or of peace in Asia and particularly Indochina and Indonesia, or of the aid to give to the developing countries in Africa, Asia and Latin America, or of the organization of the agricultural common market and consequently the future of the Community of the Six—one could not say that Germany and France have yet agreed to make together a policy and one could not dispute that this results from the fact that Bonn has not believed, up to now, that this policy should be European and independent. If this state of affairs were to last, there would be the risk, in the long run, of doubts among the French people, of misgivings among the German people and, among their four partners of the Rome Treaty, an increased tendency to leave things as they are, while waiting, perhaps, to be split up.

But, throughout the world, the force of things is doing its work. In wanting and in proposing the organization of a Europe having its own policy, France is sure of serving the balance, the peace and the progress of the world. Moreover, she is now strong enough and sure enough of herself to be able to be patient, except for major external changes which would jeopardize everything and therefore lead her to change her direction. Besides, at the last meeting just held between the Governments in Bonn and Paris, Chancellor Erhard gave an indication of a forthcoming German initiative. In waiting for the sky to clear, France is pursuing, by her own means, that which a European and independent policy can and should be. It is a fact that people everywhere are pleased with it and that for herself it is not an unsatisfactory situation.

UNITED STATES NOTE TO THE U.S.S.R. ON BERLIN[1]
August 17, 1961

The Embassy of the United States presents its compliments to the Minister of Foreign Affairs and upon instructions of its Government has the honor to direct the most serious attention of the Government of the U.S.S.R. to the following.

On August 13, East German authorities put into effect several measures regulating movement at the boundary of the western sectors and the Soviet sector of the city of Berlin. These measures have the effect of limiting, to a degree approaching complete prohibition, passage from the Soviet sector to the western sectors of the city. These measures were accompanied by the closing of the sector boundary by a sizable deployment of police forces and by military detachments brought into Berlin for this purpose.

All this is a flagrant, and particularly serious, violation of the quadripartite status of Berlin. Freedom of movement with respect to Berlin was reaffirmed by the quadripartite agreement of New York of May 4, 1949, and by the decision taken at Paris on June 20, 1949, by the Council of the Ministers of Foreign Affairs of the Four Powers. The United States Government has never accepted that limitations can be imposed on freedom of movement within Berlin. The boundary between the Soviet sector and the western sectors of Berlin is not a state frontier. The United States Government considers that the measures which the East German authorities have taken are illegal. It reiterates that it does not accept the pretension that the Soviet sector of Berlin forms a part of the so-called "German Democratic Republic" and that Berlin is situated on its territory. Such a pretension is in itself a violation of the solemnly pledged word of the U.S.S.R. in the Agreement on the Zones of Occupation in Germany and the administration of Greater Berlin. Moreover, the United States Government cannot admit the

---

[1] Reprinted from *The Department of State Bulletin*, XLV, No. 1158 (September 4, 1961), p. 397.

right of the East German authorities to authorize their armed forces to enter the Soviet sector of Berlin.

By the very admission of the East German authorities, the measures which have just been taken are motivated by the fact that an ever increasing number of inhabitants of East Germany wish to leave this territory. The reasons for this exodus are known. They are simply the internal difficulties in East Germany.

To judge by the terms of a declaration of the Warsaw Pact powers published on August 13, the measures in question are supposed to have been recommended to the East German authorities by those powers. The United States Government notes that the powers which associated themselves with the U.S.S.R. by signing the Warsaw Pact are thus intervening in a domain in which they have no competence.

It is to be noted that this declaration states that the measures taken by the East German authorities are "in the interests of the German peoples themselves." It is difficult to see any basis for this statement, or to understand why it should be for the members of the Warsaw Pact to decide what are the interests of the German people. It is evident that no Germans, particularly those whose freedom of movement is being forcibly restrained, think this is so. This would become abundantly clear if all Germans were allowed a free choice, and the principle of self-determination were also applied in the Soviet sector of Berlin and in East Germany.

The United States Government solemnly protests against the measures referred to above, for which it holds the Soviet Government responsible. The United States Government expects the Soviet Government to put an end to these illegal measures. This unilateral infringement of the quadripartite status of Berlin can only increase existing tension and dangers.

SOVIET REPLY[1]
To Identic Notes Dated August 17 of United States, United Kingdom, and France on Berlin, August 18, 1961

In connection with the note of the Government of the United States of America of August 17, 1961, the Government of the Union of Soviet Socialist Republics considers it necessary to state the following:

The Soviet Government fully understands and supports the actions of the Government of the German Democratic Republic which established effective control on the border with West Berlin in order to bar the way for subversive activity being carried out from West Berlin against the G.D.R. and other countries of the socialist community. . . .

West Berlin has been transformed into a center of subversive activity,

---

[1] Reprinted from *The Department of State Bulletin*, LXV, No. 1158 (September 4, 1961), pp. 397–400.

diversion, and espionage, into a center of political and economic provocations against the G.D.R., the Soviet Union, and other socialist countries. Former and present West Berlin municipal leaders have cynically called West Berlin an "arrow in the living body of the German Democratic Republic," a "front city," a "violator of tranquillity," the "cheapest atom bomb put in the center of a socialist state.". . .

However, West Berlin authorities and the occupation organs of the three powers did not lift a finger to put an end to this criminal activity. . . .

The question is, have such actions anything in common with the observation of the four-power status established in Berlin immediately after the defeat of Hitlerite Germany, to which the note of the Government of the U.S.A. refers? One must have an exceptionally great sense of humor to affirm that the activity carried on in West Berlin corresponds to four-power obligations. . . .

The Government of the U.S.A. should be well informed on the fact that, with the collaboration of the occupation forces, the ruling circles of the F.R.G. have turned West Berlin into the principal base of uninterrupted economic diversions against the G.D.R. At the expense of taxes collected from the population of the F.R.G., a speculative rate for the exchange of West marks for the currency of the G.D.R. was arbitrarily established and artificially maintained in West Berlin. There has never been so shameless a speculation in currency in any other city in the world as in West Berlin—and this under the protection of the occupation authorities. Buying up in the G.D.R. and export to West Berlin and the F.R.G. of valuable goods and foodstuffs was organized on an enormous scale; this inflicted colossal damage upon the population and national economy of the G.D.R. The workers of the G.D.R. were annually forced to pay at least 3½ billion marks for the open border with West Berlin. . . .

The Government organs and concerns of the F.R.G. led from West Berlin an entire army of recruiters who, by means of deception, bribery, and blackmail, instigated a certain part of the residents of the G.D.R. to migrate to West Germany. There, these people were compelled to enter into service in the Bundeswehr and to work in the war-production industry; they were drawn into various subversive organizations. . . .

Slanderous propaganda of incitement, inimical to the Soviet Union, the G.D.R., and other socialist countries, has been and is being systematically conducted by radio and television from West Berlin. The radio and television centers in West Berlin are totally subordinated to one task: to disseminate enmity among peoples, to incite war psychosis, to attempt to organize disorders, and to transmit enciphered instructions to agents of Western intelligence systems. . . .

The G.D.R. has displayed, over the course of many years, great tolerance in the face of such a completely disgraceful and impermissible situation. Implementing its consistently peace-loving and democratic policy, it has borne enormous sacrifices to facilitate the achievement of agreement between the two German states on the questions of peaceful settlement and reunification of Germany on peace-loving and democratic foundations.

Nevertheless, and particularly recently, following the introduction of proposals on the immediate conclusion of a peace treaty with Germany and on normalization on that basis of the situation in West Berlin, subversive activity from West Berlin against the G.D.R. and other socialist countries has assumed even greater proportions. At the same time, the enemies of peace and tranquillity in this area have not missed even one opportunity to interfere with the plans for socialist construction in the G.D.R., to hinder the rise in well-being of its population, and, by every means and without stopping at anything, to complicate the situation in the Republic. . . .

The Government of the U.S.A. attempts in its note to represent its effort to perpetuate the occupation of West Berlin (and this 16 years after the end of the war) as a concern for the Germans and almost as a concrete expression of the right to self-determination. Such attempts in the final analysis cannot be taken seriously. And if the taking of defensive measures on the G.D.R. border with West Berlin creates certain temporary inconveniences for the city's population, blame for this rests entirely with the occupation authorities and the F.R.G. Government, which have done everything to prevent improvement of the atmosphere in this area in accordance with the legitimate interests of all states. Thus, the protest made in the note of the Government of the U.S.A. is without foundation and is categorically rejected by the Soviet Government.

As was already stated, measures taken by the Government of the G.D.R. are temporary. The Soviet Government repeatedly has emphasized that the conclusion of a peace treaty with Germany and normalization on such a basis of the situation in West Berlin will not infringe the interests of any of the parties and will contribute to the cause of peace and security of all peoples. To this end it appeals to the Government of the U.S.A.

··{ *8* }·· *Spain*

THE SPANISH ACT OF SUCCESSION[1]
June 7, 1947

Article 1. Spain, as a political unit, is a Catholic, social, and representative state which, in accordance with its traditions, declares itself to be a kingdom.

Article 2. The office of Chief of State is held by the Caudillo of Spain and of the Crusade, Generalissimo of the Spanish Armies, Don Francisco Franco Bahamonde.

Article 3. Upon the Headship of State becoming vacant, the powers thereof will be assumed by a Regency Council formed by the President of the Cortes, the Prelate of highest hierarchical standing and seniority on the Council of the Realm, and the senior Captain General, or Lieutenant General, in active service, of the Army, Navy or Air Force, in this same order, or their respective substitutes appointed in compliance with the prescriptions of the next article. This Council will be presided over by the President of the Cortes, and for its decisions to be valid, the presence will be required of at least two of its three members, and always that of its President, or in default of him, that of the Vice-President of the Council of the Realm.

Article 4. I. A Council of the Realm, which will hold precedence over the advisory bodies of the nation, will assist the Head of State in the highly important matters and resolutions that fall exclusively within his competency.
[ ]

Article 6. At any moment the Chief of State may submit to the Cortes the name of the person he believes should succeed him, either as king or as regent, and according to the conditions stipulated by this law; he may also, likewise, submit to the Cortes the repeal of any previous proposal of succession, although this last may have already been accepted by the Cortes.

Article 7. Should the office of Chief of State be vacant and the successor

---

[1] The text of the Act of Succession was made available in translation through the courtesy of the Embassy of Spain, Washington, D.C., and appears here as amended by the Organic Law of the Spanish State, December 22, 1966.

74

appointed as by the previous article, the council of the regency shall assume the powers of this office to call a joint session of the Cortes and the council of the kingdom to take the successor's oath of office as prescribed in this law and to name him king or regent.

Article 8. I. Should the death of the Head of State occur, or his incapacity be declared, without a successor having been appointed, the Regency Council will assume the powers, except that of revoking the appointment of any of the members of the Council itself, who will in all cases conserve their posts, and will convoke, within a period of three days, the members of the Government and of the Council of the Realm so that, meeting in an uninterrupted and secret session, they may decide by a majority of two-thirds of those present, which must represent at least an absolute majority, as to the person of royal descent who possesses the conditions demanded by the present Law and whom they should propose to the Cortes as King, in view of the supreme interests of the country. Should the proposal not be accepted, the Government and the Council of the Realm may formulate, by means of the same procedure, a second proposal in favour of another person of royal descent who likewise possesses the legal conditions. II. When, in the opinion of those attending the session, there does not exist a person of the blood royal who possesses the said conditions, or when the proposals have not been accepted by the Cortes, they will propose to the latter as Regent, under the same conditions, that personality who by reason of his prestige, capabilities and possible support by the nation, should occupy this office. On formulating this proposal, they may stipulate a time-limit and conditions as to the duration of the Regency, and the Cortes must decide on each of those points. If the person proposed as Regent should not be accepted by the Cortes, the Government and the Council of the Realm must effectuate new proposals, complying with the same procedure, until such time as they obtain the acceptance of the Cortes. III. In the hypotheses to which the foregoing paragraphs refer, should the two-thirds majority not be obtained in the first division, a second and, if necessary, a third division will be called. In this last vote, a majority of three-fifths will suffice for the validity of the decision, which vote must represent at least an absolute majority. IV. The Plenary Session of the Cortes must be held within a maximum period of eight days following each proposal, and once the favourable vote of the Cortes has been obtained in accordance with the prescriptions of article 15, the successor will take the oath required by this Law, in virtue of which the Regency Council will at once transfer their powers to him. V. Until such time as the provisions established in Article 11 of this Law are fulfilled, on the Headship of State becoming vacant, the appointment of a successor will be proceeded with, in accordance with the precepts of the present article.

Article 9. To exercise the Headship of State as King or Regent it will be necessary to be of the male sex and a Spaniard, to be thirty years of age, to

profess the Catholic religion, to possess the qualities necessary for the fulfillment of this high mission, and to swear the Fundamental Laws, as also loyalty
to the principles that make up the National Movement. The same oath must
be taken by the successor after reaching the age of thirty.

[ ]

Article 11. I. Once the Crown has been established in the person of a
King, the regular order of succession will be that of primogeniture and
representation, with preference of the first line over the later ones; in the same
line, of the nearer over the more remote degree; in the same degree, of the
male over the female, who can not reign but can, if necessary transmit the
right to her heirs; and, within the same sex, of the senior in age over the
younger; all of which without prejudice to the exceptions and requisites
stipulated in the preceding articles. II. In case the heir to the Crown, in
accordance with the order established in the previous paragraph, should not
have reached the age of thirty at the moment of the throne becoming vacant,
his public functions will be exercised by a Regent appointed in accordance
with Article 8 of the Law, until such time as he is of legal age. III. The same
norm will be applied if, owing to incapacity of the King, appreciated in the
manner stipulated in Article 14 of this Law, the Cortes should declare the
opening of the Regency and the heir should not yet have reached the age of
thirty. IV. In the hypotheses of the two preceding paragraphs, the Regency
will end as soon as the cause that has motivated it has ceased to exist or has
disappeared.

Article 12. All delegation of rights before assuming the throne, abdica-
tion once the successor has been named, renunciation in any case, royal
marriage and marriage of the immediate successor must be approved by the
Cortes after report from the council of the kingdom.

Article 13. On the advice of the council of the kingdom, the Chief of
State may submit to the Cortes the exclusion from succession of those persons
of royal blood who lack the necessary capacity to govern or, because of their
noted indifference to the basic principles of the State or because of their
actions, have forfeited their rights to succession as established by this law.

Article 14. The incapacity of the Chief of State, appraised by two-thirds
of the members of the government, shall be communicated by report to the
council of the kingdom. Should the council agree to this report, by two-thirds
majority, its president shall submit it to the Cortes which, meeting within
eight days, shall adopt the necessary measures.

Article 15. I. For the decisions of the Cortes to which this Law refers to
be valid, there will be required a favourable vote of two-thirds of the Deputies
present, which must be the equivalent, at least, of the absolute majority of the
total number of Deputies. II. However, in the hypotheses to which Articles 6
and 8 of the present Law refer, should the majority of two-thirds not be
obtained in the first division, a second and, if necessary, a third division will
be called. In this last vote, it will suffice, in order for the decision to be valid,

to obtain a majority of three-fifths, which must be the equivalent at least of the absolute majority.

THE SPANIARD'S CHARTER[1]
July 16, 1945

Article 1. The Spanish State proclaims as a guiding principle of its acts, respect for the dignity, integrity, and liberty of the human person, recognizing man, as bearer of eternal values and member of the national community, to be holder of titles of duties and rights, the exercise of which it guarantees for the common good.

TITLE I. DUTIES AND RIGHTS OF THE SPANISH PEOPLE

Chapter I

Article 2. Spaniards owe faithful service to their country, loyalty to the Chief of State and obedience to its laws.

Article 3. The law protects equally the rights of all Spaniards without class preference or discrimination of persons.

Article 4. Spaniards have a right to the respect of their personal and family honor. He who should offend it, whatever be his condition, will be made responsible.

Article 5. All Spaniards have a right to receive education and instruction and the duty of acquiring them either in the family circle or in private or public centers of their own free election. The State will see that no talent is wasted because of lack of economic means.

Article 6. The profession and practice of the Roman Catholic religion, which is that of the Spanish State, will enjoy official protection.

The State will assume the protection of religious freedom, which will be guaranteed by effective judicial protection and which, in turn, will safeguard morals and public order.

Article 7. It is a title of honor for Spaniards to serve in the armed forces of their country.

All Spaniards are obliged to this service when they are called to it according to law.

Article 8. By means of laws, and always with a general character, those personal services that the interest of the nation and public need require will be obligatory.

Article 9. Spaniards will contribute to the maintenance of public charges according to their economic capacity. Nobody will be obliged to pay tributes that have not been established by law voted by the Cortes.

---

[1] The text of the Spaniard's Charter was made available in translation through the courtesy of the Embassy of Spain, Washington, D.C., and appears here as amended by the Organic Law of the Spanish State, December 22, 1966.

Article 10. All Spaniards have a right to participate in public office of a representative character, through the family, the municipality, and the syndicate (without barring other representation that the laws may establish).

Article 11. All Spaniards may hold office and public functions according to their merits and capacity.

Article 12. All Spaniards may freely express their ideas as long as they do not advocate the overthrow of the fundamental principles of government.

Article 13. Inside national territory, the State guarantees the liberty and inviolability of correspondence.

Article 14. Spaniards are at liberty to fix their residence inside national territory.

Article 15. Nobody may enter the home of a Spaniard or effect a search in it without his permission, unless with a warrant from the competent authority and in the case and form established by law.

Article 16. Spaniards may unite and associate themselves freely for lawful ends and according to what is established by law.

The State may create and maintain such agencies as are deemed necessary for the accomplishment of its service. Fundamental rulings which will have the character of law, will co-ordinate the exercise of this right with that recognized in the preceding paragraph.

Article 17. Spaniards have a right to legal security. All organisms of the State will act according to a hierarchical order of pre-established rulings, that may not be interpreted arbitrarily or altered.

Article 18. No Spaniard may be arrested except in the cases and in the form prescribed by law. Within a period of seventy-two hours all arrested persons will be set free or turned over to the juridical authorities.

Article 19. Nobody may be condemned except under a law prior to the act, under sentence by a competent tribunal, and after hearing and defense of the interested party.

Article 20. No Spaniard may be deprived of his nationality except for treason, as defined in the penal laws, or for entering the armed services or exercising public office in a foreign country against the expressed prohibition of the Chief of State.

Article 21. Spaniards may address individual petitions to the Chief of State, to the Cortes, and to public authorities.

Corporations, public officers, and members of the armed forces and institutions may only exercise this right according to the laws by which they are ruled.

Chapter II

Article 22. The State recognizes and protects the family as a natural and fundamental institution of society with rights and duties prior and superior to all human positive law.

Matrimony is one and indissoluble.

The State will specially protect families with numerous children.

Article 23. Parents are obliged to provide for, educate, and instruct their children. The State will suspend the exercise of patria potestad or will deprive of it all who do not exercise it with dignity, and will transfer the custody of minors to those to whom it corresponds by law.

Chapter III

Article 24. All Spaniards have a right to work and the duty to occupy themselves in some socially useful activity.

Article 25. Work, because of its essentially human character, cannot be reduced to the idea of merchandise, or be the object of a transaction incompatible with personal dignity. It constitutes in itself an attribute of honor and a sufficient title to demand guardianship and assistance from the State.

Article 26. The State recognizes in an enterprise a community of efforts of technique, labor, and capital in their different forms, and consequently proclaims the right of these elements to participate in gains.

The State will see that relations between them shall be maintained in the strictest equity and in an order that subordinates economic values to human values, to the interests of the nation and the exigencies of the common good.

Article 27. All workers will be protected by the State in their right to a just and sufficient return, which will as a minimum provide them and their families with well-being sufficient for a moral and dignified existence.

Article 28. The Spanish State guarantees the workers security in distress, and recognizes their rights to assistance in the cases of old age, death, sickness, maternity, accidents, invalidity, unemployment, and other hazards that are the object of social insurance.

Article 29. The State will maintain institutions of assistance and will protect and foster those created by the Church, the corporations, and private enterprise.

Article 30. The Spanish State recognizes and protects private property as a natural means for the fulfillment of individual ends.

All forms of property remain subordinated to the necessities of the nation and to the common good.

No source of wealth will be allowed to remain unproductive, unduly destroyed, or applied to illicit ends.

Article 31. The State will make available to all Spaniards the access to those forms of property more intimately connected with the human person, the home, inheritance, implements of production, and goods of daily use.

Article 32. In no case will a sentence of confiscation of property be passed.

Nobody may be expropriated except in the interest of public and/or social welfare, after corresponding indemnity and according to what the law disposes.

Article 33. The exercise of the rights that are recognized in this Charter may not prejudice the spiritual, national, and social unity of the community.

Article 34. The Cortes will vote the necessary laws for the exercise of the rights recognized by this Charter.

Article 35. The enforcement of Articles 12, 13, 14, 15, 16, and 18 may temporarily be suspended in part or in whole by the government by means of a decree which must define and limit the scope and duration of this measure.

Article 36. Any violation of any of the rights proclaimed in this Charter will be punishable by laws which will determine, in each case, the actions that may be taken in its defense before the competent jurisdictions.

PRINCIPLES OF THE NATIONAL MOVEMENT[1]
According to the Act of May 17, 1958

I   Spain is a unity of destiny in the world order. The service of the country's unity, greatness and freedom is a sacred duty and a collective undertaking for all Spaniards.

II   The Spanish nation regards it as a mark of honour to obey the law of God, according to the Holy Catholic Apostolic and Roman Church, the sole true church and the faith inseparable from the national consciousness which will inspire its legislation.

III Spain, the root of a great family of peoples, to whom she feels bound in indissoluble brotherhood, aspires to the restoration of justice and peace between the nations.

IV   The unity between the land and men of Spain is inviolable. The integrity of the country and its independence are supreme demands on the national community. The Armed Forces of Spain as the guarantee of her security and the expression of our people's heroic virtues, must possess the strength required for the best service of the country.

V   The national community is founded on man as bearer of eternal values, and on the family as the basis of social life; but individual and collective interests will always be subordinated to the common welfare of the nation, formed of past, present and future generations. The law supports the rights of all Spaniards equally.

VI   The natural entities of social life—Family, Municipality and Guild— are the basic structures of the national community. Such institutions and corporations of other kinds as meet general social needs shall be supported so that they may share efficaciously in perfecting the aims of the national community.

---

[1] The text of the Principles of the National Movement was made available in translation through the courtesy of the Embassy of Spain, Washington, D.C.

VII The Spanish people, united in an order of Law informed by the postulates of authority, freedom and service, form the National State. Its form, within the inmutable principles of the National Movement and the provisions of the Succession Act and the other Basic Laws, is that of the traditional, Catholic, social and representative Monarchy.

VIII The representative character of the political order is the basic principle of our public institutions. The people's share in legislation and the other fundamental tasks of general interest shall be provided through the Family, the Municipality, the occupational Guild and other bodies that the laws may recognize, having organic representation for the purpose. All political organizations of whatever kind, apart from this representative system, shall be deemed illegal.

All Spaniards shall have access to public office and functions in accordance with their merits and abilities.

IX All Spaniards are entitled: to independent justice, which shall be available free to those without financial means; to a general and professional education, which none need fail to obtain through want of material means; to the benefits of social assistance and security; and to an equitable distribution of the national income and of taxation. The State policy and laws shall be inspired by the Christian ideal of social justice, as reflected in the Labour Charter.

X Work is recognized as the origin of the rank, duty and honour of Spaniards, and private property in all its forms is recognized as a right conditioned by its social function. Private enterprise, the basis of economic activity, shall be encouraged, canalized, and where necessary supplemented by State action.

XI The Firm, an association of men and means for the purpose of production, forms a community of interests and a unity of aims. The relations between its components must be based on justice and mutual loyalty, and economic values shall be subordinated to those of the human and social order.

XII The State shall endeavour, by all means in its power, to improve the physical and moral health of Spaniards and to ensure them the best conditions of work; to promote the country's economic progress by the improvement of agriculture, the extension of irrigation work and the social reform of the countryside; to seek the fairest use and distribution of the public credit; to safeguard and encourage prospecting and mining; to intensify the process of industrialization, to patronize scientific research and to promote maritime activities, as befits the large seafaring population of Spain and her record as a sea power.

··{*9*}·· *Greece*

THE VARKIZA AGREEMENT[1]
Text; Signed by the Greek Government and the E.L.A.S. Delegates, February 12, 1945

Article I. Liberties. The Government will secure in accordance with the Constitution and the democratic principles everywhere recognized, the free expression of the political and social opinions of the citizens, repealing any existing illiberal law. It will also secure the unhindered functioning of individual liberties such as those of assembly, association and expression of views in the Press. More especially, the Government will fully restore Trade Union liberties.

Article II. Raising of Martial Law. Martial law will be raised immediately after the signature of the present agreement. Simultaneously with this action there will be brought into force a Constitutional Act similar in all respects to Constitutional Act No. 24, whereby the suspension of those articles of the Constitution to which reference is made in Act 24 shall be permitted.

Articles 5, 10, 12, 20 and 95 of the Constitution shall be suspended forthwith throughout the country. This suspension shall continue until the completion of disarmament, and the establishment of administrative, judicial and military authorities throughout the country. As regards Article 5 in particular, this suspension shall not take effect in the cities of Athens and Piraeus and their suburbs. Especially, however, as regards persons arrested up to the present day it is agreed that Article 5 of the Constitution is not in force, and that they will be liberated within the shortest possible period of time, the necessary orders to this effect being given to the competent authorities.

Followers of E.A.M. who may be held in captivity by other organizations shall be set free as soon as possible.

Article III. Amnesty. There shall be an amnesty for political crimes committed between the 3rd December, 1944, and the publication of the Law establishing the amnesty. From this amnesty shall be excluded common-law

---

[1] Reprinted with permission from W. Byford-Jones, *The Greek Trilogy (Resistance-Liberation-Revolution)* (Hutchinson & Co.: London and New York, 1946), pp. 266–269.

crimes against life and property which were not absolutely necessary to the achievement of the political crime concerned. The necessary Law will be published immediately after the signature of the present agreement. From this amnesty will be excluded any persons who, being under obligation to surrender their arms as being members of the organizations of E.L.A.S., the National Civil Guard or E.L.A.N., shall not have handed them over by the 15th March, 1945. This last provision concerning exclusion from the amnesty shall be annulled after verification of the fact that the disarmament of E.L.A.S. has been effected, since there will then be no further cause and justification for it. Guarantees and details of the amnesty to be provided are contained in the draft law attached to the present agreement.

Article IV. Hostages. All civilians who have been arrested by E.L.A.S. or by the National Civil Guard (E.P.), irrespective of the date on which they were arrested, shall be set at liberty immediately. Any who may be held on the charge of collaboration with the enemy or of commission of any crime shall be handed over to the justice of the State for trial by the competent Courts according to law.

Article V. National Army. The National Army, apart from the professional officers and N.C.O.s, shall consist of the soldiers of the classes which shall from time to time be called up. Reserve officers, N.C.O.s and other ranks, who have been specially trained in modern weapons, shall remain in service so long as there is a formation requiring them. The Sacred Squadron shall remain as at present, since it is under the immediate orders of the Allied High Command, and shall thereafter be merged in the united National Army in accordance with the above principle. The effort will be made to extend regular conscription to the whole of Greece in accordance with the technical facilities existing and the necessities which may arise. After the demobilization of E.L.A.S. those men who belong to classes which are to be called up in accordance with the attached protocol shall report for enrolment in the units already existing. All men who have been enrolled in the units now existing, without belonging to the classes being called up, shall be discharged. All members of the permanent cadres of the National Army shall be considered by the Councils for which provision is made in Constitutional Act No. VII. The political and social views of citizens serving in the Army shall be respected.

Article VI. Demobilization. Immediately on the publication of the present agreement the armed forces of resistance shall be demobilized and in particular the E.L.A.S., both Regular and Reserve, the E.L.A.N. and the National Civil Guard. The demobilization and surrender of arms shall take place according to the detailed provisions of the protocol drawn up by the Committee of Experts which, duly initialled, is attached hereto.

The State will settle all questions arising out of requisitioning carried out by E.L.A.S. The goods requisitioned by E.L.A.S., including beasts, motor vehicles, etc., which will be handed over to the State according to the detailed provisions of the protocol which has been drawn up and is attached hereto, will be regarded thereafter as having been requisitioned by the Greek State.

Article VII. Purge of Civil Service. The Government will proceed, by means of Committees or Councils, to be established by a special Law, to the purging of the personnel of the public services, officials of public companies, local Government officials, and those of other services dependent on the State or paid by it. The criteria of which the purge will take account will be either professional competence, or character and personality, or collaboration with the enemy or the utilization of the official as an instrument of the dictatorship. Officials of the above services who, during the occupation, joined the forces of the resistance will return to their positions and will be considered in the same manner as other officials. The above-mentioned Councils will also consider the cases of officials who have taken part or collaborated in the manifestations which have taken place between the 3rd December, 1944, and the date of signature of the present agreement. Those of them who are found to have been concerned may be placed at the disposal of the State as provided by Law. The final disposal of such officials will be decided by the Government which shall result from the elections to the Constituent Assembly. Officials who have already been placed *en disponibilité* by decisions of the Ministers will be submitted to the decision of the Council above mentioned. No official will be dismissed solely on account of his political opinion.

Article VIII. Purge of Security Services. The purge of the Security Services, the Gendarmerie and the City Police will be carried out as soon as possible by the special purge committee on the same basis as the purge of the Civil Service. All officers and other ranks of the above Corps who fall under the provisions of the Amnesty Law, who, during the period of the occupation, joined the ranks of E.L.A.S., E.L.A.N. or the National Civil Guard, will return to their positions and will be considered by the purge Councils in the same manner as the rest of their colleagues. All the officers and other ranks of the above Corps who left their positions between 3rd December, 1944, and the date of signature of the present document shall be placed *en disponibilité*, their final disposal being left for the decision of the Councils to be constituted by the Government arising from the elections.

Article IX. Plebiscite and Elections. At the earliest possible date, and in any case within the current year, there shall be conducted in complete freedom and with every care for its genuineness a plebiscite which shall finally decide on the Constitutional question, all points being submitted to the decision of the people. Thereafter shall follow as quickly as possible elections to a Constituent Assembly for the drafting of the new Constituent of the country. The representatives of both sides agree that for the verification of the genuineness of the expression of the popular will the great Allied Powers shall be requested to send observers.

Of this present agreement two similar copies have been made, whereof the one has been received by the Government Delegation and the other by the Delegation of E.A.M.

In Athens, at the Ministry of Foreign Affairs, 12th February, 1945.

STALIN'S VIEW OF THE NEED TO END THE GREEK UPRISING[1]

Stalin then turned to the uprising in Greece: "The uprising in Greece has to fold up." (He used for this the word *svernut'*, which means literally *to roll up*.) "Do you believe"—he turned to Kardelj—"in the success of the uprising in Greece?"

Kardelj replied, "If foreign intervention does not grow and if serious political and military errors are not made."

Stalin went on, without paying attention to Kardelj's opinion: "If, if! No, they have no prospect of success at all. What do you think, that Great Britain and the United States—the United States, the most powerful state in the world—will permit you to break their line of communication in the Mediterranean Sea! Nonsense. And we have no navy. The uprising in Greece must be stopped, and as quickly as possible."

Someone mentioned the recent success of the Chinese Communists. But Stalin remained adamant: "Yes, the Chinese comrades have succeeded, but in Greece there is an entirely different situation. The United States is directly engaged there—the strongest state in the world. China is a different case, relations in the Far East are different. True, we, too, can make a mistake! Here, when the war with Japan ended, we invited the Chinese comrades to reach an agreement as to how a modus vivendi with Chiang Kai-shek might be found. They agreed with us in word, but in deed they did it their own way when they got home: they mustered their forces and struck. It has been shown that they were right, and not we. But Greece is a different case—we should not hesitate, but let us put an end to the Greek uprising."

UNITED NATIONS SPECIAL COMMITTEE FOR THE BALKANS REPORT [CONCLUSION][2]
August 23, 1950

206. In conformity with the terms of General Assembly resolution 288 (IV) of 18 November 1949, the Special Committee has consistently endeavoured to promote the establishment of normal diplomatic and good-neighbourly relations between Albania, Bulgaria and Yugoslavia on the one hand

---

[1] From *Conversations with Stalin* by Milovan Djilas, pp. 181–182, © 1962 by Harcourt, Brace & World, Inc. and reprinted with their permission.

[2] Reprinted from United Nations, General Assembly, *Official Records, Fifth Session*, Supplement No. 11, pp. 26–27.

and Greece on the other. The Government of Greece has continued to co-operate with the Special Committee, while the Governments of Albania, Bulgaria and Yugoslavia, as in the past, have refused either to co-operate with it or to recognize it.

207. Diplomatic and good-neighbourly relations between Greece on the one hand and Albania and Bulgaria on the other do not exist. Diplomatic relations between Greece and Yugoslavia exist and an agreement was reached between the two Governments on 21 May 1950 for an exchange of Ministers.

208. In view of the elimination of large-scale guerrilla activity along the northern frontiers of Greece, as a result of the operations of the Greek Army in 1949, the Special Committee believes that the threat to the political independence and territorial integrity of Greece has altered in character. The organized guerrilla movement within Greece now consists of the activities of scattered bands. Nevertheless, many thousands of Greek guerrillas fled beyond the northern frontiers of Greece; the disarming and disposition of these guerrillas have not been verified by any international agency; and the Greek guerrilla leaders themselves claim that their forces still exist. While the guerrilla leaders have of necessity suspended, at any rate for the time being, their effort to dominate Greece by armed force, their aims have not been abandoned. The Greek guerrilla radio continues to operate from Romanian territory. Apart from the fact that guerrillas are being harboured outside Greece, the remnants of the movement within Greece have not been dissolved.

209. While Yugoslavia has maintained the policy, announced in July 1949, of closing her frontier with Greece, and frontier relations between the two countries have, for the most part, been correct, there is evidence to indicate that Bulgaria, in particular, has continued to give moral and material assistance to guerrilla raiding and sabotage parties on and near the Greek border. Aid of this nature to the Greek guerrillas on the part of Bulgaria and also Albania has necessarily been considerably reduced because of the flight of the bulk of the guerrillas from Greek territory, but it has not ceased. The Special Committee is of the opinion that the continuing potential threat to Greek political independence and territorial integrity is to be found at present chiefly in Bulgaria.

210. Large numbers of Greek guerrillas are known to be present in various countries of eastern Europe as a consequence of the guerrilla retreat. The States harbouring them have failed to give effect to the General Assembly's recommendations with respect to the verification by an international agency of their disarming and disposition.

211. With regard to the repatriation of Greek nationals at present in countries to the north of Greece as a result of the military operations and subsequent retreat of Greek guerrilla forces, the Special Committee has consistently endeavoured to assist in achieving a solution of the problem. It has noted that the amelioration of the situation in Greece has given rise to

conditions which would facilitate the peaceful repatriation to Greece of those Greek nationals who desire to return and live in accordance with the law of the land.

212. Likewise, the Special Committee has given serious consideration to the important problem of the repatriation of Greek military personnel captured by the Greek guerrillas and removed by them to the countries to the north of Greece. Despite repeated requests by the Government of Greece, and in violation of international practice, no lists of these prisoners have been circulated by the Governments concerned and all efforts made by the Special Committee to assist in their repatriation have proved futile.

213. The Special Committee has viewed with the gravest concern the fact that no Greek children have yet been repatriated to their homes in Greece. The Special Committee has noted the definite proposals of the Yugoslav Government indicating that it intended to fulfil the terms of the resolution of the General Assembly regarding this question, and that seventeen Greek children from Yugoslavia had been sent to their parents in Australia. But apart from this, the two unanimous resolutions of the General Assembly calling for the repatriation of the children removed from Greece during the course of the guerrilla warfare have had no practical results, despite the untiring efforts of the Secretary-General of the United Nations and the international Red Cross organizations. The failure of the States concerned to return these children to their homes has given rise to widespread indignation and sorrow. The basic failure to resolve this problem constitutes a continuing source of international friction, as well as a standing challenge to the United Nations and to the most elementary humanitarian principles.

214. The problem of international refugees in Greece has continued to develop during the course of the past year. In view of the movement of political and other refugees across the northern frontiers into Greece, the Special Committee is convinced that an international body should remain in charge of the work being accomplished in Greece at present by the International Refugee Organization. The Special Committee also believes that it would be advantageous that these refugees should be resettled outside Greece.

215. The Special Committee considers that the vigilance of the United Nations with respect to the political independence and territorial integrity of Greece has been, and remains, a significant factor in maintaining peace in the Balkans. Nevertheless, the remaining problems of the Greek guerrilla warfare and outstanding international difficulties with regard to the Greek question still constitute a source of danger, if of a modified nature.

216. Among the problems still remaining, the urgent solution of which constitutes a prerequisite for the restoration of normal relations between Greece and its northern neighbours are: international verification of the disarming and disposition of Greek guerrillas outside Greece; the repatriation of Greek children—a problem which has done much to perpetuate bad relations between Greece and its northern neighbours; the repatriation of

detained Greek soldiers and other Greek nationals; and conclusion of conventions for the regulation and control of the common frontiers between Greece and its northern neighbours. Only when these problems have been solved, in compliance with the General Assembly's recommendations, will conditions in the Balkans be such as to permit the re-establishment of normal relations between the four Governments.

··{**10**}·· *Efforts toward European Integration*

A EUROPEAN FREE TRADE AREA[1]
United Kingdom Memorandum to the Organisation for European Economic Co-operation

1. Her Majesty's Government earnestly desire a successful outcome of the continued efforts in the post-war world to strengthen the cohesion and promote the prosperity of Western Europe. They have therefore given careful thought in recent months to the widely held view that our principal economic need in Europe is to remove existing barriers to trade and develop a single market for manufactured goods. With a population of 250 million, there is clearly a great opportunity which Europe can seize provided that the free circulation of goods is not impeded by tariffs and quantitative restrictions throughout Europe. The need to take large and constructive measures to remove these barriers to trade is the more urgent in view of the pace of technical development which increasingly demands larger markets in order that its full benefits may be obtained. During the past decade a great deal has been done in the Organisation for European Economic Co-operation and elsewhere to lower trade barriers in Europe, but Her Majesty's Government believe that what is needed now is a much bolder approach.

2. With these considerations in mind Her Majesty's Government are glad that the negotiations which were set in train in June 1955 for the establishment of a Customs and Economic Union consisting of France, Germany, Italy, Belgium, Holland and Luxembourg are now approaching a successful conclusion. There are, however, substantial reasons why the United Kingdom could not become a member of such a Union. These arise in particular from the United Kingdom's interests and responsibilities in the Commonwealth. If the United Kingdom were to join the Customs and Economic Union, the United Kingdom tariff would be replaced by a single common tariff with the other member countries against the rest of the world. This would mean that goods entering the United Kingdom from the Com-

---

[1] Reprinted from *A European Free Trade Area: The United Kingdom Memorandum to the Organisation for European Economic Co-operation*, February 7, 1957, Cmnd 72 (London: H.M.S.O., 1957), pp. 3-4.

monwealth would have to pay duty at the same rate as goods coming from any other third country not a member of the Customs and Economic Union, while goods from the Union would be admitted free of duty. Her Majesty's Government could not contemplate entering arrangements which would in principle make it impossible for the United Kingdom to treat imports from the Commonwealth at least as favourably as those from Europe.

3. At the same time it is of great importance in the view of Her Majesty's Government to establish free trade over as wide an area as possible within Western Europe. It was for this reason that Her Majesty's Government strongly supported the decision taken by the Council of O.E.E.C. in July 1956 that a study should be made urgently to discover whether other member countries of the Organisation could be associated with the Customs and Economic Union.

4. The possibility of such an association has now been examined by Working Party No. 17 of the Council. Her Majesty's Government believe, with the members of that Working Party, that it is fully practicable for the United Kingdom and many other O.E.E.C. countries, including the countries which are proposing to create a Customs and Economic Union, to enter a Free Trade Area. The members of this Free Trade Area would undertake to eliminate, in respect of each other's products, protective duties and other restrictive regulations of commerce, including quantitative restrictions. They would be free to keep their own separate and different tariffs on imports from outside the Area, except that the countries which were also members of the Customs and Economic Union would in due course establish a common external tariff; they would also be able to vary these tariffs, subject to any international agreements by which they are bound from time to time.

5. Her Majesty's Government's own examination of this problem had led to the conclusion that, provided foodstuffs were excluded from its scope, a Free Trade Area in Europe could be established. On 26th November 1956 the Government informed the House of Commons of their intention to enter into negotiations in O.E.E.C. with this in view. Now that the practicability of a European Free Trade Area has been confirmed by the Working Party, Her Majesty's Government hope that other countries will also declare, either before or in the course of the forthcoming meeting of O.E.E.C., their willingness to negotiate on these lines.

6. Her Majesty's Government recognise the desirability of associating with the development of the Free Trade Area as many countries in Europe as possible. At the same time it is of the essence of the Free Trade Area that the obligations undertaken by its members progressively to remove tariffs over the whole field of trade which it includes should be reciprocal. Accordingly it is the view of Her Majesty's Government that the Free Trade Area should be open to all the member countries of O.E.E.C. who were prepared to accept its obligations. The position of any such countries which felt unable to accept the obligations of a Free Trade Area would need to be examined.

7. Her Majesty's Government believe that the establishment of a Free Trade Area would in no way prejudice the high level of employment which Europe generally has enjoyed, and that it should be an objective of member countries to maintain a high and stable level of employment. This would be an essential condition for the effective working of the Free Trade Area.

8. Her Majesty's Government advocate the establishment of a Free Trade Area in the belief that it will raise industrial efficiency by the encouragement it will afford to increase specialisation, large-scale production, and new technical and industrial developments. It should therefore strengthen the economy of Western Europe as a whole; and as a result of its formation the members of the Area should be in a stronger position progressively to remove restrictions on imports from countries outside the Area. The proposal aims at the total removal of barriers to trade over a significant proportion of world trade. It does not involve the creation of any new barriers against trade with the rest of the world. On the contrary Her Majesty's Government consider it indispensable that the Free Trade Area should be formed in such a way as to be wholly consistent with the existing objective of a collective approach to the widest possible system of multilateral trade and payments. It should also be fully consistent with the obligations of member countries as contracting parties to the G.A.T.T., the provisions of which would continue to govern the relations of the G.A.T.T. members of the Area with other G.A.T.T. countries.

THE EUROPEAN COMMON MARKET AND EURATOM[1]
Soviet Foreign Ministry Press Statement, March 16, 1957

The Soviet Union has always favoured and continues to favour the all-round development of international economic co-operation, and particularly in the peaceful use of atomic energy, because it considers that such co-operation is in the interests of all countries, strengthens trust among the peoples, and creates a firm basis for the peaceful co-existence of states.

The Soviet Union is of the opinion that the establishment of such co-operation in Europe on an all-European basis is of especial importance since it would be instrumental in overcoming the division of Europe into two opposing military groups which is the result of the policy of the western powers, and would help to consolidate peace in Europe.

The development of the peaceful uses of atomic energy in European countries on a large scale would open up favourable prospects for the development of the economy, science and culture and improve the welfare of the peoples. The use of the great possibilities opened up by the peaceful application of atomic energy naturally demands the establishment of the necessary

[1] Reprinted with permission from the *Soviet News*, No. 3591, March 18, 1957, pp. 217–18, 220.

production, scientific and technical facilities and the joint efforts of states in organising large-scale industrial production of nuclear energy. That is why the Soviet government takes cognisance of the desire of various European states, particularly those which lack sufficient resources and technical experience to work in this sphere, to unite their efforts and potential in the peaceful use of nuclear energy and make use of the experience accumulated by other countries.

The Soviet government likewise understands the concern of European countries in organising broad economic co-operation in every other sphere. The extension of economic co-operation between European countries would be very beneficial to the development of their economies, to increased employment and to a higher standard of living, and would have a positive effect on the world economic situation as a whole.

Economic co-operation on a European basis would help to re-establish the disrupted traditional trade and scientific and technical connections, and to overcome the artificial barriers and restrictions in trade and other economic relations, and would bring the European countries closer to one another, strengthening their sense of security and confidence in the future.

However, the plans for creating Euratom and the Common Market are in manifest contradiction with these aims. The first thing that strikes the eye is that all those taking part in Euratom and the Common Market are members of the military N.A.T.O. grouping. It is obvious that the activities of Euratom and the Common Market will be subjugated to N.A.T.O. aims, the aggressive character of which is widely known.

Under the circumstances the creation of Euratom and the Common Market would inevitably lead to a further widening of the rift in Europe, to an aggravation of tension in Europe, would complicate the establishment of economic and political co-operation on a European basis and give rise to fresh difficulties in the solution of the problem of European security.

New and grave obstacles would also arise on the road to re-establishing the national unity of the German people since Western Germany will be increasingly drawn into the system of exclusive military blocs of western powers opposed to other European states. . . .

The assertions of some West European leaders that Euratom and the Common Market would deal only with questions concerning the peaceful co-operation of their member-states are nothing more than a veil to cloak the real schemes of their organisers and sponsors. It should not be forgotten that certain circles in the United States who are actively supporting Euratom are working for the speediest rebirth of German militarism and the equipping of the West German Army now being created with all types of modern weapons, including nuclear weapons. Such a decision, it will be recalled, was adopted by the N.A.T.O. Council session in December 1956 at the suggestion of the United States.

The creation of Euratom will be a practical step in the realisation of these aggressive plans which spell danger for the peoples.

There is no doubt that the revenge-seeking West German groups will not fail to utilise Euratom for stockpiling fissionable materials in order to start producing their own nuclear weapons as soon as possible. In this way the creation of Euratom will pave the way for German militarism to prepare new military gambles. A dangerous centre of disquiet will emerge in the heart of Europe. In this connection, however, it should be stressed again that the equipping of the West German Army with nuclear weapons is fraught with grave consequences for the population of Western Germany above all, since it may become the target of a retaliatory atomic blow.

The hopes of the ruling circles of certain West European countries of utilising Euratom as a means to control the production of nuclear energy in Western Germany are entirely without foundation. It is well known that when the European Coal and Steel Community was set up, the French government, in its efforts to get the French Parliament to ratify the treaty, likewise declared that the community would serve to control the military and industrial potential of Western Germany. In its efforts to secure the ratification of the Paris agreements the French government asserted that these agreements would be a means of military control over Western Germany. It is now evident to all that these calculations have proved to be illusory. The creation of Euratom—willy-nilly—will inevitably lead to the removal of all restrictions in the production of nuclear weapons in Western Germany, which will create a direct threat to the French people as well as to the peoples of other West European countries.

The hopes of certain French, Italian and other West European circles that the creation of Euratom would lessen their economic dependence on the United States are equally groundless. On the contrary, their dependence on the United States would increase to the detriment of the national sovereignty of the participants in that grouping, since the United States—and this is no secret—will actually control Euratom as the chief supplier of fissionable materials and equipment for the atomic industry of Euratom countries. It is no accident that influential circles in Britain declare themselves to be against Britain's accession to Euratom because they realise the consequences of such a step.

The Common Market plan, too, is a grave menace to the peoples of Europe. Its implementation would mean that the economically stronger countries and, in effect, appropriate big monopolies would be able to impose their terms on the weaker European countries in both the Common Market and Euratom, to the detriment of their vital national interests. Not even the most rabid champions of the Common Market plan deny that it is the West German monopolies that stand to gain most from it. It would be useful to recall in this connection that the European Coal and Steel Community, set up earlier by the same six countries, is already dominated by the West German monopoly concerns to the detriment of its other members. There can be no doubt that the establishment of the Common Market would subordinate France and other West European countries to German monopolies economically, disarming them in the face of West German militarists and revenge-seekers. . . .

Some shortsighted West European policy-makers pretend that the establishment of the Common Market would place its participants on a footing of equality in their economic relations with the United States.

The groundlessness of these contentions, however, becomes obvious once we consider the facts.

It is common knowledge that American capital has further penetrated the economy of France, Western Germany, Italy and other West European countries in the post-war years. Scores of branch and daughter companies of the largest American monopolies and corporations, such as General Motors, Ford, Standard Oil and Dupont de Nemours, are now active in every one of these countries. It is obvious that American monopolies and corporations are using the Common Market in their own interests and to the detriment of the national industries of France, Italy and the other member-countries. No one can dispute the undeniable fact that advantages and profits in the capitalist world are distributed according to the strength of the competitors, which is determined by the extent of the capital, and this strength is on the side of the big American and West German monopolies first and foremost. . . .

The question presents itself: who stands to gain from the Euratom and Common Market plans? Why are these plans being pushed forward? Who expects to benefit from them? Do these plans conform to the interests of those who are seeking to strengthen peace and security in Europe, to improve the international situation, to raise the living standards of the working people of the European countries? There can be only one answer: These plans are designed to serve the interests of the western circles which want to supply West German revenge-seekers with nuclear weapons, aggravate the relations between European countries, raise new obstacles to peace and security in Europe, and further complicate the re-establishment of the national unity of the German people. They are designed to serve the interests of those who are seeking to deprive France and other West European countries of their national sovereignty, to make their economy dependent on West German monopolies and to hamper the establishment of general European economic co-operation.

The Soviet Union is convinced that a genuine solution of the economic problems affecting each European country as, indeed, a solution of the problem of the economic co-operation of the European countries and their co-operation in the sphere of the peaceful uses of atomic energy, cannot be found through the establishment of new exclusive organisations by this or that group of countries opposed to other European countries.

This solution can and should be found on an all-European basis through the use of the already existing organisations of an all-European nature or through the establishment of new European organisations on terms acceptable to all European countries regardless of their social system.

Proceeding from this, the Soviet Union has already made a number of proposals towards the establishment of genuine all-European co-operation:

1. In April 1956 the Soviet Union proposed at the 11th Session of the United Nations Economic Commission for Europe that an agency for the peaceful application of atomic energy be established within its framework. This motion has been included in the agenda of the 12th Session of the United Nations Economic Commission for Europe opening on April 29 this year.

In its statement on all-European co-operation in the peaceful uses of atomic energy of July 12, 1956, the Soviet government proposed that a conference of European countries be called to consider the establishment of an all-European organisation for the peaceful uses of atomic energy, having in mind that this organisation is to be a regional branch of the International Atomic Energy Agency. This organisation, the Soviet government believed, might be established on an inter-governmental basis with the participation of all European countries wishing to do so, and also the United States of America.

The European regional organisation for the peaceful uses of atomic energy proposed by the Soviet Union would not be directed against any state or group of states whatsoever, and would not infringe on any national interests.

Co-operation within the framework of an all-European regional atomic energy organisation would, unquestionably, contribute to the progress of every European country in the peaceful uses of atomic energy and help raise the living standards of the European peoples, besides being an important means of improving the European situation in general.

The establishment of all-European co-operation in the peaceful uses of atomic energy would greatly contribute to the solution of a pressing issue of our time—the banning of atomic and hydrogen weapons as weapons of mass destruction.

Guided by a desire to promote a positive solution of the problem of all-European co-operation in the sphere of the peaceful uses of atomic energy, the Soviet government proposes that the following questions bearing on the problem be discussed:

(a) Establishment of an atomic energy research institute or institutes on an all-European basis.

(b) Co-operation in the building of establishments for the generation of atomic energy for industrial, scientific and technical purposes, including questions concerning the provision of raw materials to these establishments.

It goes without saying that in developing all-European co-operation in the peaceful uses of atomic energy, the European countries will be able to make use of the appropriate experience of the Soviet Union.

2. With regard to the question of all-European economic co-operation, the Soviet government submitted at the same 11th Session of the United Nations Economic Commission for Europe in April, 1956, a proposal to conclude an all-European agreement on economic co-operation, providing for the establishment of more favourable conditions for the development of European trade and co-operation in the sphere of transport, scientific and technical co-operation and the exchange of production experience. A draft agreement supported by the Soviet government will likewise be considered by the 12th Session of the Economic Commission for Europe.

The Soviet government now proposes that the following questions be considered additionally:

(a) Co-operation in the construction of large hydro-electric power stations of interest to several countries, with their consent and participation.

(b) Co-operation in the development of Europe's fuel resources and power resources with a view to easing the strain on the fuel resources of many European countries.

(c) Conclusion of an agreement between all interested European countries on measures for promoting trade between them.

(d) Mutual economic and financial assistance by countries to promote their economic development.

The Soviet government is prepared to consider any other proposal concerning the principles and forms of economic co-operation and co-operation in the peaceful application of atomic energy.   [ ]

THE EUROPEAN COMMON MARKET AND
THE FREE TRADE AREA[1]
United States Department of State Press Statement,
January 15, 1957

Belgium, France, the German Federal Republic, Italy, Luxembourg, and the Netherlands have been engaged in negotiations with a view to establishing a common market among them. The common market would involve the elimination of substantially all of the barriers to trade among these six countries and the establishment by them of a common external tariff toward outside countries. The United Kingdom has expressed a desire to associate itself with the envisaged six-country common market in a free-trade-area relationship. Under this arrangement barriers to trade between the United

---

[1] Reprinted from *The Department of State Bulletin*, XXXVI, No. 919 (February 4, 1957), p. 182.

Kingdom and the six countries of the common market would be eliminated on a wide range of products. However, the United Kingdom would continue to maintain its own tariff against countries outside the free trade area, and the six countries of the common market would do the same with their unified tariff. Other Western European countries have indicated an interest in associating themselves with these arrangements on a basis similar to that of the United Kingdom.

Following is a statement of U.S. policy with respect to the proposed European common market and free trade area. This is a summary of views which have been communicated to the governments concerned.

The attitude of the United States with respect to current Western European proposals for a common market and free trade area is determined by two traditional policies of the U.S. Government: our consistent support of moves to further the political and economic strength and cohesion of Western Europe within an expanding Atlantic community and our long-standing devotion to progress toward freer nondiscriminatory multilateral trade and convertibility of currencies.

It is in the light of these complementary objectives that the United States welcomes the initiatives for a common market and free trade area in Western Europe. The details of the common-market treaty are being worked out in negotiations now taking place in Brussels among Belgium, France, the German Federal Republic, Italy, Luxembourg, and the Netherlands; the governments of these countries have indicated that it is their intention that the common market which they envisage should result in the expansion of their trade not only with each other but also with other countries.

A European common market based on provisions which hold the promise of attaining this objective will have the support of the United States. This would be consistent with U.S. support of such arrangements as the General Agreement on Tariffs and Trade and the Articles of Agreement of the International Monetary Fund, both of which have as their objective the expansion of nondiscriminatory multilateral trade.

Certain aspects of the common-market arrangements will be of particular interest to the U.S. Government: those relating to agriculture, those having a bearing on the liberalization of import controls affecting dollar goods, and measures both public and private which bear on international trade. The European market for agricultural exports from the United States is important, and we will wish therefore to study carefully the possible impact of common-market arrangements on it. The progress which Western European countries have made in recent years in liberalizing imports from the dollar area has been encouraging; it is hoped that this progress will be continued as rapidly as the circumstances permit. Since the six countries are also participants in the General Agreement on Tariffs and Trade, it is assumed that such import restrictions as may be found necessary to maintain will be consistent with the standards of the general agreement.

The United Kingdom has made known its preliminary decision to associate itself with the common-market countries in a free-trade-area arrangement. The association of the United Kingdom in such an arrangement would further strengthen the unity of the Atlantic Community and the free world. The United States hopes that such free-trade-area arrangements as may be concluded among the proposed common market, the United Kingdom, and other OEEC countries would also encourage the expansion of international trade from which all of the free-world countries, and not only those participating in the common market and free trade area, would benefit.

In summary it is our hope and expectation that the negotiations on the common market and free trade area will be carried forward and concluded in such a manner that from these European initiatives will come a new contribution to the unity and prosperity of Europe and the Atlantic Community and to the welfare of the entire free world.

BRITAIN'S PROPOSED ENTRY INTO THE COMMON MARKET[1]
French Statement, May 16, 1967

[ ]

. . . the Common Market is a sort of prodigy. To introduce into it now new and massive elements, into the midst of those that have been fit together with such difficulty, would obviously be to jeopardize the whole and the details and to raise the problem of an entirely different undertaking. All the more that if the Six have been able to build this famous edifice it is because it concerned a group of continental countries, immediate neighbors to each other, doubtless offering differences of size, but complementary in their economic structure. Moreover, the Six form through their territory a compact geographic and strategic unit. It must be added that despite, perhaps because of their great battles of the past—I am naturally speaking of France and Germany—they now find themselves inclined to support one another mutually rather than to oppose one another. Finally, aware of the potential of their material resources and their human values, all desire either aloud or in whispers that their unit constitute one day an element that might provide a balance to any power in the world.

Compared with the motives that led the Six to organize their unit, we understand for what reasons, why Britain—who is not continental, who remains, because of the Commonwealth and because she is an island, committed far beyond the seas, who is tied to the United States by all kinds of special agreements—did not merge into a Community with set dimensions and strict

---

[1] These remarks, made by President Charles de Gaulle at his fifteenth press conference on May 16, 1967, were made available through the courtesy of the French Press and Information Service, New York.

rules. While this Community was taking shape, Britain therefore first refused to participate in it and even took toward it a hostile attitude as if she saw in it an economic and political threat. Then she tried to negotiate in order to join the Community, but in such conditions that the latter would have been suffocated by this membership. The attempt having failed, the British Government then asserted that it no longer wanted to enter the Community and set about strengthening its ties with the Commonwealth and with other European countries grouped around it in a free-trade area. Yet, apparently now adopting a new state of mind, Britain declares she is ready to subscribe to the Rome Treaty, even though she is asking exceptional and prolonged delays and, as regards her, that basic changes be made in the Treaty's implementation. At the same time, she acknowledges that in order to arrive there, it will be necessary to surmount obstacles that the great perceptiveness and profound experience of her Prime Minister have qualified as formidable.

This is true, for instance, of the agricultural regulations. We know that they tend to have the countries of the Community nourish themselves on what they produce and to compensate, by what is called "financial levies," for all the advantages that each could have in importing less expensive produce from elsewhere. Now, Britain nourishes herself, to a great extent, on foodstuffs bought inexpensively throughout the world and, particularly, in the Commonwealth. If she submits to the rules of the Six, then her balance of payments will be crushed by "levies" and, on the other hand, she would then be forced to raise the price of her food to the price level adopted by the continental countries, consequently to increase the wages of her workers and, thereby, to sell her goods all the more at a higher price and with more difficulty. It is clear that she cannot do this. But, if she enters the Community without being really subjected to the agricultural system of the Six, this system will thereby collapse, completely upsetting the equilibrium of the Common Market and removing for France one of the main reasons she can have for participating in it.

Another basic difficulty arises from the fact that, among the Six, it is a rule that capital circulates freely to promote expansion, but that in Britain—if she were allowed to enter—it is forbidden for capital to leave so as to limit the balance-of-payments deficit, a deficit that, despite praiseworthy efforts and some recent progress, still remains threatening. How can this problem be solved? For it would be for the British an excessive risk to eliminate the sluice-gates which, in Britain, block the movement of money to the outside and, for the Europeans, it would be unthinkable to take into the organization a partner which, in this respect, would find itself isolated in such a costly regime.

Also, how can it not be seen that the very situation of the pound sterling prevents the Common Market from incorporating Britain. The very fact that the organization of the Six is entirely freeing their mutual trade necessarily implies that the currency of the member countries has a constant relative value and that, if it happened that one of them were disturbed, the Community would ensure its recovery. But this is possible only due to the well-established soundness of the mark, the lira, the florin, the Belgian franc and the French franc. Now, without despairing of seeing the pound hold its own, for a long time we would not be assured that it will succeed. . . . Monetary parity and solidarity are the essential conditions of the Common Market and assuredly could not be extended to our neighbors across the Channel, unless the pound appears, one day, in a new situation and such that its future value appears assured; unless it also frees itself of the character of reserve currency; unless, finally, the burden of Great Britain's deficitary balances within the sterling area disappear. When and how will this happen?

What is true, at this very moment, from the economic standpoint, would also be true, eventually, from the political standpoint. The idea, the hope which, from the beginning, led the Six continental countries to unite, tended without any doubt toward the formation of a unit which would be European in all respects, and, because of this would become capable not only of carrying its own weight in production and trade, but also of acting one day politically by itself and for itself toward anyone. Considering the special relations that tie the British to America, with the advantage and also the dependence that results for them; considering the existence of the Commonwealth and their preferential relations with it; considering the special commitment that they still have in various parts of the world and which, basically, distinguishes them from the continentals, we see that the policy of the latter, as soon as they have one, would undoubtedly concur, in certain cases, with the policy of the former. But we cannot see how both policies could merge, unless the British assumed again, particularly as regards defense, complete command of themselves, or else if the continentals renounced forever a European Europe.

[ ]

In truth, it really seems that the change in the situation of the British in relation to the Six, once we would be ready by common consent to proceed with it, might consist of a choice between three issues.

Either recognize that, as things stand at present, their entry into the Common Market, with all the exceptions that it would not fail to be accompanied by, with the irruption of entirely new facts, new both in nature and in quantity, that would necessarily result from this entry, with the participation of several other States that would certainly be its corollary, would amount to necessitating the building of an entirely new edifice, scrapping nearly all of that which has just been built. What, then, would we end up with if not, perhaps, the creation of a free-trade area of Western Europe, pending that of the Atlantic area, which would deprive our continent of any real personality?

Or, establish, between the Community on the one hand, and Britain and some States of the "little" free-trade area on the other, a system of association, such as the one provided for in the Treaty of Rome and which could, without creating an upheaval, multiply and facilitate the economic relations between the contracting parties.

Or else, lastly, before changing what exists, wait until a certain internal and external evolution, of which Great Britain seems already to be showing signs, is eventually completed, that is to say, until that great people which is endowed with tremendous ability and courage has itself accomplished first and for its part the necessary profound economic and political transformation so that it can join with the Six continental countries. I really believe that this is the desire of many people, who are anxious to see the emergence of a Europe corresponding to its natural dimensions and who have great admiration and true friendship for Britain. If, one day, she were to come to this point, how warmly France would welcome this historic conversion.

FRANCE'S VIEW OF THE ATLANTIC ALLIANCE AND NATO[1]
Speech Delivered by Foreign Minister Maurice Couve de Murville before the French National Assembly, April 14, 1966

Even before the opening of the debate on the Government's general policy, it was clear that, to a very large extent, the National Assembly's interest would concentrate on foreign policy, that is, on the highly important decisions that have just been taken by France on the Atlantic alliance and on our country's participation in the organization known as NATO, the organization set up in the years that followed the conclusion of the Treaty of Washington in 1949 and that marked, with the Korean war, the climax of the cold war. . . .

That alliance was concluded, to be sure, at a time when international conditions were quite different from what they have become. In 1949, Western Europe seemed directly threatened, and undoubtedly it actually was. Two ideological blocs—two very great powers, also—confronted each other everywhere in the world, and first of all on our continent. The European countries seemed to be the immediate stake of this confrontation. Their alliance with North America was a normal defensive reflex, just as it represented for the United States the obvious means of safeguarding some of its fundamental interests.

We then experienced many crises, the last of which, in November 1958 on Berlin, ended in 1961 with the construction of the wall that completed the brutal physical separation of the two Germanies. But at that time, and for several years already, an evolution had been evident. It had begun to change the world picture. It has continued since then, to the extent that the blocs are disintegrating, if only as a result of the Sino-Russian conflict; nuclear deterrence, which worked effectively in the Cuban crisis, now obviously plays an

---

[1] The English-language version of this speech was made available through the courtesy of the French Press and Information Service, New York.

effective role of terror. And yet, in our view the Atlantic alliance should continue to exist, and to do so doubtless for a long time still. This is because it remains, in a still disordered world, a factor of equilibrium and consequently of peace. In man's eye, it will remain as such so long as an overall European settlement has not been reached—that is, essentially a solution to the problem of Germany—so long, in other words, as a new equilibrium has not been established in Europe, a stable one that would open the way to normal relations, that is, peaceful relations within the entire continent.

Such is the first conclusion that France has made known to her associates, by officially and publicly stating to them that she had no intention of availing herself of the clause that permits each partner, in 1969, insofar as it is concerned, to terminate the alliance; that she intended, on the contrary, to stay in it so long as that appeared necessary. What I have just said shows that this is a question of long-term perspectives.

But what holds true for the alliance does not hold true for the Organization. That is quite another thing.

First, the one is in no way the condition for the other, even if, in current terminology, and through an ambiguity perhaps intentionally maintained, the term "NATO" covers both the alliance and the Organization, and even if some assert—perhaps, moreover, less often in recent weeks—that they are necessarily linked.

The Organization—what does that mean? Essentially it is a whole group of integrated international commands, placed unavoidably under the authority of the strongest, by far, of all the partners, which are set up in continental Europe, already functioning in peacetime, even if they at that time have no effective responsibilities, and to which are assigned, in the event of war, the bulk of the conventional military forces—I stress conventional—stationed in the western part of the European continent, whether it concerns European forces strictly speaking or American, British and Canadian expeditionary corps.

It is obvious that an organization of this type—outside of the maintenance of those expeditionary corps—places the United States, Great Britain and Canada under no particular constraint. It is understandable that those countries accommodate themselves to it without difficulties, even if they find the corresponding expenditures heavy.

This is not at all the case for the countries on the European continent. This is the problem raised by France.

When our American and British friends and allies extol the virtues of Atlantic integration to us, it is in reality a matter of showing the advantages of a system that offers the various parties quite different situations. For it is on French soil that two of the essential NATO general headquarters are installed —the Supreme Command for Europe and the Central Europe Command, with thousands of officers, communications networks, logistics systems and constraints of all kinds that such general headquarters entail. . . .

All these installations and all this personnel benefit, by force of circum-stances, from a status that is, in fact, a status of extraterritoriality. This inevitable infringement—but one that is serious by its scope—upon our sovereignty could be conceived of, at the most, in a situation of crisis, not to mention in time of war. How can it be imagined that it might become for decades, if not for generations, the normal international status for a country such as ours?

The analysis, however, does not end there. Due to the very fact of that vast implantation of general staffs, forces and resources—even, once again, if they do not actually exercise command in time of peace, and even if their main activity is then really their own maintenance—due to the very fact that this involves a system set up to take in charge in time of war, among other things and fully, the defense of France, France has the feeling that, precisely with regard to her defense, the matter is no longer really within her compe-tence, that she has been discharged of her essential responsibilities, and that her interest is simply to attribute to others—and it is not difficult to see what I mean—the largest possible part of the effort. . . .

I am aware that it is said repeatedly that NATO has never prevented our country from pursuing its policy in the past. France, under NATO, continued the war in Indochina, undertook the Suez expedition and conducted the Algerian war. Perhaps I might have a reservation about Suez, since neither NATO nor the United States had been consulted or warned, and when the facts were known, our American partners' reaction was swift and—I might add—effective. But, on the whole, it is true that the Atlantic Organization has been no hindrance to the action of our governments. The real problem does not lie there. It does not so much involve our being able to do what we like as it does our not being drawn into doing what we do not like. Who does not see the weight that the intermeshing, if not the integration, of general staffs and forces under the leadership of a partner infinitely more powerful than the others can bring to bear on the determination of a government, and consequently the influence that this can have in orienting its policy in a direction quite different from the one that it would have taken sponta-neously? Who does not see the hazards of such a system for France's security in the event of a major conflict in which America would be involved, without France herself being so? Is that not, moreover, what our public opinion has been vaguely feeling ever since crises have been appearing—at least temporar-ily—no longer in our regions, but in the distant confines of the Asian continent? . . .

In reality, and barring, of course, the very special and very understand-able case of Germany, Europe scarcely feels itself directly affected by the French initiatives. If Europe reacts, it is not in terms of itself, but in relation to the United States, and that is indeed the real problem.

That is the problem, for the United States occupies such an important—shall I say such a predominant—place in NATO that if one touches the

Organization, one seems to take issue with the United States itself. It happens, for the same reason, that the foreign forces stationed in Europe, outside of Germany, are almost entirely American forces. Consequently we also seem to take issue with them when we say that the fate of the foreign forces is logically linked to that of the NATO installations and commands as such with regard to their presence on French soil. . . .

It is inevitable, and beneficial to all, that Europe reassume its independence with respect to America. It is inevitable that the latter conduct its policy throughout the world, and that this policy, more and more, be outside the European countries. It is inevitable that relations between East and West not remain frozen in the situation they were in fifteen years ago and that, as a result, the Russian-American rivalry decrease, at the same time as distant prospects for a peaceful and lasting European settlement come into view. Finally, it is inevitable that, in international policy, the new factors that have appeared in the past fifteen years—that it, first the mass of newly independent countries, and second the enormous Chinese power—make their action increasingly felt and that the Atlantic alliance be transformed by this.

These are the prospects within which France's decisions on NATO should be placed. Far from being, as is claimed, naively lingering in the past; these are the prospects of the future. France is in the mainstream of world policy, she is moving in the direction of history, and that is why she is working for peace in the end.

PART III

*

The Communist World

··{*11*}·· *Domestic Changes in the Soviet Union*

THE CULT OF PERSONALITY[1]
Secret Speech Delivered by First Party Secretary N. S. Khrushchev at the Twentieth Party Congress of the Communist Party of the Soviet Union, February 25, 1956

[ ]

Comrades, in the report of the Central Committee of the party at the 20th Congress, in a number of speeches by delegates to the Congress, as also formerly during the plenary CC/CPSU sessions, quite a lot has been said about the cult of the individual and about its harmful consequences. . . .

Allow me first of all to remind you how severely the classics of Marxism-Leninism denounced every manifestation of the cult of the individual. In a letter to the German political worker, Wilhelm Bloss, Marx stated: "From my antipathy to any cult of the individual, I never made public during the existence of the International the numerous addresses from various countries which recognized my merits and which annoyed me. I did not even reply to them, except sometimes to rebuke their authors. Engels and I first joined the secret society of Communists on the condition that everything making for superstitious worship of authority would be deleted from its statute. . . .

The great modesty of the genius of the revolution, Vladimir Ilyich Lenin, is known. Lenin had always stressed the role of the people as the creator of history, the directing and organizational role of the party as a living and creative organism, and also the role of the central committee.

Marxism does not negate the role of the leaders of the workers' class in directing the revolutionary liberation movement.

While ascribing great importance to the role of the leaders and organizers of the masses, Lenin at the same time mercilessly stigmatized every manifestation of the cult of the individual, inexorably combated the foreign-to-Marxism views about a "hero" and a "crowd" and countered all efforts to oppose a "hero" to the masses and to the people.

---

[1] Reprinted from the *Congressional Record: Proceedings and Debates of the 84th Congress, 2nd Session* (May 22, 1956–June 11, 1956), CII, Part 7 (June 4, 1956), pp. 9389–9403.

106

Lenin taught that the party's strength depends on its indissoluble unity with the masses, on the fact that behind the party follow the people—workers, peasants and intelligentsia. "Only he will win and retain the power," said Lenin, "who believes in the people, who submerges himself in the fountain of the living creativeness of the people.". . .

During Lenin's life the central committee of the party was a real expression of collective leadership of the party and of the Nation. Being a militant Marxist-revolutionist, always unyielding in matters of principle, Lenin never imposed by force his views upon his coworkers. He tried to convince; he patiently explained his opinions to others. Lenin always diligently observed that the norms of party life were realized, that the party statute was enforced, that the party congresses and the plenary sessions of the central committee took place at the proper intervals.

In addition to the great accomplishments of V. I. Lenin for the victory of the working class and of the working peasants, for the victory of our party and for the application of the ideas of scientific communism to life, his acute mind expressed itself also in this that he detected in Stalin in time those negative characteristics which resulted later in grave consequences. Fearing the future fate of the party and of the Soviet nation, V. I. Lenin made a completely correct characterization of Stalin, pointing out that it was necessary to consider the question of transferring Stalin from the position of Secretary General because of the fact that Stalin is excessively rude, that he does not have a proper attitude toward his comrades, that he is capricious, and abuses his power. . . .

Vladimir Ilyich said: "Stalin is excessively rude, and this defect, which can be freely tolerated in our midst and in contacts among us Communists, becomes a defect which cannot be tolerated in one holding the position of the Secretary General. Because of this, I propose that the comrades consider the method by which Stalin would be removed from this position and by which another man would be selected for it, a man, who above all, would differ from Stalin in only one quality, namely, greater tolerance, greater loyalty, greater kindness, and more considerate attitude toward the comrades, a less capricious temper, etc.". . .

As later events have proven, Lenin's anxiety was justified; in the first period after Lenin's death Stalin still paid attention to his (i.e., Lenin's) advice, but, later he began to disregard the serious admonitions of Vladimir Ilyich.

When we analyze the practice of Stalin in regard to the direction of the party and of the country, when we pause to consider everything which Stalin perpetrated, we must be convinced that Lenin's fears were justified. The negative characteristics of Stalin, which, in Lenin's time, were only incipient, transformed themselves during the last years into a grave abuse of power by Stalin, which caused untold harm to our party. . . .

Stalin acted not through persuasion, explanation, and patient cooperation with people, but by imposing his concepts and demanding absolute submission to his opinion. Whoever opposed this concept or tried to prove his viewpoint, and the correctness of his position—was doomed to removal from the leading collective and to subsequent moral and physical annihilation. This was especially true during the period following the 17th party congress, when many prominent party leaders and rank-and-file party workers, honest and dedicated to the cause of communism, fell victim to Stalin's despotism. . . .

Stalin originated the concept enemy of the people. This term automatically rendered it unnecessary that the ideological errors of a man or men engaged in a controversy be proven; this term made possible the usage of the most cruel repression, violating all norms of revolutionary legality, against anyone who in any way disagreed with Stalin, against those who were only suspected of hostile intent, against those who had bad reputations. This concept, enemy of the people, actually eliminated the possibility of any kind of ideological fight or the making of one's views known on this or that issue, even those of a practical character. In the main, and in actuality, the only proof of guilt used, against all norms of current legal science, was the confession of the accused himself, and, as subsequent probing proved, confessions were acquired through physical pressures against the accused. . . .

Lenin used severe methods only in the most necessary cases, when the exploiting classes were still in existence and were vigorously opposing the revolution, when the struggle for survival was decidedly assuming the sharpest forms, even including a civil war.

Stalin, on the other hand, used extreme methods and mass repressions at a time when the revolution was already victorious, when the Soviet state was strengthened, when the exploiting classes were already liquidated, and Socialist relations were rooted solidly in all phases of national economy, when our party was politically consolidated and had strengthened itself both numerically and ideologically. It is clear that here Stalin showed in a whole series of cases his intolerance, his brutality, and his abuse of power. Instead of proving his political correctness and mobilizing the masses, he often chose the path of repression and physical annihilation, not only against actual enemies, but also against individuals who had not committed any crimes against the party and the Soviet Government. Here we see no wisdom but only a demonstration of the brutal force which had once so alarmed V. I. Lenin. . . .

Considering the question of the cult of an individual we must first of all show everyone what harm this caused to the interests of our party. . . .

In practice Stalin ignored the norms of party life and trampled on the Leninist principle of collective party leadership.

Stalin's willfulness vis-a-vis the party and its central committee became fully evident after the 17th party congress, which took place in 1934. . . .

It was determined that of the 139 members and candidates of the party's Central Committee who were elected at the 17th congress, 98 persons, that is,

70 percent, were arrested and shot (mostly in 1937–38). [Indignation in the hall.] . . .

The same fate met not only the central committee members but also the majority of the delegates to the 17th party congress. Of 1,966 delegates with either voting or advisory rights, 1,108 persons were arrested on charges of antirevolutionary crimes, i.e., decidedly more than a majority. This very fact shows how absurd, wild, and contrary to commonsense were the charges of counter-revolutionary crimes made out, as we now see, against a majority of participants at the 17th party congress. [Indignation in the hall.] . . .

What is the reason that mass repressions against activists increased more and more after the 17th party congress? It was because at that time Stalin had so elevated himself above the party and above the nation that he ceased to consider either the central committee or the party. While he still reckoned with the opinion of the collective before the 17th congress, after the complete political liquidation of the Trotskyites, Zinovievites and Bukharinites, when as a result of that fight and Socialist victories the party achieved unity, Stalin ceased to an ever greater degree to consider the members of the party's central committee and even the members of the Political Bureau. Stalin thought that now he could decide all things alone and all he needed were statisticians; he treated all others in such a way that they could only listen to and praise him.

After the criminal murder of S. M. Kirov, mass repressions and brutal acts of violation of Socialist legality began. On the evening of December 1, 1934, on Stalin's initiative (without the approval of the Political Bureau— which was passed 2 days later, casually) the Secretary of the Presidium of the Central Executive Committee, Yenukidze, signed the following directive:

I. Investigative agencies are directed to speed up the cases of those accused of the preparation or execution of acts of terror.

II. Judicial organs are directed not to hold up the execution of death sentences pertaining to crimes of this category in order to consider the possibility of pardon, because the Presidium of the Central Executive Committee, U.S.S.R., does not consider as possible the receiving of petitions of this sort.

III. The organs of the Commissariat of Internal Affairs are directed to execute the death sentences against criminals of the above-mentioned category immediately after the passage of sentences.

This directive became the basis for mass acts of abuse against Socialist legality. During many of the fabricated court cases the accused were charged with "the preparation" of terroristic acts; this deprived them of any possibility that their cases might be reexamined, even when they stated before the court that their confessions were secured by force, and when, in a convincing manner, they disproved the accusations against them. . . .

Mass repressions grew tremendously from the end of 1936 after a telegram from Stalin and Zhdanov, dated from Sochi on September 25, 1936, was addressed to Kaganovich, Molotov, and other members of the Political Bureau. The content of the telegram was as follows: "We deem it absolutely necessary and urgent that Comrade Yezhov be nominated to the post of People's Commissar for Internal Affairs. Yagoda has definitely proved himself to be incapable of unmasking the Trotskyite-Zinovievite bloc. The OGPU is 4 years behind in this matter. This is noted by all party workers and by the majority of the representatives of the NKVD." Strictly speaking we should stress that Stalin did not meet with and therefore could not know the opinion of party workers. . . .

The mass repressions at this time were made under the slogan of a fight against the Trotskyites. Did the Trotskyites at this time actually constitute such a danger to our party and to the Soviet state? We should recall that in 1927, on the eve of the 15th party congress, only some 4,000 votes were cast for the Trotskyite-Zinovievite opposition, while there were 724,000 for the party line. During the 10 years which passed between the 15th party congress and the February–March central committee plenum, Trotskyism was completely disarmed; many former Trotskyites had changed their former views and worked in the various sectors building socialism. It is clear that in the situation of Socialist victory there was no basis for mass terror in the country. . . .

The majority of the Central Committee members and candidates elected at the 17th congress and arrested in 1937–38 were expelled from the party illegally through the brutal abuse of the party statute, because the question of their expulsion was never studied at the Central Committee plenum.

Now when the cases of some of these so-called spies and saboteurs were examined it was found that all their cases were fabricated. Confessions of guilt of many arrested and charged with enemy activity were gained with the help of cruel and inhuman tortures. . . .

An example of vile provocation of odious falsification and of criminal violation of revolutionary legality is the case of the former candidate for the central committee political bureau, one of the most eminent workers of the party and of the Soviet Government, Comrade Eikhe, who was a party member since 1905. [Commotion in the hall.]

Comrade Eikhe was arrested on April 29, 1938, on the basis of slanderous materials, without the sanction of the prosecutor of the U.S.S.R., which was finally received 15 months after the arrest.

Investigation of Eikhe's case was made in a manner which most brutally violated Soviet legality and was accompanied by willfulness and falsification.

Eikhe was forced under torture to sign ahead of time a protocol of his confession prepared by the investigative judges, in which he and several other eminent party workers were accused of anti-Soviet activity.

On October 1, 1939, Eikhe sent his declaration to Stalin in which he categorically denied his guilt and asked for an examination of his case. In the declaration he wrote:

"There is no more bitter misery than to sit in the jail of a government for which I have always fought.". . .

On February 2, 1940, Eikhe was brought before the court. Here he did not confess any guilt and said as follows:

"In all the so-called confessions of mine there is not one letter written by me with the exception of my signatures under the protocols which were forced from me. I have made my confession under pressure from the investigative judge who from the time of my arrest tormented me. After that I began to write all this nonsense. The most important thing for me is to tell the court, the party and Stalin that I am not guilty. I have never been guilty of any conspiracy. I will die believing in the truth of party policy as I have believed in it during my whole life."

On February 4 Eikhe was shot. [Indignation in the hall.] It has been definitely established now that Eikhe's case was fabricated; he has been posthumously rehabilitated. . . .

The way in which the former NKVD workers manufactured various fictitious "anti-Soviet centers" and "blocs" with the help of provocatory methods is seen from the confession of Comrade Rozenblum, party member since 1906, who was arrested in 1937 by the Leningrad NKVD.

During the examination in 1955 of the Komarov case Rozenblum revealed the following fact: when Rozenblum was arrested in 1937 he was subjected to terrible torture during which he was ordered to confess false information concerning himself and other persons. He was then brought to the office of Zakovsky, who offered him freedom on condition that he make before the court a false confession fabricated in 1937 by the NKVD concerning "sabotage, espionage and diversion in a terroristic center in Leningrad." [Movement in the hall.] . . .

"You, yourself," said Zakovsky, "will not need to invent anything. The NKVD will prepare for you a ready outline for every branch of the center; you will have to study it carefully and to remember well all questions and answers which the court might ask. This case will be ready in 4–5 months, or perhaps a half year. During all this time you will be preparing yourself so that you will not compromise the investigation and yourself. Your future will depend on how the trial goes and on its results. If you begin to lie and to testify falsely, blame yourself. If you manage to endure it, you will save your head and we will feed and clothe you at the government's cost until your death."

This is the kind of vile things which were then practiced. [Movement in the hall.] . . .

When we look at many of our novels, films, and historical scientific studies, the role of Stalin in the patriotic war appears to be entirely improbable. Stalin had foreseen everything. The Soviet Army, on the basis of a strategic plan prepared by Stalin long before, used the tactics of so-called active defense, i. e., tactics which, as we know, allowed the Germans to come up to Moscow and Stalingrad. Using such tactics, the Soviet Army, supposedly, thanks only to Stalin's genius, turned to the offensive and subdued the enemy. The epic victory gained through the armed might of the land of the Soviets, through our heroic people, is ascribed in this type of novel, film, and scientific study as being completely due to the strategic genius of Stalin.

We have to analyze this matter carefully because it has a tremendous significance, not only from the historical but especially from the political, educational, and practical point of view. . . .

During the war and after the war, Stalin put forward the thesis that the tragedy which our nation experienced in the first part of the war was the result of the unexpected attack of the Germans against the Soviet Union. But, comrades, this is completely untrue. As soon as Hitler came to power in Germany he assigned to himself the task of liquidating communism. The Fascists were saying this openly; they did not hide their plans. In order to attain this aggressive end, all sorts of pacts and blocs were created, such as the famous Berlin-Rome-Tokyo Axis. Many facts from the prewar period clearly showed that Hitler was going all out to begin a war against the Soviet state and that he had concentrated large armed units, together with armored units, near the Soviet borders. . . .

We must assert that information of this sort concerning the threat of German armed invasion of Soviet territory was coming in also from our own military and diplomatic sources; however, because the leadership was conditioned against such information, such data was dispatched with fear and assessed with reservation. . . .

Despite these particularly grave warnings, the necessary steps were not taken to prepare the country properly for defense and to prevent it from being caught unaware.

Did we have time and the capabilities for such preparations? Yes; we had the time and capabilities. Our industry was already so developed that it was capable of supplying fully the Soviet Army with everything that it needed. . . .

Had our industry been mobilized properly and in time to supply the army with the necessary materiel, our wartime losses would have been decidedly smaller. Such mobilization had not been, however, started in time. And already in the first days of the war it became evident that our Army was badly armed, that we did not have enough artillery, tanks, and planes to throw the enemy back. . . .

Very grievous consequences, especially in reference to the beginning of the war, followed Stalin's annihilation of many military commanders and political workers during 1937–41 because of his suspiciousness and through slanderous accusations. During these years repressions were instituted against certain parts of military cadres beginning literally at the company and battallion commander level and extending to the higher military centers; during this time the cadre of leaders who had gained military experience in Spain and in the Far East was almost completely liquidated. . . .

After the conclusion of the patriotic war the Soviet nation stressed with pride the magnificent victories gained through great sacrifices and tremendous efforts. The country experienced a period of political enthusiasm. The party came out of the war even more united; in the fire of the war party cadres were tempered and hardened. Under such conditions nobody could have even thought of the possibility of some plot in the party.

And it was precisely at this time that the so-called Leningrad affair was born. As we have now proven, this case was fabricated. Those who innocently lost their lives included Comrades Voznesensky, Kuznetsov, Rodionov, Popkov, and others. . . .

Facts prove that the Leningrad affair is also the result of willfulness which Stalin exercised against party cadres. . . .

We must state that after the war the situation became even more complicated. Stalin became even more capricious, irritable, and brutal; in particular his suspicion grew. His persecution mania reached unbelievable dimensions. Many workers were becoming enemies before his very eyes. After the war Stalin separated himself from the collective even more. Everything was decided by him alone without any consideration for anyone or anything.

This unbelievable suspicion was cleverly taken advantage of by the abject provocateur and vile enemy, Beriya, who had murdered thousands of Communists and loyal Soviet people. The elevation of Voznesensky and Kuznetsov alarmed Beriya. As we have now proven, it had been precisely Beriya who had suggested to Stalin the fabrication by him and by his confidants of materials in the form of declarations and anonymous letters, and in the form of various rumors and talks. . . .

The question arises: Why is it that we see the truth of this affair only now, and why did we not do something earlier, during Stalin's life, in order to prevent the loss of innocent lives? It was because Stalin personally supervised the Leningrad affair, and the majority of the Political Bureau members did not, at that time, know all of the circumstances in these matters, and could not therefore intervene. . . .

The willfulness of Stalin showed itself not only in decisions concerning the internal life of the country but also in the international relations of the Soviet Union.

The July plenum of the Central Committee studied in detail the reasons for the development of conflict with Yugoslavia. It was a shameful role which Stalin played here. The "Yugoslav affair" contained no problems which could not have been solved through party discussions among comrades. There was no significant basis for the development of this "affair;" it was completely possible to have prevented the rupture of relations with that country. . . .

I recall the first days when the conflict between the Soviet Union and Yugoslavia began artificially to be blown up. Once, when I came from Kiev to

Moscow, I was invited to visit Stalin who, pointing to the copy of a letter lately sent to Tito, asked me, "Have you read this?"

Not waiting for my reply he answered, "I will shake my little finger and there will be no more Tito. He will fall.". . .

But this did not happen to Tito. No matter how much or how little Stalin shook, not only his little finger but everything else that he could shake, Tito did not fall. Why? The reason was that, in this case of disagreement with the Yugoslav comrades, Tito had behind him a state and a people who had gone through a severe school of fighting for liberty and independence, a people which gave support to its leaders.

You see to what Stalin's mania for greatness led. He had completely lost consciousness of reality; he demonstrated his suspicion and haughtiness not only in relation to individuals in the U.S.S.R., but in relation to whole parties and nations. . . .

Let us also recall the affair of the doctor plotters. [Animation in the hall.] Actually there was no affair outside of the declaration of the woman doctor Timashuk, who was probably influenced or ordered by someone (after all, she was an unofficial collaborator of the organs of state security) to write Stalin a letter in which she declared that doctors were applying supposedly improper methods of medical treatment.

Such a letter was sufficient for Stalin to reach an immediate conclusion that there are doctor plotters in the Soviet Union. He issued orders to arrest a group of eminent Soviet medical specialists. He personally issued advice on the conduct of the investigation and the method of interrogation of the arrested persons. He said that the academician Vinogradov should be put in chains, another one should be beaten. Present at this Congress as a delegate is the former Minister of State Security Comrade Ignatiev. Stalin told him curtly, "If you do not obtain confessions from the doctors we will shorten you by a head." [Tumult in the hall.] . . .

In organizing the various dirty and shameful cases, a very base role was played by the rabid enemy of our party, an agent of a foreign intelligence service—Beriya, who had stolen into Stalin's confidence. In what way could this provocateur gain such a position in the party and in the State, so as to become the First Deputy Chairman of the Council of Ministers of the Soviet Union and a member of the Central Committee Political Bureau? It has now been established that this villain had climbed up the government ladder over an untold number of corpses.

Were there any signs that Beriya was an enemy of the party? Yes; there were. Already in 1937, at a Central Committee plenum, former People's Commissar of Health Protection Kaminsky said that Beriya worked for the Mussavat intelligence service. But the Central Committee plenum had barely concluded when Kaminsky was arrested and then shot. Had Stalin examined Kaminsky's statement? No; because Stalin believed in Beriya, and that was enough for him. And when Stalin believed in anyone or anything, then no one could say anything which was contrary to his opinion; anyone who would dare to express opposition would have met the same fate as Kaminsky. . . .

Comrades, the cult of the individual acquired such monstrous size chiefly because Stalin himself, using all conceivable methods, supported the glorification of his own person. This is supported by numerous facts. One of the most characteristic examples of Stalin's self-glorification and of his lack of even elementary modesty is the edition of his Short Biography, which was published in 1948.

This book is an expression of the most dissolute flattery, an example of making a man into a godhead, of transforming him into an infallible sage, "the greatest leader," "sublime strategist of all times and nations." Finally no other words could be found with which to lift Stalin up to the heavens.

We need not give here examples of the loathsome adulation filling this book. All we need to add is that they all were approved and edited by Stalin personally and some of them were added in his own handwriting to the draft text of the book. . . .

Comrades, if we sharply criticize today the cult of the individual which was so widespread during Stalin's life and if we speak about the many negative phenomena generated by this cult which is so alien to the spirit of Marxism-Leninism, various persons may ask: How could it be? Stalin headed the party and the country for 30 years and many victories were gained during his lifetime. Can we deny this? In my opinion, the question can be asked in this manner only by those who are blinded and hopelessly hypnotized by the cult of the individual, only by those who do not understand the essence of the revolution and of the Soviet State, only by those who do not understand, in a Leninist manner, the role of the party and of the nation in the development of the Soviet society. . . .

Our historical victories were attained thanks to the organizational work of the party, to the many provincial organizations, and to the self-sacrificing work of our great nation. These victories are the result of the great drive and activity of the nation and of the party as a whole; they are not at all the fruit of the leadership of Stalin, as the situation was pictured during the period of the cult of the individual. . . .

Let us consider the first Central Committee plenum after the 19th party congress when Stalin, in his talk at the plenum, characterized Vyacheslav Mikhailovich Molotov and Anastas Ivanovich Mikoyan and suggested that these old workers of our party were guilty of some baseless charges. It is not excluded that had Stalin remained at the helm for another several months, Comrades Molotov and Mikoyan would probably have not delivered any speeches at this congress.

Stalin evidently had plans to finish off the old members of the political bureau. He often stated that political bureau members should be replaced by new ones. . . .

We can assume that this was also a design for the future annihilation of the old political bureau members and in this way a cover for all shameful acts of Stalin, acts which we are now considering.

Comrades, in order not to repeat errors of the past, the central committee has declared itself resolutely against the cult of the individual. We consider that Stalin was excessively extolled. However, in the past Stalin doubtless performed great services to the party, to the working class, and to the international workers' movement. . . .

We should in all seriousness consider the question of the cult of the individual. We cannot let this matter get out of the party, especially not to the press. It is for this reason that we are considering it here at a closed congress session. We should know the limits; we should not give ammunition to the enemy; we should not wash our dirty linen before their eyes. I think that the delegates to the congress will understand and assess properly all these proposals. [Tumultuous applause.]

Comrades, we must abolish the cult of the individual decisively, once and for all; we must draw the proper conclusions concerning both ideological-theoretical and practical work.

It is necessary for this purpose:

First, in a Bolshevik manner to condemn and to eradicate the cult of the individual as alien to Marxism-Leninism and not consonant with the principles of party leadership and the norms of party life, and to fight inexorably all attempts at bringing back this practice in one form or another.

To return to and actually practice in all our ideological work, the most important theses of Marxist-Leninist science about the people as the creator of history and as the creator of all material and spiritual good of humanity, about the decisive role of the Marxist party in the revolutionary fight for the transformation of society, about the victory of communism.

In this connection we will be forced to do much work in order to examine critically from the Marxist-Leninist viewpoint and to correct the widely spread erroneous views connected with the cult of the individual in the sphere of history, philosophy, economy, and of other sciences, as well as in the literature and the fine arts. It is especially necessary that in the immediate future we compile a serious textbook of the history of our party which will be edited in accordance with scientific Marxist objectivism, a textbook of the history of Soviet society, a book pertaining to the events of the civil war and the great patriotic war.

Secondly, to continue systematically and consistently the work done by the party's central committee during the last years, a work characterized by minute observation in all party organizations, from the bottom to the top, of the Leninist principles of party leadership, characterized, above all, by the main principle of collective leadership, characterized by the observation of the norms of party life described in the statutes of our party, and, finally, characterized by the wide practice of criticism and self-criticism.

Thirdly, to restore completely the Leninist principles of Soviet Socialist democracy, expressed in the constitution of the Soviet Union, to fight willful-ness of individuals abusing their power. The evil caused by acts violating revolutionary Socialist legality which have accumulated during a long time as a result of the negative influence of the cult of the individual has to be completely corrected.

Comrades, the 20th Congress of the Communist Party of the Soviet Union has manifested with a new strength the unshakable unity of our party, its cohesiveness around the central committee, its resolute will to accomplish the great task of building communism. [Tumultuous applause.] And the fact that we present in all their ramifications the basic problems of overcoming the cult of the individual which is alien to Marxism-Leninism, as well as the problem of liquidating its burdensome consequences, is an evidence of the great moral and political strength of our party. [Prolonged applause.]

We are absolutely certain that our party, armed with the historical resolutions of the 20th Congress, will lead the Soviet people along the Leninist path to new successes, to new victories. [Tumultuous, prolonged applause.]

Long live the victorious banner of our party—Leninism. [Tumultuous, prolonged applause ending in ovation. All rise.]

··{*12*}·· Communist Eastern Europe

COMINFORM COMMUNIQUÉ[1]
Resolution of the Information Bureau Concerning the Communist Party of Yugoslavia, June 28, 1948

The Information Bureau, composed of the representatives of the Bulgarian Workers' Party (Communists), Rumanian Workers' Party, Hungarian Workers' Party, Polish Workers' Party, The Communist Party of the Soviet Union (Bolsheviks), Communist Party of France, Communist Party of Czechoslovakia and the Communist Party of Italy, upon discussing the situation in the Communist Party of Yugoslavia and announcing that the representatives of the Communist Party of Yugoslavia had refused to attend the meeting of the Information Bureau, unanimously reached the following conclusions:

1. The Information Bureau notes that recently the leadership of the Communist Party of Yugoslavia has pursued an incorrect line on the main questions of home and foreign policy, a line which represents a departure from Marxism-Leninism. In this connection the Information Bureau approves the action of the Central Committee of the CPSU(B), which took the initiative in exposing this incorrect policy of the Central Committee of the Communist Party of Yugoslavia, particularly the incorrect policy of Comrades Tito, Kardelj, Djilas and Rankovic.

2. The Information Bureau declares that the leadership of the Yugoslav Communist Party is pursuing an unfriendly policy toward the Soviet Union and the CPSU (B). An undignified policy of defaming Soviet military experts and discrediting the Soviet Union, has been carried out in Yugoslavia. A special régime was instituted for Soviet civilian experts in Yugoslavia, whereby they were under surveillance of Yugoslav state security organs and were continually followed. . . .

The Information Bureau denounces this anti-Soviet attitude of the leaders of the Communist Party of Yugoslavia, as being incompatible with Marxism-Leninism and only appropriate to nationalists.

---

[1] Reprinted by permission of the Royal Institute of International Affairs from *The Soviet-Yugoslav Dispute* (London and New York, 1948), pp. 61–70.

3. In home policy, the leaders of the Communist Party of Yugoslavia are departing from the positions of the working class and are breaking with the Marxist theory of classes and class struggle. They deny that there is a growth of capitalist elements in their country, and consequently, a sharpening of the class struggle in the countryside. This denial is the direct result of the opportunist tenet that the class struggle does not become sharper during the period of transition from capitalism to socialism, as Marxism-Leninism teaches, but dies down, as was affirmed by opportunists of the Bukharin type, who propagated the theory of the peaceful growing over of capitalism into socialism.

The Yugoslav leaders are pursuing an incorrect policy in the countryside by ignoring the class differentiation in the countryside and by regarding the individual peasantry as a single entity, contrary to the Marxist-Leninist doctrine of classes and class struggle, contrary to the well-known Lenin thesis that small individual farming gives birth to capitalism and the bourgeoisie continually, daily, hourly, spontaneously and on a mass scale. . . .

Concerning the leading role of the working class, the leaders of the Yugoslav Communist Party, by affirming that the peasantry is the 'most stable foundation of the Yugoslav state' are departing from the Marxist-Leninist path and are taking the path of a populist, Kulak party. Lenin taught that the proletariat as the 'only class in contemporary society which is revolutionary to the end . . . must be the leader in the struggle of the entire people for a thorough democratic transformation, in the struggle of all working people and the exploited against the oppressors and exploiters.'

The Yugoslav leaders are violating this thesis of Marxism-Leninism. . . .

4. The Information Bureau considers that the leadership of the Communist Party of Yugoslavia is revising the Marxist-Leninist teachings about the Party. . . .

The Information Bureau believes that this policy of the Central Committee of the Communist Party of Yugoslavia threatens the very existence of the Communist Party, and ultimately carries with it the danger of the degeneration of the People's Republic of Yugoslavia.

5. The Information Bureau considers that the bureaucratic régime created inside the Party by its leaders is disastrous for the life and development of the Yugoslav Communist Party. There is no inner Party democracy, no elections, and no criticism and self-criticism in the Party. . . .

It is a completely intolerable state of affairs when the most elementary rights of members in the Yugoslav Communist Party are suppressed, when the slightest criticism of incorrect measures in the Party is brutally repressed. . . .

The Information Bureau considers that such a disgraceful, purely Turkish, terrorist régime cannot be tolerated in the Communist Party. The interests of the very existence and development of the Yugoslav Communist Party demand that an end be put to this régime.

6. The Information Bureau considers that the criticism made by the

Central Committee of the Communist Party of the Soviet Union (B) and Central Committees of the other Communist Parties of the mistakes of the Central Committee of the Communist Party of Yugoslavia, and who in this way rendered fraternal assistance to the Yugoslav Communist Party, provides the Communist Party of Yugoslavia with all the conditions necessary to speedily correct the mistakes committed.

However, instead of honestly accepting this criticism and taking the Bolshevik path of correcting these mistakes, the leaders of the Communist Party of Yugoslavia, suffering from boundless ambition, arrogance and conceit, met this criticism with belligerence and hostility. . . .

7. Taking into account the situation in the Communist Party of Yugoslavia, and seeking to show the leaders of the Party the way out of this situation, the Central Committee of the Communist Party of the Soviet Union (B) and the Central Committees of other fraternal parties, suggested that the matter of the Yugoslav Communist Party should be discussed at a meeting of the Information Bureau, on the same, normal party footing as that on which the activities of other Communist Parties were discussed at the first meeting of the Information Bureau.

However, the Yugoslav leaders rejected the repeated suggestions of the fraternal Communist Parties to discuss the situation in the Yugoslav Party at a meeting of the Information Bureau. . . .

8. In view of this, the Information Bureau expresses complete agreement with the estimation of the situation in the Yugoslav Communist Party, with the criticism of the mistakes of the Central Committee of the Party, and with the political analysis of these mistakes contained in letters from the Central Committee of the Communist Party of the Soviet Union (B) to the Central Committee of the Communist Party of Yugoslavia between March and May 1948.

The Information Bureau unanimously concludes that by their anti-Party and anti-Soviet views, incompatible with Marxism-Leninism, by their whole attitude and their refusal to attend the meeting of the Information Bureau, the leaders of the Communist Party of Yugoslavia have placed themselves in opposition to the Communist Parties affiliated to the Information Bureau, have taken the path of seceding from the united socialist front against imperialism, have taken the path of betraying the cause of international solidarity of the working people, and have taken up a position of nationalism.

The Information Bureau condemns this anti-Party policy and attitude of the Central Committee of the Communist Party of Yugoslavia.

The Information Bureau considers that, in view of all this, the Central Committee of the Communist Party of Yugoslavia has placed itself and the Yugoslav Party outside the family of the fraternal Communist Parties, outside the united Communist front and consequently outside the ranks of the Information Bureau.

[ ]

The Information Bureau does not doubt that inside the Communist Party of Yugoslavia there are sufficient healthy elements, loyal to Marxism-Leninism, to the international traditions of the Yugoslav Communist Party and to the United Socialist front.

Their task is to compel their present leaders to recognize their mistakes openly and honestly and to rectify them; to break with nationalism, return to internationalism; and in every way to consolidate the united socialist front against imperialism.

Should the present leaders of the Yugoslav Communist Party prove incapable of doing this, their job is to replace them and to advance a new internationalist leadership of the Party.

The Information Bureau does not doubt that the Communist Party of Yugoslavia will be able to fulfill this honourable task.

TREATY OF FRIENDSHIP, CO-OPERATION AND MUTUAL ASSISTANCE[1]
Between the People's Republic of Albania, the People's Republic of Bulgaria, the Hungarian People's Republic, the German Democratic Republic, the Polish People's Republic, the Rumanian People's Republic, the Union of Soviet Socialist Republics, and the Czechoslovak Republic, May 1, 1955

The contracting parties,

Reaffirming their desire for the organisation of a system of collective security in Europe, with the participation of all the European states, irrespective of their social and state systems, which would make it possible to combine their efforts in the interests of securing peace in Europe,

Taking into consideration at the same time the situation obtaining in Europe as the result of ratification of the Paris agreements, which provide for the formation of a new military grouping in the shape of the "Western European Union" together with a remilitarised Western Germany, and for the integration of Western Germany in the North Atlantic bloc, which increases the threat of another war and creates a menace to the national security of the peaceloving states,

Convinced that, under these circumstances, the peaceloving states of Europe should take the necessary measures for safeguarding their security, and in the interests of maintaining peace in Europe,

Guided by the purposes and principles of the United Nations Charter,

In the interests of further strengthening and promoting friendship, co-operation and mutual assistance, in accordance with the principles of respect for

---

[1] Reprinted with permission from the *Soviet News*, No. 3165 (May 16, 1955), pp. 1–2.

the independence and sovereignty of states, and also with the principle of noninterference in their internal affairs,

Have resolved to conclude this Treaty of Friendship, Co-operation and Mutual Assistance, . . .

Article 1. The contracting parties undertake, in accordance with the Charter of the United Nations Organisation, to refrain in their international relations from the threat or use of force, and to settle their international disputes by peaceful means so as not to endanger international peace and security.

Article 2. The contracting parties declare their readiness to take part, in the spirit of sincere co-operation, in all international undertakings intended to safeguard international peace and security and they shall use all their energies for the realisation of these aims.

Moreover, the contracting parties shall work for the adoption, in agreement with other states desiring to co-operate in this matter, of effective measures towards a general reduction of armaments and prohibition of atomic, hydrogen and other weapons of mass destruction.

Article 3. The contracting parties shall take council among themselves on all important international questions relating to their common interests, guided by the interests of strengthening international peace and security.

They shall take council among themselves immediately, whenever, in the opinion of any of them, there has arisen the threat of an armed attack on one or several states that are signatories of the treaty, in the interests of organising their joint defence and of upholding peace and security.

Article 4. In the event of an armed attack in Europe on one or several states that are signatories of the treaty by any state or group of states, each state that is a party to this treaty shall, in the exercise of the right to individual or collective self-defence in accordance with Article 51 of the Charter of the United Nations Organisation, render the state or states so attacked immediate assistance, individually and in agreement with other states that are parties to this treaty, by all the means it may consider necessary, including the use of armed force. The states that are parties to this treaty shall immediately take council among themselves concerning the necessary joint measures to be adopted for the purpose of restoring and upholding international peace and security.

In accordance with the principles of the Charter of the United Nations Organisation, the Security Council shall be advised of the measures taken on the basis of the present article. These measures shall be stopped as soon as the Security Council has taken the necessary measures for restoring and upholding international peace and security.

Article 5. The contracting parties have agreed on the establishment of a joint command for their armed forces, which shall be placed, by agreement among these parties, under this command, which shall function on the basis of jointly defined principles. They shall also take other concerted measures necessary for strengthening their defence capacity, in order to safeguard the peaceful labour of their peoples, to guarantee the inviolability of their frontiers and territories and to provide safeguards against possible aggression.

Article 6. For the purpose of holding the consultations provided for in the present treaty among the states that are parties to the treaty, and for the purpose of considering problems arising in connection with the implementation of this treaty, a political consultative committee shall be formed in which each state that is a party to this treaty shall be represented by a member of the government, or any other specially appointed representative.

The committee may form the auxiliary organs for which the need may arise.

Article 7. The contracting parties undertake not to participate in any coalitions and alliances, and not to conclude any agreements the purposes of which would be at variance with those of the present treaty.

The contracting parties declare that their obligations under existing international treaties are not at variance with the provisions of this treaty.

Article 8. The contracting parties declare that they will act in the spirit of friendship and co-operation with the object of furthering the development of, and strengthening the economic and cultural relations between them, adhering to the principles of mutual respect for their independence and sovereignty, and of non-interference in their internal affairs.

Article 9. The present treaty is open to be acceded to by other states—irrespective of their social and state systems—which may express their readiness to assist, through participation in the present treaty, in combining the efforts of the peaceloving states for the purpose of safeguarding the peace and security of nations. This act of acceding to the treaty shall become effective, with the consent of the states that are parties to this treaty, after the instrument of accedence has been deposited with the government of the Polish People's Republic.

Article 10. The present treaty is subject to ratification, and the instruments of ratification shall be deposited with the government of the Polish People's Republic.

The treaty shall take effect on the date on which the last ratification instrument is deposited. The government of the Polish People's Republic shall advise the other states that are parties to the treaty of each ratification instrument deposited with it.

Article 11. The present treaty shall remain in force for 20 years. For the contracting parties which will not have submitted to the government of the Polish People's Republic a statement denouncing the treaty a year before the expiration of its term, it shall remain in force throughout the following ten years.

In the event of the organisation of a system of collective security in Europe and the conclusion of a general European treaty of collective security to that end, which the contracting parties shall unceasingly seek to bring about, the present treaty shall cease to be effective on the date the general European treaty comes into force.

Done in Warsaw, on May 1, 1955, in one copy each in the Russian, Polish, Czech, and German languages, all the texts being equally authentic. Certified copies of the present treaty shall be transmitted by the government of the Polish People's Republic to all the parties to this treaty.

RESOLUTION ADOPTED AT PLENARY MEETING OF THE BUILDING INDUSTRY TECHNOLOGY UNIVERSITY[1]
Sixteen Political, Economic, and Ideological Points, October 22, 1956

Students of Budapest!

The following resolution was born on 22 October 1956, at the dawn of a new period in Hungarian history, in the Hall of the Building Industry Technological University as a result of the spontaneous movement of several thousand of the Hungarian youth who love their Fatherland:

(1) We demand the immediate withdrawal of all Soviet troops in accordance with the provisions of the Peace Treaty.

(2) We demand the election of new leaders in the Hungarian Workers' Party on the low, medium and high levels by secret ballot from the ranks upwards. These leaders should convene the Party Congress within the shortest possible time and should elect a new central body of leaders.

(3) The Government should be reconstituted under the leadership of Comrade Imre Nagy; all criminal leaders of the Stalinist-Rákosi era should be relieved of their posts at once.

(4) We demand a public trial in the criminal case of Mihály Farkas and his accomplices. Mátyás Rákosi, who is primarily responsible for all the crimes of the recent past and for the ruin of this country, should be brought home and brought before a People's Court of Judgment.

(5) We demand general elections in this country, with universal suffrage, secret ballot and the participation of several Parties for the purpose of electing a new National Assembly. We demand that the workers should have the right to strike.

(6) We demand a re-examination and re-adjustment of Hungarian-Soviet and Hungarian-Yugoslav political, economic and intellectual relations on the basis of complete political and economic equality and of non-intervention in each other's internal affairs.

(7) We demand the re-organization of the entire economic life of Hungary, with the assistance of specialists. Our whole economic system based on planned economy should be re-examined with an eye to Hungarian conditions and to the vital interests of the Hungarian people.

(8) Our foreign trade agreements and the real figures in respect of

---

[1] Reprinted from *Report of the Special Committee on the Problem of Hungary*, U.N. General Assembly, Official Records: Eleventh Session, Supplement No. 18 (A/3592) p. 69.

reparations that can never be paid should be made public. We demand frank and sincere information concerning the country's uranium deposits, their exploitation and the Russian concession. We demand that Hungary should have the right to sell the uranium ore freely at world market prices in exchange for hard currency.

(9) We demand the complete revision of norms in industry and an urgent and radical adjustment of wages to meet the demands of workers and intellectuals. We demand that minimum living wages for workers should be fixed.

(10) We demand that the delivery system should be placed on a new basis and that produce should be used rationally. We demand equal treatment of peasants farming individually.

(11) We demand the re-examination of all political and economic trials by independent courts and the release and rehabilitation of innocent persons. We demand the immediate repatriation of prisoners-of-war and of civilians deported to the Soviet Union, including prisoners who have been condemned beyond the frontiers of Hungary.

(12) We demand complete freedom of opinion and expression, freedom of the Press and a free Radio, as well as a new daily newspaper of large circulation for the MEFESZ* organization. We demand that the existing 'screening material' should be made public and destroyed.

(13) We demand that the Stalin statue—the symbol of Stalinist tyranny and political oppression—should be removed as quickly as possible and that a memorial worthy of the freedom fighters and martyrs of 1848–49 should be erected on its site.

(14) In place of the existing coat of arms, which is foreign to the Hungarian people, we wish the re-introduction of the old Hungarian Kossuth arms. We demand for the Hungarian Army new uniforms worthy of our national traditions. We demand that 15 March should be a national holiday and a non-working day and that 6 October should be a day of national mourning and a school holiday.

(15) The youth of the Technological University of Budapest unanimously express their complete solidarity with the Polish and Warsaw workers and youth in connexion with the Polish national independence movement.

(16) The students of the Building Industry Technological University will organize local units of MEFESZ as quickly as possible, and have resolved to convene a Youth Parliament in Budapest for the 27th of this month (Saturday) at which the entire youth of this country will be represented by their delegates. The students of the Technological University and of the various other Universities will gather in the Gorkij Fasor before the Writers' Union Headquarters tomorrow, the 23rd of this month, at 2.30 P.M., whence they will proceed to the Pálffy Tér (Bem Ter) to the Bem statue, on which

* MEFESZ—League of Hungarian University and College Student Associations.

they will lay wreaths in sign of their sympathy with the Polish freedom movement. The workers of the factories are invited to join in this procession.

CLEAR CURRENT AND SCUM[1]
Editorial of the Polish Newspaper Trybuna Ludu on the Events of 1956 in Poland, October 25, 1956

In these exciting and uncommon times the Polish working class has clearly made its voice heard. This class leads the nation not by someone's appointment or decree, but by virtue of its position in society. In these exciting and unusual days, it is evident that the leading role of the Party has been tangibly confirmed. The Party has been united as never before with the class which gave it birth, with the peasant masses, with the student youth, with the progressive intelligentsia, and with the Polish People's Army. The Party is united with the nation.

We perceive the strength of this bond, hearing with deep emotion the clear and wise voice of our working class, our people, and our soldiers.

This voice supports the leadership of the Party elected in accordance with the will of the people. It supports the correction of abuses, further democratization, and the strengthening of the alliance and friendship with the Soviet Union and all people of the great socialist family on the basis of the Leninist foundation of equality and mutual respect for the sovereignty and independence of each country.

Love for the fatherland and the cause of socialism have burst forth in Poland with a bright flame. The political maturity and discipline of the working class arouse admiration.

But, as in the time of any great mass movement, evidences of irresponsibility and thoughtlessness, diverging from the current of reform, are revealed in a few places.

It would be naive to think that the forces which have been attempting to poison this great, renovating, and pure current with the poison of anti-Soviet demagogy have capitulated.

Utilizing the understandable agitation in society, reactionary scum have tried to come to the surface of this life-giving wave of exalted reform, in order to sow anti-Soviet sentiments. The majority of these who let themselves temporarily be infected by nationalistic demagogy, as was the case in Wroclaw, certainly are unaware of the motives which guide the Polish and foreign reactionaries, motives which are directed against the national interests of Poland and against the cause of socialism in Poland. But the triumph of this hostile propaganda is short-lived.   [ ]

Our Party and our working classes desire a strengthening of the alliance

---

[1] Editor's translation. The translation was made from a reprint of this editorial which appeared in *Pravda* on October 25, 1956.

and friendship with the land of the Soviets, and it is for this reason that they want to cleanse that friendship of everything which weakened its strength. Therefore, we desire a strengthening of this alliance through the observance of the principles of equality and mutual recognition of independence.   [ ]

Even within a family, misunderstandings and groundless suspicions sometimes arise. Is not the same thing true in the case of states? But between socialist states misunderstandings can, should, and will be eliminated.

In these critical days, we are aware that a considerable number of prejudices concerning the Soviet Union are concealed in Poland behind the official facade which has existed until this moment. Everything that was half-true or even false nourished these prejudices. This was a vestige of a bygone era against which the Twentieth Congress of the C.P.S.U. directed its struggle to eliminate lack of respect for the equality, sovereignty, and independence of socialist Poland.

We desire friendship between Poland and the Soviet Union, a living, complete, and thus dependable friendship based on the Leninist norms of equality and built on a clear understanding of the Polish nation.

At this moment, all necessary conditions exist to finally free Polish-Soviet relations and Polish-Soviet friendship from everything which, until now (to the delight of the enemies of socialism and peace), has harmed these relations and this friendship.

To irresponsibility, and especially to the reactionary work of their enemies, the Polish working class, the Polish toilers, and the Polish students will counterpose their militant revolutionary vigilance and their political sagacity.

The Polish working class, defending the program which it has so vigorously formulated during the past few days, will suppress all statements incompatible with this program.

If anyone thinks that in Poland it is possible to arouse anti-Soviet sentiments, he is sadly mistaken. We shall not permit anyone to harm the vital interests of the Polish state and the cause of building socialism in Poland.

These words of Comrade Wladyslaw [Gomulka] show all of us, young and old, Party members and non-Party members, what needs to be done in these times of great reform.

FRIENDSHIP AND COOPERATION BETWEEN THE SOVIET UNION AND OTHER SOCIALIST STATES[1]
Soviet Statement, October 30, 1956

The principles of peaceful coexistence, friendship, and cooperation among all states have always been and still form the unshakable foundation of

---

[1] Reprinted from *The Department of State Bulletin*, XXXV, No. 907 (November 12, 1956), pp. 745–747.

the foreign relations of the U.S.S.R. This policy finds its most profound and consistent expression in the relationship with socialist countries. United by the common ideal of building a socialist society and the principles of proletarian internationalism, the countries of the great commonwealth of socialist nations can build their relations only on the principle of full equality, respect of territorial integrity, state independence and sovereignty, and noninterference in one another's domestic affairs.

This does not exclude, but on the contrary presupposes, close fraternal cooperation and mutual aid between the countries of the socialist commonwealth in the economic, political, and cultural spheres. It is on this basis that after World War II and after the rout of fascism the regimes of the people's democracies came into being in a number of countries of Europe and Asia, which were strengthened and display great vitality.

In the process of the establishment of the new regime and the deep revolutionary transformation in social relations there were not a few difficulties, unsolved problems, and out-and-out mistakes, including some in the relations between the socialist states—violations and mistakes which infringed the principles of equality in relations between socialist states.

The 20th Congress of the Communist Party of the Soviet Union resolutely condemned these mistakes and violations and demanded that the Soviet Union apply Lenin's principles of the equality of nations in its relations with other socialist states. This statement took complete cognizance of the historical past and the peculiarities of each country which has taken the road of building a new life. . . .

As recent events have shown, the need has arisen for an appropriate declaration to be made on the position of the Soviet Union in the mutual relations between the U.S.S.R. and other socialist countries, primarily in the economic and military spheres. The Soviet Government is ready to discuss with the governments of other socialist states measures insuring the further development and strengthening of economic ties between socialist countries, in order to remove any possibilities of violating the principle of national sovereignty, mutual advantage, and equality in economic relations.

This principle should extend also to advisers. It is common knowledge that during the first period of the formation of the new social order, at the request of the governments of the people's democracies, the Soviet Union sent to these countries a certain number of specialists—engineers, agronomists, scientific workers, and military advisers. During the later period the Soviet Government on many occasions asked the socialist states about the recall of its advisers.

In view of the fact that by now the people's democracies have formed their own qualified national cadres in all spheres of economic and military construction, the Soviet Government considers it as urgent to examine, together with other socialist states, the question whether a further stay of U.S.S.R. advisers in these countries is expedient.

In the military sphere, the Warsaw Treaty is an important foundation for mutual relations between the Soviet Union and the people's democracies. Its participants took upon themselves appropriate political and military obligations, including obligations to adopt agreed measures essential for strengthening their defense potential, so as to protect the peaceful labors of their people, guarantee the inviolability of their frontiers and territories, and insure defense against possible aggression.

It is known that, in accordance with the Warsaw Treaty and with government agreements, Soviet units are stationed in the Hungarian and the Rumanian Republics. In the Polish Republic, Soviet military units are stationed on the basis of the Potsdam Four-Power Agreement and the Warsaw Treaty. In other people's democratic countries there are no Soviet military units.

With a view to insuring the mutual security of the socialist countries, the Soviet Government is ready to examine with other socialist countries that are parties to the Warsaw Treaty the question of Soviet troops stationed on the territory of these countries. In this the Soviet Government proceeds from the general principle that the stationing of troops of one state that is a party to the Warsaw Treaty on the territory of another state that is a party to the Warsaw Treaty should take place on the basis of an agreement among all its participants and not only with the agreement of the state on whose territory these troops are stationed or are planned to be stationed at its request. . . .

The Soviet Government and all the Soviet people deeply regret that the development of events in Hungary has led to bloodshed. On the request of the Hungarian People's Government the Soviet Government consented to the entry into Budapest of the Soviet Army units to assist the Hungarian People's Army and the Hungarian authorities to establish order in the town. Believing that the further presence of Soviet Army units in Hungary can serve as a cause for even greater deterioration of the situation, the Soviet Government has given instructions to its military command to withdraw the Soviet Army units from Budapest as soon as this is recognized as necessary by the Hungarian Government.

At the same time, the Soviet Government is ready to enter into relevant negotiations with the Government of the Hungarian People's Republic and other participants of the Warsaw Treaty on the question of the presence of Soviet troops on the territory of Hungary. . . .

The Soviet Government expresses confidence that the peoples of the socialist countries will not permit foreign and internal reactionary forces to undermine the basis of the people's democratic regimes, won and consolidated by the heroic struggle and toil of the workers, peasants, and intelligentsia of each country.

They will make all efforts to remove all obstacles that lie in the path of further strengthening the democratic basis of the independence and sovereignty of their countries, to develop further the socialist basis of each country, its economy and culture, for the sake of the constant growth of the material welfare and the cultural level of all the workers. They will consolidate the fraternal unity and mutual assistance of the socialist countries for the strengthening of the great cause of peace and socialism.

·{*13*}·· *Cuba—Communist Bastion in the Western Hemisphere*

KHRUSHCHEV'S SPEECH TO THE R.F.S.R. TEACHERS' CONGRESS[1]
Moscow, July 9, 1960

[ ]

A few days ago the Governor of New York State, Rockefeller, openly called for struggle against the government of Cuba and the Cuban people. He advised that a course directed against Cuba should be taken and that the regime chosen by the people should be stifled through economic blockade.

Rockefeller's pronouncements are an obvious example of the aggressive actions of American politicians who are not accustomed to taking the will of the people into account.

But the time when the United States *diktat* prevailed is over. The Soviet Union is raising its voice on behalf of, and is offering help to, the people of Cuba who are fighting for their independence. The times are not now the same as they were when only one working class—the working people of former tsarist Russia—was raising the banner of struggle, when not only economic blockade but also armed intervention was organised against us.

Times are quite different now. Over 1,000 million people live in states where the working class and the working people have triumphed and where the glorious banner of Marxism-Leninism is flying. The world socialist camp is now stronger than ever before. The peoples of the socialist countries will help their Cuban brothers to uphold their independence with the object of frustrating the economic blockade the United States of America has just declared against Cuba.

And not only we, the working people of the socialist camp, but the peoples of all countries must be vigilant against the intrigues of the American imperialists.

---

[1] Reprinted with permission from the *Soviet News*, No. 4304 (July 11, 1960), pp. 28–29.

It is clear to everybody that economic blockade by the American monopolists can be a prelude to intervention against Cuba. Therefore we must speak up in defence of Cuba and give warning that the imperialists can no longer rob and divide the world as they please, each choosing any piece for himself, as they used to do in the past. Today the peoples of the colonial and dependent countries rebel and fight successfully to rid themselves of the shameful colonial yoke and of enslavement by the United States imperialists. For our part, we shall do everything to support Cuba and her courageous people in their struggle for the freedom and national independence which they have won under the leadership of their national leader Fidel Castro.

The socialist states and all peoples who stand for peace will support the Cuban people in their just struggle and no one will succeed in enslaving the Cubans.

It should be borne in mind that the United States is now not at such an inaccessible distance from the Soviet Union as formerly. Figuratively speaking, if need be, Soviet artillerymen can support the Cuban people with their rocket fire, should the aggressive forces in the Pentagon dare to start intervention against Cuba. And the Pentagon would be well advised not to forget that, as has been shown by the latest tests, we have rockets which land accurately in a predetermined square target 13,000 kilometres [about 8,000 miles] away. This, if you wish, is a warning to those who might like to solve international problems by force and not by reason.

I have a note here that has been handed to me which says that I have apparently made a slip. The rocket covered not 30,000 kilometres, but 13,000. Well, that is enough! Of course, 30,000 kilometres was a slip and I want to correct the figure, for my speech is being broadcast. Let the Pentagon record that it was a slip; so far we have shot over a distance of 13,000 kilometres, and there is no need to shoot over 30,000. Am I correct, Comrade Malinovsky? Rodion Yakolevich Malinovsky has confirmed this.   [ ]

THE LESSON OF CUBA[1]
Speech Delivered by President Kennedy before the American Society of Newspaper Editors at Washington, D.C., April 20, 1961

The President of a great democracy such as ours, and the editors of great newspapers such as yours, owe a common obligation to the people: an obligation to present the facts, to present them with candor, and to present them in perspective. It is with that obligation in mind that I have decided in the last 24 hours to discuss briefly at this time the recent events in Cuba.

On that unhappy island, as in so many other areas of the contest for

[1] Reprinted from The Department of State Bulletin, XLIV, No. 1141 (May 8, 1961), pp. 659–661.

freedom, the news has grown worse instead of better. I have emphasized before that this was a struggle of Cuban patriots against a Cuban dictator. While we could not be expected to hide our sympathies, we made it repeatedly clear that the armed forces of this country would not intervene in any way. . . .

It is not the first time that Communist tanks have rolled over gallant men and women fighting to redeem the independence of their homeland. Nor is it by any means the final episode in the eternal struggle of liberty against tyranny, anywhere on the face of the globe, including Cuba itself.

Mr. Castro has said that these were mercenaries. According to press reports, the final message to be relayed from the refugee forces on the beach came from the rebel commander when asked if he wished to be evacuated. His answer was: "I will never leave this country." That is not the reply of a mercenary. . . .

The Cuban people have not yet spoken their final piece, and I have no doubt that they and their Revolutionary Council, led by Dr. Miró Cardona— and members of the families of the Revolutionary Council, I am informed by the Doctor yesterday, are involved themselves in the islands—will continue to speak up for a free and independent Cuba.

Meanwhile we will not accept Mr. Castro's attempts to blame this Nation for the hatred with which his onetime supporters now regard his repression. But there are from this sobering episode useful lessons for all to learn. Some may be still obscure and await further information. Some are clear today.

First, it is clear that the forces of communism are not to be underestimated; in Cuba or anywhere else in the world. The advantages of a police state—its use of mass terror and arrests to prevent the spread of free dissent— cannot be overlooked by those who expect the fall of every fanatic tyrant. . . .

Secondly, it is clear that this Nation, in concert with all the free nations of this hemisphere, must take an even closer and more realistic look at the menace of external Communist intervention and domination in Cuba. The American people are not complacent about Iron Curtain tanks and planes less than 90 miles from our shores. . . .

The evidence is clear—and the hour is late. We and our Latin friends will have to face the fact that we cannot postpone any longer the real issue of the survival of freedom in this hemisphere itself. . . .

Third, and finally, it is clearer than ever that we face a relentless struggle in every corner of the globe that goes far beyond the clash of armies or even nuclear armaments. The armies are there, and in large number. The nuclear armaments are there. But they serve primarily as the shield behind which subversion, infiltration, and a host of other tactics steadily advance, picking off vulnerable areas one by one in situations which do not permit our own armed intervention.

Power is the hallmark of this offensive—power and discipline and deceit. The legitimate discontent of yearning peoples is exploited. The legitimate trappings of self-determination are employed. But once in power, all talk of discontent is repressed—all self-determination disappears—and the promise of a revolution of hope is betrayed, as in Cuba, into a reign of terror. . . .

The message of Cuba, of Laos, of the rising din of Communist voices in Asia and Latin America—these messages are all the same. The complacent, the self-indulgent, the soft societies are about to be swept away with the debris of history. Only the strong, only the industrious, only the determined, only the courageous, only the visionary who determine the real nature of our struggle can possibly survive.   [ ]

CUBAN MISSILE CRISIS DEBATE[1]
Between Adlai Stevenson and V. A. Zorin in the United Nations Security Council, October 23, 1962

[ ]
Mr. STEVENSON (United States of America): I have asked for an emergency meeting of the Security Council to bring to your attention a grave threat to the Western Hemisphere and to the peace of the world.

Last night, the President of the United States reported the recent alarming military developments in Cuba. . . .

In view of this transformation of Cuba into a base for offensive weapons of sudden mass destruction, the President announced the initiation of a strict quarantine on all offensive military weapons under shipment to Cuba. He did so because, in the view of my Government, the recent developments in Cuba —the importation of the cold war into the heart of the Americas—constitute a threat to the peace of this hemisphere, and, indeed, to the peace of the world.

[ ]
The time has come for this Council to decide whether to make a serious attempt to bring peace to the world—or to let the United Nations stand idly by while the vast plan of piecemeal aggression unfolds, conducted in the hope that no single issue will seem consequential enough to mobilize the resistance of the free peoples. For my own Government, this question is not in doubt. We remain committed to the principles of the United Nations, and we intend to defend them. . . .

[ ]
Let me make it absolutely clear what the issue of Cuba is. It is not an issue of revolution. This hemisphere has seen many revolutions, including the one which gave my own nation its independence.

---

[1] Reprinted from United Nations, *Security Council, Official Records*, XVIIth year, 1022nd Meeting: October 23, 1962, S/PV.1022, pp. 1–39.

It is not an issue of reform. My nation has lived happily with other countries which have had thorough-going and fundamental social transformations, like Mexico and Bolivia. The whole point of the Alliance for Progress is to bring about an economic and social revolution in the Americas.

It is not an issue of socialism. As Secretary of State Rusk said in February, "our hemisphere has room for a diversity of economic systems."

It is not an issue of dictatorship. The American Republics have lived with dictators before. If this were his only fault, they could live with Mr. Castro.

The foremost objection of the States of the Americas to the Castro régime is not because it is revolutionary, not because it is socialistic, not because it is dictatorial, not even because Mr. Castro perverted a noble revolution in the interests of a squalid totalitarianism. It is because he has aided and abetted an invasion of this hemisphere—an invasion just at the time when the hemisphere is making a new and unprecedented effort for economic progress and social reform.

The crucial fact is that Cuba has given the Soviet Union a bridgehead and staging area in this hemisphere; that it has invited an extra-continental, antidemocratic and expansionist Power into the bosom of the American family; that it has made itself an accomplice in the communist enterprise of world dominion.

[ ]

In our passion for peace we have forborne greatly. There must, however, be limits to forbearance if forbearance is not to become the diagram for the destruction of this Organization. Mr. Castro transformed Cuba into a totalitarian dictatorship with impunity; he extinguished the rights of political freedom with impunity; he aligned himself with the Soviet bloc with impunity; he accepted defensive weapons from the Soviet Union with impunity; he welcomed thousands of Communists into Cuba with impunity: but when, with cold deliberation, he turns his country over to the Soviet Union for a long-range missile launching base, and thus carries the Soviet programme for aggression into the heart of the Americas, the day of forbearance is past.

If the United States and the other nations of the Western Hemisphere should accept this new phase of aggression we would be delinquent in our obligations to world peace. If the United States and the other nations of the Western Hemisphere should accept this basic disturbance of the world's structure of power we would invite a new surge of aggression at every point along the frontier. If we do not stand firm here our adversaries may think that we will stand firm nowhere—and we guarantee a heightening of the world civil war to new levels of intensity and peril. . . .

The issue which confronts the Security Council is grave. Were it not, I should not have detained you so long. Since the end of the Second World War, there has been no threat to the vision of peace so profound—no challenge to the world of the Charter so fateful. The hopes of mankind are concentrated in this room. The action we take may determine the future of civilization. I know that this Council will approach the issue with a full sense of our responsibility and a solemn understanding of the import of our deliberations.

There is a road to peace. The beginning of that road is marked out in the draft resolution I have submitted for your consideration. If we act promptly, we will have another chance to take up again the dreadful questions of nuclear arms and military bases and the means and causes of aggression and of war—to take them up and do something about them.

This is, I believe, a solemn and significant day for the life of the United Nations and the hope of the world community. Let it be remembered not as the day when the world came to the edge of nuclear war, but as the day when men resolved to let nothing thereafter stop them in their quest for peace.   [ ]

The PRESIDENT [Mr. V. A. ZORIN] (translated from Russian): I should now like to make a statement in my capacity as the representative of the Union of Soviet Socialist Republics. . . .

I must say that even a cursory examination of Mr. Stevenson's statement reveals the totally untenable nature of the position taken by the United States Government on the question which it has thought necessary to place before the Council, and its complete inability to defend this position in the Council and before world public opinion.

Mr. Stevenson touched on many subjects. . . . He spoke about the history of the Cuban revolution—although it is difficult to understand what the United States has to do with the internal affairs of the sovereign State of Cuba—and he drew an idyllic picture of the history of the Western Hemisphere for the past 150 years, seeming to forget about the policy of the "big stick" followed by the United States President McKinley, the Olney Doctrine, the actions taken by Theodore Roosevelt in connexion with the Panama Canal, the boastful statement made by the American General Butler to the effect that with his marines he could hold elections in any Latin American country.

He made no mention of all this. The United States is even now attempting to apply this policy of the "big stick." But Mr. Stevenson apparently forgot that times have changed. . . .

Yesterday, the United States Government placed the Republic of Cuba under a virtual naval blockade. Insolently flouting the rules of international conduct and the principles of the Charter, the United States has arrogated to itself—and has so stated—the right to attack the ships of other States on the high seas, which is nothing less than undisguised piracy. At the same time, the landing of additional United States troops has begun at the United States Guantánamo base in Cuban territory, and the United States armed forces are being placed in a state of combat readiness.

[ ]

The present aggressive actions of the United States of America against

Cuba represent a logical stage in that aggressive policy, fraught with the most serious international consequences, which the United States began to pursue towards Cuba in the days of the Eisenhower Administration and which has been continued and intensified by the present United States Government, in the era of the "new frontier" that it proclaimed at the outset of its activities.

[ ]

Everyone will remember Mr. Stevenson's statement on 15 April that the United States was not planning any aggression against Cuba, while on 17 April United States mercenaries landed at Playa Girón. What credence are we to attach to the statements of the representative of a great Power who dared to mislead world public opinion and the official organs of the United Nations in order to conceal the activities of the United States intelligence agency which was preparing for aggression and had ordered Mr. Stevenson to say nothing about it?

[ ]

The falsity of the charges now levelled by the United States against the Soviet Union, which consist in the allegation that the Soviet Union has set up offensive weapons in Cuba, is perfectly clear from the start. First of all, the Soviet delegation hereby officially confirms the statements already made by the Soviet Union in this connexion, to the effect that the Soviet Government has never sent and is not now sending offensive weapons of any kind to Cuba. The Soviet delegation would recall, in particular, the statement issued by Tass on 11 September of this year on the instructions of the Soviet Government, in which the following passage occurs:

> The Government of the Soviet Union has authorized Tass to state, further, that the Soviet Union does not need to transfer to any other country, such as Cuba, its existing means for the repelling of aggression and the delivering of a retaliatory blow. The explosive force of our nuclear resources is so great, and the Soviet Union has such powerful rockets for the delivery of these nuclear charges, that there is no need to seek places for their installation anywhere outside the borders of the Soviet Union.

[ ]

The United States delegation is now trying to use its own fabrications in the Security Council for absolutely monstrous purposes—in order to try to obtain the retroactive approval of the Security Council of the illegal acts of aggression already undertaken by the United States against Cuba, acts which the United States is undertaking unilaterally and in manifest violation of the United Nations Charter and of the elementary rules and principles of international law.

The peoples of the world must clearly realize, however, that in openly embarking on this venture the United States of America is taking a step along the road which leads to a thermo-nuclear world war. Such is the heavy price which the world may have to pay for the present reckless and irresponsible actions of the United States.

[ ]

Peace-loving nations have long been afraid that the reckless aggressive policy of the United States with regard to Cuba may push the world to the brink of disaster. The alarm of the peace-loving elements and their efforts to induce the United States Government to listen to the voice of reason and accept a peaceful settlement of its differences with Cuba have been manifested in the course of the general debate during the seventeenth session of the General Assembly, which ended only a few days ago.

[ ]

When it announced the introduction of its blockade against Cuba, the United States took a step which is unprecedented in relations between States not formally at war. By its arbitrary and piratical action, the United States menaced the shipping of many countries—including its allies—which do not agree with its reckless and dangerous policy in respect of Cuba. By this aggressive action, which put the whole world under the threat of war, the United States issued a direct challenge to the United Nations and to the Security Council as the principal organ of the United Nations responsible for maintaining international peace and security.

[ ]

The Security Council would not be carrying out its bounden duty, as the principal organ responsible for maintaining world and international security, if it ignored the aggressive actions of the United States, which mean nothing less than that the United States has set out to destroy the United Nations and to unleash a world war.

What, then, are the actual facts now facing the Security Council? These facts may be summarized as follows:

(a) The United States Government has stated that it will take action against the ships of other countries, sailing on the high seas, of a type for which there can be no other name but piracy. The decision of the United States to stop and search Cuba-bound ships of other countries will lead to an extreme heightening of international tension, and is a step towards provoking a thermo-nuclear world war, because no self-respecting State will permit its ships to be interfered with.

(b) In order to cover up its actions, the United States is putting forward pretexts which are made up out of whole cloth. It is trying to misrepresent the measures taken by the Cuban Government to ensure the defence of Cuba. Like any State which values its sovereignty and independence, Cuba can hardly fail to display serious anxiety for its security in the face of aggression.

(c) From the very first days of its existence, post-revolutionary Cuba has been subjected to continuous threats and provocation by the United States, which has stopped at nothing, including armed intervention in Cuba in April 1961.

(d) The United States imperialists have openly declared that they intend to impose their policies on other countries, and they are brazenly demanding that armaments intended for national defence should be removed from Cuban soil.

(*e*) The Soviet Government has consistently advocated that all foreign armed forces and armaments should be withdrawn from the territory of other countries to within their own national boundaries. This Soviet proposal is intended to clear the international atmosphere and set up conditions of mutual trust and understanding among nations. However, the United States Government, which has stationed its troops and military equipment all over the world, stubbornly refuses to accept this proposal of the Soviet Union. . . .

(*f*) The United States has no right whatever, either from the point of view of the accepted rules of international law relating to freedom of shipping, or from that of the provisions of the United Nations Charter, to put forward the demands contained in the statements of President Kennedy. No State, no matter how powerful it may be, has any right to rule on the quantities or types of arms which another State considers necessary for its defence. According to the United Nations Charter, each State has the right to defend itself and to possess weapons to ensure its security. . . .

(*g*) The attitude of the United States, as set forth in President Kennedy's statement, is a complete contradiction of the principles of the United Nations Charter and other generally accepted rules of international law. . . . The road which the United States is taking with regard to Cuba and the Soviet Union leads to the destruction of the United Nations and to the unleashing of war.

(*h*) The Soviet Government calls on all the peoples of the world to raise their voices in defence of the United Nations, to refuse to permit the break-up of this Organization, and to oppose the policy of piracy and thermo-nuclear warmongering followed by the United States. . . .

We call on all the members of the Security Council and—so serious is this question—even on the allies of the United Sates to weigh carefully all the possible consequences of the present aggressive actions of the United States and to realize to what a disastrous course of action the United States is trying to commit the Security Council and the world as a whole. . . .

The realization by delegations of their responsibility for the outcome of the train of events set in motion by the aggressive actions of the United States against Cuba is, in the present situation, of direct significance not only for the settling of the present difficulties in the Caribbean, but also for the fate of peace throughout the world. [ ]

CASTRO'S STATEMENT ON SOVIET MISSILES IN CUBA[1]

WHY THE MISSILES WERE INSTALLED

There is one point on which I want to give you new information right away. I have refrained from doing this until now; but today an attempt is being made to frighten all mankind by propagating the idea that Cuba, and in particular I, might provoke a nuclear war, so I feel the world should know the true story of the missile emplacement.

Six months before these missiles were installed in Cuba, we had received an accumulation of information warning us that a new invasion of the island was being prepared under sponsorship of the Central Intelligence Agency, whose administrators were humiliated by the Bay of Pigs disaster and by the spectacle of being ridiculed in the eyes of the world and berated in US government circles. We also knew that the Pentagon was vesting the CIA preparations with the mantle of its authority, but we had doubts as to the attitude of the President. There were those among our informants who even thought it would suffice to alert the President and give him cause for concern in order to arrest these preparations. Then one day Khrushchev's son-in-law, Adzhubei, came to pay us a visit before going on to Washington at the invitation of Kennedy's associates. Immediately upon arriving in Washington, Adzhubei had been received by the American Chief Executive, and their talk centered particularly on Cuba. A week after this interview, we received in Havana a copy of Adzhubei's report to Khrushchev. It was this report which triggered the whole situation.

What did Kennedy say to Adzhubei? Now listen to this carefully, for it is very important: he had said that the new situation in Cuba was intolerable for the United States, that the American government *had decided it would not tolerate it any longer*; he had said that peaceful coexistence was seriously compromised by the fact that 'Soviet influences' in Cuba altered the balance of strength, was destroying the equilibrium agreed upon and [at this point Castro emphasized his statement by pronouncing each syllable separately] *Kennedy reminded the Russians that the United States had not intervened in Hungary*, which was obviously a way of demanding Russian non-intervention in the event of a possible invasion. To be sure, the actual word 'invasion' was not mentioned and Adzhubei, at the time, lacking any background information, could not draw the same conclusions as we did. But when we communicated to Khrushchev all our previous information, the Russians too began to interpret the Kennedy-Adzhubei conversation as we saw it and they went to the source of our information. By the end of a month, the Russian and Cuban governments had reached the *definite conviction* that an invasion might take place from one moment to the next. This is the truth.

---

[1] Reprinted with permission from Jean Daniel, "Unofficial Envoy: An Historic Report from Two Capitals," *New Republic*, December 14, 1963, pp. 18–20.

What was to be done? How could we prevent the invasion? We found that Khrushchev was concerned about the same things that were worrying us. He asked us what we wanted. We replied: *do whatever is needed to convince the United States that any attack on Cuba is the same as an attack on the Soviet Union.* And how to realize this objective? All our thinking and discussions revolved around this point. We thought of a proclamation, an alliance, conventional military aid. The Russians explained to us that their concern was twofold: first, they wanted to save the Cuban revolution (in other words, their socialist honor in the eyes of the world), and at the same time they wished to avoid a world conflict. They reasoned that if conventional military aid was the extent of their assistance, the United States might not hesitate to instigate an invasion, in which case Russia would retaliate and this would inevitably touch off a world war. . . .

It is true that it was said then by other factions that the real reason for installing the missiles was because certain internal problems were driving the Russians to use us to provoke the United States. I am here to tell you that the Russians didn't want and do not today want war. One only need visit them on their home territory, watch them at work, share their economic concerns, admire their intense efforts to raise the workers' standard of living, to understand right away that they are far, very far, from any idea of provocation or domination. However, Soviet Russia was confronted by two alternatives: an absolutely inevitable war (because of their commitments and their position in the socialist world), if the Cuban revolution was attacked; or the risk of a war if the United States, refusing to retreat before the missiles, would not give up the attempt to destroy Cuba. They chose socialist solidarity and the risk of war.

Under these circumstances, how could we Cubans have refused to share the risks taken to save us? It was, in the final analysis, a question of honor, don't you agree? Don't you believe that honor plays a role in politics? You think we are romantics, don't you? Perhaps we are. And why not? In any event, we are militants. In a word, then, we agreed to the emplacement of the missiles. And I might add here that for us Cubans it didn't really make so much difference whether we died by conventional bombing or a hydrogen bomb. Nevertheless, we were not gambling with the peace of the world. The United States was the one to jeopardize the peace of mankind by using the threat of war to stifle revolutions.

And so in June, 1962, my brother Raoul and Che Guevara went to Moscow to discuss ways and means of installing the missiles. The convoy arrived by sea in three weeks. The United States was able to find out that weapons were being shipped in, of course; but it took them two months to discover that these weapons were guided missiles. Two months . . . in other words, longer than we had calculated. Because, of course, we were seeking intimidation, not aggression.

··{14}·· Communist China, 1949–1967

LET FLOWERS OF MANY KINDS BLOSSOM, DIVERSE SCHOOLS OF THOUGHT CONTEND![1]

Speech Delivered by Lu Ting-yi, Director of the Propaganda Department of the Central Committee of the Chinese Communist Party, on the Party's Policy on Art, Literature, and Science, May 26, 1956

Mr. Kuo Mo-jo, President of the Chinese Academy of Sciences and Chairman of the All-China Federation of Literary and Art Circles, has asked me to speak on the policy of the Chinese Communist Party on the work of artists, writers and scientists.

To artists and writers, we say, "Let flowers of many kinds blossom." To scientists we say, "Let diverse schools of thought contend." This is the policy of the Chinese Communist Party. It was announced by Chairman Mao Tse-tung at the Supreme State Conference. . . .

If we want our country to be prosperous and strong, we must, besides consolidating the people's state power, developing our economy and education and strengthening our national defence, have a flourishing art, literature and science. That is essential.

If we want art, literature and science to flourish, we must apply a policy of letting flowers of many kinds blossom, letting diverse schools of thought contend. . . .

"Letting flowers of many kinds blossom, diverse schools of thought contend" means that we stand for freedom of independent thinking, of debate, of creative work; freedom to criticize and freedom to express, maintain and reserve one's opinions on questions of art, literature or scientific research.

The freedom we uphold is not the same as that based on the type of democracy advocated by the bourgeoisie. The freedom advocated by the bourgeoisie really means freedom for only a minority, with little or no freedom for the working people. The bourgeoisie exercises a dictatorship over the working people. Jingos in the United States bellow about the "free world"

---

[1] Reprinted from Lu Ting-yi, *Let Flowers of Many Kinds Blossom, Diverse Schools of Thought Contend* (Peking: Foreign Languages Press, 1957), pp. 3–35.

—a free world in which jingos and reactionaries have all the freedom and every freedom, while the Rosenbergs are put to death because they stand for peace. We, on the contrary, hold that there must be democratic liberties among the people, but that no freedom should be extended to counter-revolutionaries: for them we have only dictatorship. This is a question of drawing a political demarcation line. A clear political line must be drawn between friend and foe.

"Let flowers of many kinds blossom, diverse schools of thought contend": that means freedom among the people. And we urge that, as the people's political power becomes progressively consolidated, such freedom should be given ever fuller scope.

Among the people there are points of agreement and points of difference. Our country has a constitution and it is a public duty to abide by it—this is an agreement among the people. That is to say, the people agree among themselves that they should love their country and support socialism. But there are other matters on which they do not agree with one another. In ideology there is the difference between materialism and idealism. . . .

Members of the Communist Party are dialectical materialists. We Communists of course stand for materialism and against idealism—nothing can change that. But, precisely because we are dialectical materialists and understand the laws governing the development of society, we hold that a strict distinction must be made between the battle of ideas among the people and the struggle against counter-revolutionaries. Among the people themselves there is freedom not only to spread materialism but also to propagate idealism. Provided he is not a counter-revolutionary, everyone is free to expound materialism or idealism. There is also freedom of debate between the two. This is a struggle between conflicting ideas among the people, but that is quite different from the struggle against counter-revolutionaries. We must suppress and put an end to the activities of counter-revolutionaries. We also have to wage a struggle against backward, idealist ways of thinking among the people. The latter struggle can be quite sharp, too; but we embark on it with the intention of strengthening unity, ending backwardness and creating an ever closer unity among the people. When it comes to questions of ideas, administrative measures will get us nowhere. Only through open debate can materialism gradually conquer idealism.

There will be diverse opinions, too, on matters of a purely artistic, academic or technological nature. This is, of course, quite all right. In matters of this sort, there is freedom to voice different opinions, to criticize, counter-criticize and debate.

In short, we hold that while it is necessary to draw a clear political line between friend and foe, we must have freedom among the people. . . .

Let flowers of many kinds blossom, diverse schools of thought contend: that is a policy to mobilize all the positive elements. It is also, therefore, a policy that will in the end strengthen unity.

On what basis are we to unite? On the basis of patriotism and socialism.

What do we unite for? To build a new, socialist China and combat our enemies both at home and abroad.

There are two kinds of unity: one is built on mechanical obedience and the other on our own conscious, free will. What we want is the latter.

Are those engaged in art, literature and science united? Yes, they are. Compare the situation in the days when the Chinese People's Republic was just founded with what we have now and you find we now have a far closer unity among artists, writers and scientists. This has come about as a result of our work for social reforms and changes in our ways of thought. It would be wrong to deny or ignore this. But even so, we cannot say that our unity is all it should be: there is still room for improvement.

In what respect? Well, first and foremost, some Communist Party members have forgotten Comrade Mao Tse-tung's warning about the evils of sectarianism. Success turns some people's heads and they get swelled-headed and sectarian. . . .

As everyone knows, in the past few years we have fought a series of battles in the Party against sectarianism in artistic, literary and scientific circles. We have waged this struggle in organizations dealing with public health and research in the natural sciences, in literature and art, and in the social sciences. We shall go on waging this struggle and we call on all Party members working in these fields to make an end of this sectarianism. . . .

Finish with sectarianism and unite with all who are ready to co-operate, all who possibly can co-operate with us. Put aside the desire to monopolize things. Get rid of unreasonable rules and commandments, and apply the policy of letting flowers of many kinds blossom, letting diverse schools of thought contend. Do not think only of the interests of your own department; try to give more help to others and to other departments. Don't be self-conceited and cocksure. Be modest and discreet and respect others. That is how to rid themselves of the shortcomings which have marred our work in building up unity; that is how to strengthen our unity to the utmost. . . .

In regard to criticism, our policy of letting flowers of many kinds blossom, diverse schools of thought contend means freedom to criticize and freedom to counter-criticize. . . .

There are two kinds of criticism. One is criticism directed against the enemy—what people call criticism that "kills at a blow," criticism with no holds barred. The other is criticism directed against the honestly mistaken— well-meant, comradely criticism, made in the cause of unity, intended to achieve unity through struggle. In making this kind of criticism, one must always bear the whole situation in mind. The critic should rely on reasoning, and his aim should be to help others. . . .

It is quite common for people to make mistakes in all innocence. There is no such person as a man who never makes mistakes. We must make a sharp distinction between mistakes like this and statements consciously directed against the revolution. Criticism of such mistakes must only be made for the good of others; it must be cool-headed criticism, well reasoned. In making it, we must bear the whole situation in mind and act in a spirit of unity, with the intention of achieving unity. We must do all we can to help those who have made mistakes correct them, and those criticized should have no apprehensions about being criticized.

It is easy to make mistakes. But mistakes should be rectified immediately, the sooner the better. It is sticking to one's mistakes that does the harm. As far as being criticized is concerned, one should stick to what is right, and dissent if others are wrong in their criticism. But if the other party is right you must rectify your mistakes and humbly accept others' criticism. To admit a mistake frankly, to root out the causes of it, to analyse the situation in which it was made and thoroughly discuss how to correct it is, as far as a political party is concerned, the hallmark of a mature party. As far as the individual is concerned, it is the hallmark of a realist. To accept criticism when one has made a mistake is to accept the help of others. Besides helping the person concerned, that also helps the progress of science, art and literature in our country; and there is certainly nothing wrong with that!

As regards study in general, we must continue to see to it that the study of Marxism-Leninism is organized on a voluntary basis. At the same time, we must acquire a broad range of general knowledge; we must critically study things both past and present, things at home and from abroad, and critically learn from both friends and foes.

Marxism-Leninism is being enthusiastically studied by most of our intellectuals. That is a good thing. The scientific theories of Marx and Lenin are the cream of human knowledge, truth that is everywhere applicable. Once there were people who thought that Marxism-Leninism was not applicable in China; but such ideas have been proved sheer nonsense. Without scientific Marxist-Leninist theory to guide us, it is unthinkable that the revolution could have been victorious in China. It is also unthinkable that we could have achieved the tremendous successes and made the rapid progress that we have in construction and in scientific and cultural work. . . .

As they come from the people things are often not systematically developed or are crude or lack theoretical explanation. Some of them have more than a bit of the "quack" about them, or a taint of the superstitious. There is nothing surprising about that. It is the duty of our scientists, artists and writers not to despise these things but to make a careful study of them, to select, cherish and foster the good in them, and, where necessary, put them on a scientific basis.

We must have our national pride, but we must not become national nihilists. We oppose that misguided attitude known as "wholesale Westernization." But that does not mean that we can afford to be arrogant and refuse to learn good things from abroad. Our country is still a very backward one; we can make it prosperous and strong only by doing our best to learn all we can from foreign countries. Under no circumstances is national arrogance justified.

We must learn from the Soviet Union, from the People's Democracies, and from the peoples of all lands.

To learn from the Soviet Union—that is a correct watchword. We have already learnt a little, but much remains to be learnt. The Soviet Union is the world's first socialist state, the leader of the world camp of peace and democracy. It has the highest rate of industrial development. It has a rich experience in socialist construction. In not a few important branches of science it has caught up with and surpassed the most advanced capitalist countries. It stands to reason that it is worth our while to learn from such a country and such a people. It is utterly wrong not to learn from the Soviet Union.

Nevertheless, in learning from the Soviet Union we must not mechanically copy everything in the Soviet Union in a doctrinaire way. We must make what we have learnt fit our actual conditions. That is a point we must pay attention to. Otherwise, we shall run into trouble. . . .

Apart from learning from our friends, we must see what we can learn from our enemies—not to learn what is reactionary in their systems but to study what is good in their methods of management or in their scientific techniques. Our aim in this is to speed the progress of our socialist construction, so as to build up our strength to ward off aggression and safeguard peace in Asia and throughout the world. . . .

Now that this policy—"let flowers of many kinds blossom, diverse schools of thought contend"—has been put forward, many problems will crop up one after the other and demand solutions. I hope all of you will do some hard thinking on such questions. Today I have only touched upon some matters of principle, and anything I say is open to correction.

THE ATOMIC BOMB[1]
Statement of the Government of the People's Republic of China, October 16, 1964

China exploded an atomic bomb at 15:00 hours on October 16, 1964, thereby successfully carrying out its first nuclear test. This is a major achievement of the Chinese people in their struggle to strengthen their national defence and oppose the U.S. imperialist policy of nuclear blackmail and nuclear threats.

To defend oneself is the inalienable right of every sovereign state. To safeguard world peace is the common task of all peace-loving countries. China cannot remain idle in the face of the ever increasing nuclear threats from the United States. China is conducting nuclear tests and developing nuclear weapons under compulsion.

The Chinese Government has consistently advocated the complete pro-

---

[1] Reprinted from *Break the Nuclear Monopoly, Eliminate Nuclear Weapons* (Peking: Foreign Languages Press, 1965), pp. 1–5.

hibition and thorough destruction of nuclear weapons. If this had been achieved, China need not have developed nuclear weapons. But our proposal has met with stubborn resistance from the U.S. imperialists. The Chinese Government pointed out long ago that the treaty on the partial halting of nuclear tests signed in Moscow in July 1963 by the United States, Britain and the Soviet Union was a big fraud to fool the people of the world, that it was an attempt to consolidate the nuclear monopoly of the three nuclear powers and tie the hands of all peace-loving countries, and that it had increased, and not decreased, the nuclear threat of U.S. imperialism against the people of China and of the whole world. . . .

The atomic bomb is a paper tiger. This famous statement by Chairman Mao Tse-tung is known to all. This was our view in the past and this is still our view at present. China is developing nuclear weapons not because it believes in their omnipotence nor because it plans to use them. On the contrary, in developing nuclear weapons, China's aim is to break the nuclear monopoly of the nuclear powers and to eliminate nuclear weapons.

The Chinese Government is loyal to Marxism-Leninism and proletarian internationalism. We believe in the people. It is the people, and not any weapons, that decide the outcome of a war. The destiny of China is decided by the Chinese people, while the destiny of the world is decided by the people of the world, and not by nuclear weapons. China is developing nuclear weapons for defence and for protecting the Chinese people from U.S. threats to launch a nuclear war.

The Chinese Government hereby solemnly declares that China will never at any time or under any circumstances be the first to use nuclear weapons. . . .

The Chinese Government will, as always, exert every effort to promote, through international consultations, the realization of the lofty aim of com plete prohibition and thorough destruction of nuclear weapons. Until that day comes, the Chinese Government and people will firmly and unswervingly follow their own path to strengthen their national defence, defend their motherland and safeguard world peace.

We are convinced that man, who creates nuclear weapons, will certainly be able to eliminate them.

THE NATURE OF PEOPLE'S WAR[1]
Statement by Defense Minister Lin Piao, September 3, 1965

[ ]
Comrade Mao Tse-tung's theory of people's war has been proved by the long practice of the Chinese revolution to be in accord with the objective laws of such wars and to be invincible. It has not only been valid for China, it is a

---

[1] Reprinted from Lin Piao, *Long Live the Victory of People's War!* (Peking: Foreign Languages Press, 1965), pp. 42–58.

great contribution to the revolutionary struggles of the oppressed nations and peoples throughout the world. . . .

It was on the basis of the lessons derived from the people's wars in China that Comrade Mao Tse-tung, using the simplest and the most vivid language, advanced the famous thesis that "political power grows out of the barrel of a gun."

He clearly pointed out:

The seizure of power by armed force, the settlement of the issue by war, is the central task and the highest form of revolution. This Marxist-Leninist principle of revolution holds good universally, for China and for all other countries.

[ ]

Since World War II, U.S. imperialism has stepped into the shoes of German, Japanese and Italian fascism and has been trying to build a great American empire by dominating and enslaving the whole world. It is actively fostering Japanese and West German militarism as its chief accomplices in unleashing a world war. Like a vicious wolf, it is bullying and enslaving various peoples, plundering their wealth, encroaching upon their countries' sovereignty and interfering in their internal affairs. It is the most rabid aggressor in human history and the most ferocious common enemy of the people of the world. Every people or country in the world that wants revolution, independence and peace cannot but direct the spearhead of its struggle against U.S. imperialism. . . .

U.S. imperialism is stronger, but also more vulnerable, than any imperialism of the past. It sets itself against the people of the whole world, including the people of the United States. Its human, military, material and financial resources are far from sufficient for the realization of its ambition of dominating the whole world. U.S. imperialism has further weakened itself by occupying so many places in the world, over-reaching itself, stretching its fingers out wide and dispersing its strength, with its rear so far away and its supply lines so long. As Comrade Mao Tse-tung has said, "Wherever it commits aggression, it puts a new noose around its neck. It is besieged ring upon ring by the people of the whole world.". . .

Everything is divisible. And so is this colossus of U.S. imperialism. It can be split up and defeated. The peoples of Asia, Africa, Latin America and other regions can destroy it piece by piece, some striking at its head and others at its feet. That is why the greatest fear of U.S. imperialism is that people's wars will be launched in different parts of the world, and particularly in Asia, Africa and Latin America, and why it regards people's war as a mortal danger.

U.S. imperialism relies solely on its nuclear weapons to intimidate people. But these weapons cannot save U.S. imperialism from its doom. Nuclear weapons cannot be used lightly. . . .

However highly developed modern weapons and technical equipment may be and however complicated the methods of modern warfare, in the final analysis the outcome of a war will be decided by the sustained fighting of the ground forces, by the fighting at close quarters on battlefields, by the political consciousness of the men, by their courage and spirit of sacrifice. Here the weak points of U.S. imperialism will be completely laid bare, while the superiority of the revolutionary people will be brought into full play. The reactionary troops of U.S. imperialism cannot possibly be endowed with the courage and the spirit of sacrifice possessed by the revolutionary people. The spiritual atom bomb which the revolutionary people possess is a far more powerful and useful weapon than the physical atom bomb.

Viet Nam is the most convincing current example of a victim of aggression defeating U.S. imperialism by a people's war. The United States has made South Viet Nam a testing ground for the suppression of people's war. It has carried on this experiment for many years, and everybody can now see that the U.S. aggressors are unable to find a way of coping with people's war. On the other hand, the Vietnamese people have brought the power of people's war into full play in their struggle against the U.S. aggressors. The U.S. aggressors are in danger of being swamped in the people's war in Viet Nam. They are deeply worried that their defeat in Viet Nam will lead to a chain reaction. They are expanding the war in an attempt to save themselves from defeat. But the more they expand the war, the greater will be the chain reaction. The more they escalate the war, the heavier will be their fall and the more disastrous their defeat. The people in other parts of the world will see still more clearly that U.S. imperialism can be defeated, and that what the Vietnamese people can do, they can do too.

History has proved and will go on proving that people's war is the most effective weapon against U.S. imperialism and its lackeys. All revolutionary people will learn to wage people's war against U.S. imperialism and its lackeys. They will take up arms, learn to fight battles and become skilled in waging people's war, though they have not done so before. U.S. imperialism like a mad bull dashing from place to place, will finally be burned to ashes in the blazing fires of the people's wars it has provoked by its own actions.   [ ]

MAO TSE-TUNG'S THOUGHT IS THE TELESCOPE AND MICROSCOPE OF OUR REVOLUTIONARY CAUSE[1]
Editorial of the Liberation Army Daily (Jiefangjun Bao) *of June 7, 1966*

The current great socialist cultural revolution is a great revolution to sweep away all monsters and a great revolution that remoulds the ideology of people and touches their souls. What weapon should be used to sweep away

---

[1] Reprinted from *The Great Socialist Cultural Revolution in China* (Peking: Foreign Languages Press, 1966), III, 11–17.

all monsters? What ideology should be applied to arm people's minds and remould their souls? The most powerful ideological weapon, the only one, is the great Mao Tse-tung's thought.

Mao Tse-tung's thought is our political orientation, the highest instruction for our actions; it is our ideological and political telescope and microscope for observing and analysing all things. In this unprecedented great cultural revolution, we should use Mao Tse-tung's thought to observe, analyse and transform everything, and, in a word, put it in command of everything. We should use Mao Tse-tung's thought to storm the enemy's positions and seize victory. . . . Our struggle against the black anti-Party, anti-socialist line and gangsters is a mighty, life-and-death class struggle. The enemies without guns are more hidden, cunning, sinister and vicious than the enemies with guns. The representatives of the bourgeoisie and all monsters, including the modern revisionists, often oppose the red flag by hoisting a red flag and oppose Marxism-Leninism and Mao Tse-tung's thought under the cloak of Marxism-Leninism and Mao Tse-tung's thought when they attack the Party and socialism, because Marxism-Leninism and Mao Tse-tung's thought are becoming more popular day by day, our Party and Chairman Mao enjoy an incomparably high prestige and the dictatorship of the proletariat in our country is becoming more consolidated. These are the tactics that the revisionists always use in opposing Marxism-Leninism. This is a new characteristic of the class struggle under the conditions of the dictatorship of the proletariat.

The many facts exposed during the great cultural revolution show us more clearly that the anti-Party and anti-socialist elements are all careerists, schemers and hypocrites of the exploiting classes. They indulge in double-dealing. They feign compliance while acting in opposition. They appear to be men but are demons at heart. They speak human language to your face, but talk devil's language behind your back. They are wolves in sheep's clothing and man-eating tigers with smiling faces. They often use the phrases of Marxism-Leninism and Mao Tse-tung's thought as a cover while greatly publicizing diametrically opposed views behind the word "but" and smuggling in bourgeois and revisionist stuff. Enemies holding a false red banner are ten times more vicious than enemies holding a white banner. Wolves in sheep's clothing are ten times more sinister than ordinary wolves. Tigers with smiling faces are ten times more ferocious than tigers with their fangs bared and their claws sticking out. Sugar-coated bullets are ten times more destructive than real bullets. A fortress is most vulnerable when attacked from within. Enemies who have wormed their way into our ranks are far more dangerous than enemies operating in the open. We must give this serious attention and be highly vigilant.

In such a very complicated and acute class struggle, how are we to draw a clear-cut line between the enemy and ourselves and maintain a firm stand? How are we to distinguish between revolutionaries and counter-revolutionaries, genuine revolutionaries and sham revolutionaries, and Marxism-Leninism and revisionism? We must master Mao Tse-tung's thought, the powerful ideological weapon, and use it as a telescope and a microscope to observe all matters. With the invincible Mao Tse-tung's thought, with the scientific world outlook and methodology of dialectical materialism and historical materialism which have been developed by Chairman Mao, and with the sharp weapon of Chairman Mao's theory of classes and class struggle, we have the highest criterion for judging right and wrong. . . .

Chairman Mao teaches us, "The proletariat seeks to transform the world according to its own world outlook, so does the bourgeoisie." In the sharp clash between the two world outlooks, either you crush me, or I crush you. It will not do to sit on the fence; there is no middle road. The overthrown bourgeoisie, in their plots for restoration and subversion, always give first place to ideology, take hold of ideology and the superstructure. The representatives of the bourgeoisie, by using their position and power, usurped and controlled the leadership of a number of departments, did all they could to spread bourgeois and revisionist poison through the media of literature, the theatre, films, music, the arts, the press, periodicals, the radio, publications and academic research and schools, etc., in an attempt to corrupt people's minds and perpetrate "peaceful evolution" as ideological preparation and preparation of public opinion for capitalist restoration. If our proletarian ideology does not take over the position, then the bourgeois ideology will have free rein; it will gradually nibble away and chew you up bit by bit. Once proletarian ideology gives way, so will the superstructure and the economic base and this means the restoration of capitalism. Therefore, we must arm our minds with Mao Tse-tung's thought and establish a firm proletarian world outlook. We must use the great Mao Tse-tung's thought to fight and completely destroy the bourgeois ideological and cultural positions.

Mao Tse-tung's thought is the acme of Marxism-Leninism in the present era. It is living Marxism-Leninism at its highest. It is the powerful, invincible weapon of the Chinese people, and it is also a powerful, invincible weapon of the revolutionary people the world over. Mao Tse-tung's thought has proved to be the invincible truth through the practice of China's democratic revolution, socialist revolution and socialist construction, and through the struggle in the international sphere against U.S. imperialism and its lackeys and against Khrushchov revisionism. Chairman Mao has, with the gifts of genius, creatively and comprehensively developed Marxism-Leninism. Basing himself on the fundamental theses of Marxism-Leninism, Chairman Mao has summed up the experience of the practice of the Chinese revolution and the world revolution, and the painful lesson of the usurpation of the leadership of the Party and the state of the Soviet Union by the modern revisionist clique, systematically put forward the theory concerning classes, class contradictions and class struggle that exist in socialist society, greatly enriched and developed the Marxist-Leninist theory on the dictatorship of the proletariat, and put forward a series of wise policies aimed at opposing and preventing revisionism and the restoration of capitalism. . . . Every sentence by Chairman Mao is the truth, and carries more weight than ten thousand ordinary sentences. As the Chinese people master Mao Tse-tung's thought, China will be prosperous and ever-victorious. Once the world's people master Mao Tse-tung's thought which is living Marxism-Leninism, they are sure to win their emancipation, bury imperialism, modern revisionism and all reactionaries lock, stock and barrel, and realize communism throughout the world step by step.

The most fundamental task in the great socialist cultural revolution in our country is to eliminate thoroughly the old ideology and culture, the old customs and habits which were fostered by all the exploiting classes for thousands of years to poison the minds of the people, and to create and form an entirely new, proletarian ideology and culture, new customs and habits among the masses of the people. This is to creatively study and apply Mao Tse-tung's thought in tempestuous class struggle, popularize it and let it become closely integrated with the masses of workers, peasants and soldiers. Once the masses grasp it, Mao Tse-tung's thought will be transformed into a mighty material force. Facts show that those armed with Mao Tse-tung's thought are the bravest, wisest, most united, most steadfast in class stand and have the sharpest sight. In this great, stormy cultural revolution, the masses of workers, peasants and soldiers are playing the role of the main force —this is the result of their efforts in creatively studying and applying Mao Tse-tung's thought and arming their ideology with it. This is another eloquent proof of the fact that when the masses of workers, peasants and soldiers master the political telescope and microscope of Mao Tse-tung's thought, they are invincible and ever-triumphant. . . .

The attitude towards Mao Tse-tung's thought, whether to accept it or resist it, to support it or oppose it, to love it warmly or be hostile to it, this is the touchstone to test and the watershed between true revolution and sham revolution, between revolution and counter-revolution, between Marxism-Leninism and revisionism. He who wants to make revolution must accept Mao Tse-tung's thought and act in accordance with it. A counter-revolutionary will inevitably disparage, distort, resist, attack and oppose Mao Tse-tung's thought. The "authorities" of the bourgeoisie and all monsters, including the modern revisionists, use every means to slander Mao Tse-tung's thought, and they are extremely hostile to the creative study and application of Mao Tse-tung's works by the masses of workers, peasants and soldiers. They wildly attack the creative study and application of Mao Tse-tung's works by workers, peasants and soldiers as "philistinism," "over-simplification" and "pragmatism." The only explanation is that this flows from their exploiting class instinct. They fear Mao Tse-tung's thought, the revolutionary truth of the proletariat, and particularly the integration of Mao Tse-tung's thought with the worker, peasant and soldier masses. Once the workers, peasants and soldiers master the sharp weapon of Mao Tse-tung's thought, all monsters have no ground left to stand on. All their intrigues and plots will be thoroughly exposed, their ugly features will be brought into the broad light of day and their dream to restore capitalism will be utterly shattered.

The class enemy won't fall down if you don't hit him. He still tries to rise to his feet after he has fallen. When one black line is eliminated, another appears. When one gang of representatives of the bourgeoisie has been laid low, a new one takes the stage. We must follow the instructions of the Central Committee of the Communist Party of China and never forget the class struggle, never forget the dictatorship of the proletariat, never forget to give prominence to politics, never forget to hold aloft the great red banner of Mao Tse-tung's thought. We must firmly give prominence to politics. We must creatively study and apply still better Chairman Mao Tse-tung's works, putting stress on the importance of application. We must consider Chairman Mao's works the supreme directive for all our work. We must master Mao Tse-tung's thought and pass it on from generation to generation. This is dictated by the needs of the revolution, the situation, the struggle against the enemy, the preparations to smash aggressive war by U.S. imperialism, of opposing and preventing revisionism, preventing the restoration of capitalism, of building socialism with greater, faster, better and more economical results and of ensuring the gradual transition from socialism to communism in China. Chairman Mao is the radiant sun lighting our minds. Mao Tse-tung's thought is our lifeline. Those who oppose Mao Tse-tung's thought, no matter when they do so and what kind of "authorities" they are, will be denounced by the entire Party and the whole nation.

··{15}·· The Sino-Soviet Conflict

THE LEADERS OF THE CPSU ARE THE GREATEST SPLITTERS OF OUR TIMES[1]
February 4, 1964

Never before has the unity of the international communist movement been so gravely threatened as it is today when we are witnessing a deluge of modern revisionist ideology. Both internationally and inside individual Parties, fierce struggles are going on between Marxism-Leninism and revisionism. The international communist movement is confronted with an unprecedentedly serious danger of a split.

It is the urgent task of the Communists, the proletariat and the revolutionary people of the world to defend the unity of the socialist camp and of the international communist movement.

The Communist Party of China has made consistent and unremitting efforts to defend and strengthen the unity of the socialist camp and the international communist movement in accordance with Marxism-Leninism and the revolutionary principles of the 1957 Declaration and the 1960 Statement. It has been and remains the unswerving position of the Chinese Communist Party to uphold principle, uphold unity, eliminate differences and strengthen the struggle against our common enemy.

Ever since they embarked on the path of revisionism, the leaders of the CPSU have tirelessly professed their devotion to the unity of the international communist movement. Of late, they have been particularly active in crying for "unity." This calls to mind what Engels said ninety years ago. "One must not allow oneself to be misled by the cry for 'unity.' Those who have this word most often on their lips are the ones who sow the most dissension. . . ." ". . . the biggest sectarians and the biggest brawlers and rogues at times shout loudest for unity." ("Engels to A. Bebel, June 20, 1873," *Selected Correspondence of Marx and Engels*, Foreign Languages Publishing House, Moscow, p. 345.)

---

[1] Reprinted from *The Leaders of the CPSU Are the Greatest Splitters of Our Times: Comment on the Open Letter of the Central Committee of the CPSU* (Peking: Foreign Languages Press, 1964), VII, pp. 1–2, 16–26, 59–63.

While presenting themselves as champions of unity, the leaders of the CPSU are trying to pin the label of splittism on the Chinese Communist Party. In its Open Letter the Central Committee of the CPSU says:

The Chinese leaders are undermining the unity not only of the socialist camp but of the entire world communist movement, trampling on the principles of proletarian internationalism and grossly violating accepted standards of relations between fraternal parties.

And the subsequent articles published in the Soviet press have been condemning the Chinese Communists as "sectarians" and "splitters."

But what are the facts? Who is undermining the unity of the socialist camp? Who is undermining the unity of the international communist movement? Who is trampling on the principles of proletarian internationalism? And who is grossly violating the accepted standards of relations between fraternal Parties? In other words, who are the real, out-and-out splitters? . . .

The events of recent years show that the leaders of the CPSU headed by Khrushchov have become the chief representatives of modern revisionism as well as the greatest splitters in the international communist movement.

Between the 20th and 22nd Congresses of the CPSU, the leaders of the CPSU developed a rounded system of revisionism. They put forward a revisionist line which contravenes the proletarian revolution and the dictatorship of the proletariat, a line which consists of "peaceful coexistence," "peaceful competition," "peaceful transition," "a state of the whole people" and "a party of the entire people." They have tried to impose this revisionist line on all fraternal Parties as a substitute for the common line of the international communist movement which was laid down at the meetings of fraternal Parties in 1957 and 1960. And they have attacked anyone who perseveres in the Marxist-Leninist line and resists their revisionist line.

The leaders of the CPSU have themselves undermined the basis of the unity of the international communist movement and created the present grave danger of a split by betraying Marxism-Leninism and proletarian internationalism and pushing their revisionist and divisive line. . . .

They have violated the principles guiding relations among fraternal countries as laid down in the Declaration and the Statement, pursued a policy of great-power chauvinism and national egoism towards fraternal socialist countries and thus disrupted the unity of the socialist camp.

They have arbitrarily infringed the sovereignty of fraternal countries, interfered in their internal affairs, carried on subversive activities and striven in every way to control fraternal countries.

In the name of the "international division of labour," the leaders of the CPSU oppose the adoption by fraternal countries of the policy of building socialism by their own efforts and developing their economies on an independent basis, and attempt to turn them into economic appendages. They have tried to force those fraternal countries which are comparatively backward economically to abandon industrialization and become their sources of raw materials and markets for surplus products.

The leaders of the CPSU are quite unscrupulous in their pursuit of the policy of great-power chauvinism. They have constantly brought political, economic and even military pressure to bear on fraternal countries.

The leaders of the CPSU have openly called for the overthrow of the Party and government leaders of Albania, brashly severed all economic and diplomatic relations with her and tyrannically deprived her of her legitimate rights as a member of the Warsaw Treaty Organization and the Council of Economic Mutual Assistance.

The leaders of the CPSU have violated the Sino-Soviet Treaty of Friendship, Alliance and Mutual Assistance, made a unilateral decision to withdraw 1,390 Soviet experts working in China, to tear up 343 contracts and supplementary contracts on the employment of experts and to cancel 257 projects of scientific and technical co-operation, and pursued a restrictive and discriminatory trade policy against China. They have provoked incidents on the Sino-Soviet border and carried on large-scale subversive activities in Sinkiang. On more than one occasion, Khrushchov went so far as to tell leading comrades of the Central Committee of the CPC that certain anti-Party elements in the Chinese Communist Party were his "good friends." He has praised Chinese anti-Party elements for attacking the Chinese Party's general line for socialist construction, the big leap forward and the people's communes, describing their action as a "manly act.". . .

The great-power chauvinism and splittism of the leaders of the CPSU are equally glaring in their conduct vis-a-vis fraternal Parties.

Since the 20th Congress of the CPSU its leaders have tried, on the pretext of "combating the personality cult," to change the leadership of other fraternal Parties to conform to their will. Right up to the present they have insisted on "combating the personality cult" as a pre-condition for the restoration of unity and as a "principle" which is "obligatory on every Communist Party."

Contrary to the principles guiding relations among fraternal Parties laid down in the Declaration and the Statement, the leaders of the CPSU ignore the independent and equal status of fraternal Parties, insist on establishing a kind of feudal patriarchal domination over the international communist movement and turn the relations between brother Parties into those between a patriarchal father and his sons. Khrushchov has more than once described a fraternal Party as a "silly boy" and called himself its "mother." With his feudal psychology of self-exaltation, he has absolutely no sense of shame.

The leaders of the CPSU have completely ignored the principle of achieving unanimity through consultation among fraternal Parties and habitually make dictatorial decisions and order others about. They have recklessly torn up joint agreements with fraternal Parties, taken arbitrary decisions on important matters of common concern to fraternal Parties and forced *faits acccomplis* on them. . . .

The leaders of the CPSU regard fraternal Parties as pawns on their diplomatic chessboard. Khrushchov plays fast and loose, he blows hot and cold, he talks one way one day and another the next, and yet he insists on the fraternal Parties dancing to his every tune without knowing whence or whither.

The leaders of the CPSU have stirred up trouble and created splits in many Communist Parties by encouraging the followers of their revisionist line in these Parties to attack the leadership, or usurp leading positions, persecute Marxist-Leninists and even expel them from the Party. It is this divisive policy of the leaders of the CPSU that has given rise to organizational splits in the fraternal Parties of many capitalist countries. . . .

The leaders of the CPSU have completely reversed enemies and comrades. They have directed the edge of struggle, which should be against U.S. imperialism and its lackeys, against the Marxist-Leninist fraternal Parties and countries.

The leaders of the CPSU are bent on seeking Soviet-U.S. co-operation for the domination of the world, they regard U.S. imperialism, the most ferocious enemy of the people of the world, as their most reliable friend, and they treat the fraternal Parties and countries adhering to Marxism-Leninism as their enemy. They collude with U.S. imperialism, the reactionaries of various countries, the renegade Tito clique and the Right-wing social democrats in a partnership against the socialist fraternal countries, the fraternal Parties, the Marxist-Leninists and the revolutionary people of all countries.

When they snatch at a straw from Eisenhower or Kennedy or others like them,· or think that things are going smoothly for them, the leaders of the CPSU are beside themselves with joy, hit out wildly at the fraternal Parties and countries adhering to Marxism-Leninism, and endeavour to sacrifice fraternal Parties and countries on the altar of their political dealings with U.S. imperialism. . . .

These facts show that the leaders of the CPSU have taken the road of complete betrayal of proletarian internationalism, in contravention of the interests of the Soviet people, the socialist camp and the international communist movement and those of all revolutionary people. . . .

We would like to advise the leaders of the CPSU to think matters over calmly: what will your clinging to revisionism and splittism lead to? Once again, we would like to make a sincere appeal to the leaders of the CPSU: We hope you will be able to return to Marxism-Leninism and proletarian internationalism, to the revolutionary principles of the 1957 Declaration and the 1960 Statement and to the principles guiding relations among fraternal Parties and countries as laid down in these documents, so that the differences will be eliminated and the unity of the international communist movement and the socialist camp and unity between China and the Soviet Union will be strengthened on these principled bases.

Despite our serious differences with the leaders of the CPSU, we have full confidence in the vast membership of the CPSU and in the Soviet people, who grew up under the guidance of Lenin and Stalin. As always, the Communists and the people of China will unswervingly safeguard the unity between China and the Soviet Union, and consolidate and develop the deep-rooted friendship between our two peoples.

Communists of the world, unite on the basis of Marxism-Leninism!

THE SINO-SOVIET DISPUTE[1]
Statement by the Rumanian Workers' Party, April 22, 1964

Of late, the divergencies in the international communist and working-class movement have deepened, and the public polemic has assumed particular sharpness. Instead of a debate imbued with the endeavour to bring standpoints closer to each other and to find solutions based on Marxist-Leninist ideology, forms and methods have been adopted in the course of the public polemic which considerably envenom relations between parties, and offensive judgements, as well as accusations and the ascribing of certain intentions are being resorted to.

Particularly serious is the fact that almost all fraternal parties are drawn into the polemic, and that the key is set by parties that owing to their merits and revolutionary experience have a great influence in the communist movement.

The elaboration of a common general line and of the norms to ensure the unity of action of the communist and workers' parties can only be a result of their collective wisdom. Considering the great variety of conditions in which the Marxist-Leninist parties carry on their activity, the cohesion of the communist movement has to be conceived in the light of the historical necessities to ensure, while paying heed to this variety, unity on the issues of common interest, on the fundamental problems of social development. This unity does not, of course, preclude different opinions in one problem or another of domestic or international life.

When differences of opinion appear with regard to the general problems of the communist and working-class movement, it is essential that they should not lead to tension in the relations between parties, to irreconcilable contradictions, to reciprocal accusations and excommunications from the family of Marxist-Leninist parties. . . .

---

[1] Reprinted from *Statement on the Stand of the Rumanian Workers' Party Concerning the Problems of the World Communist and Working-Class Movement Endorsed by the Enlarged Plenum of the C.C. of the R.W.P. Held in April 1964* (Rumanian News Agency, 1964), pp. 46–55.

There does not and cannot exist a "parent" party and a "son-party," parties that are "superior" and parties that are "subordinate," but there exists the great family of communist and workers' parties, which have equal rights. No party has or can have a privileged place, or can impose its line and opinions on other parties. Each party makes its own contribution to the development of the common treasure store of Marxist-Leninist teaching, to enriching the forms and practical methods of revolutionary struggle for winning power and building the socialist society.

In discussing and confronting different points of view on problems concerning the revolutionary struggle or socialist construction, no party must label as anti-Marxist, anti-Leninist the fraternal party whose opinions it does not share.

We consider as unjust the practice of using in Party documents, in the press and over the radio, at meetings of international organizations, etc., offensive assessments, accusations and epithets against fraternal parties and their leadership, of expounding in an unfriendly and distorted manner within the ranks of the Party or among the mass of the people the stand of other parties, of condemning at congresses or in the resolutions of a Party the point of view of other communist parties and the stand taken by them.

No Party is allowed to bypass the Party leadership in one country or another, and so much the less, to launch appeals for the removal, or the change of the leadership of a party. Appraisals and manifestations which lack respect for a communist party and its leadership, may justly be interpreted as a lack of respect for the working class, for the people who trust the party and the leadership of the communist party of their country; and this further worsens the relations between parties, between socialist states, and affects the friendship of the respective peoples.

Unfortunately, in the heat of the polemic, reciprocal accusations have gone so far as to take the place of a scientific analysis of the differences of opinion, to overshadow the fundamental issues, overstepping all bounds.

It is inconceivable that in relations between communist parties reciprocal and deeply offensive accusations be levelled against the leaders of a fraternal party as being "the biggest revisionists of our time," who are in "collusion with U.S. imperialism," and "throw wide open the gates for the restoration of capitalism," or that they are "trotzkyites" who "furiously attack world socialism," "partners on the right-flank of the American 'wild men,' " etc.

Such grave invectives cannot but lead to tension in interparty relations, to rendering difficult the contacts between leaderships of the respective parties and drive things towards a break, towards a split of the communist movement. . . .

Particularly serious is the fact that in such a situation the central press organs of one of the largest fraternal parties, the Communist Party of China, assert that in the conditions now prevailing in the communist movement a split, both on the international plane and within various parties, becomes necessary and unavoidable and that the dialectics of the development of the international working-class movement is "unity, struggle and even splits, as well as unity on a new basis."

In our opinion, this means to give a theoretical foundation for a split, it means a call for a split.

Taking advantage of the present state of affairs in the communist movement, all kinds of dissatisfied, anti-party and dissolving elements of a series of parties are rising against the party leaderships, set up splitter groups, call themselves "true Marxist-Leninist parties" and struggle to split the working-class movement of the respective country.

It is regrettable that these groups meet with favourable appraisals and support on the part of the Chinese comrades.

The conferences, sessions and congresses held in the last years by various international democratic organizations, and especially the recent ones, go to show that open polemic leads to undermining the influence and prestige enjoyed by the Communists, by the socialist countries in these organizations, leads to weakening the unity and the fighting power of the international working-class and democratic organizations.

We note with regret that in the materials of some communist and workers' parties the fraternal parties are advised to sharpen the public polemic —which causes tension in relations, intensifying the danger of a split.

The Communist Party of the Soviet Union and the Communist Party of China have, owing to their prestige, a particular responsibility and role in re-establishing the unity of the communist movement. We address an appeal to all the fraternal parties and above all to the two big parties, the Communist Party of the Soviet Union and the Communist Party of China: let all of us unite to bar the road of a split, to safeguard the unity and cohesion of the countries of the socialist camp, of the world communist and working-class movement!

The first and most important step, at the present moment, is the immediate termination, under all forms, of the public polemic between the communist and workers' parties. . . .

If a complete cessation of the open polemic cannot be achieved, differences of opinion should be discussed in a principled, objective manner. Invectives and offensive appraisals, reciprocal charges, the ascribing of certain intentions, the distortion and mystification of the stands taken by other parties, cannot be taken for convincing arguments, helping to solve the issues.

The Rumanian Workers' Party deems it necessary that immediate consultations should be started between the Communist Party of the Soviet Union, the Communist Party of China and the other fraternal parties with a view to setting up a Commission consisting of representatives of a number of parties; this Commission should proceed to preparing a Conference of representatives of the communist and workers' parties.

Such a Conference should be organized only on the basis of the participation of all communist and workers' parties and should be convened only after having been thoroughly prepared.

The C.C. of the Rumanian Workers' Party considers that a Conference with the participation of only part of the communist and workers' parties would run counter to the cause of unity, and would lead to an aggravation of the situation, to the isolation of some of the fraternal parties, to the establishing of a split in the world communist and working-class movement. . . .

The C.C. of the Rumanian Workers' Party reiterates its conviction that above any divergencies stands what is common to all the communist and workers' parties; everything that is essential unites them and is infinitely stronger than any difference of opinion. We are united in the common goals of achieving working-class power, of the victory of socialism and communism throughout the world. We are united in the common struggle against imperialism, for the vital interests and democratic rights of the people at large, against colonialism in all its forms, for the national liberation of the peoples; we are united in the common goal of establishing a lasting world peace, as vital task of the whole of mankind. We are united by proletarian internationalism and internationalist class solidarity, by our historic responsibility before the international proletariat and the working people everywhere; we are united by our common ideology, the Marxist-Leninist teaching.

These bonds unite the communist and workers' parties in a great family of fraternal parties, they form the unshakable foundation of the cohesion of the world communist and working-class movement and furnish the objective factors for a comradely solution of any issues among our parties.   [ ]

THE ANTI-SOVIET POLICY OF COMMUNIST CHINA[1]
Pravda *Editorial, February 16, 1967*

During the past half century our party and our people have more than once had to withstand fierce attacks by hostile forces against the first socialist state in the history of mankind. If, however, we omit the periods of war, the periods of direct armed aggression against the Soviet Union, it can be said that never before has such a fierce campaign been waged against it as the one launched by the present leaders of China. . . .

In their shameless violations of the existing standards and customs of international law the Chinese authorities go to lengths which even the most reactionary of imperialist governments have rarely permitted themselves. . . .

What are the organisers of the campaign of hatred against the Soviet Union trying to achieve?

The facts show that the persons who are today directing the policy of China, are setting themselves the goal not only of bringing up the Chinese

---

[1] Reprinted with permission from "The Anti-Soviet Policy of Mao Tse-tung and His Group," *Soviet News*, No. 5370 (February 17, 1967), pp. 93–96.

people in a spirit of enmity towards the U.S.S.R. but of worsening Soviet-Chinese relations to the limit, and, in the last analysis, bringing those relations to the point of a complete break. . . .

Another question arises in this connection: Why does the Mao Tse-tung group need this worsening of the position and what goals is it pursuing? The answer to this question should be sought in the entire nationalistic, great-power policy of the present Chinese leadership. . . .

Nor can there be any doubt either about the fact that one of the direct reasons for the anti-Soviet policy and the anti-Soviet propaganda of the present Chinese leadership is a desire to divert the attention of the Chinese people from the privations and difficulties they are experiencing and from the many mistakes and failures in the domestic and foreign policy of China. Here we are actually confronted with the old and hackneyed method employed by all unprincipled politicians when facing bankruptcy. . . .

It was by no means accidental that they fired their first shots in the political war against the Soviet state and the C.P.S.U. shortly after the failure of the ill-starred policy of the "Great Leap" and the "people's communes." As the scale of the setbacks in domestic policy and the failure of the line in the foreign policy pursued by the C.P.C. leadership, which led the country to isolation, became increasingly clear, the intensity of the anti-Soviet campaign grew more and more. . . .

In an atmosphere of tense struggle inside the party and among the people, Mao Tse-tung's group needed this slander precisely in the interests of the power struggle. Mao Tse-tung simply could not have remained in power without such slander, because the Soviet Union's successes in building communism and the successes in building socialism in other countries expose his apostasy and the bankruptcy of his political line. . . .

The entire practice of the C.P.S.U. and the other Communist Parties which are consistently developing Leninist standards in inner-party life, strengthening the principles of collective leadership and strictly adhering to democratic principles in the activities of all party organisations from top to bottom, naturally creates a danger to Mao Tse-tung and his power, for Mao Tse-tung's group has long been attacking its own party. The most elementary standards and principles of inner party life—the elective nature of party bodies, the responsibility of leaders to the party and party organisations, publicity in the discussion of the party line, etc.—have been trampled underfoot in China. The cult of the personality of Mao Tse-tung has reached absurd lengths and has become actual idolatry. . . .

The anti-Soviet campaign of the Chinese leaders is being waged in the most outrageous ways, with real hooliganism.

However, the fact that it apparently assumes the character of an offensive should not deceive anyone. In reality, the actions of Mao Tse-tung's group are motivated not by their strength but by their weakness, by their fear of their own party and their own people. The most recent events show that the

Peking leaders have sufficient grounds for that fear. The "cultural revolution" has brought to light the great degree of dissatisfaction that exists among the workers, peasants and intellectuals—dissatisfaction which has spread even to the army and the youth on whom Mao Tse-tung's group is gambling. The events which began under the banner of the "cultural revolution" have actually developed into a fierce struggle by Mao Tse-tung and his followers to retain power. Their policy shows that for the sake of power they are ready to sacrifice everything—the interests of socialism, the interests of their people and the interests of the revolution. . . .

The main thing is, however, that already today Mao Tse-tung and his entourage, by their policy, are rendering invaluable services to the imperialists. This group has actually replaced the struggle against imperialism by a struggle against the Soviet Union and the other socialist countries, and against the communist movement. It is thereby weakening the front of the anti-imperialist forces and worsening the entire political situation in Asia. All this is, in the first place, a stab in the back for the heroic Vietnamese people in their struggle against the American aggressors.

Imperialist circles fully approve of this line of Mao Tse-tung's group. The *Washington Post* has said that officials in Washington believe that Mao is serving American interests and they are therefore even thinking of cultivating Maoism as a means of bringing pressure to bear on Moscow. The magazine *United States News and World Report* has directly stated in this connection that the United States is gambling on Mao and that American officials tend to prefer a victory for Mao Tse-tung in his struggle to destroy more moderate elements, because that would mean more trouble for Soviet Russia.

Such is the reaction of imperialist circles to Mao Tse-tung's policy, which is advertised in Peking propaganda as the very latest thing in "revolutionariness." Praise of this kind from the class enemy is yet another proof of the extent to which the domestic and foreign policy of Mao Tse-tung and his group is contrary to the interests of socialism, to the interests of the revolution, and plays into the hands of imperialism, and in the first place, United States imperialism. . . .

Having replaced the struggle against imperialism with a struggle against the Soviet Union, against the whole socialist community, and against the international communist and liberation movements, Mao Tse-tung's group is doing considerable harm to the cause of world socialism, including harm to the Chinese people and the cause of building socialism in China. The adventurist anti-Leninist policy of this group has in store for the Chinese people only a further worsening of economic difficulties, a lowering of living standards, a deterioration in the international situation and the prospect of China becoming completely isolated from the socialist community.   [ ]

Part IV

*

The Western Hemisphere

··{*16*}·· *Domestic Developments in the United States*

THE HISTORY OF GEORGE CATLETT MARSHALL[1]
Speech Delivered by Senator Joseph McCarthy before the Senate on June 14, 1951

[ ]
How can we account for our present situation unless we believe that men high in this Government are concerting to deliver us to disaster? This must be the product of a great conspiracy, a conspiracy on a scale so immense as to dwarf any previous such venture in the history of man. A conspiracy of infamy so black that, when it is finally exposed, its principals shall be forever deserving of the maledictions of all honest men.

Who constitutes the highest circles of this conspiracy? About that we cannot be sure. We are convinced that Dean Acheson, who steadfastly serves the interests of nations other than his own, the friend of Alger Hiss, who supported him in his hour of retribution, who contributed to his defense fund, must be high on the roster. The President? He is their captive. I have wondered, as have you, why he did not dispense with so great a liability as Acheson to his own and his party's interests. It is now clear to me. In the relationship of master and man, did you ever hear of man firing master? Truman is a satisfactory front. He is only dimly aware of what is going on.

I do not believe that Mr. Truman is a conscious party to the great conspiracy, although it is being conducted in his name. I believe that if Mr. Truman had the ability to associate good Americans around him, he would have behaved as a good American in this most dire of all our crises.

It is when we return to an examination of General Marshall's record since the spring of 1942 that we approach an explanation of the carefully planned retreat from victory. Let us again review the Marshall record, as I have disclosed it from all the sources available and all of them friendly. This

---

[1] Reprinted from *The Congressional Record: Proceedings and Debates of the 82nd Congress, First Session*, Volume 97, Part 5 (May 28, 1951–June 27, 1951), pp. 6556–6603.

166

grim and solitary man it was who, early in World War II, determined to put his impress upon our global strategy, political and military.

It was Marshall who, amid the din for a "second front now" from every voice of Soviet inspiration, sought to compel the British to invade across the Channel in the fall of 1942 upon penalty of our quitting the war in Europe.

It was Marshall who, after North Africa had been secured, took the strategic direction of the war out of Roosevelt's hands and who fought the British desire, shared by Mark Clark, to advance from Italy into the eastern plains of Europe ahead of the Russians.

It was a Marshall-sponsored memorandum, advising appeasement of Russia in Europe and the enticement of Russia into the far-eastern war, circulated at Quebec, which foreshadowed our whole course at Tehran, at Yalta, and until now in the Far East.

It was Marshall who, at Tehran, made common cause with Stalin on the strategy of the war in Europe and marched side by side with him thereafter.

It was Marshall who enjoined his chief of military mission in Moscow under no circumstances to "irritate" the Russians by asking them questions about their forces, their weapons, and their plans, while at the same time opening our schools, factories, and gradually our secrets to them in this count.

It was Marshall who, as Hanson Baldwin asserts, himself referring only to the "military authorities," prevented us having a corridor to Berlin. So it was with the capture and occupation of Berlin and Prague ahead of the Russians.

It was Marshall who sent Deane to Moscow to collaborate with Harriman in drafting the terms of the wholly unnecessary bribe paid to Stalin at Yalta. It was Marshall, with Hiss at his elbow and doing the physical drafting of agreements at Yalta, who ignored the contrary advice of his senior, Admiral Leahy, and of MacArthur and Nimitz in regard to the folly of a major land invasion of Japan; who submitted intelligence reports which suppressed more truthful estimates in order to support his argument, and who finally induced Roosevelt to bring Russia into the Japanese war with a bribe that reinstated Russia in its pre-1904 imperialistic position in Manchuria—an act which, in effect, signed the death warrant of the Republic of China.

It was Marshall, with Acheson and Vincent eagerly assisting, who created the China policy which, destroying China, robbed us of a great and friendly ally, a buffer against the Soviet imperialism with which we are now at war.

It was Marshall who, after long conferences with Acheson and Vincent, went to China to execute the criminal folly of the disastrous Marshall mission.

It was Marshall who, upon returning from a diplomatic defeat for the United States at Moscow, besought the reinstatement of forty millions in lend-lease for Russia.

It was Marshall who, for 2 years suppressed General Wedemeyer's report, which is a direct and comprehensive repudiation of the Marshall policy.

It was Marshall who, disregarding Wedemeyer's advices on the urgent need for military supplies, the likelihood of China's defeat without ammunition and equipment, and our "moral obligation" to furnish them, proposed instead a relief bill bare of military support.

It was the State Department under Marshall, with the wholehearted support of Michael Lee and Remington in the Commerce Department, that sabotaged the $125,000,000 military-aid bill to China in 1948.

It was Marshall who fixed the dividing line for Korea along the thirty-eighth parallel, a line historically chosen by Russia to mark its sphere of interest in Korea.

It is Marshall's strategy for Korea which has turned that war into a pointless slaughter, reversing the dictum of Von Clausewitz and every military theorist since him that the object of a war is not merely to kill but to impose your will on the enemy.

It is Marshall-Acheson strategy for Europe to build the defense of Europe solely around the Atlantic Pact nations, excluding the two great wells of anti-Communist manpower in Western Germany and Spain and spurning the organized armies of Greece and Turkey—another case of following the Lattimore advice of "let them fall but don't let it appear that we pushed them."

It is Marshall who, advocating timidity as a policy so as not to annoy the forces of Soviet imperialism in Asia, had admittedly put a brake on the preparations to fight, rationalizing his reluctance on the ground that the people are fickle and if war does not come, will hold him to account for excessive zeal.

What can be made of this unbroken series of decisions and acts contributing to the strategy of defeat? They cannot be attributed to incompetence. If Marshall were merely stupid, the laws of probability would dictate that part of his decisions would serve this country's interest. If Marshall is innocent of guilty intention, how could he be trusted to guide the defense of this country further? We have declined so precipitously in relation to the Soviet Union in the last 6 years. How much swifter may be our fall into disaster with Marshall at the helm? Where will all this stop? That is not a rhetorical question: Ours is not a rhetorical danger. Where next will Marshall carry us? It is useless to suppose that his nominal superior will ask him to resign. He cannot even dispense with Acheson.

What is the objective of the great conspiracy? I think it is clear from what has occurred and is now occurring: to diminish the United States in world affairs, to weaken us militarily, to confuse our spirit with talk of surrender in the Far East and to impair our will to resist evil. To what end? To the end that we shall be contained, frustrated and finally fall victim to Soviet intrigue from within and Russian military might from without. Is that farfetched? There have been many examples in history of rich and powerful states which have been corrupted from within, enfeebled and deceived until they were unable to resist aggression. . . .

It is the great crime of the Truman administration that it has refused to undertake the job of ferreting the enemy from its ranks. I once puzzled over that refusal. The President, I said, is a loyal American; why does he not lead in this enterprise? I think that I know why he does not. The President is not master in his own house. Those who are master there not only have a desire to protect the sappers and miners—they could not do otherwise. They themselves are not free. They belong to a larger conspiracy, the world-wide web of which has been spun from Moscow. It was Moscow, for example, which decreed that the United States should execute its loyal friend, the Republic of China. The executioners were that well-identified group headed by Acheson and George Catlett Marshall.

How, if they would, can they break these ties, how return to simple allegiance to their native land? Can men sullied by their long and dreadful record afford us leadership in the world struggle with the enemy? How can a man whose every important act for years had contributed to the prosperity of the enemy reverse himself? The reasons for his past actions are immaterial. Regardless of why he has done what he did, he has done it and the momentum of that course bears him onward. . . .

The time has come to halt this tepid, milk-and-water acquiescence which a discredited administration, ruled by disloyalty, sends down to us. The American may belong to an old culture, he may be beset by enemies here and abroad, he may be distracted by the many words of counsel that assail him by day and night, but he is nobody's fool. The time has come for us to realize that the people who sent us here expect more than time-serving from us. The American who has never known defeat in war, does not expect to be again sold down the river in Asia. He does not want that kind of betrayal. He has had betrayal enough. He has never failed to fight for his liberties since George Washington rode to Boston in 1775 to put himself at the head of a band of rebels unversed in war. He is fighting tonight, fighting gloriously in a war on a distant American frontier made inglorious by the men he can no longer trust at the head of our affairs.

The America that I know, and that other Senators know, this vast and teeming and beautiful land, this hopeful society where the poor share the table of the rich as never before in history, where men of all colors, of all faiths, are brothers as never before in history, where great deeds have been done and great deeds are yet to do, that America deserves to be led not to humiliation or defeat, but to victory.

The Congress of the United States is the people's last hope, a free and open forum of the people's representatives. We felt the pulse of the people's response to the return of MacArthur. We know what it meant. The people, no longer trusting their executive, turn to us, asking that we reassert the constitutional prerogative of the Congress to declare the policy for the United States.

The time has come to reassert that prerogative, to oversee the conduct of this war, to declare that this body must have the final word on the disposition of Formosa and Korea. They fell from the grasp of the Japanese empire through our military endeavors, pursuant to a declaration of war made by the Congress of the United States on December 8, 1941. If the Senate speaks, as is its right, the disposal of Korea and Formosa can be made only by a treaty which must be ratified by this body. Should the administration dare to defy such a declaration, the Congress has abundant recourses which I need not spell out.

PILGRIMAGE TO NONVIOLENCE[1]
Martin Luther King, Jr.

During the Christmas holidays of 1949 I decided to spend my spare time reading Karl Marx to try to understand the appeal of communism for many people. For the first time I carefully scrutinized *Das Kapital* and *The Communist Manifesto*. I also read some interpretive works on the thinking of Marx and Lenin. In reading such Communist writings I drew certain conclusions that have remained with me as convictions to this day. First I rejected their materialistic interpretation of history. Communism, avowedly secularistic and materialistic, has no place for God. This I could never accept, for as a Christian I believe that there is a creative personal power in this universe who is the ground and essence of all reality—a power that cannot be explained in materialistic terms. History is ultimately guided by spirit, not matter. Second, I strongly disagreed with communism's ethical relativism. Since for the Communist there is no divine government, no absolute moral order, there are no fixed, immutable principles; consequently almost anything—force, violence, murder, lying—is a justifiable means to the "millennial" end. This type of relativism was abhorrent to me. Constructive ends can never give absolute moral justification to destructive means, because in the final analysis the end is preëxistent in the mean. Third, I opposed communism's political totalitarianism. In communism the individual ends up in subjection to the state. True, the Marxist would argue that the state is an "interim" reality which is to be eliminated when the classless society emerges; but the state is the end while it lasts, and man only a means to that end. And if any man's so-called rights or liberties stand in the way of that end, they are simply swept aside. His liberties of expression, his freedom to vote, his freedom to listen to what news he likes or to choose his books are all restricted. Man becomes hardly more, in communism, than a depersonalized cog in the turning wheel of the state.

---

[1] From *Stride toward Freedom* by Martin Luther King, Jr., copyright © 1958 by Martin Luther King, Jr., Harper & Brothers, Inc. Reprinted with the permission of Harper & Row, Publishers, Inc., New York, pp. 92–101.

This deprecation of individual freedom was objectionable to me. I am convinced now, as I was then, that man is an end because he is a child of God. Man is not made for the state; the state is made for man. To deprive man of freedom is to relegate him to the status of a thing, rather than elevate him to the status of a person. Man must never be treated as a means to the end of the state, but always as an end within himself. . . .

My reading of Marx also convinced me that truth is found neither in Marxism nor in traditional capitalism. Each represents a partial truth. Historically capitalism failed to see the truth in collective enterprise and Marxism failed to see the truth in individual enterprise. Nineteenth-century capitalism failed to see that life is social and Marxism failed and still fails to see that life is individual and personal. The Kingdom of God is neither the thesis of individual enterprise nor the antithesis of collective enterprise, but a synthesis which reconciles the truths of both. . . .

During this period I had about despaired of the power of love in solving social problems. Perhaps my faith in love was temporarily shaken by the philosophy of Nietzsche. I had been reading parts of *The Genealogy of Morals* and the whole of *The Will to Power*. Nietzsche's glorification of power—in his theory all life expressed the will to power—was an outgrowth of his contempt for ordinary morals. He attacked the whole of the Hebraic-Christian morality—with its virtues of piety and humility, its other-worldliness and its attitude toward suffering—as the glorification of weakness, as making virtues out of necessity and impotence. He looked to the development of a superman who would surpass man as man surpassed the ape.

Then one Sunday afternoon I traveled to Philadelphia to hear a sermon by Dr. Mordecai Johnson, president of Howard University. He was there to preach for the Fellowship House of Philadelphia. Dr. Johnson had just returned from a trip to India, and, to my great interest, he spoke of the life and teachings of Mahatma Gandhi. His message was so profound and electrifying that I left the meeting and bought a half-dozen books on Gandhi's life and works.

Like most people, I had heard of Gandhi, but I had never studied him seriously. As I read I became deeply fascinated by his campaigns of nonviolent resistance. I was particularly moved by the Salt March to the Sea and his numerous fasts. The whole concept of "Satyagraha" (*Satya* is truth which equals love, and *agraha* is force; "Satyagraha," therefore, means truth-force or love force) was profoundly significant to me. As I delved deeper into the philosophy of Gandhi my skepticism concerning the power of love gradually diminished, and I came to see for the first time its potency in the area of social reform. Prior to reading Gandhi, I had about concluded that the ethics of Jesus were only effective in individual relationship. The "turn the other cheek" philosophy and the "love your enemies" philosophy were only valid, I felt, when individuals were in conflict with other individuals; when racial groups and nations were in conflict a more realistic approach seemed necessary. But after reading Gandhi, I saw how utterly mistaken I was.

Gandhi was probably the first person in history to lift the love ethic of Jesus above mere interaction between individuals to a powerful and effective social force on a large scale. Love for Gandhi was a potent instrument for social and collective transformation. It was in this Gandhian emphasis on love and nonviolence that I discovered the method for social reform that I had been seeking for so many months. . . .

But my intellectual odyssey to nonviolence did not end here. During my last year in theological school, I began to read the works of Reinhold Niebuhr. The prophetic and realistic elements in Niebuhr's passionate style and profound thought were appealing to me, and I became so enamored of his social ethics that I almost fell into the trap of accepting uncritically everything he wrote.

About this time I read Niebuhr's critique of the pacifist position. Niebuhr had himself once been a member of the pacifist ranks. For several years, he had been national chairman of the Fellowship of Reconciliation. His break with pacifism came in the early thirties, and the first full statement of his criticism of pacifism was in *Moral Man and Immoral Society*. . . .

At first, Niebuhr's critique of pacifism left me in a state of confusion. As I continued to read, however, I came to see more and more the shortcomings of his position. For instance, many of his statements revealed that he interpreted pacifism as a sort of passive nonresistance to evil expressing naïve trust in the power of love. But this was a serious distortion. My study of Gandhi convinced me that true pacifism is not nonresistance to evil, but nonviolent resistance to evil. Between the two positions, there is a world of difference. Gandhi resisted evil with as much vigor and power as the violent resister, but he resisted with love instead of hate. True pacifism is not unrealistic submission to evil power, as Niebuhr contends. It is rather a courageous confrontation of evil by the power of love, in the faith that it is better to be the recipient of violence than the inflicter of it, since the latter only multiplies the existence of violence and bitterness in the universe, while the former may develop a sense of shame in the opponent, and thereby bring about a transformation and change of heart.

In spite of the fact that I found many things to be desired in Niebuhr's philosophy, there were several points at which he constructively influenced my thinking. Niebuhr's great contribution to contemporary theology is that he has refuted the false optimism characteristic of a great segment of Protestant liberalism, without falling into the anti-rationalism of the continental theologian Karl Barth, or the semi-fundamentalism of other dialectical theologians. Moreover, Niebuhr has extraordinary insight into human nature, especially the behavior of nations and social groups. He is keenly aware of the complexity of human motives and of the relation between morality and power. His theology is a persistent reminder of the reality of sin on every level of man's existence. These elements in Niebuhr's thinking helped me to recognize the illusions of a superficial optimism concerning human nature and the dangers of a false idealism. While I still believed in man's potential for good, Niebuhr made me realize his potential for evil as well. Moreover, Niebuhr helped me to recognize the complexity of man's social involvement and the glaring reality of collective evil.

. . . After reading Niebuhr, I tried to arrive at a realistic pacifism. In other words, I came to see the pacifist position not as sinless but as the lesser evil in the circumstances. I felt then, and I feel now, that the pacifist would have a greater appeal if he did not claim to be free from the moral dilemmas that the Christian nonpacifist confronts.

The next stage of my intellectual pilgrimage to nonviolence came during my doctoral studies at Boston University. Here I had the opportunity to talk to many exponents of nonviolence, both students and visitors to the campus. Boston University School of Theology, under the influence of Dean Walter Muelder and Professor Allen Knight Chalmers, had a deep sympathy for pacifism. Both Dean Muelder and Dr. Chalmers had a passion for social justice that stemmed, not from a superficial optimism, but from a deep faith in the possibilities of human beings when they allowed themselves to become co-workers with God. It was at Boston University that I came to see that Niebuhr had overemphasized the corruption of human nature. His pessimism concerning human nature was not balanced by an optimism concerning divine nature. He was so involved in diagnosing man's sickness of sin that he overlooked the cure of grace. . . .

In 1954 I ended my formal training with all of these relatively divergent intellectual forces converging into a positive social philosophy. One of the main tenets of this philosophy was the conviction that nonviolent resistance was one of the most potent weapons available to oppressed people in their quest for social justice. At this time, however, I had merely an intellectual understanding and appreciation of the position, with no firm determination to organize it in a socially effective situation.

When I went to Montgomery as a pastor, I had not the slightest idea that I would later become involved in a crisis in which nonviolent resistance would be applicable. I neither started the protest nor suggested it. I simply responded to the call of the people for a spokesman. When the protest began, my mind, consciously or unconsciously, was driven back to the Sermon on the Mount, with its sublime teachings on love, and the Gandhian method of nonviolent resistance. As the days unfolded, I came to see the power of nonviolence more and more. Living through the actual experience of the protest, nonviolence became more than a method to which I gave intellectual assent; it became a commitment to a way of life. Many of the things that I had not cleared up intellectually concerning nonviolence were now solved in the sphere of practical action.

THE INAUGURAL ADDRESS OF PRESIDENT KENNEDY[1]
January 20, 1961

We observe today not a victory of party but a celebration of freedom—symbolizing an end as well as a beginning—signifying renewal as well as change. For I have sworn before you and Almighty God the same solemn oath our forebears prescribed nearly a century and three quarters ago.

The world is very different now. For man holds in his mortal hands the power to abolish all forms of human poverty and all forms of human life. And yet the same revolutionary beliefs for which our forebears fought are still at issue around the globe—the belief that the rights of man come not from the generosity of the state but from the hand of God.

We dare not forget today that we are the heirs of that first revolution. Let the word go forth from this time and place, to friend and foe alike, that the torch has been passed to a new generation of Americans—born in this century, tempered by war, disciplined by a hard and bitter peace, proud of our ancient heritage—and unwilling to witness or permit the slow undoing of those human rights to which this Nation has always been committed, and to which we are committed today at home and around the world.

Let every nation know, whether it wishes us well or ill, that we shall pay any price, bear any burden, meet any hardship, support any friend, oppose any foe to assure the survival and the success of liberty.

This much we pledge—and more.

To those old allies whose cultural and spiritual origins we share, we pledge the loyalty of faithful friends. United, there is little we cannot do in a host of cooperative ventures. Divided, there is little we can do—for we dare not meet a powerful challenge at odds and split asunder.

To those new states whom we welcome to the ranks of the free, we pledge our word that one form of colonial control shall not have passed away merely to be replaced by a far more iron tyranny. We shall not always expect to find them supporting our view. But we shall always hope to find them strongly supporting their own freedom—and to remember that, in the past, those who foolishly sought power by riding the back of the tiger ended up inside.

To those people in the huts and villages of half the globe struggling to break the bonds of mass misery, we pledge our best efforts to help them help themselves, for whatever period is required—not because the Communists may be doing it, not because we seek their votes, but because it is right. If a free society cannot help the many who are poor, it cannot save the few who are rich.

To our sister republics south of our border, we offer a special pledge—to

---

[1] Reprinted from *The Department of State Bulletin* (February 6, 1961), pp. 175–176.

convert our good words into good deeds—in a new alliance for progress—to assist free men and free governments in casting off the chains of poverty. But this peaceful revolution of hope cannot become the prey of hostile powers. Let all our neighbors know that we shall join with them to oppose aggression or subversion anywhere in the Americas. And let every other power know that this hemisphere intends to remain the master of its own house.

To that world assembly of sovereign states, the United Nations, our last best hope in an age where the instruments of war have far outpaced the instruments of peace, we renew our pledge of support—to prevent it from becoming merely a forum for invective—to strengthen its shield of the new and the weak—and to enlarge the area in which its writ may run.

Finally, to those nations who would make themselves our adversary, we offer not a pledge but a request: that both sides begin anew the quest for peace, before the dark powers of destruction unleashed by science engulf all humanity in planned or accidental self-destruction.

We dare not tempt them with weakness. For only when our arms are sufficient beyond doubt can we be certain beyond doubt that they will never be employed.

But neither can two great and powerful groups of nations take comfort from our present course—both sides overburdened by the cost of modern weapons, both rightly alarmed by the steady spread of the deadly atom, yet both racing to alter that uncertain balance of terror that stays the hand of mankind's final war.

So let us begin anew—remembering on both sides that civility is not a sign of weakness, and sincerity is always subject to proof. Let us never negotiate out of fear. But let us never fear to negotiate.

Let both sides explore what problems unite us instead of belaboring those problems which divide us.

Let both sides, for the first time, formulate serious and precise proposals for the inspection and control of arms—and bring the absolute power to destroy other nations under the absolute control of all nations.

Let both sides seek to invoke the wonders of science instead of its terrors. Together let us explore the stars, conquer the deserts, eradicate disease, tap the ocean depths, and encourage the arts and commerce.

Let both sides unite to heed in all corners of the earth the command of Isaiah—to "undo the heavy burdens . . . [and] let the oppressed go free."

And if a beachhead of cooperation may push back the jungle of suspicion, let both sides join in creating a new endeavor, not a new balance of power, but a new world of law, where the strong are just and the weak secure and the peace preserved.

All this will not be finished in the first one hundred days. Nor will it be finished in the first one thousand days, nor in the life of this administration, nor even perhaps in our lifetime on this planet. But let us begin.

In your hands, my fellow citizens, more than mine, will rest the final success or failure of our course. Since this country was founded, each generation of Americans has been summoned to give testimony to its national loyalty. The graves of young Americans who answered the call to service surround the globe.

Now the trumpet summons us again—not as a call to bear arms, though arms we need—not as a call to battle, though embattled we are—but as a call to bear the burden of a long twilight struggle year in and year out, "rejoicing in hope, patient in tribulation"—a struggle against the common enemies of man: tyranny, poverty, disease, and war itself.

Can we forge against these enemies a grand and global alliance, North and South, East and West that can assure a more fruitful life for all mankind? Will you join in that historic effort?

In the long history of the world, only a few generations have been granted the role of defending freedom in its hour of maximum danger. I do not shrink from this responsibility—I welcome it. I do not believe that any of us would exchange places with any other people or any other generation. The energy, the faith, the devotion which we bring to this endeavor will light our country and all who serve it—and the glow from that fire can truly light the world.

And so, my fellow Americans: ask not what your country can do for you —ask what you can do for your country.

My fellow citizens of the world: ask not what America will do for you, but what together we can do for the freedom of man.

Finally, whether you are citizens of America or citizens of the world, ask of us here the same high standards of strength and sacrifice which we ask of you. With a good conscience our only sure reward, with history the final judge of our deeds let us go forth to lead the land we love, asking His blessing and His help, but knowing that here on earth God's work must truly be our own.

PROPOSAL FOR A NATIONWIDE WAR ON THE SOURCES OF POVERTY[1]
Lyndon B. Johnson's Special Message to Congress, March 16, 1964

[ ]

Because it is right, because it is wise, and because, for the first time in our history, it is possible to conquer poverty, I submit, for the consideration of the Congress and the country, the Economic Opportunity Act of 1964.

The Act does not merely expand old programs or improve what is already being done.

It charts a new course.

It strikes at the causes, not just the consequences of poverty.

---

[1] Reprinted from *Public Papers of U.S. Presidents, Lyndon B. Johnson, 1963–1964* (Washington: G.P.O., 1965), I, pp. 375–380.

It can be a milestone in our one-hundred eighty year search for a better life for our people.

This Act provides five basic opportunities.

It will give almost half a million underprivileged young Americans the opportunity to develop skills, continue education, and find useful work.

It will give every American community the opportunity to develop a comprehensive plan to fight its own poverty—and help them to carry out their plans.

It will give dedicated Americans the opportunity to enlist as volunteers in the war against poverty.

It will give many workers and farmers the opportunity to break through particular barriers which bar their escape from poverty.

It will give the entire nation the opportunity for a concerted attack on poverty through the establishment, under my direction, of the Office of Economic Opportunity, a national headquarters for the war against poverty.

This is how we propose to create these opportunities.

First we will give high priority to helping young Americans who lack skills, who have not completed their education or who cannot complete it because they are too poor. . . .

I therefore recommend the creation of a Job Corps, a Work-Training Program, and a Work Study Program.

A new national Job Corps will build toward an enlistment of 100,000 young men. They will be drawn from those whose background, health and education make them least fit for useful work. . . .

Half of these young men will work, in the first year, on special conservation projects to give them education, useful work experience and to enrich the natural resources of the country.

Half of these young men will receive, in the first year, a blend of training, basic education and work experience in Job Training Centers. . . .

A new national Work-Training Program operated by the Department of Labor will provide work and training for 200,000 American men and women between the ages of 16 and 21. This will be developed through state and local governments and non-profit agencies. . . .

A new national Work-Study Program operated by the Department of Health, Education, and Welfare will provide federal funds for part-time jobs for 140,000 young Americans who do not go to college because they cannot afford it.

There is no more senseless waste than the waste of the brainpower and skill of those who are kept from college by economic circumstance. Under this program they will, in a great American tradition, be able to work their way through school. . . .

Second, through a new Community Action program we intend to strike at poverty at its source—in the streets of our cities and on the farms of our countryside among the very young and the impoverished old.

This program asks men and women throughout the country to prepare long-range plans for the attack on poverty in their own local communities. . . .

Third, I ask for the authority to recruit and train skilled volunteers for the war against poverty.

Thousands of Americans have volunteered to serve the needs of other lands.

Thousands more want the chance to serve the needs of their own land.

They should have that chance.

Among older people who have retired, as well as among the young, among women as well as men, there are many Americans who are ready to enlist in our war against poverty.

They have skills and dedication. They are badly needed. . . .

Fourth, we intend to create new opportunities for certain hard-hit groups to break out of the pattern of poverty.

Through a new program of loans and guarantees we can provide incentives to those who will employ the unemployed.

Through programs of work and retraining for unemployed fathers and mothers we can help them support their families in dignity while preparing themselves for new work.

Through funds to purchase needed land, organize cooperatives, and create new and adequate family farms we can help those whose life on the land has been a struggle without hope.

Fifth, I do not intend that the war against poverty become a series of uncoordinated and unrelated efforts—that it perish for lack of leadership and direction.

Therefore this bill creates, in the Executive Office of the President, a new Office of Economic Opportunity. Its Director will be my personal Chief of Staff for the War against poverty. I intend to appoint Sargent Shriver to this post. . . .

What you are being asked to consider is not a simple or an easy program. But poverty is not a simple or an easy enemy.

It cannot be driven from the land by a single attack on a single front. Were this so we would have conquered poverty long ago.

Nor can it be conquered by government alone. . . .

Today, for the first time in our history, we have the power to strike away the barriers to full participation in our society. Having the power, we have the duty. . . .

We are fully aware that this program will not eliminate all the poverty in America in a few months or a few years. Poverty is deeply rooted and its causes are many.

But this program will show the way to new opportunities for millions of our fellow citizens.

It will provide a lever with which we can begin to open the door to our prosperity for those who have been kept outside.

It will also give us the chance to test our weapons, to try our energy and ideas and imagination for the many battles yet to come. As conditions change, and as experience illuminates our difficulties, we will be prepared to modify our strategy.

And this program is much more than a beginning.

Rather it is a commitment. It is a total commitment by this President, and this Congress, and this nation, to pursue victory over the most ancient of mankind's enemies. [ ]

··{17}·· Latin America

OPERATION PAN AMERICA[1]
Aide Mémoire Sent by the Government of Brazil to Governments of Other American States, August 9, 1958

I. DEFINITION AND OBJECTIVES

The Brazilian Government considers that a clearer definition of the objectives of Operation Pan America is necessary in order that this movement, which has been initiated at the right time and under the best auspices, may not be impaired or lose its impact.

A. *General definition:* Operation Pan America is not an undertaking limited by time, with objectives to be attained in a short period; rather, it is a reorientation of hemispheric policy, intended to place Latin America, by a process of full appraisement, in a position to participate more effectively in the defense of the West, with a growing sense of vitality and a greater development of its capacities. Thus, Operation Pan America is more than a mere program; it is an entire policy.

B. *Strategic political concept:* Operation Pan America must be understood as a corollary of the general strategy of the West, and among its fundamental purposes the following are particularly outstanding: preservation of the democratic system, based on political and religious freedom and on respect for private ownership and free enterprise, and the defense of all areas that concern the security of the free world. Because of its intrinsic, political, economic, social and strategic importance, and because "a threat to the peace in any part of the world is now a threat to the peace of the entire world," it is opportune to re-examine, with a view to strengthening it, the contribution to the resources of the free world that may be made by the nations that are signatories of the Treaty of Rio de Janeiro.

C. *Economic concept:* The more rapid development of Latin America's

---

[1] Reprinted from Council of the Organization of American States, Special Committee to Study the Formulation of New Measures for Economic Cooperation, *Volume I: Report and Documents, First Meeting, Washington, D.C., November 17–December 12, 1958* (Washington, D.C.: 1959), pp. 29–31.

economic strength will result in a growing sense of vitality and will enable it to increase its contribution to the defense of the West.

II. CHARACTERISTICS

A. *Joint multilateral action:* Operation Pan America is conceived as involving the joint action of the twenty-one republics of the Western Hemisphere, the preservation of its strictly multilateral nature being indispensable. Bilateral matters will continue to be handled through the channels normally followed in such cases, without becoming part of the aforesaid Operation.

B. *Struggle for democracy:* Within the framework of Operation Pan America, the struggle for democracy becomes identified with the struggle against stagnation and underdevelopment. The underdevelopment that prevails in this Hemisphere morally and materially involves the cause that we are defending. Underdeveloped areas are open to the penetration of antidemocratic ideology. From many standpoints and in all of its implications, the battle of the West is the battle for development. Materialist ideologies feed upon the poverty and misery that give rise to them in the first place; to combat these factors is the only sure way to combat those ideologies. Where there is poverty, our cause will always be in danger. It is illusory to expect positive action on behalf of a cause embracing such complex factors from peoples whose isolation in the rigors of extreme poverty prevents them from thinking or feeling anything beyond the narrow limits of their urgent needs for survival.

C. *Latin America's participation in world policy:* According to the Brazilian concept, Operation Pan America is a reflection of the need for more active and more vigorous participation and cooperation by the Latin American countries .in international policy, and it reveals these countries' full awareness of their moral, political, and demographic importance. Latin America's contribution may become highly significant in the struggle for a balance of power.

III. WESTERN POSTWAR POLICY

A. *Inter-American political reorientation:* The Brazilian Government believes that the time has come for a revision of inter-American policy, with a view to strengthening hemispheric unity in the face of the increasing common danger. A stronger, more courageous, creative, and dynamic initiative is urgently needed in the Western Hemisphere at this time.

It is imperative that the West become ever more conscious of its mission in the modern world. The principal objective of this mission is to defend and to perfect man's spiritual and moral achievements. Spiritual and moral forces should be the ones to guide and regulate a world expanded and profoundly transformed by technology. This is what is important to the West; this is its own Cause.

B. *Economic reorientation of Pan Americanism:* The reasons for underdevelopment are many and complex. One could not in good faith fix responsibility for Latin America's chronic anemic condition and the consequent organic weakening of Pan Americanism. Although it is understood that efforts toward economic development devolve primarily upon each country individually, it is now understood better than ever before that there must be cooperation on international bases.

IV. THE OPERATION'S COURSE OF ACTION

A. *Advance preparation:* The Brazilian Government wishes to clarify the fact that it was never its intention or plan to hold a conference of American Chiefs of State without the most careful advance preparation. Furthermore, the Brazilian Government is not committed to any rigid plans for carrying out the Operation in question, and it believes that only after a series of contacts and consultations among the countries of our community will it be possible to make a definitive determination of the best methods for achieving the common objective.

B. *Preliminary inquiries:* The Brazilian Government would now be willing to assume responsibility for making diplomatic inquiries with a view to the preparation of a basic agenda and toward ascertaining whether the American governments would agree with the idea of reaching informal understanding and carrying out preliminary negotiations in Washington through the embassies accredited to the Government of the United States.

C. *Initiation of the Operation:* The preparatory work could be done at the diplomatic or technical level, and it is anticipated that the participation by members of the delegations accredited to the Organization of American States would be desirable. These informal understandings would become more clearly defined and be better coordinated if a *Committee of Twenty-one* were created. Brazil does not wish to propose any date, but nonetheless it does state that it would be ready to begin its work in the said committee during the latter part of September.

D. *High-level meeting:* Once the bases for an agreement have been established and significant results obtained that might be looked upon as substantial progress, then the competent organs of the Organization of American States could study the idea of a high-level meeting among the republics of the Hemisphere to approve and to sign that group of resolutions and proclamations that could become the plan of action for achieving Pan American unity; among these would be included, with special emphasis, the preparation of a dynamic and progressive program for the struggle against underdevelopment, and this would be the crowning feature of Operation Pan America.

V. BASIC OBJECTIVES OF THE OPERATION

The following points might be the basic objectives of the Operation:
1. Reaffirmation of the principles of hemispheric solidarity;
2. Recognition of underdevelopment as a problem of common interest;

3. Adaptation of inter-American organs and agencies, if necessary, to the requirements of more dynamic action to carry on the struggle against underdevelopment;
4. Technical assistance for increased productivity;
5. Measures to stabilize the market for basic commodities;
6. Adaptation to present needs and expansion of the resources of international financial institutions;
7. Reaffirmation of private initiative in the struggle against underdevelopment; and
8. Revision by each country, where necessary, of its fiscal and economic policy, for the purpose of assuring means to promote economic development.

PRELIMINARY FORMULATIONS OF THE ALLIANCE FOR PROGRESS[1]
Address by President Kennedy at a White House Reception for Latin American Diplomats and Members of Congress, March 13, 1961

[ ]
We meet together as firm and ancient friends, united by history and experience and by our determination to advance the values of American civilization. For this new world of ours is not merely an accident of geography. Our continents are bound together by a common history—the endless exploration of new frontiers. Our nations are the product of a common struggle—the revolt from colonial rule. And our people share a common heritage—the quest for the dignity and the freedom of man. . . .

As a citizen of the United States let me be the first to admit that we North Americans have not always grasped the significance of this common mission, just as it is also true that many in your own countries have not fully understood the urgency of the need to lift people from poverty and ignorance and despair. But we must turn from these mistakes—from the failures and the misunderstandings of the past—to a future full of peril but bright with hope.

Throughout Latin America—a continent rich in resources and in the spiritual and cultural achievements of its people—millions of men and women suffer the daily degradations of hunger and poverty. They lack decent shelter or protection from disease. Their children are deprived of the education or the jobs which are the gateway to a better life. . . .

If we are to meet a problem so staggering in its dimensions, our approach must itself be equally bold, an approach consistent with the majestic concept of Operation Pan America. Therefore I have called on all the people of the hemisphere to join in a new Alliance for Progress—*alianza para Progreso*—a

---

[1] Reprinted from *The Department of State Bulletin*, XLIV, No. 1136 (April 3, 1961), pp. 471–474.

vast cooperative effort, unparalleled in magnitude and nobility of purpose, to satisfy the basic needs of the American people for homes, work and land, health and schools—*techo, trabajo y tierra, salud y escuela.*

First, I propose that the American Republics begin on a vast new 10-year plan for the Americas, a plan to transform the 1960's into an historic decade of democratic progress. . . .

And if we are successful, if our effort is bold enough and determined enough, then the close of this decade will mark the beginning of a new era in the American experience. The living standards of every American family will be on the rise, basic education will be available to all, hunger will be a forgotten experience, the need for massive outside help will have passed, most nations will have entered a period of self-sustaining growth, and, although there will be still much to do, every American Republic will be the master of its own revolution and its own hope and progress.

Let me stress that only the most determined efforts of the American nations themselves can bring success to this effort. They, and they alone, can mobilize their resources, enlist the energies of their people, and modify their social patterns so that all, and not just a privileged few, share in the fruits of growth. If this effort is made, then outside assistance will give a vital impetus to progress; without it, no amount of help will advance the welfare of the people. . . .

Secondly, I will shortly request a ministerial meeting of the Inter-American Economic and Social Council, a meeting at which we can begin the massive planning effort which will be at the heart of the Alliance for Progress.

For if our alliance is to succeed, each Latin nation must formulate long-range plans for its own development—plans which establish targets and priorities, insure monetary stability, establish the machinery for vital social change, stimulate private activity and initiative, and provide for a maximum national effort. . . .

Third, I have this evening signed a request to the Congress for $500 million as a first step in fulfilling the Act of Bogotá. . . . The money will be used to combat illiteracy, improve the productivity and use of their land, wipe out disease, attack archaic tax and land-tenure structures, provide educational opportunities, and offer a broad range of projects designed to make the benefits of increasing abundance available to all. We will begin to commit these funds as soon as they are appropriated.

Fourth, we must support all economic integration which is a genuine step toward larger markets and greater competitive opportunity. The fragmentation of Latin American economies is a serious barrier to industrial growth. . . .

Fifth, the United States is ready to cooperate in serious, case-by-case examinations of commodity market problems. Frequent violent changes in commodity prices seriously injure the economies of many Latin American countries, draining their resources and stultifying their growth. Together we must find practical methods of bringing an end to this pattern.

Sixth, we will immediately step up our food-for-peace emergency program, help to establish food reserves in areas of recurrent drought, and help provide school lunches for children and offer feed grains for use in rural development. For hungry men and women cannot wait for economic discussions or diplomatic meetings; their need is urgent, and their hunger rests heavily on the conscience of their fellow men.

Seventh, all the people of the hemisphere must be allowed to share in the expanding wonders of science—wonders which have captured man's imagination, challenged the powers of his mind, and given him the tools for rapid progress. I invite Latin American scientists to work with us in new projects in fields such as medicine and agriculture, physics and astronomy, and desalinization, and to help plan for regional research laboratories in these and other fields, and to strengthen cooperation between American universities and laboratories. . . .

Eighth, we must rapidly expand the training of those needed to man the economies of rapidly developing countries. This means expanded technical training programs, for which the Peace Corps, for example, will be available when needed. It also means assistance to Latin American universities, graduate schools, and research institutes.

We welcome proposals in Central America for intimate cooperation in higher education, cooperation which can achieve a regional effort of increased effectiveness and excellence. We are ready to help fill the gap in trained manpower, realizing that our ultimate goal must be a basic education for all who wish to learn.

Ninth, we reaffirm our pledge to come to the defense of any American nation whose independence is endangered. As confidence in the collective security system of the OAS [Organization of American States] spreads, it will be possible to devote to constructive use a major share of those resources now spent on the instruments of war. Even now, as the Government of Chile has said, the time has come to take the first steps toward sensible limitations of arms. And the new generation of military leaders has shown an increasing awareness that armies can not only defend their countries—they can, as we have learned through our own Corps of Engineers, help to build them.

Tenth, we invite our friends in Latin America to contribute to the enrichment of life and culture in the United States. We need teachers of your literature and history and tradition, opportunities for our young people to study in your universities, access to your music, your art, and the thought of your great philosophers. For we know we have much to learn.

In this way you can help bring a fuller spiritual and intellectual life to the people of the United States and contribute to understanding and mutual respect among the nations of the hemisphere.

With steps such as these we propose to complete the revolution of the Americas, to build a hemisphere where all men can hope for a suitable standard of living and all can live out their lives in dignity and in freedom.

To achieve this goal political freedom must accompany material progress.

Our Alliance for Progress is an alliance of free governments—and it must work to eliminate tyranny from a hemisphere in which it has no rightful place. Therefore let us express our special friendship to the people of Cuba and the Dominican Republic—and the hope they will soon rejoin the society of free men, uniting with us in our common effort.

This political freedom must be accompanied by social change. For unless necessary social reforms, including land and tax reform, are freely made, unless we broaden the opportunity of all of our people, unless the great mass of Americans share in increasing prosperity, then our alliance, our revolution, our dream, and our freedom will fail. But we call for social change by free men—change in the spirit of Washington and Jefferson, of Bolvíar and San Martín and Martí—not change which seeks to impose on men tyrannies which we cast out a century and a half ago. Our motto is what it has always been—progress yes, tyranny no—*progreso sí, tiranía no!*

But our greatest challenge comes from within—the task of creating an American civilization where spiritual and cultural values are strengthened by an ever-broadening base of material advance, where, within the rich diversity of its own traditions, each nation is free to follow its own path toward progress.

The completion of our task will, of course, require the efforts of all the governments of our hemisphere. But the efforts of governments alone will never be enough. In the end the people must choose and the people must help themselves.

And so I say to the men and women of the Americas—to the *campesino* in the fields, to the *obrero* in the cities, to the *estudiante* in the schools—prepare your mind and heart for the task ahead, call forth your strength, and let each devote his energies to the betterment of all so that your children and our children in this hemisphere can find an ever richer and a freer life.

Let us once again transform the American Continent into a vast crucible of revolutionary ideas and efforts, a tribute to the power of the creative energies of free men and women, an example to all the world that liberty and progress walk hand in hand. Let us once again awaken our American revolution until it guides the struggles of people everywhere—not with an imperialism of force or fear but the rule of courage and freedom and hope for the future of man.

REPORT ON THE ALLIANCE FOR PROGRESS[1]
PREAMBLE

On October 26, 1962, the First Annual Meeting of the Inter-American Economic and Social Council at the Ministerial Level approved Resolution

---

[1] Reprinted from Alberto Lleras, *Report on the Alliance for Progress* (Washington, D.C.: Organization of American States, June 15, 1963), pp. v–x.

A-8 designed to initiate a study of the inter-American system to determinate whether its present structure is adapted to the needs of the new Alliance for Progress program. The resolution commences by recognizing "that the inter-American system, as presently constituted, was in the main established prior to the Alliance for Progress and, in consequence, may not possess a type of structure permitting of achievement of the objectives of the Charter of Punta del Este in the dynamic and efficient way called for." . . .

Pursuant to this resolution, the Council of the OAS agreed to appoint the former president of Brazil, Mr. Juscelino Kubitschek, and the author of this report to carry out the aforementioned task.

I accepted the commission entrusted to me by the OAS even though I was thereby temporarily interrupting my intention to retire from all public activity, in the national or international fields, and even though my state of health made it inadvisable. I felt obligated particularly to fulfil this honorable commission because, owing to circumstances that it is not pertinent to recall at this time, I was closely associated with all the antecedents that led to the creation of the Alliance for Progress, since its remote origin in Operation Pan America, proposed by President Kubitschek, who has now been designated as my associate in the fulfillment of this task.

It became clear in December of last year that from several sources and for conflicting reasons an offensive was being launched against the new program, which like the Marshall Plan, had been greeted from the beginning with volleys of indignation, distortions, and malicious propaganda by the pro-communist forces throughout the world and particularly in the Latin American countries themselves. President Kennedy alone, in the entire hemisphere, defended the audacious plan to transform the lives of millions of human beings in the face of their own political opposition and the indifference of a major part of those whom it was to serve directly.

The reactionary right wing of the American world, therefore, was and is working against the objectives of Punta del Este. In the United States it was represented by the systematic enemies of all foreign aid, even more exalted now with the apparent initiation of a new program of expenditures; by those who maintain that loans and donations to governments only serve to encourage socialization in Latin America and weaken private enterprise; by the adversaries of the type of social-welfare investments recommended in the Charter of Punta del Este. In Latin America, by the system of the latifundia, which is always alert to any type of agrarian reform, entrenched in the governments and congresses; by a certain native capitalism, which accepts no restrictions upon its action but which defends itself with the same arguments as United States private enterprise, which is actually subject to strict competition and to anti-monopoly regulations; and, in general, by all the present beneficiaries of the social situation that was boldly denounced in the daring document signed in a moment of inspiration and, why not, of anxiety at the meeting in Uruguay.

In the United States Congress the opposing elements of the Alliance had already found an echo and obtained substantial victories, both in reducing the allocations for aid to Latin America and in introducing conditions for investment that were destined to protect United States capital unnecessarily and excessively, thereby succeeding in giving a displeasing aspect to the generous project. Taking advantage of the terms of the Foreign Trade Act, United States business men were already beginning to threaten the governments of Latin America with a suspension of the aid foreseen in the Alliance, if conditions arose that they considered intolerable and, even worse, the citizens themselves were approaching foreign authorities requesting them to intervene in this respect. The danger of a serious corruption of the spirit of the Alliance, its progressive weakening, and the disappointment of the people with it, in addition to the continual risk that it might become a bureaucratic operation, was obvious towards the end of 1962, when the enormous rehabilitation enterprise of Latin America began to be talked of as a new form of imperialism, as a policy on the part of the United States to soothe Latin American discontent, as a gigantic publicity stunt. These fears made it even more compulsory for me to accept the mission entrusted to me by the Council of the OAS, jointly with President Kubitschek, to examine the structure and procedures of the inter-American system to the end that the Alliance be carried out expeditiously and efficiently.

President Kubitschek and I began the study immediately after traveling to Washington, and contacted the organizations and entities that participated directly in the Alliance or that had correlating functions. We were received with the greatest interest and courtesy by the highest authorities of the OAS, members of the Council, the Secretary General, the Assistant Secretaries; the Director of ECLA, who up to that time was the coordinator of the Committee of Nine; by the members of this Committee individually; by the President and other high officials of the International Bank for Reconstruction and Development; by the President and directors of the Inter-American Development Bank; by administrative heads of the Agency for International Development (AID), and by the President of the International Monetary Fund. We also received, in due course, sufficient information from most of these international and national agencies regarding the manner in which their functions having to do with the Alliance were carried out within their respective spheres, together with very important suggestions, some of which are included in this report.

President Kubitschek returned to Brazil and I to Colombia, where we continued to receive documentation and to prepare the conclusions of the report that we would present to the governments. But from the first moment of our interview in Washington we agreed on some points that were to be dealt with in the two projects and that we intended to discuss at a second meeting in Rio de Janeiro.

Some of these concepts were mentioned in our addresses to the Council of the OAS at the time we began our assignment. As for myself, it was clear that our task would have to take the following facts into account:

a. Even though it is possible to visualize an organization different from the present one and, in theory, much more efficient, our mission should limit itself to recommending partial changes that would not affect the Charter of the Organization of American States, or introduce radical changes in the procedures and institutional machinery created in Punta del Este.

b. Any amendment implying a modification of the Charter of the OAS would require an Inter-American Conference, which is the only organ empowered to make such amendments, and the mere process of ratification by the member states would probably involve a longer period than the decade that the Charter of Punta del Este has established for the task of the Alliance.

c. The creation of the Alliance is very recent and any opinion on the efficiency of its organization, which obviously requires time in which to develop fully, would be premature. The agencies called for in the Charter of Punta del Este could not be established at the very beginning, and in most cases there was no planning body in the Latin American countries to undertake the preparation of the programs required.

d. The administrative reorganization of United States agencies devoted to the management of foreign aid signified another initial impediment.

e. The mechanism established in the General Secretariat of the OAS to handle the Alliance should not be abandoned in order to create an agency independent of the OAS and outside the system. The autonomy that is required can be achieved without the need of increasing bureaucracy or creating new agencies, which according to the Charter of the OAS would always be subordinated to the Council and controlled from the technical point of view by the respective organ, namely, the IA-ECOSOC.

f. The opinions of Kubitschek and Lleras may have political value, but they cannot claim to have value in the technical field. The organization that the IA-ECOSOC has been establishing and that the Council of the OAS has approved, as a development of the provisions of the Charter of Punta del Este, may have defects but, in principle, it responds to a system that should not be modified by improvising. The weaknesses of the Alliance for Progress and its consequent slowness or lack of active implementation are due mainly to political elements that it is possible to correct with a minimum of structural changes. It is a mistake to believe that policies can be changed through organization; organization does whatever the governments want it to do. The important change in the position of the United States and Latin America in their collaboration in the economic field took place precisely within the Organization and with the same instruments and elements that had been preventing it until the Punta del Este meeting.

At the meeting in Rio de Janeiro, President Kubitschek had already prepared the basis for a report with whose conclusions, still tentative, Lleras was in agreement even though there were differences of opinion regarding the aim of the Alliance for Progress, as well as some of the procedures and the cause of its faults and deficiencies. Nevertheless, it was possible to eliminate these differences, and it was agreed that a new text prepared by Lleras would attempt to reconcile the two frames of mind.

Then I became ill and was prevented from meeting on time the commitment I had entered into with the OAS; in addition, this illness made it impossible for President Kubitschek and I to coordinate texts. The difficulty of communicating between Rio de Janeiro and Bogotá is unlikely, but we both chose to communicate through the coordinator appointed by the General Secretariat for this purpose, the Assistant Secretary for Cultural, Scientific, and Informational Affairs, Dr. Jaime Posada. It was planned to hold another meeting in Bogotá, but this was not possible. Finally, I suggested that two reports should be made. The reason for this is very clear: there is very little difference between President Kubitschek's ideas and mine, and the conclusions are almost identical, but the desire to adapt our opinions to a common text would probably bring about a loss in the shades of criterion of each one that may be of use to the OAS in making its decisions.

The conclusions I have reached after examining the initial program of Punta del Este and the changes it has undergone in practice, are a result of the conviction that the Alliance cannot achieve its transforming and revolutionary effectiveness as long as the Latin American countries do not take the full responsibility that the document appeared to assign them but that unfortunately was not clearly defined in the document and that, finally, the Government of the United States assumed by itself, saving the program from immediate failure but turning it aside from its original meaning and making it appear, involuntarily, as a national policy and program of that country towards its sister nations to the South.

I therefore propose, as President Kubitschek will probably do, the creation of a new inter-American organ that will take over the functions delegated to it by the IA-ECOSOC for the direction and orientation of the program in its final phase—financing between the various channels: some banking, others governmental, some national, others international, and still others inter-American—in order that the Alliance will not be subject, as it has been up to now, to the occasional good-will of entities that are alien to the program itself; and that will at the same time represent the Alliance in all its relations with other non-American countries and, naturally, with the members of the inter-American Organization themselves, particularly with respect to supervising the fulfilment of national programs and foreign investments in such programs. Thus, President Kubitschek and I believe that important objectives will be achieved and certain serious faults will be corrected that are weakening the Alliance by presenting it to the world as a United States program and not as the collective understanding of 20 countries to develop one of the most important regions in the West. It should be mentioned that an immense majority of the reports we have received coincide in this point of view, and that, up to now, we have encountered no opposition to the procedure we are going to propose.   [ ]

SPECIFIC PROBLEMS FACED WITHIN THE LATIN AMERICAN ECONOMIES[1]
Excerpts from a Policy Statement by the Inter-American Committee on the Alliance for Progress (CIAP)

A. THE MODERIZATION OF RURAL LIFE

One problem emerges above any other in a broad view of the Latin American scene, based on the country reviews and the Secretariat assessment; that is, the problem of modernizing rural life. The statistics reflecting industrial production and development in Latin America by and large are moving forward with high and reasonably regular momentum. On the other hand, food output is lagging behind the increase in population, and the gap between rural and urban ways of life within Latin America is becoming more acute. As ECLA has recently stated, the industrialization of Latin America can no longer be based on the substitution of manufactured imports at the national level. The Latin American nations must look outward—to Latin America as a whole and to the world—to expand their exports of primary products and manufactured goods, and must simultaneously look inward to the modernization of agriculture not merely to supplying food for a rapidly expanding population but also as a source of industrial raw materials, diversified export commodities and as markets for the products of Latin American industry.

It is heartening to observe the beginning in one Latin American country after another, of a new emphasis and priority for agricultural development. Many countries have enacted legal measures of agrarian reform, but this is still a field where a much greater and deeper effort is needed. One essential element of the agricultural policy should be the reform of the structure of land tenure, in order to establish a sound economic and social basis for that development, which implies an increase in the agricultural productivity necessary to sustain the development of the economy as a whole.

There are many complex factors to be dealt with in promoting improved performance in agricultural development, of which the following five against the background of adequate transport and infrastructure are critical: a reliable and equitable price to the farmer, which in turn requires radically improved marketing arrangements and often changes in price policies; provision to the farmer at equitable price of necessary agricultural inputs and desired incentive goods; improved credit at reasonable rates and of sufficiently long term;

---

[1] Reprinted from *The Alliance for Progress: Its Third Year, 1963–1964* (Washington, D.C.: The Pan American Union, General Secretariat, Organization of American States, 1965), pp. 5–8.

relevant technical assistance; and research. Ultimately, all of these interrelated elements in the agricultural productive "system" must be dealt with in an organized way (via producer's cooperatives, food processing firms, regional development institutions, etc.).

Besides, as CIAP noted at its Mexico City meeting, a critical and hitherto neglected aspect of the linking of the urban and rural life must be the modernization of marketing arrangements and institutions. A concerted program designed to yield this result is already under way within the Alliance for Progress.

B. INFLATION

A second major problem affecting some of the Latin American nations—including those which weigh most heavily within the indexes of over-all performance—is the problem of inflation. At the present time inflation in those countries is restricting and distorting the use of resources in Latin America and endangering the objectives of the Punta del Este Charter.

Specifically, inflation has these major effects:

a. It diverts investment away from channels which would yield the highest rate of return in terms of the development of the nation into channels which represent the best possible hedge against a rise in prices.

b. It leads, through the creation of economic instability and the expectation of future devaluations, to the holding of substantial Latin American assets abroad.

c. Through unrealistic exchange rates, it restricts undertakings which could generate export earnings, and reduces the incentive to export.

d. It renders unattractive saving in the form of money; impedes the development of modern banking systems; and places an unnatural pressure and responsibility upon the central banks as the primary source of working capital.

e. The need to hedge against possible future rises in costs leads to industrial price policies which are unsound, and which do not exploit the possibility of selling more at lower prices.

f. It damages disproportionately the poorer sections of the population which have the least possibility of taking action to hedge against price increases.

g. It restricts and renders more expensive Latin American borrowing from abroad.

h. By placing each element of the community in competition with others in the struggle to avoid damage through inflation, it renders difficult the creation of that sense of communal purpose and enterprise which is essential for the success of the development process.

From the discussions of inflation in the reviews of countries that faced these problems, a consensus emerges concerning the major steps required to prevent inflation where it does not exist and to attack inflation where it does exist.

Evidently specific measures must be designed in the light of specific circumstances in each country since each case is, in an important sense, unique. On the other hand, without going into the details of the importance of this policy in the development process it is possible to state the key general headings for a program to end inflation, assuming, of course, a framework of monetary and credit policy which is geared to stabilization itself.

a. Reduction of the government deficit via: improved tax collection; reduction of subsidies to and inefficiencies in government-owned and operated corporations; adjustments of rates; and generally increased efficiency in and control over government expenditures.

b. Systematic efforts to reduce the cost of living from the supply side are necessary. This should include high priority efforts within the over-all limits of monetary and credit ceilings to insure that foodstuffs in distant parts of the country are brought to major urban markets; agriculture production is expanded along the lines suggested in section A, above. In this effort to attack the cost of living from the supply side, the United States should consider modifications of legislation in order to permit a more effective use of its food surpluses to help reduce inflationary pressures, with due attention to the interest of other producers.

c. With respect to manufactured goods specifically those important in the cost of living as well as manufactured goods relevant to agricultural expansion, government should seek arrangements with the private sector to expand output and to pass along the benefits of lowered average costs and in the form of lowered or relatively lowered prices. In this connection, textiles, shoes, household equipment, as well as farm equipment, tools, fertilizers and insecticides, should be considered. On a selective, qualitative basis, the central banks should induce the banking system to supply the working capital for this expansion.

d. Against the background of efforts to constrain government deficits and to enlarge supplies particularly relevant to the cost of living, wage policies are required which do not have built into them self-fulfilling inflationary consequences. At the present time escalatory arrangements which automatically relate cost of living and wages in the short run, immediately set in motion price policies designed to protect industry against future wage increases. Such price policies, based upon the expectation of higher wages, produce the cost of living increases which then bring about the wage increases that were feared. In certain countries inflation continues quite independently of autonomous inflationary pressure from the monetary side. The banking system then finances by inflationary means the price-wage spiral set in motion by escalatory clauses in order to avoid unemployment. There is, in short, no substitution for a deep communal understanding between government, industry and labor in the form of wage-price policies which avoid the process of inflation via mutual expectation, and which systematically relate wage increases to the average increase in productivity.

e. As Latin American governments undertake effective measures to bring inflation to a halt through this three-sided attack (reduction of government deficits, increased supplies, and income policy), the financing agencies of the international community should be prepared to make a maximum effort in the form of economic assistance.

Part V

*

The Third World

··{*18*}·· *The Decolonization of Sub-Saharan Africa*

SPEECH DELIVERED BY JOMO KENYATTA[1]
At the Kenya African Union Meeting at Nyeri, July 26, 1952

. . . I want you to know the purpose of K.A.U. It is the biggest purpose the African has. It involves every African in Kenya and it is their mouthpiece which asks for freedom. K.A.U. is you and you are the K.A.U. If we unite now, each and every one of us, and each tribe to another, we will cause the implementation in this country of that which the European calls democracy. True democracy has no colour distinction. It does not choose between black and white. We are here in this tremendous gathering under the K.A.U. flag to find which road leads us from darkness into democracy. In order to find it we Africans must first achieve the right to elect our own representatives. That is surely the first principle of democracy. We are the only race in Kenya which does not elect its own representatives in the Legislature and we are going to set about to rectify this situation. We feel we are dominated by a handful of others who refuse to be just. God said this is our land. Land in which we are to flourish as a people. We are not worried that other races are here with us in our country, but we insist that we are the leaders here, and what we want we insist we get. We want our cattle to get fat on our land so that our children grow up in prosperity; we do not want that fat removed to feed others. He who has ears should now hear that K.A.U. claims this land as its own gift from God and I wish those who are black, white or brown at this meeting to know this. K.A.U. speaks in daylight. He who calls us the *Mau Mau* is not truthful. We do not know this thing *Mau Mau*. We want to prosper as a nation, and as a nation we demand equality, that is equal pay for equal work. Whether it is a chief, headman or labourer he needs in these days increased salary. He needs a salary that compares with a salary of a European who does equal work. We will never get our freedom unless we succeed in this issue. We do not want equal pay for equal work tomorrow—we want it right now. Those who profess to be just must realize that this is the foundation of justice. It has never been known in history that a country prospers without

---

[1] Reprinted from F. D. Cornfield, *The Origins and Growth of Mau Mau*, Sessional Paper No. 5 of 1959–1960 (Nairobi: 1960), pp. 301–308.

196

equality. We despise bribery and corruption, those two words that the European repeatedly refers to. Bribery and corruption is prevalent in this country, but I am not surprised. As long as a people are held down, corruption is sure to rise and the only answer to this is a policy of equality. If we work together as one, we must succeed.

Our country today is in a bad state for its land is full of fools—and fools in a country delay the independence of its people. K.A.U. seeks to remedy this situation and I tell you now it despises thieving, robbery and murder for these practices ruin our country. I say this because if one man steals, or two men steal, there are people sitting close by lapping up information, who say the whole tribe is bad because a theft has been committed. Those people are wrecking our chances of advancement. They will prevent us getting freedom. If I have my own way, let me tell you I would butcher the criminal, and there are more criminals than one in more senses than one. The policeman must arrest an offender, a man who is purely an offender, but he must not go about picking up people with a small horn of liquor in their hands and march them in procession with his fellow policemen to Government and say he has got a *Mau Mau* amongst the Kikuyu people. The plain clothes man who hides in the hedges must, I demand, get the truth of our words before he flies to Government to present them with false information. I ask this of them who are in the meeting to take heed of my words and do their work properly and justly. . . .

. . . Do not be scared of the few policemen under those trees who are holding their rifles high in the air for you to see. Their job is to seize criminals, and we shall save them a duty today. I will never ask you to be subversive but I ask you to be united, for the day of Independence is the day of complete unity and if we unite completely tomorrow, our independence will come tomorrow. This is the day for you to work hard for your country, it is not words but deeds that count and the deeds I ask for come from your pockets. The biggest subscribers to K.A.U. are in this order. First, Thomson's Falls branch, second, Elburgon branch and third Gatundu branch. Do you, in Nyeri branch, want to beat them? Then let us see your deeds come forth.

. . . I want to touch on a number of points, and I ask you for the hundredth time to keep quiet whilst I do this. We want self-government, but this we will never get if we drink beer. It is harming our country and making people fools and encouraging crime. It is also taking all our money. Prosperity is a prerequisite of independence and, more important, the beer we are drinking is harmful to our birthrate. You sleep with a woman for nothing if you drink beer. It causes your bones to weaken and if you want to increase the population of the Kikuyu you must stop drinking.

. . . K.A.U. is not a fighting union that uses fists and weapons. If any of you here think that force is good, I do not agree with you: remember the old saying that he who is hit with a *rungu* returns, but he who is hit with justice never comes back. I do not want people to accuse us falsely—that we steal and that we are *Mau Mau*. I pray to you that we join hands for freedom and freedom means abolishing criminality. Beer harms us and those who drink it do us harm and they may be the so-called *Mau Mau*. Whatever grievances we have, let us air them here in the open. The criminal does not want freedom and land—he wants to line his own pocket. Let us therefore demand our rights justly. The British Government has discussed the land problem in Kenya and we hope to have a Royal Commisson to this country to look into the land problem very shortly. When this Royal Commission comes, let us show it that we are a good peaceful people and not thieves and robbers.   [ ]

THE "LOI-CADRE" OF JUNE 23, 1956[1]
Authorizing the French Government to Carry out the Reforms and Take the Measures Calculated to Ensure the Development of the Territories under the Jurisdiction of the Ministry of France Overseas

Article First. Without prejudice to the expected reform of Title VIII of the Constitution, in order to give the overseas peoples a more direct share in the management of their own interests, measures of administrative decentralization and devolution shall be introduced within the territories, groups of territories and central services under the jurisdiction of the Ministry of France Overseas.

To this end, decrees taken . . . on the basis of the report given by the Minister of France Overseas and, on occasion, by the Ministers concerned, may:

1) Modify the role and powers of administration and management of the general governments with a view to transforming them into coordinating bodies, and modify the composition and attributes of the grand councils and of the representative assembly of Madagascar;

2) Institute government councils in all the territories and in addition, in Madagascar, provincial councils charged, in particular, with administering the territorial services;

3) Grant broadened deliberative powers, notably for the organization and management of the territorial services, to the assemblies of the territories as well as to the representative assembly and provincial assemblies of Madagascar; regarding the exercise of their attributes, which shall be defined in the decrees to be introduced, and when the decrees taken in pursuance of the present article shall authorize them to do so, the assemblies may abrogate or modify any regulatory text governing matters which fall under said attributes;

4) Determine the conditions of the institution and functioning, as well

---

[1] The text of the "loi-cadre" was supplied in an English translation through the courtesy of the French Press and Information Service, New York.

as the attributes of the councils in the administrative circumscriptions and rural communities, and the modalities of granting legal status to these circumscriptions, without this impeding in any way the establishment of new municipalities.

The decrees taken in pursuance of the present article may modify, abrogate or revive in the form of regulations existing legislative provisions.

[ ]

Article 3. The Government may, by decree taken in the Council of Ministers on the basis of the report given by the Minister of France Overseas and, on occasion, by the Ministers concerned, and after consultation with the Council of State, inaugurate a reform of the public services charged with managing the interests of the State and, on the other hand, the territorial services charged with managing the interests of the territories, as well as the division of attributes between those services. The purpose of this reform shall be:

On the one hand, to facilitate the access of native-born civil servants to all ranks in the administration;

On the other hand, to institute independent regulations pertaining to the civil service overseas, as far as the territorial services are concerned. . . .

Article 4. The Government may, in the manner stipulated in Article 3 above, without interfering in any way with Law No. 46–860 of April 30, 1946 and the legislative provisions referring to it, take all measures intended to raise the standard of living in the territories under the jurisdiction of the Ministry of France Overseas, to promote economic development and social progress and to facilitate economic and financial cooperation between Metropolitan France and those territories, especially:

By generalizing and standardizing education;

By organizing and supporting the production of goods necessary to the economic equilibrium of the territories and to the needs of the franc area;

By inaugurating modern methods of rural development and establishing a cadastral plan in which the customary rights of the autochthones will be respected;

By setting up and enforcing the registration of births, marriages and deaths;

By setting up suitable structures in the field of credit and savings;

By effecting all modifications, in matters of financial law and regulations, calculated to promote private investment overseas, without derogating in any way from the prerogatives of the territorial assemblies;

By taking all measures calculated to ensure a successful social program.

The Government must make all useful arrangements to ensure on a permanent basis and at the level of the presidency of the council the coordination of economic and financial measures concerning the Metropolitan-Overseas complex.

[ ]

Article 10. In the territories under the jurisdiction of the Ministry of France Overseas, elections to the National Assembly, to the territorial assemblies, to the provincial assemblies of Madagascar, to the circumscription councils and to the municipal assemblies shall be held on the basis of universal suffrage of citizens of both sexes, without regard to their personal status, who are twenty-one years of age or over, who are regularly inscribed on the election rolls and who are not disqualified for any reason stipulated by law.

[ ]

Article 12. The election of members of the National Assembly, members of the Council of the Republic, members of the territorial assemblies, members of the representative assembly and the provincial assemblies of Madagascar, of the circumscription councils, and also members of the municipal assemblies of the fully organized communes, the semi-organized communes and the mixed communes shall be by a single electoral college.   [ ]

CONFERENCE RESOLUTION ON IMPERIALISM AND COLONIALISM[1]
All-African People's Conference, Accra, December 5–13, 1958

Whereas the great bulk of the African continent has been carved out arbitrarily to the detriment of the indigenous African peoples by European Imperialists, namely: Britain, France, Belgium, Spain, Italy and Portugal.

(2) Whereas in this process of colonisation two groups of colonial territories have emerged, to wit:

(a) Those territories where indigenous Africans are dominated by foreigners who have their seats of authority in foreign lands, for example, French West Africa, French Equatorial Africa, Nigeria, Sierra Leone, Gambia, Belgian Congo, Portuguese Guinea, Basutoland, Swaziland and Bechuanaland.

(b) Those where indigenous Africans are dominated and oppressed by foreigners who have settled permanently in Africa and who regard the position of Africa under their sway as belonging more to them than to the Africa, e.g. Kenya, Union of South Africa, Algeria, Rhodesia, Angola and Mozambique.

(3) Whereas world opinion unequivocally condemns oppression and subjugation of one race by another in whatever shape or form.

(4) Whereas all African peoples everywhere strongly deplore the economic exploitation of African peoples by imperialist countries thus reducing Africans to poverty in the midst of plenty.

(5) Whereas all African peoples vehemently resent the militarisation of

---

[1] Reprinted from the *All-African People's Conference News Bulletin*, Vol. I, No. 4 (Accra: 1959), pp. 1–2.

Africans and the use of African soldiers in a nefarious global game against their brethren as in Algeria, Kenya, South Africa, Cameroons, Ivory Coast, Rhodesia and in the Suez Canal invasion.

(6) Whereas fundamental human rights, freedom of speech, freedom of association, freedom of movement, freedom of worship, freedom to live a full and abundant life, as approved by the All-African People's Conference on 13th December, 1958, are denied to Africans through the activities of imperialists.

(7) Whereas denial of the franchise to Africans on the basis of race or sex has been one of the principal instruments of colonial policy by imperialists and their agents, thus making it feasible for a few white settlers to lord it over millions of indigenous Africans as in the proposed Central African Federation, Kenya, Union of South Africa, Algeria, Angola, Mozambique and the Cameroons.

(8) Whereas imperialists are now co-ordinating their activities by forming military and economic pacts such as NATO, European Common Market, Free Trade Area, Organisation for European Economic Co-operation, Common Organisation in Sahara for the purpose of strengthening their imperialist activities in Africa and elsewhere,

Be it resolved and it is hereby resolved by the All-African People's Conference meeting in Accra 5th to 13th December, 1958, and comprising over 300 delegates representing over 200 million Africans from all parts of Africa as follows:

1. That the All-African People's Conference vehemently condemns colonialism and imperialism in whatever shape or form these evils are perpetuated.

2. That the political and economic exploitation of Africans by imperialist Europeans should cease forthwith.

3. That the use of African manpower in the nefarious game of power politics by imperialists should be a thing of the past.

4. That independent African States should pursue in their international policy principles which will expedite and accelerate the independence and sovereignty of all dependent and colonial African territories.

5. That fundamental human rights be extended to all men and women in Africa and that the rights of indigenous Africans to the fullest use of their lands be respected and preserved.

6. That universal adult franchise be extended to all persons in Africa regardless of race or sex.

7. That independent African states ensure that fundamental human rights and universal adult franchise are fully extended to everyone within their states as an example to imperial nations who abuse and ignore the extension of those rights to Africans.

8. That a permanent secretariat of the All-African People's Conference be set up to organise the All-African Conference on a firm basis.

9. That a human rights committee of the Conference be formed to examine complaints of abuse of human rights in every part of Africa and to take appropriate steps to ensure the enjoyment of the rights by everyone.

10. That the All-African People's Conference in Accra declares its full support to all fighters for freedom in Africa, to all those who resort to peaceful means of non-violence and civil disobedience, as well as to all those who are compelled to retaliate against violence to attain national independence and freedom for the people. Where such retaliation becomes necessary, the Conference condemns all legislations which consider those who fight for their independence and freedom as ordinary criminals.

··{*19*}·· *Sub-Saharan Africa since Independence— Remaining Areas of White Supremacy*

THE NATIONAL PARTY'S COLOUR POLICY[1]
Statement by the National Party of South Africa, March 29, 1948

There are two sections of thought in South Africa in regard to the policy affecting the non-European community. On the one hand there is the policy of equality, which advocates equal rights within the same political structure for all civilized and educated persons, irrespective of race or colour, and the gradual granting of the franchise to non-Europeans as they become qualified to make use of democratic rights.

On the other hand there is the policy of separation (*apartheid*) which has grown from the experience of established European population of the country, and which is based on the Christian principles of justice and reasonableness.

Its aim is the maintenance and protection of the European population of the country as a pure White race, the maintenance and protection of the indigenous racial groups as separate communities, with prospects of developing into self-supporting communities within their own areas, and the stimulation of national pride, self-respect, and mutual respect among the various races of the country.

We can act in only one of two directions. Either we must follow the course of equality, which must eventually mean national suicide for the White race, or we must take the course of separation (*apartheid*) through which the character and the future of every race will be protected and safeguarded with full opportunities for development and self-maintenance in

---

[1] United Nations, General Assembly, *Official Records: Eighth Session*, Supplement No. 16 (A/2505 and A/2505/Add.1), "Report of the United Nations Commission on the Racial Situation in the Union of South Africa," Annex V (New York: 1952), pp. 139–140.

their own ideas, without the interests of one clashing with the interests of the other, and without one regarding the development of the other as undermining or a threat to himself.

The party therefore undertakes to protect the White race properly and effectively against any policy, doctrine or attack which might undermine or threaten its continued existence. At the same time the party rejects any policy of oppression and exploitation of the non-Europeans by the Europeans as being in conflict with the Christian basis of our national life and irreconcilable with our policy.

The party believes that a definite policy of separation (*apartheid*) between the White races and the non-White racial groups, and the application of the policy of separation also in the case of the non-White racial groups, is the only basis on which the character and future of each race can be protected and safeguarded and on which each race can be guided so as to develop his own national character, aptitude and calling.

All marriages between Europeans and non-Europeans will be prohibited.

In their areas the non-European racial groups will have full opportunities for development in every sphere and will be able to develop their own institutions and social services whereby the forces of the progressive non-Europeans can be harnessed for their own national development (*volkeepbou*). The policy of the country must be so planned that it will eventually promote the ideal of complete separation (*algehele apartheid*) in a national way.

A permanent advisory body of experts on non-European affairs will be established.

The State will exercise complete supervision over the moulding of the youth. The party will not tolerate interference from without or destructive propaganda from the outside world in regard to the racial problems of South Africa.

The party wishes all non-Europeans to be strongly encouraged to make the Christian religion the basis of their lives and will assist churches in this task in every possible way. Churches and societies which undermine the policy of *apartheid* and propagate doctrines foreign to the nation will be checked.

The Coloured community takes a middle position between the European and the Natives. A policy of separation (*apartheid*) between the Europeans and Coloureds and between Natives and Coloureds will be applied in the social, residential, industrial and political spheres. No marriage between Europeans and Coloureds will be permitted. The Coloureds will be protected against unfair competition from the Natives in so far as where they are already established.

The Coloured community will be represented in the Senate by a European representative to be appointed by the Government by reason of his knowledge of Coloured affairs.

The present unhealthy system which allows Coloureds in the Cape to be registered on the same voters' roll as Europeans and to vote for the same candidate as Europeans will be abolished and the Coloureds will be represented in the House of Assembly by three European representatives.

These Coloured representatives will be elected by a Coloured representative council. They will not vote on:

(1) Votes on confidence in the Government.

(2) A declaration of war, and

(3) A change in the political rights of non-Europeans.

A State Department of Coloured Affairs will be established.

The Coloured community will be represented in the Cape Provincial Council by three Europeans elected by the Coloured representative council.

A Coloured representative council will be established in the Cape Province consisting of representatives elected by the Coloured community, divided into constituencies with the present franchise qualifications, the head of the Department of Coloured Affairs and representatives nominated by the Government. In their own areas the Coloured community will have their own councils with their own public services which will be managed by themselves within the framework of the existing councils with higher authority.

Attention will be given to the provision of social, medical and welfare services in which the efforts of the Coloured themselves can be harnessed, and in which they will be taught as far as possible to be self-supporting.

THE NATURE OF BELGIAN COLONIAL RULE IN THE CONGO[1]
Speech by King Baudouin of Belgium

The independence of the Congo constitutes the crowning of the work conceive'd by the genius of King Leopold II, undertaken by him with firm resolve and continued with perseverance by Belgium. This independence marks a decisive hour not only in the destiny of the Congo, but also, I do not hesitate to maintain, in the destiny of all Africa.

For eighty years, Belgium has sent to your land the best of her sons, first in order to deliver the Congo Basin from the odious slave trade which was decimating its population, later to bring together the various tribes which, though formerly enemies, are now preparing to form the largest of the independent African states, and finally, to call to a more prosperous life the various regions of the Congo, which you represent here, united in a single Parliament.

In this historic moment, our thoughts ought to turn to the pioneers of African emancipation and to those coming after them who have made the Congo what it is today. They deserve both our admiration and your recogni-

---

[1] Editor's translation from the French. This speech was delivered at the Independence Day ceremonies at Leopoldville, the Congo, on June 30, 1960.

tion, for these are the men who, dedicating all their energies and even their lives to a great ideal, brought you peace and enriched your intellectual and material heritage. They must never be forgotten, either by Belgium or by the Congo.

When Leopold II undertook the great task which reaches its completion today, he did not come to you as a conqueror, but as a bearer of civilization.

The Congo has been endowed with railroads, roads, and both shipping and air lines which, by putting your people in contact with each other, have encouraged their unity and have extended the contacts of your country to the edges of the world.

We are happy to have thus given to the Congo, in spite of the greatest difficulties, those elements which are essential to the structure of a country embarking upon the path of development.

The great independence movement, which involves all of Africa, has found in Belgium the greatest understanding. In the face of the unanimous desire of your people, we have not hesitated to recognize your independence.

It is up to you, gentlemen, to show that we were right in trusting you.

Your task is immense and you are the first to recognize it. The principal dangers which threaten you are the inexperience of the population in governing themselves; tribal feuds, which have done so much harm in the past and which must not return at any price; and the influence which certain foreign powers, ready to profit from the least show of weakness, can exercise on certain regions.

Independence will require work and sacrifice from everyone. It will be necessary to adapt institutions to your ideas and needs in a way which will make them stable and balanced. It will be necessary to form experimental administrative structures to intensify the intellectual and moral development of the Congolese people, to maintain a stable currency, and to safeguard and develop your economic, social, and financial organizations.

Do not compromise the future by hasty reforms, and do not replace the systems which Belgium has turned over to you until you are certain that you have the means to create better ones.

Do not fear to turn to us for help. We are ready to remain in your land to aid you with our advice and to train the technicians and officials which you will need.

The entire world has its eyes on you. At the time when the Congo independently chooses its way of life, I hope that the Congolese people will preserve and develop that heritage of spiritual, moral, and religious values which we have in common, and which transcends political vicissitudes and the differences of race or frontier.

Remain united and you will be able to show yourselves worthy of the great role which you have been called upon to play in the history of Africa.

My country and I recognize with joy and emotion that, on this 30th day of June 1960, in full agreement and friendship with Belgium, the Congo accedes to independence and international sovereignty.

ON THE NATURE OF BELGIAN COLONIAL RULE AND THE AIMS OF HIS GOVERNMENT[1]
Speech by Patrice Lumumba, Prime Minister and Minister of National Defense of the Republic of the Congo

I ask all of you, my friends, who have struggled unceasingly in our land, to make this 30th day of June 1960 an illustrious event which you will preserve indelibly engraved in your hearts—a day, the significance of which you will teach to your children with pride, so that they, in their turn, can tell their sons and their grandsons of the glorious history of our struggle for freedom.

No Congolese worthy of the name should ever forget that this independence of the Congo, proclaimed today in agreement with Belgium, a friendly country with which we deal as equals, has been gained only by an unceasing, ardent, and idealistic struggle, a struggle in which we have spared neither strength, losses, suffering, nor our blood. It was a battle of tears, of fire, and of blood, a battle of which we are extremely proud, for this was a noble and just battle, and one which was essential to put an end to the humiliating slavery which was imposed on us by force.

This was our lot during eighty years of colonialist rule; our wounds are too fresh and painful for us to be able to erase them from our memory.

We have known the back-breaking toil demanded of us in exchange for wages which would not permit us to satisfy our hunger, or to clothe and house ourselves decently, or to raise our children properly. We have known sarcasm, insults, and blows to which we have had to submit morning, noon, and night because we were Negroes. Who could forget that one used the intimate form of address to a Negro not because he was a friend, but because the formal term of address was reserved for whites alone?

We have seen our lands plundered in the name of supposedly legal regulations which only recognized the rights of power; we have known that the law was never the same for whites as it was for blacks, being permissive for the former and cruel and inhuman for the latter. We have known the atrocious sufferings of exile for political opinions or religious beliefs. Exiles in our own country, our lot was truly worse than death. We have known that in the towns there were magnificent homes for the whites and miserable shacks

---

[1] Editor's translation. This speech was delivered at the Independence Day ceremonies at Leopoldville, the Congo, on June 30, 1960.

for the blacks, that a black was admitted neither to the cinemas nor to restaurants, nor to the so-called European shops, and that a black travelled in the hold of a ship while the white man travelled in a deluxe cabin.

Who could forget, finally, the shootings in which so many of our brothers perished, or the prisons into which those who did not wish to submit to a regime of injustice were thrown?

From all that, my brethren, we have suffered greatly, but we, as the representatives elected to guide our cherished country, we who have suffered in body and spirit from the colonialist oppression, tell you that all this is forever ended.

The Republic of the Congo has been proclaimed and our beloved land is now in the hands of her own children.

Together, my brothers, we are going to begin a new struggle, a lofty struggle which will bring our country peace, prosperity, and greatness.

At the same time, we are going to establish social justice and ensure that everyone will receive an equitable reward for his work.

We are going to show the world what the black man can accomplish when he works in freedom, and we are going to make the Congo the center of radiance for all Africa.

The independence of the Congo marks a decisive step in the liberation of the entire African Continent.

That, Excellencies, ladies and gentlemen, my racial brothers, my comrades in battle, my fellow countrymen, is what I wished to say in the name of the government on this magnificent day of our complete and sovereign independence.   [ ]

THE CONGO PROBLEM[1]
Comments by Secretary-General of the United Nations, U Thant, August 20, 1962

[ ]

Since in press and corridor recently there has been much comment and speculation about certain "proposals" which I am said to have in mind, some clarifying words from me on this subject would seem appropriate. . . .

I am instructing my representative in Leopoldville, Mr. Robert Gardiner, to present a programme of measures to Mr. Adoula, the Prime Minister, and, with his agreement, to Mr. Tshombé, the Provincial President of Katanga.

---

[1] Reprinted from United Nations, Security Council, Official Records, Seventeenth year, Supplement for July, August, and September 1962, Document S/5053/Add.11, pp. 15–18.

These measures have my full support. The main elements of the programme are set forth in the following paragraphs.

A constitution for a federal system of government in the Congo is now in preparation and all provincial governments and interested political groups have been invited to submit their views. The United Nations, on request of the Government of the Congo, is assisting this process by making available international experts in federal constitutional law. It is my hope that work on a draft constitution will be completed in thirty days.

A new law is needed to establish definitive arrangements for the division of revenues between the Central Government and the provincial governments, as well as regulations and procedures for the utilization of foreign exchange. The Central Government should submit such new law to Parliament only after consultations with provincial governments. Until that process is completed, the Central Government and the Provincial authorities of Katanga should agree: (*a*) to share on a fifty-fifty basis revenues from all taxes or duties on exports and imports and all royalties from mining concessions; (*b*) to pay to the Monetary Council or institution designated by it, which is acceptable to the parties concerned, all foreign exchange earned by any part of the Congo. The Monetary Council should control the utilization of all foreign exchange and make available for the essential needs of Katanga at least 50 per cent of the foreign exchange generated in that province.

The Central Government should request assistance from the International Monetary Fund in working out a national plan of currency unification, and put such a plan into effect in the shortest possible time.

Rapid integration and unification of the entire Congolese army is essential. A three-member commission of representatives from the Central Government, Katanga Province and the United Nations, should prepare within thirty days a plan to bring this about. Two months thereafter should be adequate to put the plan into effect.

Only the Central Government should maintain government offices or representation abroad.

As an essential aspect of national reconciliation, the Central Government should be reconstituted to provide representation for all political and provincial groups. It is noted that Mr. Adoula, the Prime Minister, has already made certain specific offers in this regard.

Reconciliation should be served by a general amnesty for political prisoners. In addition, all Congolese authorities, national, state, and local, should co-operate fully with the United Nations in its task of carrying out United Nations resolutions.

The proposed steps toward national reconciliation are fully in accord with the statement made on 29 July by Mr. Adoula. They likewise should be acceptable to Katanga and all other provinces of the Congo, judging from recent statements of Congolese leaders. Mr. Tshombé, therefore, should be able to indicate his acceptance promptly. The United Nations, of course, stands ready to give all possible assistance in their implementation. I urge Member Governments to support these approaches by urging Congolese of all sectors and views to accept them forthwith.

While consultations on these approaches are going on I would hope that no actions will be taken to distract from this new effort to achieve agreement. At the same time certain actions are required by the Central Government, by the Provincial authorities of Katanga and by neighbouring States, both to begin putting the proposals into effect, and to prevent any distracting incidents from any quarter. All Member States of the United Nations should take the necessary measures to assure that there are no unauthorized movements to the Congo of mercenaries, arms, war material or any kind of equipment capable of military use.

I believe that the Katanga authorities must consider these proposals and respond to them affirmatively within a quite brief period so that concrete steps can begin, according to a time-table which Mr. Gardiner is authorized to propose. If, however, after this period Katangese agreement is not forthcoming, I will emphatically renew an appeal to all governments of Member States of the United Nations to take immediate measures to ensure that their relations with the Congo will be in conformity with laws and regulations of the Government of the Congo.

Further, failing such agreement, as I indicated in my statement of 31 July: "I have in mind economic pressure upon the Katangese authorities of a kind that will bring home to them the realities of their situation and the fact that Katanga is not a sovereign State and is not recognized by any Government in the world as such . . . this could justifiably go to the extent of barring all trade and financial relations." In pursuance of this, a firm request would be made by me to all Member Governments to apply such a ban especially to Katangese copper and cobalt.   [ ]

THE CHARTER OF THE ORGANIZATION OF AFRICAN UNITY[1]
May 25, 1963

We, the Heads of African States and Governments assembled in the City of Addis Ababa, Ethiopia;

Convinced that it is the inalienable right of all people to control their own destiny;

Conscious of the fact that freedom, equality, justice and dignity are essential objectives for the achievement of the legitimate aspirations of the African peoples;

---

[1] Reprinted from *Organization of African Unity: Basic Documents and Resolutions* (Addis Ababa: n.d., The Provisional Secretariat of the Organization of African Unity), pp. 7–13.

Conscious of our responsibility to harness the natural and human resources of our continent for the total advancement of our peoples in spheres of human endeavour;

Inspired by a common determination to promote understanding among our peoples and co-operation among our States in response to the aspirations of our peoples for brotherhood and solidarity, in a larger unity transcending ethnic and national differences;

Convinced that, in order to translate this determination into a dynamic force in the cause of human progress, conditions for peace and security must be established and maintained;

Determined to safeguard and consolidate the hard-won independence as well as the sovereignty and territorial integrity of our States, and to fight against neo-colonialism in all its forms;

Dedicated to the general progress of Africa;

Persuaded that the Charter of the United Nations and the Universal Declaration of Human Rights, to the principles of which we reaffirm our adherence, provide a solid foundation for peaceful and positive co-operation among States;

Desirous that all African States should henceforth unite so that the welfare and well-being of their peoples can be assured;

Resolved to reinforce the links between our states by establishing and strengthening common institutions;

Have agreed to the present Charter.

Establishment

Article I

1. The High Contracting Parties do by the present Charter establish an Organization to be known as the ORGANIZATION OF AFRICAN UNITY.

2. The Organization shall include the Continental African States, Madagascar and other Islands surrounding Africa.

Purposes

Article II

1. The Organization shall have the following purposes:
   a. to promote the unity and solidarity of the African States;
   b. to co-ordinate and intensify their co-operation and efforts to achieve a better life for the peoples of Africa;
   c. to defend their sovereignty, their territorial integrity and independence;
   d. to eradicate all forms of colonialism from Africa; and
   e. to promote international co-operation, having due regard to the

Charter of the United Nations and the Universal Declaration of Human Rights.

2. To these ends, the Member States shall co-ordinate and harmonize their general policies, especially in the following fields:

    a. political and diplomatic co-operation;

    b. economic co-operation, including transport and communications;

    c. educational and cultural co-operation;

    d. health, sanitation, and nutritional co-operation;

    e. scientific and technical co-operation; and

    f. co-operation for defence and security.

PRINCIPLES

Article III

The Member States, in pursuit of the purposes stated in Article II, solemnly affirm and declare their adherence to the following principles:

    1. the sovereign equality of all Member States;

    2. non-interference in the internal affairs of States;

    3. respect for the sovereignty and territorial integrity of each State and for its inalienable right to independent existence;

    4. peaceful settlement of disputes by negotiation, mediation, conciliation or arbitration;

    5. unreserved condemnation, in all its forms, of political assassination as well as of subversive activities on the part of neighboring States or any other State;

    6. absolute dedication to the total emancipation of the African territories which are still dependent;

    7. affirmation of a policy of non-alignment with regard to all blocs.

MEMBERSHIP

Article IV

Each independent sovereign African State shall be entitled to become a Member of the Organization.

RIGHTS AND DUTIES OF MEMBER STATES

Article V

All Member States shall enjoy equal rights and have equal duties.

Article VI

The Member States pledge themselves to observe scrupulously the principles enumerated in Article III of the present Charter.   [ ]

CESSATION OF MEMBERSHIP

CESSATION OF MEMBERSHIP

Article XXXII

Any State which desires to renounce its membership shall forward a written notification to the Administrative Secretary-General. At the end of one year from the date of such notification, if not withdrawn, the Charter shall cease to apply with respect to the renouncing State, which shall thereby cease to belong to the Organization.   [ ]

ANNOUNCEMENT OF THE UNILATERAL DECLARATION OF INDEPENDENCE BY RHODESIA[1]
Speech by Prime Minister Ian Smith, November 11, 1965

[ ]
Now I would like to say a few words to you. Today, now that the final stalemate in negotiations has become evident, the end of the road has been reached.

It has become abundantly clear that it is the policy of the British Government to play us along with no real intention of arriving at a solution which we could possibly accept. Indeed, in the latest verbal and confidential message delivered to me last night we find that on the main principle which is in dispute the two Governments have moved further apart.

I promised the people of this country that I would continue to negotiate to the bitter end and that I would leave no stone unturned in my endeavours to secure an honourable and mutually accepted settlement.

It now falls to me to tell you that negotiations have come to an end. No one could deny that we have striven with might and main and at times bent over backwards to bridge the gap which divides us from the British Government.

. . . Let no one believe that this action today marks a radical departure from the principles by which we have lived, or be under any misconception that now the Constitution will be torn up and that the protection of the rights of all peoples which are enshrined in that Constitution will be abrogated and disregarded.

Neither let it be thought that this event marks a diminution in the opportunities which our African people have to advance and prosper in Rhodesia. Far from this being the case, it is our intention, in consultation with the chiefs, to bring them into the Government and administration as the acknowledged leaders of the African people on a basis acceptable to them.

It is our firm intention to abide by the Constitution. Indeed, we have

---

[1] Reprinted from the *East Africa and Rhodesia Newspaper*, November 18, 1965, pp. 204–205.

never asked for anything other than independence on the basis of the present Constitution, and only such amendments are included as are necessary to adapt it to that of an independent country.

With regard to the position of Members of Parliament, judges, civil servants, and members of the armed forces, as well as the police, provision has been made for all of them to carry on their duties, and all are deemed to have complied with the requirements of the New Constitution. They will continue to carry on their normal work. All present laws shall continue to operate and the courts will enforce them in the normal manner.

We are doing no more than assuming the right which various British Ministers have in the past indicated were ours. And in fact this Constitution was the one which would carry us to independence.

Let no one be persuaded that this action marks a change in our attitude towards our neighbours in Africa, to whom we have ceaselessly extended the hand of friendship and to whom we have nothing but goodwill and the best of intentions.

We have never sought, nor will we ever seek, to interfere or in any way attempt to influence their policy and their internal affairs. All we ask in return is their goodwill in permitting us to look after what are, after all, our own private and domestic matters. . . .

There can be no solution to our racial problems while African nationalists believe that, provided they stirred up sufficient trouble, they will be able to blackmail the British Government into bringing about a miracle on their behalf by handing the country over to irresponsible rule.

There can be no happiness in this country while the absurd situation continues to exist where people such as ourselves, who have ruled ourselves with an impressive record for over 40 years, are denied what is freely granted to other countries, who have ruled themselves in some cases for no longer than a year.

There can never be long-term prosperity, which is so necessary for the nurturing of our endeavours to improve the standard of living and increase the happiness and better the lot of all our people, whilst the present uncertainty exists.

No businessman could ever seriously contemplate massive long-term investment in a country in which chaos and confusion will always be future possibilities.

Whatever the short-term economic disadvantages may be, in the long term steady economic progress could never be achieved unless we are masters in our own house. . . .

That some economic retributions will be visited upon us there is no doubt. Those who seek to damage us do not have any great concern for the principles to which they endlessly pay lip service; for if they really believed in these principles, which they ceaselessly proclaim, then they could not possibly deny the many disasters which have been brought about by the premature withdrawal of European influence from countries in Africa and Asia who were nowhere near ready for it.

There is no doubt that the talk of threats and sanctions is no more than appeasement to the United Nations, the Afro-Asian bloc, and certain members of the Commonwealth; and undoubtedly some action will be taken.

But I cannot conceive of a rational world uniting in an endeavour to destroy the economy of this country, knowing, as they undoubtedly do, that in many cases the hardest hit will be the very people on whose behalf they would like to believe they are invoking these sanctions. We for our part will never do anything in the nature of taking revenge on any neighbouring African State for what other countries may do to us. . . .

We may be a small country, but we are a determined people who have been called upon to play a rôle of world-wide significance.

We Rhodesians have rejected the doctrinaire philosophy of appeasement and surrender. The decision which we have taken today is a refusal by Rhodesians to sell their birthright. And, even if we were to surrender, does anyone believe that Rhodesia would be the last target of the Communists in the Afro-Asian block?

We have struck a blow for the preservation of justice, civilization, and Christianity; and in the spirit of this belief we have this day assumed our sovereign independence. God bless you all.

THE POSITION OF THE BRITISH GOVERNMENT ON THE UNILATERAL DECLARATION OF INDEPENDENCE BY RHODESIA[1]

Speech by Prime Minister Harold Wilson to Parliament, November 11, 1965

[ ]

I still find it incredible—and the House, when it reads the records, will find it incredible—that this action should have taken place this morning. But, as I have previously warned the House, the differences between us have not been differences of legal drafting; they have not been the differences of normal political interchange. They have represented a deep difference of philosophy—a gulf that we now know could never be bridged because it was a gulf covering all the differences between different worlds and different centuries. At every point when agreement was near we were told that our positions were irreconcilable. This was because there were men in the then Rhodesian Cabinet who were determined at all costs that agreement should not be reached. I challenged Mr. Smith today, as I did—and my right hon. Friends will confirm this—in my last meeting in Salisbury, with this fact, and to his

---

[1] Reprinted from Hansard, *Parliamentary Debates*, House of Commons, Official Report, 5th Series, Vol. 720 (H.M.S.O., 1966), columns 349–356.

credit Mr. Smith had the honesty to admit it in my telephone conversation this morning.

. . . Now I must inform the House of the action that has been taken, the action that is being taken, and that will be taken—some of it subject to the necessary powers being given by Parliament to the Government.

I repeat that the British Government condemn the purported declaration of Independence by the former Government of Rhodesia as an illegal act and one which is ineffective in law. It is an act of rebellion against the Crown and against the Constitution as by law established, and actions taken to give effect to it will be treasonable. The Governor, in pursuance of the authority vested in him by Her Majesty The Queen, has today informed the Prime Minister and other Ministers of the Rhodesian Government that they cease to hold office. They are now private persons and can exercise no legal authority in Rhodesia.

The British Government wish to make it clear that it is the duty of all British subjects in Rhodesia, including all citizens of Rhodesia, to remain loyal to The Queen and to the law of the land, and to recognise the continuing authority and responsibility for Rhodesia of the Government of the United Kingdom.

The British Government are in close touch with all other Commonwealth Governments about the consequences of this illegal act and about the measures we should take. The British Government will, of course, have no dealings with the rebel régime. The British High Commissioner is being withdrawn and the Southern Rhodesian High Commissioner in London has been asked to leave. Export of arms, including spares have, of course, been stopped. All British aid will cease. Rhodesia has been removed from the sterling area. Special exchange control restrictions will be applied. Exports of United Kingdom capital to Rhodesia will not be allowed. Rhodesia will no longer be allowed access to the London capital market.

Our Export Credits Guarantee Department will give no further cover for exports to Rhodesia. The Ottawa Agreement of 1932 which governs our trading relations with Rhodesia is suspended. Rhodesia will be suspended forthwith from the Commonwealth Preference Area and her goods will no longer receive preferential treatment on entering the United Kingdom. There will be a ban on further purchases of tobacco from Southern Rhodesia. We propose to suspend the Commonwealth Sugar Agreement in its relation to Rhodesia and to ban further purchases of Rhodesian sugar. We shall not recognise passports issued or renewed by the illegal Southern Rhodesian régime. . . .

It is the duty of everyone owing allegiance to the Crown in Rhodesia or elsewhere to refrain from all acts which would assist the illegal régime to continue in their rebellion against the Crown. Members of the armed forces and the police in Southern Rhodesia should refrain from taking up arms in support of the illegal régime, and from doing anything which will help them to pursue their unlawful courses. Public servants in Rhodesia should not do any work for the illegal régime which would tend to further the success of the rebellion. It is the duty of all private citizens owing allegiance to the Crown, wherever they may be, in Rhodesia or outside, to refrain from acts which will give support to the illegal régime. . . .

But I cannot end this statement about a problem with which my right hon. Friend the Secretary of State and other colleagues and myself have been so intimately concerned for so long without expressing the deep sense of tragedy which each of us feels—personal tragedy, but not only personal tragedy. It is a tragedy affecting a great people, including many thousands who have made their homes there and who are plunged into a maelstrom not of their own making, and of millions more who are denied the inalienable human right of self-expression and self-determination.

Heaven knows what crimes will be committed against the concept of the rule of law and of human freedom for which this House has always stood: this progressive unfolding of the regulations which have been signed under the state of emergency—and there are more to come—are an ominous warning.

The illegal régime which now claims power and authority in Rhodesia marked its usurpation of authority with a proclamation which borrowed for the purposes of small and frightened men the words of one of the historic documents of human freedom, even to the point of appropriating the historic reference to "a respect for the opinions of mankind."

I would repeat to them and to the Rhodesian people as a whole the words I used in my farewell statement on leaving Salisbury, which also quoted these words:

> When, nearly two centuries ago, the American States declared their independence from a British Government, which, to say the least, was remote, oppressive and unimaginative, they insisted that their actions be inspired by "a proper respect for the opinions of mankind." Nor were they alone in the world. Could anyone say that either of these things would be true of a Rhodesia which chose illegally to claim its independence?

It would be unworthy of this Government, of any British Government, as it would be unworthy of this House, to allow this challenge, offensive as it is to all our cherished traditions, and to the wider aspirations of the whole of mankind, to go unanswered.

We did not seek this challenge. The House will concede that we did everything in our power to avoid it, but now it has been made, then, with whatever sadness, we shall face this challenge with resolution and determination. Whatever measures the Government, with the support of this House, judge are needed to restore Rhodesia to the rule of law, to allegiance to the Crown, these measures will be taken. And I am confident that we shall have not only the support of this House, not only the support of the nations of the world, but we shall have the clear and decisive verdict of history.

THE SITUATION IN SOUTHERN RHODESIA[1]
The Soviet Government's Statement, November 15, 1965

The colonialists have committed a new crime against the African peoples. On November 11 the racialist régime of Ian Smith proclaimed the "independence" of Southern Rhodesia. These actions are aimed at perpetuating in Southern Rhodesia a colonial system based on inhuman oppression of the Zimbabwe people, four million strong, by a handful of racialists and on ruthless suppression of the just struggle of this people for real independence, freedom and social justice. . . .

The South Rhodesian racialists would not have dared to carry out their criminal plans without a deal with the colonialists, who have permitted the racialist régime in Salisbury to acquire economic and military strength and who have rendered it all-out support.

Nor could this crime have taken place without the blessing of the governments of other N.A.T.O. countries, and in the first place the United States of America. The creation of yet another centre of racialism—this time in Southern Rhodesia—is part of the overall plan of imperialist circles to erect an obstacle in the way of the national liberation movement of the African peoples, the waves of which are drawing nearer and nearer to the last bulwarks of colonialism.

The Soviet government fully shares the view of the independent African states, expressed in decisions of the Organisation of African Unity, that the ruling circles of Britain will never be able to escape responsibility for this crime against the African peoples, for the national tragedy of the Zimbabwe people, who for many years now have been waging a stubborn struggle for their rights.

At the present time the government of Great Britain, in words, is condemning the actions of the South Rhodesian authorities and is asking the Security Council to examine the question of Southern Rhodesia. It is clear, however, that these statements of the British government are at present only an attempt to whitewash its actual policy.

As long ago as 1961, having put into effect a "constitution" worked out by the British government itself which formalised the racialist system, Britain laid the foundations for the present régime of the racialists' colonial rule over millions of Africans.

Following that, she armed the South Rhodesian racialists and helped them to consolidate their positions by encouraging the colonial alliance of Southern Rhodesia with the racialist régime in the Republic of South Africa and the Portuguese colonialists in Angola and Mozambique. As a result,

---

[1] Reprinted with permission from the *Soviet News*, No. 5206 (November 16, 1965), p. 70.

Southern Rhodesia turned into a police state, into a land of jails, concentration camps and terror for the African population of the country.

The racialist régime in Southern Rhodesia also constitutes a hotbed of danger for all other African peoples, including those which have already freed themselves from colonial oppression. It is a bayonet pointed at the heart of liberated Africa, a constant threat to peace on the African continent and a threat to world peace. . . .

The Soviet government, guided by its principled stand in questions of abolishing colonialism, strongly condemns the new crime against the peoples of Africa and declares that it does not recognise the racialist regime which has usurped power in Southern Rhodesia. The Soviet Union fully supports the decisions adopted by the United Nations Security Council and General Assembly on the situation in Southern Rhodesia and will carry them out unswervingly.

Loyal to its steadfast policy of supporting the national liberation movement of the peoples, the Soviet government declares its full solidarity with the Zimbabwe people and again confirms its readiness to co-operate with the African countries in rendering them all-out support in their just struggle for genuine national independence.

AFRICAN DEVELOPMENT AND FOREIGN AID[1]
Speech by President Kaunda of Zambia, March 18, 1966

Recently a very close friend of mine declared it would take us another twenty years to be *really* independent. Was he right? I am afraid there is a lot of truth in this. I do not know what he had in mind but I respect his intelligence and depth of analysing problems. For my own reasons, I agree with him, and here I am not talking about freeing Mozambique, Angola, Portugese Guinea, Rhodesia, South West Africa and South Africa: I am talking now of countries like ours and many other independent African States.

In a calm, friendly world these problems might not have existed; our Independence might have been real. Unfortunately, we do not have the ideal world as yet; ours is a world in which the jungle law is still very much in evidence in spite of claims of civilisation, etc., etc., etc. We live in a world in which survival is for the fittest. . . .

Now we, the so called emerging countries, whether in Africa, parts of Asia or Latin America, are saddled with so many problems that to organise ourselves locally as well as internationally presents a Himalayan challenge.

---

[1] The text of this speech, which was delivered at the opening of the University of Zambia, was made available through the courtesy of the Embassy of Zambia, Washington, D.C.

Most of our weaknesses derive from lack of finance, trained personnel, etc., etc., etc.

We are left with no choice but to fall on either the east or west, or indeed, on both of them. Some of us choose to be non-aligned, believing that this might give us a breathing space to work out our own systems from which we might grow from strength to strength.

In the latter case we are not trusted by either the east or the west. When we preach the importance of man, whether he be from the east or the west, this is dismissed as a meaningless platitude from immature politicians. A very cruel world you might say, but then it is the one in which we live.

When we go to any of these big powers for help they readily will give us that help. They will say aid is being given to us without any strings because this is what they know is popular fancy with us. In fact, there is no such a thing as aid without strings.

A few examples might help to give meaning to what I say. Take training in any field—wherever you send your people they will be indoctrinated, consciously or unconsciously. They will be taught, very vigorously, to look at problems from the aid-giving country's point of view. In most cases, we like to think in terms of getting aid from various sources—that is, from both the east and west—hoping against hope that this will be a shield against interference from either. In fact we end up with a mixture of various explosive gasses in one bottle, and inevitably, explosions follow.

The question, of course, is—what are we supposed to do? We are in a hurry to reassert our Independence—it is human; it is natural. The strong beliefs we hold about the importance of man wherever he may come from lead us to believe that it is right and proper for us to mix with all our fellow men without regard to ideological differences or, indeed any other differences.

Because of this approach and, as I have already said, we feel we are justified in sending our young people to all corners of the world to attain the necessary knowledge. This is the field in which we find ourselves helpless and yet we see it so very often that this is one of the real sources of danger to our own Independence.

At home we have got to build these extensive civil and military organisations to develop and defend our countries. We have no choice but to train our people in other countries. Some of our civil and military people are those very ones who were used by colonising powers to suppress freedom movements. In most cases, they have been trained, again by the same powers when they colonised us.

When we make changes that do not conform to the pattern they have been used to, they take offence and the people's Government is first of all doubted, deceived and then overthrown. This often comes without the help of countries and organisations outside our own borders. The sources will depend on which side feels let down.

This is such an important subject that I do not think we should approach it from one side only. If we are honest to the cause we fought and suffered for; if we are honest to our own people, we must see that from time to time we take a critical look of self-inspection.

We are pioneers and, in a way, we are faced with more problems than a pathfinder who has no beaten track before him. The pathfinder who enters a forest has got to find his own track. This in many ways is easier, because certain things have been done in a certain way by certain people from whom we have taken over and we are trying now to redirect things in our own way. Various vested interests will not be happy with us and will naturally react and cause difficulties. We tread on a very rough road for we are not only trying to change the course of history but are also laying down a foundation. The will is there; the path is clear in our own minds; alas, the resources are limited.

I cannot help but mention, once again, that the cornerstone of our constitutions, governments and peoples must be service to man. I know this sounds so simple as to warrant no serious thought, but really when you come to think about this it is the all in all. Without man there is no constitution—there is no government—there is no law—there is no factory—there is no country. In fact, there is nothing that you can think of that would be meaningful. So those of us who are leaders of our people must not only think about the importance of man, it must be an *obsession*.

We must think and think and think again about how best we shall *serve* and *not* about how important we are as leaders of our people, or how we can safeguard our own positions as leaders. Why must we, don't we hold these in trust for our people? We must remember we are *not* elected kings, and that if we believe so much in the importance of man, we must not devise artificial methods of bottling his feelings. On the other hand, those who elected us and those who are our advisers must help their leaders by not doing things that will go to their leaders' heads so that they begin to feel that they are superhuman. . . .

Selfishness in leaders and followers inevitably leads to corruption. I cannot see, however, that uniformed men replacing elected leaders by either killing them, imprisoning them, or, indeed, sending them into exile is the answer to this problem. In some cases, Africa has witnessed the release of thousands, and in a few hours, their places were taken up by tens of thousands.

We should not, however, be over critical at this time because with the exception of one or two of those who have taken over, they have stated that they will hand power back to civil authorities. I do hope they do. If they do not do that, then I can foresee the sad growth of a second Middle East or Latin America right here on the continent. Africa cannot afford that.

To my fellow leaders on the continent of Africa I would venture to send this message—that our task and challenge is to try and help establish Governments of the people, by the people and for the people on the basis of "do unto others as you would have them do unto you"—all the time bearing in mind the application of this to the common man.

There is an obvious danger here that leaders on the continent of Africa might become so frightened of what is happening as to be preoccupied only with their own safety. I might say here that looking at the short list of my heroes I see that they have all got one thing in common, whether they were religious, philosophical, political or military, and this is that sincerely and relentlessly they served—almost without exception they were misunderstood and, indeed, all of them were misunderstood to the point where they died at the hands of the very people they served.

I am sure my heroes must be happy people because later generations understood them, worshipped them and followed them. Of course this cannot be the case with us if we suffered at the hands of our own people for corruptive practices. In other words, much as we deplore violent overthrowing of established governments our main concern is to leave behind us stable and genuine *people's* systems of government.   [ ]

THE ARUSHA DECLARATION[1]
On the Policy of Self-Reliance in Tanzania, February 5, 1967

[ ]
It is obvious that in the past we have chosen the wrong weapon for our struggle, because we chose money as our weapon. We are trying to overcome our economic weakness by using the weapons of the economically strong— weapons which in fact we do not possess. By our thoughts, words, and actions it appears as if we have come to the conclusion that without money we cannot bring about the revolution we are aiming at. It is as if we have said, "Money is the basis of development. Without money there can be no development." . . .

It is stupid to rely on money as the major instrument of development when we know only too well that our country is poor. It is equally stupid, indeed it is even more stupid, for us to imagine that we shall rid ourselves of our poverty through foreign financial assistance rather than our own financial resources. . . .

Let us therefore always remember the following. We have made a mistake to choose money, something which we do not have, to be our major instrument of development. We are mistaken when we imagine that we shall get money from foreign countries, firstly because, to say the truth, we cannot get enough money for our development and, secondly, because even if we could get it, such complete dependence on outside help would have endangered our independence and the other policies of our country.

Because of our emphasis on money, we have made another big mistake.

---

[1] Reprinted with permission from *Africa Report*. These, and other excerpts from the Arusha Declaration, appeared in the March 1967 issue of *Africa Report*, pp. 11–13.

We have put too much emphasis on industries. Just as we have said "Without money there can be no development," we also seem to say "Industries are the basis of development." This is true. The day when we have lots of money we shall be able to say we are a developed country. . . .

The mistake we are making is to think that development *begins* with industries. It is a mistake because we do not have the means to establish many modern industries in our country. We do not have either the necessary finances or the technical know-how. It is not enough to 'say that we shall borrow the finances and the technicians from other countries to come and start the industries. The answer to this is the same one we gave earlier, that we cannot get enough money and borrow enough technicians to start all the industries we need. And even if we could get the necessary assistance, dependence on it could interfere with our policy of socialism. The policy of inviting a chain of capitalists to come and establish industries in our country might succeed in giving us all the industries we need, but it would also succeed in preventing the establishment of socialism unless we believe that without first building capitalism, we cannot build socialism. . . .

The development of a country is brought about by people, not by money. Money, and the wealth it represents, is the result and not the basis of development. . . .

A great part of Tanzania's land is fertile and gets sufficient rains. Our country can produce various crops for home consumption and for export. We can produce food crops (which can be exported if we produce in large quantities) such as maize, rice, wheat, beans, and groundnuts. And we can produce such cash crops as sisal, cotton, coffee, tobacco, pyrethrum, and tea. Our land is also good for grazing cattle, goats, sheep, and for raising chickens; we can get plenty of fish from our rivers, lakes, and from the sea. All of our farmers are in areas which can produce two or three or even more of the food and cash crops enumerated above, and each farmer could increase his production so as to get more food or more money. And because the main aim of development is to get more food, and more money for our other needs, our purpose must be to increase production of these agricultural crops. This is in fact the only road through which we can develop our country—in other words, only by increasing our production of these things can we get more food and more money for every Tanzanian.

Everybody wants development, but not everybody understands and accepts the basic requirements for development. The biggest requirement is hard work. Let us go to the villages and talk to our people and see whether or not it is possible for them to work harder.

In towns, for example, the average paid worker works seven-and-a-half or eight hours a day for six or six-and-a half days a week. This is about 45 hours a week, excluding two or three weeks' leave every year. This means that an urban worker works for 45 hours a week in 48 to 50 weeks a year.

For a country like ours, these are really quite short working hours. In other countries, even those which are more developed than we are, people work for more than 45 hours a week. It is not normal for a young country to start with such a short working week. The normal thing is to begin with long working hours and decrease them as the country becomes more and more prosperous. By starting with such short working hours and asking for even shorter hours, we are in fact imitating the more developed countries. And we shall regret this imitation. . . .

It would be appropriate to ask our farmers, especially the men, how many hours a week and how many weeks a year they work. Many do not even work for half as many hours as the wage-earner does. The truth is that in the villages the women work very hard. At times they work for 12 or 14 hours a day. They even work on Sundays and public holidays. Women who live in the villages work harder than anybody else in Tanzania. But the men who live in villages (and some of the women in towns) are on leave for half of their life. The energies of the millions of men in the villages and thousands of women in the towns which are at present wasted in gossip, dancing, and drinking, are a great treasure which could contribute more toward the development of our country than anything we could get from rich nations. . . .

The second condition of development is the use of intelligence. Unintelligent hard work would not bring the same good results as the two combined. Using a big hoe instead of a small one; using a plough pulled by oxen instead of an ordinary hoe; the use of fertilizers; the use of insecticides; knowing the right crop for a particular season or soil; choosing good seeds for planting; knowing the right time for planting, weeding, etc.; all these things show the use of knowledge and intelligence. And all of them combine with hard work to produce more and better results.

The money and time we spend on passing on this knowledge to the peasants are better spent and bring more benefits to our country than the money and the great amount of time we spend on other things which we call development. . . .

None of this means that from now on we will not need money or that we will not start industries or embark upon development projects which require money. Furthermore, we are not saying that we will not accept, or even that we shall not look for, money from other countries for our development. This is *not* what we are saying. We will continue to use money; and each year we will use more money for the various development projects than we used the previous year because this will be one of the signs of our development.

What we are saying, however, is that from now on we shall know what is the foundation and what is the fruit of development. Between *money* and *people* it is obvious that the people and their *hard work* are the foundation of development, and money is one of the fruits of that hard work.

From now on we shall stand upright and walk forward on our feet rather than look at this problem upside down. Industries will come and money will come, but their foundation is *the people* and their *hard work*, especially in *agriculture*. This is the meaning of self-reliance. . . .   [ ]

··{20}·· North Africa and the Middle East

SOVIET REACTION TO THE BAGHDAD PACT[1]
Statement by U.S.S.R. Ministry of Foreign Affairs on Security in the Near and Middle East, April 16, 1955

The situation in the Near and Middle East has recently become considerably more tense. The explanation of this is that certain western powers have been making new attempts to draw the countries of the Near and Middle East into the military groupings which are being set up as appendages to the aggressive North Atlantic bloc. . . .

It is not difficult to see that, lying at the basis of the policy of setting up military groupings in the Near and Middle East—just as in the establishment of the aggressive military grouping in South-East Asia (the so-called S.E.A.-T.O.)—is the desire of certain western powers for the colonial enslavement of these countries. The western powers wish to carry on exploiting the peoples of the countries of the Near and Middle East so as to enrich their big monopolies which are making greedy use of the natural wealth of these countries. Unable to establish and preserve their domination by the old methods, these powers are trying to involve the countries of the Near and Middle East in aggressive blocs, on the false pretext that this is in the interests of the defence of the countries of this area.

Military blocs in the Near and Middle East are needed, not by the countries of that area, but by those aggressive American circles which are trying to establish domination there. They are also needed by those British circles which, by means of these blocs, are trying to retain and restore their shaken positions, in spite of the vital interests of the peoples of the Near and Middle East who have taken the road of independent national development. . . .

As has frequently happened in the past, now, too, efforts are being made to cloak the aggressive nature of the Near and Middle Eastern plans of the United States and Britain with ridiculous fabrications about a "Soviet menace" to the countries of that area. Such inventions have nothing in common

[1] Reprinted with permission from the *Soviet News*, No. 3146 (April 19, 1955), pp. 1–2.

with reality, for it is a matter of record that the underlying basis of the Soviet Union's foreign policy is an unalterable desire to ensure peace among the peoples, a peace founded on observance of the principles of equality, non-interference in domestic affairs, and respect for national independence and state sovereignty.

From the very first days of its existence, the Soviet state has decisively condemned the policy of imperialist usurpations and colonial oppression; and it annulled all the unequal treaties which the tsarist government had concluded with the countries of the east.

Regarding the national aspirations of the peoples of the east with full understanding and sympathy, the Soviet government was the first to recognise the independence of Afghanistan and helped her to restore her state sovereignty.

The Soviet government cancelled the tsarist government's unequal treaties with Iran, and transferred to her great material wealth which Russia owned in Iran.

During the years of Turkey's hard struggle for national independence, the Soviet Union stretched out the hand of friendship and gave her all-round assistance—a fact which played a decisive part in the struggle of the Turkish people against the foreign interventionists.

The Soviet government was the first to recognise Saudi Arabia as an independent state and supported the struggle for state independence of the Yemen, Syria and Lebanon, and Egypt's rightful demands for the withdrawal of foreign troops from her territory.

In international bodies, the Soviet government always supports the legitimate demands of the countries of the Near and Middle East aimed at strengthening their national independence and state sovereignty.

The Soviet Union has unswervingly pursued, and continues to pursue a policy of peace and the easing of international tension. Proof of this, in particular, can be seen in its proposal to end the arms drive; to prohibit atomic and hydrogen weapons; for an immediate and substantial reduction of armaments and, first and foremost, of the armaments of the five great powers; and for the establishment of a system of collective security in Europe. . . .

Of course, the Soviet Union cannot remain indifferent to the situation arising in the region of the Near and Middle East, since the formation of these blocs and the establishment of foreign military bases on the territory of the countries of the Near and Middle East have a direct bearing on the security of the U.S.S.R. This attitude of the Soviet government should be all the more understandable since the U.S.S.R. is situated very close to these countries—something which cannot be said of other foreign powers, for instance, of the United States, which is thousands of kilometres from this area.

The refusal of the countries of the Near and Middle East to take part in aggressive military blocs would be an important prerequisite to the ensuring of their security, and the best guarantee of these countries not being drawn into dangerous military adventures.

Striving for the development of peaceful co-operation among all countries, the Soviet government is prepared to support and develop co-operation with the countries of the Near and Middle East, in the interests of strengthening peace in this area. In its declaration of February 9, 1955, the Supreme Soviet of the Union of Soviet Socialist Republics declared that it considered it of exceedingly great importance that relations among countries, large and small, should be based on those international principles which would facilitate the development of friendly co-operation among the nations, in conditions of a peaceful and tranquil life.

The Soviet Union believes that relations among states, and real security can be ensured on the basis of the practical application of the well-known principles enumerated in that declaration—namely: equality; non-interference in domestic affairs; non-aggression and the renunciation of encroachment on the territorial integrity of other states; and on respect for sovereignty and national independence.

The government of the Soviet Union would support any steps by the countries of the Near and Middle East towards putting these principles into practice in the relations between them and the Soviet Union, towards strengthening the national independence of these countries and consolidating peace and friendly co-operation among the peoples.

If the policy of pressure and threats with regard to the countries of the Near and Middle East is continued, the question should be examined by the United Nations Organisation.

Upholding the cause of peace, the Soviet government will defend the freedom and independence of the countries of the Near and Middle East and will oppose interference in their domestic affairs.

DENOUNCEMENT OF THE PROPOSAL FOR A CANAL USERS ASSOCIATION[1]
Speech by President Nasser of the United Arab Republic, September 15, 1956

In these decisive days in the history of mankind, these days in which truth struggles to have itself recognized in international chaos where powers of evil domination and imperialism have prevailed, Egypt stands firmly to preserve her sovereignty. Your country stands solidly and stanchly to preserve her dignity against imperialistic schemes of a number of nations who have uncovered their desires for domination and supremacy.

In these days and in such circumstances Egypt has resolved to show the

---

[1] Reprinted from *The Suez Canal Problem, 26 July–22 September 1956*, U.S. Department of State Publication No. 6392 (Washington: G.P.O., 1956), pp. 345–351.

world that when small nations decide to preserve their sovereignty, they will do that all right and that when these small nations are fully determined to defend their rights and maintain their dignity, they will undoubtedly succeed in achieving their ends. . . .

I am speaking in the name of every Egyptian Arab and in the name of all free countries and of all those who believe in liberty and are ready to defend it. I am speaking in the name of principles proclaimed by these countries in the Atlantic Charter. But they are now violating these principles and it has become our lot to shoulder the responsibility of reaffirming and establishing them anew. . . .

We have tried by all possible means to cooperate with those countries which claim to assist smaller nations and which promised to collaborate with us but they demanded their fees in advance. This we refused so they started to fight with us. They said they will pay toward building the High Dam and then they withdrew their offer and cast doubts on the Egyptian economy. Are we to declaim [*disclaim?*] our sovereign right? Egypt insists her sovereignty must remain intact and refuses to give up any part of that sovereignty for the sake of money.

Egypt nationalized the Egyptian Suez Canal company. When Egypt granted the concession to de Lesseps it was stated in the concession between the Egyptian Government and the Egyptian company that the company of the Suez Canal is an Egyptian company subject to Egyptian authority. Egypt nationalized this Egyptian company and declared freedom of navigation will be preserved.

But the imperialists became angry. Britain and France said Egypt grabbed the Suez Canal as if it were part of France or Britain. The British Foreign Secretary forgot that only two years ago he signed an agreement stating the Suez Canal is an integral part of Egypt.

Egypt declared she was ready to negotiate. But as soon as negotiations began threats and intimidations started. . . .

Eden stated in the House of Commons there shall be no discrimination between states using the canal. We on our part reaffirm that and declare there is no discrimination between canal users. He also said Egypt shall not be allowed to succeed because that would spell success for Arab nationalism and would be against their policy, which aims at the protection of Israel.

Today they are speaking of a new association whose main objective would be to rob Egypt of the canal and deprive her of rightful canal dues. Suggestions made by Eden in the House of Commons which have been backed by France and the United States are a clear violation of the 1888 convention, since it is impossible to have two bodies organizing navigation in the canal. . . .

By stating that by succeeding, Abdel Nasser would weaken Britain's stand against Arab nationalism, Eden is in fact admitting his real objective is not Abdel Nasser as such but rather to defeat Arab nationalism and crush its cause. Eden speaks and finds his own answer. A month ago he let out the cry that he was after Abdel Nasser. Today the Egyptian people are fully conscious of their sovereign rights and Arab nationalism is fully awakened to its new destiny. . . .

Those who attack Egypt will never leave Egypt alive. We shall fight a regular war, a total war, a guerrilla war. Those who attack Egypt will soon realize they brought disaster upon themselves. He who attacks Egypt attacks the whole Arab world. They say in their papers the whole thing will be over in forty-eight hours. They do not know how strong we really are.

We believe in international law. But we will never submit. We shall show the world how a small country can stand in the face of great powers threatening with armed might. Egypt might be a small power but she is great inasmuch as she has faith in her power and convictions. I feel quite certain every Egyptian shares the same convictions as I do and believes in everything I am stressing now.

We shall defend our freedom and independence to the last drop of our blood. This is the stanch feeling of every Egyptian. The whole Arab nation will stand by us in our common fight against aggression and domination. Free peoples, too, people who are really free will stand by us and support us against the forces of tyranny.   [ ]

THE EISENHOWER DOCTRINE[1]
President Eisenhower's Message to Congress, January 5, 1957

I

[ ]
The Middle East has abruptly reached a new and critical stage in its long and important history. In past decades many of the countries in that area were not fully self-governing. Other nations exercised considerable authority in the area and the security of the region was largely built around their power. But since the First World War there has been a steady evolution toward self-government and independence. This development the United States has welcomed and has encouraged. Our country supports without reservation the full sovereignty and independence of each and every nation of the Middle East.

The evolution to independence has in the main been a peaceful process. But the area has been often troubled. Persistent cross-currents of distrust and fear with raids back and forth across national boundaries have brought about a high degree of instability in much of the Mid East. Just recently there have been hostilities involving Western European nations that once exercised

---

[1] Reprinted from *The Department of State Bulletin*, XXXVI, No. 917 (January 21, 1957), pp. 83–87.

much influence in the area. Also the relatively large attack by Israel in October has intensified the basic differences between that nation and its Arab neighbors. All this instability has been heightened and, at times, manipulated by International Communism.

II

Russia's rulers have long sought to dominate the Middle East. That was true of the Czars and it is true of the Bolsheviks. The reasons are not hard to find. They do not affect Russia's security, for no one plans to use the Middle East as a base for aggression against Russia. Never for a moment has the United States entertained such a thought.

The Soviet Union has nothing whatsoever to fear from the United States in the Middle East, or anywhere else in the world, so long as its rulers do not themselves first resort to aggression.

That statement I make solemnly and emphatically. . . .

The reason for Russia's interest in the Middle East is solely that of power politics. Considering her announced purpose of Communizing the world, it is easy to understand her hope of dominating the Middle East. . . .

International Communism, of course, seeks to mask its purposes of domination by expressions of good will and by superficially attractive offers of political, economic and military aid. But any free nation, which is the subject of Soviet enticement, ought, in elementary wisdom, to look behind the mask.

Remember Estonia, Latvia and Lithuania. In 1939 the Soviet Union entered into mutual assistance pacts with these then independent countries; and the Soviet Foreign Minister, addressing the Extraordinary Fifth Session of the Supreme Soviet in October 1939, solemnly and publicly declared that "we stand for the scrupulous and punctilious observance of the pacts on the basis of complete reciprocity, and we declare that all the nonsensical talk about the Sovietization of the Baltic countries is only to the interest of our common enemies and of all anti-Soviet provocateurs." Yet in 1940, Estonia, Latvia and Lithuania were forcibly incorporated into the Soviet Union.

Soviet control of the satellite nations of Eastern Europe has been forcibly maintained in spite of solemn promises of a contrary intent, made during World War II.

Stalin's death brought hope that this pattern would change. And we read the pledge of the Warsaw Treaty of 1955 that the Soviet Union would follow in satellite countries "the principles of mutual respect for their independence and sovereignty and non-interference in domestic affairs." But we have just seen the subjugation of Hungary by naked armed force. In the aftermath of this Hungarian tragedy, world respect for and belief in Soviet promises have sunk to a new low. International Communism needs and seeks a recognizable success.

Thus, we have these simple and indisputable facts:

1. The Middle East, which has always been coveted by Russia, would today be prized more than ever by International Communism.

2. The Soviet rulers continue to show that they do not scruple to use any means to gain their ends.

3. The free nations of the Mid East need, and for the most part want, added strength to assure their continued independence.

IV

[ ]
Under all the circumstances I have laid before you, a greater responsibility now devolves upon the United States. We have shown, so that none can doubt, our dedication to the principle that force shall not be used internationally for any aggressive purpose and that the integrity and independence of the nations of the Middle East should be inviolate. Seldom in history has a nation's dedication to principle been tested as severely as ours during recent weeks.

There is general recognition in the Middle East, as elsewhere, that the United States does not seek either political or economic domination over any other people. Our desire is a world environment of freedom, not servitude. On the other hand many, if not all, of the nations of the Middle East are aware of the danger that stems from International Communism and welcome closer cooperation with the United States to realize for themselves the United Nations goals of independence, economic well-being and spiritual growth. . . .

V

Under these circumstances I deem it necessary to seek the cooperation of the Congress. Only with that cooperation can we give the reassurance needed to deter aggression, to give courage and confidence to those who are dedicated to freedom and thus prevent a chain of events which would gravely endanger all of the free world. . . .

VI

[ ]
The action which I propose would have the following features.

It would, first of all, authorize the United States to cooperate with and assist any nation or group of nations in the general area of the Middle East in the development of economic strength dedicated to the maintenance of national independence.

It would, in the second place, authorize the Executive to undertake in the same region programs of military assistance and cooperation with any nation or group of nations which desires such aid.

It would, in the third place, authorize such assistance and cooperation to include the employment of the armed forces of the United States to secure and protect the territorial integrity and political independence of such nations, requesting such aid, against overt armed aggression from any nation controlled by International Communism.

These measures would have to be consonant with the treaty obligations of the United States, including the Charter of the United Nations and with any action or recommendations of the United Nations. They would also, if armed attack occurs, be subject to the overriding authority of the United Nations Security Council in accordance with the Charter.

The present proposal would, in the fourth place, authorize the President to employ, for economic and defensive military purposes, sums available under the Mutual Security Act of 1954, as amended, without regard to existing limitations. . . .

VII

[ ]
The proposed legislation is primarily designed to deal with the possibility of Communist aggression, direct and indirect. There is imperative need that any lack of power in the area should be made good, not by external or alien force, but by the increased vigor and security of the independent nations of the area.

Experience shows that indirect aggression rarely if ever succeeds where there is reasonable security against direct aggression; where the government possesses loyal security forces, and where economic conditions are such as not to make Communism seem an attractive alternative. The program I suggest deals with all three aspects of this matter and thus with the problem of indirect aggression. . . .

And as I have indicated, it will also be necessary for us to contribute economically to strengthen those countries, or groups of countries, which have governments manifestly dedicated to the preservation of independence and resistance to subversion. Such measures will provide the greatest insurance against Communist inroads. Words alone are not enough.

VIII

Let me refer again to the requested authority to employ the armed forces of the United States to assist to defend the territorial integrity and the political independence of any nation in the area against Communist armed aggression. Such authority would not be exercised except at the desire of the nation attacked. Beyond this it is my profound hope that this authority would never have to be exercised at all. . . .

In the situation now existing, the greatest risk, as is often the case, is that ambitious despots may miscalculate. If power-hungry Communists should either falsely or correctly estimate that the Middle East is inadequately defended, they might be tempted to use open measures of armed attack. If so, that would start a chain of circumstances which would almost surely involve the United States in military action. I am convinced that the best insurance against this dangerous contingency is to make clear now our readiness to cooperate fully and freely with our friends of the Middle East in ways consonant with the purposes and principles of the United Nations. I intend promptly to send a special mission to the Middle East to explain the cooperation we are prepared to give.

IX

The policy which I outline involves certain burdens and indeed risks for the United States. Those who covet the area will not like what is proposed. Already, they are grossly distorting our purpose. However, before this Americans have seen our nation's vital interests and human freedom in jeopardy, and their fortitude and resolution have been equal to the crisis, regardless of hostile distortion of our words, motives and actions. . . .

In those momentous periods of the past, the President and the Congress have united, without partisanship, to serve the vital interests of the United States and of the free world.

The occasion has come for us to manifest again our national unity in support of freedom and to show our deep respect for the rights and independence of every nation—however great, however small. We seek not violence, but peace. To this purpose we must now devote our energies, our determination, ourselves.

TASS STATEMENT ON THE EISENHOWER DOCTRINE[1]
January 14, 1957

The President of the United States of America, Mr. Dwight D. Eisenhower, on January 5 addressed a special message to Congress on the policy of the United States in the Middle East countries. In his message, which abounds in anti-Soviet remarks, the President, describing the present situation in the Middle East as "critical," demanded the authority to use the armed forces of the United States in the Middle East at any moment he might consider it necessary, without asking for the consent of Congress as is envisaged in the country's Constitution. The President of the United States also demanded that he be empowered to render military and economic "aid" to the countries of the Middle East. It is envisaged, specifically, that 200 million dollars will be spent for "economic support" to countries of that area.

President Eisenhower's message runs counter to the principles and the purposes of the United Nations and is fraught with grave danger to peace and security in the Middle East area. . . .

In his message to Congress the President of the United States speaks of

---

[1] Reprinted with permission from the *Soviet News*, No. 3549 (January 14, 1957), pp. 33–34.

the sympathy which, he claims, the United States entertains for the Arab countries. Life, however, shows that in actual fact the American ruling circles are setting themselves obviously selfish aims in that area. It is a fact that when Egypt, as a result of the military aggression of Britain, France and Israel, was threatened with the loss of her national independence, the United States refused to pool its efforts with the Soviet Union in the United Nations in order to take resolute measures to cut short the aggression. The primary concern of the United States was not the defence of peace and the national independence of the Arab countries, but the desire to take advantage of the weakening of Britain and France in the Middle East to capture their positions.

At present, when a favourable situation has developed in the Middle East and real possibilities for consolidating peace and settling outstanding issues in that area have been created, the government of the United States has come forward with a programme which envisages flagrant interference by the United States in the affairs of the Arab countries, up to and including military intervention. The aggressive trend of this programme and its colonialist nature with regard to the Arab countries are so obvious that this cannot be disguised by any nebulous phrases about the love for peace and the concern claimed to be shown by the United States for the Middle East countries.

It is permissible to ask: Of what love for peace do the authors of the "Eisenhower doctrine" speak when the threat to the security of the Middle East countries emanates precisely from member-states of N.A.T.O., in which the United States plays first fiddle? What concern for the aforementioned countries can be in question when it is the United States and its N.A.T.O. partners that regard those countries merely as sources of strategic raw materials and spheres for the investment of capital, with the object of extracting maximum profits? Is it not clear that the uninvited "protectors" of the Middle East countries are trying to impose on that area nothing else but the régime of a kind of military protectorate, and to set back the development of these countries for many years? . . .

The United States ruling circles consider that the weakening of the positions of the Anglo-French colonialists in the Middle East and the successes of the Arab countries in consolidating their independence have produced a "vacuum," which they would like to fill by their military and economic intervention in the internal affairs of those countries. But what "vacuum" can be in question here? Since when do countries which have liberated themselves from colonial oppression and have taken the road of independent national development constitute a "vacuum"? It is clear that the strengthening of the national independence of the Arab countries, the intensification of their struggle against colonial oppression by no means create some kind of "vacuum," but are a restoration of the national rights of the Middle East peoples and constitute a progressive factor in social development. The United States tries to present its policy as an anti-colonialist one. But it is not difficult to see the falseness of these assertions, clearly designed to blunt the vigilance of the peoples in the Middle East. The programme of the United States insistently stresses that the Middle East must recognise its interdependence with the western countries, that is, with the colonialists—specifically with regard to oil, the Suez Canal, etc. In other words, the United States is stubbornly seeking to impose a "trusteeship" of the colonialists on the peoples of the Middle East countries. . . .

The authors of the colonialist programme try to sweeten it by a promise of economic "aid" to the Middle East countries. Every intelligent person, however, understands that in reality the United States is offering as charity to the peoples of the Arab countries only a small fraction of what the American monopolies have received and are receiving by plundering, by exploiting the natural wealth belonging to those countries. The United States promises the countries of the Middle East 200 million dollars in the financial years of 1958 and 1959, whereas in 1955 alone the American and British oil monopolies extracted 150 million tons of oil in the Middle East at a total cost of 240 million dollars, and made a net profit of 1,900 million dollars on this oil. Such is the real picture of American "philanthropy.". . .

Seeking to cover up gross intervention in the internal affairs of the Middle East countries and their aggressive policy with regard to these countries, the United States ruling circles resort to inventions about a threat to the Arab countries emanating from the Soviet Union. These slanderous assertions will deceive no one. The peoples of the Middle East have not forgotten that the Soviet Union has always defended the self-determination of peoples, the gaining and consolidating of their national independence. They have learned from experience that in relations with all countries the Soviet Union steadfastly pursues the policy of equality and non-interference in internal affairs. They also know very well that the Soviet Union is actively supporting the right of each people to dispose of its natural wealth and use it at its own discretion.

It was not the Soviet Union, but Britain and France—the United States' chief partners in the North Atlantic bloc—which committed aggression against Egypt, inflicting great losses and suffering on the Egyptian people. This is borne out by the fresh ruins of Port Said and other Egyptian cities, as well as by the new plans for United States economic, political and military expansion in the Middle East proclaimed by the American President. These aggressive plans of the American imperialists express their striving for world domination, of which they speak now quite shamelessly, presenting this aspiration as the need for "energetic leadership" of the world by the United States.

In the days of hard trials for the Arab peoples it was the Soviet Union, and no one else, who came out as their sincere friend and, together with the peaceloving forces of the whole world, took steps to end the aggression against Egypt. All this is well known. . . .

It is well known that the Soviet Union, as distinct from the United States, does not have and does not seek to have any military bases or concessions in the Middle East with the object of extracting profits, does not strive to gain any privileges in that area, since all this is incompatible with the principles of Soviet foreign policy.

The Soviet Union is vitally interested in the maintenance of peace in the Middle East area, situated as it is in direct proximity to its frontiers. It is sincerely interested in consolidating the national independence of those countries and in their economic prosperity and regards this as a reliable guarantee of peace and security in that area.

In our age the national liberation movement of the peoples is a historical force that cannot be repressed.

The Soviet Union, loyal to the great Leninist principles of recognising and respecting the rights of peoples, large and small, to independent development, regards as one of its prime tasks the rendering of every assistance and support to the countries fighting to consolidate their national independence and their sovereignty. That is why it welcomes the growing unity of the peoples of the Arab countries in their struggle for peace, security, national freedom and independence.

The Soviet Union opposes any manifestations of colonialism, any "doctrines" which protect and cover up colonialism. It is opposed to unequal treaties and agreements, the setting up of military bases on foreign territories, dictated by strategic considerations, and plans for establishing the world domination of imperialism. It proceeds from the premise that the natural wealth of the underdeveloped countries is the inalienable national possession of the peoples of those countries, who have the full right to dispose of it independently and to use it for their economic prosperity and progress. The need to strengthen peace and security demands the wide development of political, economic and cultural ties between all countries. The development of these ties is an important prerequisite for using the achievements of contemporary science and technology for the good of mankind. The policy of establishing closed aggressive military blocs, such as N.A.T.O., S.E.A.T.O. and the Baghdad Pact, and the raising of artificial economic barriers hampering normal relations between states seriously impairs the cause of peace. The Soviet Union, striving to render assistance to peoples fighting for the consolidation of their national independence and the earliest elimination of the aftermath of colonial oppression, is willing to develop all-round co-operation with them on the principles of full equality and mutual benefit. . . .

Authoritative Soviet circles hold that the steps with regard to the Middle East area outlined by the United States government, which envisage the possibility of employing United States armed forces in that area, might lead to dangerous consequences, the responsibility for which will rest entirely with the United States government.

AFRO-ASIAN SOLIDARITY AND THE WORLD MISSION OF THE PEOPLES OF AFRICA AND ASIA[1]

Address Delivered by Mr. Anwar el Sadat at the First Afro-Asian People's Solidarity Conference, December 26, 1957

[ ]

More than two years ago twenty nine governments of independent states convened together at the Bandung Conference to declare to the world at large that the tide of history has changed its course, and that Asia and Africa, which hitherto have been common play ground, where trespassers went by unheeded or a forest in which foreign beasts of prey roamed at leisure, have now become free world powers, majestic and serene, with a decisive role in shaping the future of the whole family of Nations. The Conference of Bandung was likewise convened to stress to the peoples of Africa and Asia the great importance of solidarity and the great weight they would have on the trend of world affairs when united. Today this people's Conference of ours meets, partly in honour of the spirit of Bandung and as a reminder of the principles and ideals it stands for, and partly to push it a step forward. Because our Conference is a Conference of peoples, it has been able to muster, not only the countries recognized by International Law as independent units, but also those peoples whose status is a foregone conclusion, a historical fact, and a reality endorsed by the whole of mankind, in addition to peoples who are still trodden under the heel of imperialism in one form or another. But our Conference takes the interest of these very peoples to heart. They are the diseased organs in the body of Asia and Africa: consequently they stand in dire need of the greatest of care and attention. A body cannot continue to exist with half of its structure safe and sound while the other half is diseased and decayed. . . .

The idea of Afro-Asian Solidarity did not emanate out of naught, so as to be born and see daylight at Bandung all of a sudden. But before materializing as an historical event, it was an impression and an innate volition instinctively developing in the mind of the colonized and the exploited—the human being whom imperialism had reduced to a typefied specimen of a subjugated specie and bondsman recognisable in every colonized country. Indeed the idea of solidarity was deeply rooted in the hearts of those subjected peoples, continually aspiring through diverse national movements to smash the fetters of bondage and redeem their salvation. In the course of time these national movements were destined to meet, to consolidate and to react with one

---

[1] Reprinted from *The First Afro-Asian People's Solidarity Conference, 26 December 1957 to January 1, 1958*, 2nd edition (Cairo: The Permanent Secretariat of the Organization for Afro-Asian People's Solidarity, 1958), pp. 7–12.

another, purposefully in some instances, but unconsciously and spontaneously in the majority of cases.

It is evident therefore, that the Bandung Conference was not a haphazard event, but rather a natural psychological factor which led to the awakening of the peoples of Africa and Asia and roused them from their slumber to solve the problem of their very existence and survival, and to resume the struggle for the recovery of their liberty and freedom. This awakening would have been devoid of any historical significance had it not marked a point of departure towards a new progressive future, the fundamental broad lines of which have been laid down by the Bandung Conference. It is up to the Peoples' Cairo Conference to reap from it, to the fullest extent, the benefits of the positive results which have blossomed in the political, economic, social and cultural fields alike. It is here that we shall necessarily be confronted by a number of difficult problems, but to find adequate solutions to these problems is not an impossible task, if we succeed in overcoming the first difficulty from the outset. It is a problem which comes within our own selves. It is the problem of sound and unbiased judgment. . . .

No doubt each country has its own particular problems for which she is more competent than any one else to gauge the nature of the difficulties they represent; but at the same time, there is not a shadow of a doubt also that it is within the power of each of us to extend a helping hand to his brother in time of need, in an endeavour to assist in solving his problems, be it only in the form of a genuine, friendly counsel or an expert advice. Thus it becomes evident that it is the duty of each of us to foster a double interest—an interest in his own problems, and an interest in the problems of others.

In addition, there are problems which present a common interest to us all. They react on us, and reflect on all of us one and the same homogeneous picture. Consequently, our particular national problems, and the problems common to us all, must of necessity go along, side by side. . . .

These are not the only responsibilities we have to shoulder in our Conference; for in addition to the host of responsibilities we have towards our diverse specific countries, there are others we have towards our two Continents, Africa and Asia. Besides, we have definite responsibilities towards the whole of mankind as an entire, indivisible unit.

We cannot live peacefully in a world threatened by the shadow of war. We can no longer enjoy the products of our hands and the fruits of our labour in a world where plunder prevails and flourishes. We can no longer build and reconstruct in a world which manufactures weapons for destruction and devastation. We can no longer raise the standard of living of our peoples and stamp out diseases and epidemics in a world where nations vie with each other for the production of lethal weapons of massacre and annihilation. Gone for ever is the era where the future of war and peace was decided upon in a few European capitals, because today we happen to be strong enough to make the decision ourselves in that respect.

Our weight in the international balance has now become preponderant.

Only think of the colossal number of our people, our natural resources, the vastness of the area covered by our respective countries, and our strategic positions. You will surely come to the conclusion that the outbreak of war is impossible so long as we insist on peace, especially if we do not content ourselves with a mere negative attitude, but assume one of positiveness in favour of Peace. This transition from the negative to the positive is a fundamental basis worthy of our adoption.

Here in Egypt we, for instance, believe in the principle of neutrality and non-alignment. Many of our friends in Asia and Africa share this belief. We are confident that by adopting this attitude, we eliminate the shadow of war and limit the area of conflict between the two belligerent blocks, thus creating a vast region for Peace, imposing its existence and its atmosphere day after day, until it prevails over the whole world. But this neutrality in which we believe, though it defines the principle of abstaining from entering into international blocks, yet it also means that we shall spare no positive effort in reconciliating these belligerent blocks. . . . It is the very principle which has been stressed by the President Gamal Abdul Nasser in his speech at Port Said on the anniversary of its liberation, when he said:

Today in Port Said we turn to the whole world demanding the corroboration of the fundamental principles of justice, which is the right to self-determination. We look from Port Said towards the whole world and demand that every colonized State should be granted its independence, and the right to govern itself. . . .

In the name of Egypt, I address a message to the world at large, for the preservation of Peace, and the abolition of war; for the removal of world tension, and the cessation of the cold war of nerves. We have seen war at Port Said. We have been hit by it, and faced its ravages and woes. But a World War, once it breaks out with its nuclear weapons and hydrogen bombs, will unquestionably annihilate mankind and destroy for ever our existing civilization. As a section of humanity, which has been treacherously attacked by imperialistic States, we demand that atomic experiments should be abolished, and that manufacture and use of nuclear weapons should be prohibited. We further press for disarmament in the interests of World Peace.

The People of Egypt who are sparing no effort for the establishment of universal justice, equity, liberty and peace, welcome you as messengers of justice, equity, liberty and peace.

THE DISPATCH OF UNITED STATES TROOPS TO LEBANON[1]
Statement by President Eisenhower, July 15, 1958

Yesterday morning, I received from President Chamoun of Lebanon an urgent plea that some United States forces be stationed in Lebanon to help

---

[1] Reprinted from *The Department of State Bulletin*, XXXIX, No. 997 (August 4, 1958), pp. 181–182.

maintain security and to evidence the concern of the United States for the integrity and independence of Lebanon. President Chamoun's appeal was made with the concurrence of all of the members of the Lebanese Cabinet. . . .

In response to this appeal from the government of Lebanon, the United States has dispatched a contingent of United States forces to Lebanon to protect American lives and by their presence there to encourage the Lebanese government in defense of Lebanese sovereignty and integrity. These forces have not been sent as any act of war. They will demonstrate the concern of the United States for the independence and integrity of Lebanon, which we deem vital to the national interest and world peace. Our concern will also be shown by economic assistance. We shall act in accordance with these legitimate concerns.

The United States, this morning, will report its action to an emergency meeting of the United Nations Security Council. As the United Nations charter recognizes, there is an inherent right of collective self-defense. In conformity with the spirit of the charter, the United States is reporting the measures taken by it to the Security Council of the United Nations, making clear that these measures will be terminated as soon as the Security Council has itself taken the measures necessary to maintain international peace and security.

The United States believes that the United Nations can and should take measures which are adequate to preserve the independence and integrity of Lebanon. It is apparent, however, that in the face of the tragic and shocking events that are occurring nearby, more will be required than the team of United Nations observers now in Lebanon. Therefore, the United States will support in the United Nations measures which seem to be adequate to meet the new situation and which will enable the United States forces promptly to be withdrawn.

Lebanon is a small peace-loving state with which the United States has traditionally had the most friendly relations. There are in Lebanon about 2,500 Americans and we cannot, consistently with our historic relations and with the principles of the United Nations, stand idly by when Lebanon appeals itself for evidence of our concern and when Lebanon may not be able to preserve internal order and to defend itself against indirect aggression.

THE DISPATCH OF UNITED STATES TROOPS TO LEBANON ON JULY 15, 1958[1]
Soviet Government's Statement, July 16, 1958

On July 15 the whole world learned with indignation of the armed intervention by the United States of America in Lebanon. Ships of the

---

[1] Reprinted with permission from the Soviet News, No. 3879 (July 17, 1958), pp. 53–54.

United States Sixth Fleet entered the port of Beirut and landed marines on the territory of Lebanon.

On the same day the White House—in the name of the President of the United States—issued a statement attempting somehow to justify this flagrant military intervention in Lebanon's internal affairs. The statement alleges that the United States has sent its troops to Lebanon to demonstrate United States concern for the integrity and independence of Lebanon, which, so it claims, are being threatened from without, and also to protect American citizens in that country. . . .

The real reason for United States armed intervention in Lebanon is the desire of the oil monopolies of the United States and other western powers to retain their colonial hold on countries of the Middle East, and also the obvious bankruptcy of their policy in the Arab East and the collapse of the Baghdad Pact and of the notorious Dulles-Eisenhower doctrine. . . .

It is well known that on the night of July 13 to 14, the monarchy in Iraq was overthrown by the army, supported by the people; a republic was proclaimed and a government of the Republic of Iraq was set up.

The first acts of this government, led by General Abdel Kerim Kassem, in the sphere of foreign policy were statements expressing full support for the principles of the Bandung Conference, withdrawal from the aggressive military Baghdad Pact, and recognition of the United Arab Republic.

The government of the Republic of Iraq declared that it would "act in accordance with the principles of the United Nations," would "follow an Arab policy and strictly abide by the decisions of the Bandung Conference," and that it was prepared "to honour commitments and treaties springing from the interests of the motherland." It also announced that it guaranteed the security of foreign nationals and their property.

These actions are evidence of the government's intention to defend the country's national independence and to strive, together with the other freedom-loving Arab peoples, to overcome the grievous aftermath of colonialism, to develop the national economy and to raise the living standards of the people. . . .

This turn in events in the Middle East obviously does not suit the colonial powers, which received the news of the establishment of the Republic of Iraq with undisguised hostility. Feverish activity began immediately in Washington, London and Ankara.

The existence of plans for large-scale intervention by the colonial powers in the internal affairs of countries of the Arab East is also borne out by the statement by the British Foreign Secretary, Mr. Selwyn Lloyd, that the British government had been informed in advance of the United States government's intention to land its troops in Lebanon, that the British government fully supported this action of the United States and that the British armed forces in the area were being kept ready.

In order to provide a pretext for armed intervention in the internal affairs of the Arab countries a statement by the Lebanese President Chamoun asking

the governments of the United States, Britain and France to send troops to
Lebanon, was inspired. It is well known, however, that the present events in
Lebanon are a result of purely internal causes and that only interference by
countries of the Baghdad Pact and the United States, seeking to preserve an
anti-national régime at any cost, has led to civil war and to a worsening of the
entire situation in the area. . . .

Armed intervention by the United States in Lebanon shows clearly that
the imperialists have cast off their disguise and have begun open aggression
against peaceloving Arab peoples. In this connection it becomes particularly
clear why the government of the United States did not accept the Soviet
government's proposal of February 11, 1957, concerning non-interference by
the great powers in the internal affairs of the countries of the area. The
government of the United States refused to undertake commitments which
would have ensured peace and eased the tension in that part of the
world. . . .

United States armed intervention in Lebanon creates a grave threat to
peace and is fraught with far-reaching consequences. The peoples cannot
remain unconcerned in face of this brazen imperialist aggression, this gross
encroachment on the sovereignty and national independence of the Arab
countries and this unceremonious violation of the principles of the United
Nations.

The White House plea that American troops are being sent to Lebanon
for purposes of self-defence and in the national interests of the United States
is open mockery of these principles. Who does not know that the United
States lies thousands of kilometres from Lebanon and that the people of
Lebanon and other Arab countries can in no way threaten either the national
interests or the security of the United States? As for Lebanon, it is precisely
American armed intervention that is the main threat to the security of this
small Arab country.

Having taken to the road of flagrant violation of the United Nations
Charter, the government of the United States is now attempting to confront
the Security Council and the whole of the United Nations with a *fait
accompli* and to bring pressure to bear on the United Nations to make it
approve the unilateral aggressive actions of the U.S.A.

The Soviet government considers that the situation in the Middle East
—a situation created by open aggression on the part of the United States,
supported by other colonial powers—is an alarming one and is dangerous to
world peace. In these circumstances, the Security Council and the United
Nations General Assembly should take urgent and vigorous measures to curb
aggression and to protect the national independence of Arab states which
have fallen victim to an unprovoked attack.

The Soviet government urges the government of the United States to
cease its armed intervention in the internal affairs of Arab countries and to
withdraw its troops from Lebanon immediately.

The Soviet government declares that the Soviet Union cannot remain indifferent to events creating a grave menace in an area abutting on its frontiers, and reserves the right to take the necessary measures dictated by the interests of peace and security.

··{21}·· *The Independent Nations of Southeast Asia*

THE TASK BEFORE US[1]
Convocation Address by Prime Minister U Nu of Burma at the University of Rangoon, December 22, 1951

To-day I am to confer degrees to the candidates who have succeeded in the University examination. But I want to do more than that. I want to confer a charge to all students, not only to the students here assembled, but to all students all over Burma. This charge is none other than to bring about in this country of ours a state of affairs which will no longer be fluid and unstable like the surface of the sea but as firm as *terra firma*.

Before I expatiate on the magnitude of this charge let me go a little into the past history of our Union of Burma. Then only you will realize—

(1) how badly dilapidated this Union of Burma is,
(2) why she is so dilapidated,
(3) and how much hard work lies ahead of us to build her up again.

The history of Burma from the beginning at Tagaung of Abhiraja to the end of Thibaw's reign has been a history of kings and kingdoms. As you know, kings were not elected by the people but derived their power from their own might and succession, so that, apart from such great kings as Anawrahta, Bayinnaung, Alaungpaya and Mindonmin, most kings had very little to do with the mass of the people.

They seldom bothered themselves about the five main pillars of Health, Education, Morals, Economics and National Solidarity which must support a nation. It was the people themselves who had to build and tend these pillars as far as they were able throughout the course of history. Thus throughout the course of history these five pillars had never been well and truly set up. After Thibaw, there were the British rulers. They too were not elected by the

---

[1] U Nu, *Burma Looks Ahead* (Ministry of Information, Government of the Union of Burma, 1953), pp. 28–39.

244

people. They were here not to bother about the five pillars but to exploit our country of rice, timber, oil and minerals. . . .

. . . Any country under the Imperialist regime, whether it be Burma, India or America, is sure to have its moral pillars shaken and dilapidated. In such a state unrest and disorders will be the order of the day.

Therefore, in order to bring about a change from the fluid and unstable state of affairs to one which is firm and stable like *terra firma*, we have no other method but to rebuild and renovate to our utmost capacity the five pillars which are in a sorry state. Mere crying over this mess will not do. Mere clamouring to Government to restore immediate peace will not do. Heaping blame on others and launching attacks on Government in a spirit of desperado will not do. Longing for distant friends and beckoning them will not solve our problems. Such measures, instead of improving matters, will make them worse. In fact mere guns will not solve our problems. Stability wrought by guns is never enduring. It will vanish once the guns are withdrawn. We do not want that type of stability brought about by means of guns. We want that type of stability which will endure whether there are guns or not, certain political organizations or not, certain leaders or not. The nature of stability must be spontaneous and natural. Only then will it be safe for everybody. To achieve this type of stability it is up to every one of us in the Union to do our utmost to rebuild the sadly dilapidated five pillars which I have enumerated.

In this noble task of rebuilding the five pillars, you students with your brains and your background will form the vanguard. . . .

To rebuild the pillar of Education, the country needs skilled technicians both in the mechanical and handicraft spheres, skilled educationists, skilled scientists, learned historians, men of letters and leaders of religions.

To rebuild the pillar of Economics, the country needs men and women skilled in Banking, Foreign Exchange, External trade and technicians who have a thorough knowledge of modern factories, administration, etc.

To rebuild the pillar of Morals, the country needs men and women who have made a life-long study of various methods of moral uplift.

To rebuild the pillar of National Solidarity, the country needs able leaders who are endowed with foresight, forbearance, public esteem and exemplary character.

Who are those architects worthy of being entrusted with the task of rebuilding these pillars? It is certain that ignoramuses cannot be our architects. It is you, educated men and women, who can play the role of the country's architects.

On behalf of the Government I have the privilege to lead, let me tell you that we are not here like the British Imperialists to gain dividends. We are here just to serve the people. Therefore if there is anything which is beneficial to the people and which is capable of being done by the Government, please see the authorities concerned and frankly exchange points of views. There is now absolutely no need for you to be rigidly formal and stage threats and struggles, as in the days of the British regime. We are prepared to meet you more than half-way if your proposal is beneficial to the country and is capable of being done by the Government. I declare this both as Chancellor of this University and in the capacity of Prime Minister. . . .

I know for certain that the vast majority of the students in this University are eager to discharge their responsibilities with the sincere desire for the good of the masses, free from political influences and political attachments. Let me address the leaders of these sincere workers. The task of rebuilding the five pillars is not small. Mere attainment of independence will not make these pillars strong. Independence merely entails opportunities for carrying out works for the good of the people. It is up to all of us to carry out these works in our respective spheres to our utmost capacity. You must bear this in mind. If you fail to take advantage of the opportunity thus offered and waste your valuable time in fights and struggles and playing with insurrection, then the country will go to the dogs. . . .

I pray that the students who have graduated this year may turn out to be worthy architects of the five pillars I have just mentioned.

SPEECH BY MR. NEHRU OF INDIA TO THE BANDUNG CONFERENCE POLITICAL COMMITTEE[1]
April 22, 1955

Mr. Chairman, the turn this discussion has taken is a much wider one than that we had already expected. In fact, it has covered the whole major heading. We have just had the advantage of listening to the distinguished leader of the Turkish Delegation who told us what he, as a responsible leader of the nation must do and must not do. He gave us an able statement of what I might call one side representing the views of one of the major blocs existing at the present time in the world. I have no doubt that an equally able disposition could be made on the part of the other bloc. I belong to neither and I propose to belong to neither whatever happens in the world. If we have to stand alone, we will stand by ourselves, whatever happens (and India has stood alone without any aid against a mighty Empire, the British Empire) and we propose to face all consequences. . . .

We do not agree with the communist teachings, we do not agree with the anti-communist teachings, because they are both based on wrong principles. I never challenged the right of my country to defend itself; it has to. We will defend ourselves with whatever arms and strength we have, and if we have no arms we will defend ourselves without arms. I am dead certain that no country can conquer India. Even the two great power blocs together

---

[1] Reprinted from G. M. Kahin, *The Asian-African Conference* (Cornell University Press, 1956), pp. 64–72. Copyright 1956 by Cornell University. Used by permission of Cornell University Press.

cannot conquer India; not even the atom or the hydrogen bomb. I know what my people are. But I know also that if we rely on others, whatever great powers they might be if we look to them for sustenance, then we are weak indeed. . . .

My country has made mistakes. Every country makes mistakes. I have no doubt we will make mistakes; we will stumble and fall and get up. The mistakes of my country and perhaps the mistakes of other countries here do not make a difference; but the mistakes the Great Powers make do make a difference to the world and may well bring about a terrible catastrophe. I speak with the greatest respect of these Great Powers because they are not only great in military might but in development, in culture, in civilization. But I do submit that greatness sometimes brings quite false values, false standards. When they begin to think in terms of military strength—whether it be the United Kingdom, the Soviet Union or the U.S.A.—then they are going away from the right track and the result of that will be that the overwhelming might of one country will conquer the world. Thus far the world has succeeded in preventing that; I cannot speak for the future. . . .

. . . So far as I am concerned, it does not matter what war takes place; we will not take part in it unless we have to defend ourselves. If I join any of these big groups I lose my identity. . . . If all the world were to be divided up between these two big blocs what would be the result? The inevitable result would be war. Therefore every step that takes place in reducing that area in the world which may be called the *unaligned area* is a dangerous step and leads to war. It reduces that objective, that balance, that outlook which other countries without military might can perhaps exercise.

Honorable Members laid great stress on moral force. It is with military force that we are dealing now, but I submit that moral force counts and the moral force of Asia and Africa must, in spite of the atomic and hydrogen bombs of Russia, the U.S.A. or another country, count. . . .

. . . Many members present here do not obviously accept the communist ideology, while some of them do. For my part I do not. I am a positive person, not an 'anti' person. I want positive good for my country and the world. Therefore, are we, the countries of Asia and Africa, devoid of any positive position except being pro-communist or anti-communist? Has it come to this, that the leaders of thought who have given religions and all kinds of things to the world have to tag on to this kind of group or that and be hangers-on of this party or the other carrying out their wishes and occasionally giving an idea? It is most degrading and humiliating to any self-respecting people or nation. It is an intolerable thought to me that the great countries of Asia and Africa should come out of bondage into freedom only to degrade themselves or humiliate themselves in this way. . . .

I submit to you, every pact has brought insecurity and not security to the countries which have entered into them. They have brought the danger of atomic bombs and the rest of it nearer to them than would have been the case otherwise. They have not added to the strength of any country, I submit, which it had singly. It may have produced some idea of security, but it is a false security. It is a bad thing for any country thus to be lulled into security. . . .

. . . Today in the world, I do submit, not only because of the presence of these two colossuses but also because of the coming of the atomic and hydrogen-bomb age, the whole concept of war, of peace, of politics, has changed. We are thinking and acting in terms of a past age. No matter what generals and soldiers learned in the past, it is useless in this atomic age. They do not understand its implications or its use. As an eminent military critic said: 'The whole conception of War is changed. There is no precedent.' It may be so. Now it does not matter if one country is more powerful than the other in the use of the atomic bomb and the hydrogen bomb. One is more powerful in its ruin than the other. That is what is meant by saying that the point of saturation has been reached. However powerful one country is, the other is also powerful. To hit the nail on the head, the world suffers; there can be no victory. It may be said perhaps rightly that owing to this very terrible danger, people refrain from going to war. I hope so. The difficulty is that while Governments want to refrain from war, something suddenly happens and there is war and utter ruin. There is another thing: because of the present position in the world there can be aggression. If there is aggression anywhere in the world, it is bound to result in world war. It does not matter where the aggression is. If one commits the aggression there is world war.

I want the countries here to realise it and not to think in terms of any limitation. Today, a war however limited it may be is bound to lead to a big war. Even if tactical atomic weapons, as they are called, are used, the next step would be the use of the big atomic bomb. You cannot stop these things. In a country's life and death struggle, it is not going to stop short of this. It is not going to decide on our or anybody else's resolutions but it would engage in war, ruin and annihilation of others before it annihilates itself completely. Annihilation will result not only in the countries engaged in war, but owing to the radioactive waves which go thousands and thousands of miles it will destroy everything. That is the position. It is not an academic position; it is not a position of discussing ideologies; nor is it a position of discussing past history. It is looking at the world as it is today.   [ ]

THE MANILA ACCORD[1]
July 31, 1963

The Governments of the Federation of Malaya, the Republic of Indonesia and the Republic of the Philippines, prompted by their keen and common

---

[1] The text of this document was made available through the courtesy of the Embassy of the Philippines, Washington, D.C.

desire to have a general exchange of views on current problems concerning stability, security, economic development and social progress of the three countries and of the region and upon the initiative of President Diosdado Macapagal, agreed that a Conference of Ministers of the three countries be held in Manila on 7th June 1963 for the purpose of achieving common understanding and close fraternal cooperation among themselves. Accordingly, Tun Abdul Razak, Deputy Prime Minister of the Federation of Malaya; Dr. Subandrio, Deputy First Minister/Minister of Foreign Affairs of the Republic of Indonesia; and Honorable Emmanuel Pelaez, Vice President of the Philippines and concurrently Secretary of Foreign Affairs, met in Manila from 7 to 11 June 1963.

2. The deliberations were held in a frank manner and in a most cordial atmosphere in keeping with the spirit of friendship prevailing in the various meetings held between President Soekarno of the Republic of Indonesia, and Prime Minister Tunku Abdul Rahman Putra of the Federation of Malaya, and President Diosdado Macapagal. This Ministerial Conference was a manifestation of the determination of the nations in this region to achieve closer cooperation in their endeavour to chart their common future.

3. The Ministers were of one mind that the three countries share a primary responsibility for the maintenance of the stability and security of the area from subversion in any form or manifestation in order to preserve their respective national identities, and to ensure the peaceful development of their respective countries and of their region, in accordance with the ideals and aspirations of their peoples.

4. In the same spirit of common and constructive endeavour, they exchanged views on the proposed Confederation of nations of Malay origin, the proposed Federation of Malaysia, the Philippine claim to North Borneo and related problems.

THE MACAPAGAL PLAN

5. Recognising that it is in the common interest of their countries to maintain fraternal relations and to strengthen co-operation among their peoples who are bound together by ties of race and culture, the three Ministers agreed to intensify the joint and individual efforts of their countries to secure lasting peace, progress and prosperity for themselves and for their neighbours.

6. In this context, the three Ministers supported President Macapagal's plan envisaging the grouping of the three nations of Malay origin working together in closest harmony but without surrendering any portion of their sovereignty. This calls for the establishment of the necessary common organs.

7. The three Ministers agreed to take the initial steps towards this ultimate aim by establishing machinery for frequent and regular consultations. The details of such machinery will be further defined. This machinery will enable the three governments to hold regular consultations at all levels to deal with matters of mutual interest and concern consistent with the national,

regional and international responsibilities or obligations of each country without prejudice to its sovereignty and independence. The Ministers agreed that their countries will endeavour to achieve close understanding and cooperation in dealing with common problems relating to security, stability, economic, social and cultural development.

8. In order to accelerate the process of growth towards the ultimate establishment of President Macapagal's plan, the Ministers agreed that each country shall set up its own National Secretariat. Pending the establishment of a Central Secretariat for the consultative machinery, the National Secretaries should coordinate and cooperate with each other in the fulfillment of their tasks.

9. The Ministers further agreed to recommend that Heads of Government and Foreign Ministers meet at least once a year for the purpose of consultations on matters of importance and common concern.

MALAYSIA AND NORTH BORNEO

10. The Ministers reaffirmed their countries' adherence to the principle of self-determination for the peoples of non-self-governing territories. In this context, Indonesia and the Philippines stated that they would welcome the formation of Malaysia provided the support of the people of the Borneo territories is ascertained by an independent and impartial authority, the Secretary-General of the United Nations or his representative.

11. The Federation of Malaya expressed appreciation for this attitude of Indonesia and the Philippines and undertook to consult the British Government and the Governments of the Borneo territories with a view to inviting the Secretary-General of the United Nations or his representative to take the necessary steps in order to ascertain the wishes of the people of those territories.

12. The Philippines made it clear that its position on the inclusion of North Borneo in the Federation of Malaysia is subject to the final outcome of the Philippine claim to North Borneo. The Ministers took note of the Philippine claim and the right of the Philippines to continue to pursue it in accordance with international law and the principle of the pacific settlement of disputes. They agreed that the inclusion of North Borneo in the Federation of Malaysia would not prejudice either the claim or any right thereunder. Moreover, in the context of their close association, the three countries agreed to exert their best endeavours to bring the claim to a just and expeditious solution by peaceful means, such as negotiation, conciliation, arbitration, or judicial settlement as well as other peaceful means of the parties' own choice, in conformity with the Charter of the United Nations and the Bandung Declaration.

13. In particular, considering the close historical ties between the peoples of the Philippines and North Borneo as well as their geographical propin-

quity, the Ministers agreed that in the event of North Borneo joining the proposed Federation of Malaysia the Government of the latter and the Government of the Philippines should maintain and promote the harmony and the friendly relations subsisting in their region to ensure the security and stability of the area.

MEETING OF HEADS OF GOVERNMENT

14. The Ministers agreed to recommend that a Meeting of their respective Heads of Government be held in Manila not later than the end of July 1963.

15. The Ministers expressed satisfaction over the atmosphere of brotherliness and cordiality which pervaded their Meeting and considered it as a confirmation of their close fraternal ties and as a happy augury for the success of future consultations among their leaders.

16. The Ministers agreed to place on record their profound appreciation of and gratitude for the statesmanlike efforts of President Macapagal whose courage, vision and inspiration not only facilitated the holding of this historic Meeting but also contributed towards the achievement for the first time of a unity of purpose and a sense of common dedication among the peoples of Malaya, Indonesia and the Philippines.

JOINT DECLARATION OF PAKISTAN AND INDIA[1]
Signed by President Ayub Khan of Pakistan and Prime Minister Shastri of India at the Final Meeting of the Tashkent Conference, January 10, 1966

The Prime Minister of India and the President of Pakistan, having met at Tashkent and having discussed the relations existing between India and Pakistan, hereby declare their firm resolve to restore normal peaceful relations between their countries and to promote understanding and friendly relations between their peoples.

They consider the attainment of these objectives of vital importance for the welfare of the 600 million people of India and Pakistan.

The Prime Minister of India and the President of Pakistan agree that both sides will exert every effort to create good-neighbourly relations between India and Pakistan in accordance with the United Nations Charter.

They reaffirm their obligation under the Charter not to have recourse to force and to settle their disputes through peaceful means.

They considered that the interests of peace in their region and particularly in the Indian-Pakistani subcontinent and, indeed, the interests of all

---

[1] Reprinted with permission from the *Soviet News*, No. 5228 (January 10, 1966), p. 17.

peoples of India and Pakistan, were not served by the continuance of tension between the two countries.

It was against this background that Jammu and Kashmir was discussed, and each of the sides set out its respective position.

The Prime Minister of India and the President of Pakistan have agreed that all armed personnel of the two countries shall be withdrawn, not later than February 25, 1966, to the positions they held prior to August 5, 1965 and both sides shall observe the cease-fire terms on the cease-fire line.

The Prime Minister of India and the President of Pakistan have agreed that relations between India and Pakistan shall be based on the principle of non-interference in each other's internal affairs.

The Prime Minister of India and the President of Pakistan have agreed that both sides will discourage any propaganda directed against the other country, and will encourage propaganda which promotes the development of friendly relations between the two countries.

The Prime Minister of India and the President of Pakistan have agreed that the Indian High Commissioner to Pakistan and the Pakistani High Commissioner to India will return to their posts and that the normal functioning of diplomatic missions of both countries will be restored. Both governments shall observe the 1961 Vienna Convention on diplomatic relations.

The Prime Minister of India and the President of Pakistan have agreed to consider measures towards the restoration of economic and trade relations and communications, as well as cultural exchanges between India and Pakistan, and to take measures to implement the existing agreements between India and Pakistan.

The Prime Minister of India and the President of Pakistan have agreed that they will give instructions to their respective authorities to carry out the repatriation of prisoners-of-war.

The Prime Minister of India and the President of Pakistan have agreed that the sides will continue the discussion of questions relating to the problems of refugees and evictions, and illegal immigrations. They also agreed that both sides will prevent the exodus of people.

They further agreed to discuss the return of the property and assets taken over by either side in connection with the conflict.

The Prime Minister of India and the President of Pakistan have agreed that the sides will continue meetings both at the highest and at other levels on matters of direct concern to both countries.

Both sides have recognised the need to set up joint Indian-Pakistani bodies which will report to their governments in order to decide what further steps should be taken.

The Prime Minister of India and the President of Pakistan record their feelings of deep appreciation and gratitude to the leaders of the Soviet Union, the Soviet government and personally to the Chairman of the U.S.S.R. Council of Ministers, for their constructive, friendly and noble part in bringing about the present meeting which has resulted in mutually satisfactory results.

They also express to the government and friendly people of Uzbekistan their sincere gratitude for their overwhelming reception and generous hospitality.

They invite the Chairman of the Council of Ministers of the U.S.S.R. to witness this Declaration.

··{**22**}·· *Japan*

THE CONSTITUTION OF JAPAN[1]
November 3, 1946

We, the Japanese people, acting through our duly elected representatives in the National Diet, determined that we shall secure for ourselves and our posterity the fruits of peaceful cooperation with all nations and the blessings of liberty throughout this land, and resolved that never again shall we be visited with the horrors of war through the action of government, do proclaim that sovereign power resides with the people and do firmly establish this Constitution. Government is a sacred trust of the people, the authority for which is derived from the people, the powers of which are exercised by the representatives of the people, and the benefits of which are enjoyed by the people. This is a universal principle of mankind upon which this Constitution is founded. We reject and revoke all constitutions, laws, ordinances and rescripts in conflict herewith.

We, the Japanese people, desire peace for all time and are deeply conscious of the high ideals controlling human relationship, and we have determined to preserve our security and existence, trusting in the justice and faith of the peace-loving peoples of the world. We desire to occupy an honored place in an international society striving for the preservation of peace, and the banishment of tyranny and slavery, oppression and intolerance for all time from the earth. We recognize that all peoples of the world have the right to live in peace, free from fear and want.

We believe that no nation is responsible to itself alone, but that laws of political morality are universal; and that obedience to such laws is incumbent upon all nations who would sustain their own sovereignty and justify their sovereign relationship with other nations.

We, the Japanese people, pledge our national honor to accomplish these high ideals and purposes with all our resources.

---

[1] The English-language version of this document was made available through the courtesy of the Embassy of Japan, Washington, D.C.

Chapter I. The Emperor

Article 1. The Emperor shall be the symbol of the State and of the unity of the people, deriving his position from the will of the people with whom resides sovereign power.

Article 2. The Imperial Throne shall be dynastic and succeeded to in accordance with the Imperial House Law passed by the Diet.

Article 3. The advice and approval of the Cabinet shall be required for all acts of the Emperor in matters of state, and the Cabinet shall be responsible therefor.

Article 4. The Emperor shall perform only such acts in matters of state as are provided for in this Constitution and he shall not have powers related to government.

The Emperor may delegate the performance of his acts in matters of state as may be provided by law.

Article 5. When, in accordance with the Imperial House Law, a Regency is established the Regent shall perform his acts in matters of state in the Emperor's name. In this case, paragraph one of the preceding article will be applicable.

Article 6. The Emperor shall appoint the Prime Minister as designated by the Diet.

The Emperor shall appoint the Chief Judge of the Supreme Court as designated by the Cabinet.

Article 7. The Emperor, with the advice and approval of the Cabinet, shall perform the following acts in matters of state on behalf of the people:

Promulgation of amendments of the constitution, laws, cabinet orders and treaties.

Convocation of the Diet.

Dissolution of the House of Representatives.

Proclamation of general election of members of the Diet.

Attestation of the appointment and dismissal of Ministers of State and other officials as provided for by law, and of full powers and credentials of Ambassadors and Ministers.

Attestation of general and special amnesty, commutation of punishment, reprieve, and restoration of rights.

Awarding of honors.

Attestation of instruments of ratification and other diplomatic documents as provided for by law.

Receiving foreign ambassadors and ministers.

Performance of ceremonial functions.

Article 8. No property can be given to, or received by, the Imperial House, nor can any gifts be made therefrom, without the authorization of the Diet.

CHAPTER II. RENUNCIATION OF WAR

Article 9. Aspiring sincerely to an international peace based on justice and order, the Japanese people forever renounce war as a sovereign right of the nation and the threat or use of force as means of settling international disputes.

In order to accomplish the aim of the preceding paragraph, land, sea, and air forces, as well as other war potential, will never be maintained. The right of belligerency of the state will not be recognized.

CHAPTER III. RIGHTS AND DUTIES OF THE PEOPLE

Article 10. The conditions necessary for being a Japanese national shall be determined by law.

Article 11. The People shall not be prevented from enjoying any of the fundamental human rights. These fundamental human rights guaranteed to the people by this Constitution shall be conferred upon the people of this and future generations as eternal and inviolate rights.

Article 12. The freedom and rights guaranteed to the people by this Constitution shall be maintained by the constant endeavor of the people, who shall refrain from any abuse of these freedoms and rights and shall always be responsible for utilizing them for the public welfare.

Article 13. All of the people shall be respected as individuals. Their right to life, liberty, and the pursuit of happiness shall, to the extent that it does not interfere with the public welfare, be the supreme consideration in legislation and in other governmental affairs.

Article 14. All of the people are equal under the law and there shall be no discrimination in political, economic or social relations because of race, creed, sex, social status or family origin.

Peers and peerage shall not be recognized.

No privilege shall accompany any award of honor, decoration or any distinction, nor shall any such award be valid beyond the lifetime of the individual who now holds or hereafter may receive it.

Article 15. The people have the inalienable right to choose their public officials and to dismiss them.

All public officials are servants of the whole community and not of any group thereof.

Universal adult suffrage is guaranteed with regard to the election of public officials.

In all elections, secrecy of the ballot shall not be violated. A voter shall not be answerable, publicly or privately, for the choice he has made.

Article 16. Every person shall have the right of peaceful petition for the redress of damage, for the removal of public officials, for the enactment, repeal or amendment of laws, ordinances or regulations and for other matters, nor shall any person be in any way discriminated against for sponsoring such a petition.

Article 17. Every person may sue for redress as provided by law from the State or a public entity, in case he has suffered damage through illegal act of any public official.

Article 18. No person shall be held in bondage of any kind. Involuntary servitude, except as punishment for crime, is prohibited.

Article 19. Freedom of thought and conscience shall not be violated.

Article 20. Freedom of religion is guaranteed to all. No religious organization shall receive any privileges from the State, nor exercise any political authority.

No person shall be compelled to take part in any religious act, celebration, rite or practice.

The State and its organs shall refrain from religious education or any other religious activity.

Article 21. Freedom of assembly and association as well as speech, press and all other forms of expression are guaranteed.

No censorship shall be maintained, nor shall the secrecy of any means of communication be violated.

Article 22. Every person shall have freedom to choose and change his residence and to choose his occupation to the extent that it does not interfere with the public welfare.

Freedom of all persons to move to a foreign country and to divest themselves of their nationality shall be inviolate.

Article 23. Academic freedom is guaranteed.

Article 24. Marriage shall be based only on the mutual consent of both sexes and it shall be maintained through mutual cooperation with the equal rights of husband and wife as a basis.

With regard to choice of spouse, property rights, inheritancy, choice of domicile, divorce and other matters pertaining to marriage and the family, laws shall be enacted from the standpoint of individual dignity and the essential equality of the sexes.

Article 25. All people shall have the right to maintain the minimum standards of wholesome and cultured living.

In all spheres of life, the State shall use its endeavors for the promotion and extension of social welfare and security, and of public health.

Article 26. All people shall have the right to receive an equal education correspondent to their ability, as provided by law.

All people shall be obligated to have all boys and girls under their protection receive ordinary education as provided for by law. Such compulsory education shall be free.

Article 27. All people shall have the right and the obligation to work.

Standards for wages, hours, rest and other working conditions shall be fixed by law.

Children shall not be exploited.

Article 28. The right of workers to organize and to bargain and act collectively is guaranteed.

Article 29. The right to own or to hold property is inviolable.

Property rights shall be defined by law, in conformity with the public welfare.

Private property may be taken for public use upon just compensation therefor.

Article 30. The people shall be liable to taxation as provided by law.

Article 31. No person shall be deprived of life or liberty, nor shall any other criminal penalty be imposed, except according to procedure established by law.

Article 32. No person shall be denied the right of access to the courts.

Article 33. No person shall be apprehended except upon warrant issued by a competent judicial officer which specifies the offense with which the person is charged, unless he is apprehended, the offense being committed.

Article 34. No person shall be arrested or detained without being at once informed of the charges against him or without the immediate privilege of counsel; nor shall he be detained without adequate cause; and upon demand of any person such cause must be immediately shown in open court in his presence and the presence of his counsel.

Article 35. The right of all persons to be secure in their homes, papers and effects against entries, searches and seizures shall not be impaired except upon warrant issued for adequate cause and particularly describing the place to be searched and things to be seized, or except as provided by Article 33.

Each search or seizure shall be made upon separate warrant issued by a judicial officer.

Article 36. The infliction of torture by any public officer and cruel punishments are absolutely forbidden.

Article 37. In all criminal cases the accused shall enjoy the right to a speedy and public trial by an impartial tribunal.

He shall be permitted full opportunity to examine all witnesses, and he shall have the right of compulsory process for obtaining witnesses on his behalf at public expense.

At all times the accused shall have the assistance of competent counsel who shall, if the accused is unable to secure the same by his own efforts, be assigned to his use by the State.

Article 38. No person shall be compelled to testify against himself.

Confession made under compulsion, torture or threat, or after prolonged arrest or detention shall not be admitted in evidence.

No person shall be convicted or punished in cases where the only proof against him is his own confession.

Article 39. No person shall be held criminally liable for an act which was lawful at the time it was committed, or of which he has been acquitted, nor shall he be placed in double jeopardy.

Article 40. Any person, in case he is acquitted after he has been arrested or detained, may sue the State for redress as provided by law.   [ ]

REMARKS OF THE U.S.S.R. ON THE DRAFT OF THE JAPANESE PEACE TREATY[1]
May 7, 1951

The Government of the U.S.S.R. received on March 29, 1951, from the Government of the United States of America a draft of a peace treaty with Japan. In connection with this, the Soviet Government considers it necessary to make the following remarks.

In spite of the fact that more than 5 years have already passed since the time of the termination of war with Japan, the question of a peaceful settlement for Japan remains unresolved. Such a situation has been created, first of all, as a result of the position taken by the Government of the U.S.A., which under various pretexts has postponed not only the conclusion but the very preparation of a peace treaty. In this connection, the Government of the U.S.A. has repeatedly rejected the proposals of the Soviet Government for the preparation of a peace treaty with Japan jointly with other Governments, as envisaged by the appropriate international agreements. As a result of this, the occupation of Japan by foreign troops has impermissibly dragged on.

1. The remarks of the Soviet Government, concern, first of all, the incorrect preparation of a peace treaty with Japan. . . .

In accordance with the Potsdam Agreement of August 2, 1945, a Council of Foreign Ministers of the five powers—U.S.A., U.S.S.R., China, Great Britain, and France—was established, in which connection it was directly stated in the Potsdam Agreement that the Council of Foreign Ministers was being created, in the first instance, for "preparatory work on peaceful settle-ment," and that in drawing up the corresponding peace treaties "the Council would consist of members representing those states which have signed the terms of capitulation dictated to that enemy state which the given task concerns." The peace treaties with Italy, Rumania, Hungary, Bulgaria and Finland were prepared and concluded in conformity with this. That the drafting of a peace treaty with Japan has been laid upon the U.S.A., the U.S.S.R., China and Great Britain, who, as is known, signed the Japanese

---

[1] The text of these remarks, submitted by the U.S.S.R. to the United States on May 7, 1951, is reprinted from *The Department of State Bulletin*, Vol. XXIV, No. 621 (May 28, 1951), pp. 856–858.

surrender document, also flows from the Potsdam Agreement referred to. As early as 1947 the Soviet Government proposed calling a special session of the Council of Foreign Ministers composed of the representatives of China, U.S.A., U.S.S.R. and Great Britain in order to embark upon the preparation of a peace treaty with Japan. In this connection, it was envisaged that all states who participated with their armed forces in the war with Japan would be drawn into the preparatory work for drawing up a peace treaty with Japan. But this proposal as well as other repeatedly renewed efforts of the Soviet Government directed toward hastening the conclusion of a peace treaty with Japan have furnished no positive results, since the Government of the U.S.A. ignores the necessity of calling a Council of Foreign Ministers for the preparation of a peace treaty with Japan as well as calling a peace conference for the consideration of this treaty.

The Soviet Government considers it necessary to mention particularly the impermissibility of excluding China from the preparation of a peace treaty with Japan. It is known that China was subjected during the course of many years to cruel aggression on the part of militaristic Japan, waged a protracted hard war against Japanese imperialism and bore the greatest sacrifices from the aggression of Japan. It is natural, therefore, that the Government of the Chinese People's Republic, being the only legal representative of the Chinese people, has a special interest in the preparation of a peace treaty with Japan and in the establishment of lasting peace in the Far East. It is perfectly obvious that without the participation of the Chinese People's Republic in the work of preparing a peace treaty with Japan a real peaceful settlement in the Far East is not possible.

From this it is seen that the Government of the United States is endeavoring to exclude the U.S.S.R., the Chinese People's Republic and other countries from the preparation of a peace treaty with Japan and to take this matter exclusively into its own hands in order unilaterally to impose upon Japan through the procedure of a dictate conditions of this treaty satisfactory to the Government of the U.S.A., utilizing for this purpose the dependence of the present Government of Japan upon the American occupation authorities.

2. The remarks of the Soviet Government concern, secondly, the fact that the American draft of a peace treaty with Japan contains, from the point of view of the substance of the matter, several incorrect contentions incompatible with existing agreements between the powers.

In such known international documents as the Cairo Declaration of 1943, the Potsdam Declaration of 1945, and the Yalta Agreement of 1945 the Governments of the United States of America, Great Britain, China, and the U.S.S.R. took upon themselves definite obligations with relation to a future peace treaty with Japan. . . .

The American draft of a peace treaty with Japan ignores in one degree or another these obligations of the powers which flow from the documents referred to above.

First of all, this must be said of territorial questions.

For example, in the Cairo Declaration of 1943 it is directly stated that the Island of Taiwan and the Pescadores Islands should be returned to China. In this American draft it is stated only that Japan renounces all rights to Taiwan and Pescadores Islands, but nothing is said regarding the transfer of Taiwan and Pescadores Islands to China. From this the conclusion can be drawn that the draft leaves the present situation with Taiwan and the Pescadores Islands, which have actually been torn away from China, without change, in violation of the Cairo Agreement concerning the return of these islands to China.

The American draft provides, further, for taking the Ryukyu, Bonin, Rosario, Volcano, Parece Vela, and Marcus Islands out from under the sovereignty of Japan and transferring them under the administration of the U.S.A. under the pretext of establishing a trusteeship over them, allegedly on the part of the United Nations Organization. Inasmuch, however, as the wresting of the islands named away from Japan is envisaged neither by agreement between the powers nor by decision of United Nations in the person of the Security Council, such wresting away does not have any justification.

Those deviations on military matters from the international agreements mentioned above which are contained in the American draft of a peace treaty with Japan possess even greater significance. It suffices to say that the American draft not only does not contain a guarantee against the restoration of Japanese militarism but in general does not set forth any limitations with relation to the size of the armed forces in Japan. . . .

Likewise the fact cannot be passed over that the American draft does not establish any period for the withdrawal of occupation troops from Japan and is directly designed to leave American occupation troops and military bases in Japan even after the conclusion of a peace treaty. Consequently, even after that "peaceful settlement" which the United States is preparing for Japan, the military occupation of Japan will not be discontinued and the United States of America will remain the real master in Japan. . . .

It is necessary to add to this that already at the present time the Government of the U.S.A. is utilizing the occupation of Japan by American troops for other purposes than were agreed among the states signing the Japanese surrender document. American occupation troops located on Japanese territory are utilizing the territory of Japan, its material and human resources for armed intervention in Korea, which is incompatible with international agreements according American troops the right of occupation in Japan only for the purposes of carrying out measures for the demilitarization and democratization of Japan.

Finally, the American draft ignores the necessity of removing limitations with respect to the free development of the peaceful economy of Japan. It is quite clear that without the development of the peaceful economy of the country and without the existence of normal trade with other countries it is not possible to create a reliable basis for the economic upsurge of Japan and growth in the welfare of the Japanese people. . . .

3. The Soviet Government, constantly insisting on a speedy conclusion of a peace treaty with Japan, considers that a peace treaty should be drawn up on the basis of international agreements which were concluded between the powers during the period of the Second World War, and the preparation of a draft treaty should be carried on jointly by representatives of the U.S.A., the Chinese People's Republic, U.S.S.R. and Great Britain with all the member states of the Far Eastern Commission being drawn into the matter.

In conformity with this, the Soviet Government proposes:

First—To call in June or July of 1951 a session of the Council of Ministers of Foreign Affairs composed of representatives of U.S.A., China, Great Britain and U.S.S.R. in order to embark upon the preparation of a peace treaty with Japan having in view bringing into the preparatory work for drawing up a peace treaty with Japan representatives of all states participating with their armed forces in the war with Japan, in order that a draft of a peace treaty may be submitted for the consideration of a peace conference.

Second—To conduct the drafting of a peace treaty with Japan on the basis of the Cairo Declaration, the Potsdam Declaration, and the Yalta Agreement, governed by the following basic aims:

A. Japan should become a peace-loving, democratic, independent state.

B. Democratic rights should be guaranteed to the population of Japan and the existence of such organizations be they political, military, or of military character whose purpose is to deprive the people of their democratic rights, as was provided in the peace treaty with Italy, should not be allowed.

C. As a guarantee against the revival of Japanese militarism limitations should be established in the treaty on the size of Japanese armed forces in order that they may not exceed the requirements of self-defense, as was established in the peace treaty with Italy.

D. No limitations be put upon Japan in the matter of the development of her peaceful economy.

E. All limitations with respect to the trade of Japan with other states be removed.

Third—To provide in the treaty that Japan will not enter any coalition directed against any of the states participating with their armed forces in the war against militaristic Japan.

Fourth—To specify precisely in the treaty that after the conclusion of a peace treaty with Japan all occupation troops will be withdrawn from Japanese territory in the course of not more than 1 year and no foreign state will have troops or military bases in Japan.

Fifth—To agree that the states signing the peace treaty with Japan will support the entry of Japan into the United Nations Organization.

TREATY OF MUTUAL COOPERATION AND SECURITY[1]
Between Japan and the United States, January 19, 1960

The United States of America and Japan,

[ ]

Having resolved to conclude a treaty of mutual cooperation and security, Therefore agree as follows:

Article I. The Parties undertake, as set forth in the Charter of the United Nations, to settle any international disputes in which they may be involved by peaceful means in such a manner that international peace and security and justice are not endangered and to refrain in their international relations from the threat or use of force against the territorial integrity or political independence of any state, or in any other manner inconsistent with the purposes of the United Nations.

The Parties will endeavor in concert with other peace-loving countries to strengthen the United Nations so that its mission of maintaining international peace and security may be discharged more effectively.

Article II. The Parties will contribute toward the further development of peaceful and friendly international relations by strengthening their free institutions, by bringing about a better understanding of the principles upon which these institutions are founded, and by promoting conditions of stability and well-being. They will seek to eliminate conflict in their international economic policies and will encourage economic collaboration between them.

Article III. The Parties, individually and in cooperation with each other, by means of continuous and effective self-help and mutual aid will maintain and develop, subject to their constitutional provisions, their capacities to resist armed attack.

Article IV. The Parties will consult together from time to time regarding the implementation of this Treaty, and, at the request of either Party, whenever the security of Japan or international peace and security in the Far East is threatened.

Article V. Each Party recognizes that an armed attack against either Party in the territories under the administration of Japan would be dangerous to its own peace and safety and declares that it would act to meet the common danger in accordance with its constitutional provisions and processes.

Any such armed attack and all measures taken as a result thereof shall be immediately reported to the Security Council of the United Nations in

---

[1] Reprinted from the United States Department of State, *Treaties and Other International Acts*, Series 4509, pp. 2–4.

accordance with the provisions of Article 51 of the Charter. Such measures shall be terminated when the Security Council has taken the measures necessary to restore and maintain international peace and security.

Article VI. For the purpose of contributing to the security of Japan and the maintenance of international peace and security in the Far East, the United States of America is granted the use by its land, air and naval forces of facilities and areas in Japan.

The use of these facilities and areas as well as the status of United States armed forces in Japan shall be governed by a separate agreement, replacing the Administrative Agreement under Article III of the Security Treaty between the United States of America and Japan, signed at Tokyo on February 28, 1952, as amended, and by such other arrangements as may be agreed upon.

Article VII. This Treaty does not affect and shall not be interpreted as affecting in any way the rights and obligations of the Parties under the Charter of the United Nations or the responsibility of the United Nations for the maintenance of international peace and security.

Article VIII. This Treaty shall be ratified by the United States of America and Japan in accordance with their respective constitutional processes and will enter into force on the date on which the instruments of ratification thereof have been exchanged by them in Tokyo.

Article IX. The Security Treaty between the United States of America and Japan signed at the city of San Francisco on September 8, 1951 shall expire upon the entering into force of this Treaty.

Article X. This Treaty shall remain in force until in the opinion of the Governments of the United States of America and Japan there shall have come into force such United Nations arrangements as will satisfactorily provide for the maintenance of international peace and security in the Japan area.

However, after the Treaty has been in force for ten years, either Party may give notice to the other Party of its intention to terminate the Treaty, in which case the Treaty shall terminate one year after such notice has been given.

··{23}·· *The Divided Nations of East Asia*

SUMMARY OF SECURITY COUNCIL SUBCOMMITTEE ON LAOS REPORT[1]
Established under the Resolution of September 7, 1959, November 3, 1959

The Sub-Committee, through the study of the statements made and the documents submitted before the Security Council and those submitted to it by the Royal Laotian Government, from the hearings of many witnesses held in Vientiane, Sam Neua, Sam Teu and Luang Prabang, by the visits made to the northern and north-eastern Provinces, considers it useful to make the following summary concerning the appeal of the Royal Laotian Government of 4 September 1959 and the mandate entrusted to it by the resolution of the Security Council of 7 September 1959.

The Sub-Committee desires to recall that the members of the Security Council during the two meetings of 7 September 1959 expressed the view that the situation in Laos at the time was fraught with danger.

According to the documents presented to the Sub-Committee by the Laotian authorities it appears that, especially since 16 July 1959, military actions have taken place on Laotian territory against Laotian army posts and units. According to the same documents these actions increased progressively, reaching their maximum intensity between 30 August and the middle of September, particularly in the province of Sam Neua, along the river Ma and in the area of Sam Teu.

According to a document of the Laotian Government, presented to the Sub-Committee on 15 October 1959, the military situation especially in the two provinces of Sam Neua and Phong Saly appears to reflect a regression after 15 September, and the general scope of the military actions has taken the characteristics of guerrilla activity, scattered practically throughout the territory of the Kingdom.

Generally speaking, the Sub-Committee considers that although there were actions of different scope and magnitude, all of them—throughout the four periods (from 16 July to 11 October)—were of a guerrilla character.

---

[1] United Nations, Security Council, *Official Report, Fourteenth Year, Supplement for October, November and December*, Document S/4236, pp. 33–34.

From the statements of the Laotian authorities, and from those of some witnesses, it appears, however, that certain of these hostile operations must have had a centralized co-ordination.

Practically all witnesses (forty out of forty-one) stated that the hostile elements received support from the territory of the Democratic Republic of Viet-Nam consisting mainly of equipment, arms, ammunition, supplies, and the help of political cadres. The same emerges from the official Laotian documents submitted and from some of the material exhibits.

Hostile elements seemed centred around former members of the *Unités combattantes du Pathet-Lao* previously integrated in 1957, the 2nd battalion of Pathet Lao, which deserted from the Plaine des Jarres on 11 May 1959, and sections of the frontier minorities (Thais, Meos and a few Khas). According to a document presented to the Sub-Committee by the Laotian Government, participation of regular army units from the Democratic Republic of Viet-Nam were reported during the attacks of the river Ma area on 30 August. The Laotian Government states in another document presented to the Sub-Committee on 15 October, that after 15 September, these units re-crossed the border into North Viet-Nam, excepting those who occupied the section of Laotian territory between the left bank of the river Ma and the frontier. Witnesses reported that in certain cases there had been participation of armed elements with ethnic Vietnamese characteristics, but they did not identify them as belonging to North Vietnamese regular army units. The body of information submitted to the Sub-Committee did not clearly establish whether there were crossings of the frontier by regular troops of the Democratic Republic of Viet-Nam.   [ ]

SOVIET NOTE TO THE UNITED STATES[1]
Concerning Events in Laos, December 13, 1960

The Government of the Union of Soviet Socialist Republics considers it necessary to state the following to the United States Government.

In the declaration of September 22, 1960 concerning events in Laos, the Soviet Government already drew attention to the serious threat to peace in this area of Southeast Asia arising from the unceremonious intervention of the United States and several of its partners in the aggressive SEATO bloc in Laos internal affairs. However, if two or three months ago the United States Government somehow tried to camouflage its illegal action in Laos, recently the United States has in fact become a direct participant in military operations on the side of the rebels against the legal government of Laos and the Laotian people.

Flouting the sovereign rights of the Laotian government headed by

---

[1] Reprinted from *The Department of State Bulletin* (January 2, 1961), p. 16.

Prince Souvanna Phoumi, the United States now extends overt support to the rebel group of Nosavan, supplies it with arms, military equipment, military stores, and money. Rebel troops have proved to be supplied with such arms as have never until the present been in the Laotian Army: 105mm howitzers, 120mm mortars, heavy tanks, military aircraft, helicopters, armored launches, and other equipment.

The rebels have been trained in the use of these arms by numerous American advisers and instructors, whom the United States Government has sent and continues to send to their camp. Moreover, near the town of Pakadin there was shot down by government troops a reconnaissance aircraft No. 830 on board which were four American officers. During engagements between government troops and the rebels, American helicopters of "Sikorsky" type regularly fly over Thailand territory, directing the artillery fire of the rebels. From this it is evident that American military advisers and instructors not only train the rebels, but also directly lead their military actions against troops of the legal government of Laos. The United States Government also widely uses its ally in the SEATO military pact, Thailand, which makes available the territory of the country for active military operations against government units and carries out a tight economic blockade of Laos.

As the facts show, the United States Government completely ignores the repeated appeals and also the official demand of the legal government of Prince Souvanna Phoumi, expressed in the December 5 declaration, that the United States cease delivery of weapons and military supplies to the rebels.

All this is a glaring violation on the part of the United States Government of Article 12 of the final declaration of the 1954 Geneva Conference on Indo-China, in which is contained the obligation of each participant of the conferences, including the United States, to respect the sovereignty, independence, unity and territorial integrity of Laos, and refrain from any interference in its internal affairs.

With its overt actions against the legal Laotian government of Prince Souvanna Phoumi, which has proclaimed as its program a policy of peace, neutrality, and national unity, the United States Government seeks to compel the Laotian people to leave this path which it has chosen, and to put Laos again in the service of a policy of military pacts and aggressive preparations, foreign to the people of Laos.

However, it is appropriate to recall that once such a policy already suffered failure in Laos. The Laotian people overthrew the government which carried out the policy of turning Laos into a United States military base and semi-colony. Realization of the legitimate striving of the Laotian people for cessation at last of fratricidal war and for national unity in conditions excluding any foreign intervention must not be hindered.

Being one of the participants and chairmen of the Geneva Conference on Indo-China, the Soviet Government decisively protests the United States intervention in the internal affairs of Laos and condemns this intervention.

This undermines the Geneva agreements and is directed against the freedom and independence of the Laotian people, against its inalienable right to conduct a policy of peace, neutrality, and friendship with all peoples.

The Soviet Government cannot ignore the threat to peace and security in Southeast Asia arising from the crude United States interference in the internal affairs of Laos, and places on the United States Government all responsibility for the consequences which can arise as a result of the aggressive actions of the United States and some of its allies in the SEATO military bloc in relation to the Laotian people.

UNITED STATES REPLY TO SOVIET NOTE ON LAOS[1]
December 17, 1960

The Government of the United States acknowledges the receipt of the note of the Government of the Union of Soviet Socialist Republics dated December 13, 1960.

The Government of the United States categorically rejects the charges leveled against it in the Soviet Government's note. The United States condemns as a violation of every standard of legal conduct the recent Soviet action in airlifting weapons and ammunition in Soviet planes to rebel military forces fighting the loyal armed forces of the Royal Government in Vientiane. Thus the responsibility for the present fratricidal war in Laos, about which the Soviet Government claims to be concerned, rests squarely and solely upon the Soviet Government and its partners.

The United States has repeatedly made clear its consistent policy of supporting the Kingdom of Laos in its determination to maintain its independence and integrity. Such support will continue. The United States has warned against efforts to seize control of or to subvert that free nation.

The Soviet allegation that Lao Army troops have been recently armed with weapons which they have not had before is completely false. Such supplies as have been furnished by the United States to the forces in Laos, in whatever region, have been provided pursuant to a long-standing agreement with Laos, and with the approval of the legal Government of Laos. The Lao Army had been equipped with M-24 tanks and 105 millimeter howitzers long before the August 9, 1960 rebellion against the Royal Lao Government. The United States has not in fact supplied any equipment of this type to Laos since 1957. The United States has never supplied 120 millimeter mortars, armed aircraft, or armed or armored vessels to Laos. The United States has not brought any arms or ammunition into Laos since the end of November. No United States–supplied helicopters have been used to direct artillery fire. Furthermore, such American advisers as have been in the country either ad-

---

[1] Reprinted from *The Department of State Bulletin* (January 2, 1961), p. 15.

ministering the American Military Aid Program or in the Franco-American training program are located at various training sites and supply depots and have not led any military actions.

It is communist and communist-fostered subversive activities, the guerrilla warfare of the Pathet Lao forces, and now the Soviet airlift of weapons which have led directly to the suffering and chaos which have befallen Laos. The Soviet Government and its agents have attempted to carry out this latest, grave action clandestinely, under the cover of delivering food and petroleum products. However, their haste to strengthen the rebel forces in Laos has resulted in widespread knowledge of these Soviet arms deliveries, which have included the howitzers which the rebels are now using against loyal troops of the Lao Government, a government formed at Royal request pursuant to the National Assembly's action. The destruction which these Soviet weapons have brought to the capital city of Laos and the suffering and loss to its people is the direct result of this Soviet intervention.

At the same time, communist-controlled north Viet-Nam, which has long aided and furnished direction to the Pathet Lao guerrillas in Laos, has been making war-like preparations, calling up additional troops and moving military units westward toward the Lao border.

In the light of these facts the Government of the United States, in rejecting the false charges of the Soviet Government in its note of December 13, places the responsibility for the current strife in Laos where that responsibility properly belongs—squarely upon the U.S.S.R. and its agents. The Government of the United States, furthermore, condemns in strongest terms the illegal Russian delivery of military equipment to the rebels in Laos.

It has always been the objective of the United States to assist the people of Laos in developing their free political institutions, in improving their social and economic well being and in preserving their national integrity. The policy of the United States towards Laos remains the same today.

PROGRAM OF THE PEOPLE'S REVOLUTIONARY PARTY OF VIETNAM[1]
January, 1962

1. We will overthrow the Ngo Dinh Diem government and form a national democratic coalition government.

2. We will carry out a program involving extension of democratic liberties, general amnesty for political detainees, abolition of agrovilles and resettlement centers, abolition of the special military tribunal law and other undemocratic laws.

3. We will abolish the economic monopoly of the U.S. and its hench-

---

[1] Reprinted from *Viet Cong* by Douglas Pike by permission of The M. I. T. Press, Cambridge, Massachusetts; copyright 1966 by the Massachusetts Institute of Technology, p. 141.

men, protect domestically made products, promote development of the economy, and allow forced evacuees from North Vietnam to return to their place of birth.

4. We will reduce land rent and prepare for land reform.

5. We will eliminate U.S. cultural enslavement and depravity and build a nationalistic progressive culture and education.

6. We will abolish the system of American military advisers and close all foreign military bases in Vietnam.

7. We will establish equality between men and women and among different nationalities and recognize the autonomous rights of the national minorities in the country.

8. We will pursue a foreign policy of peace and will establish diplomatic relations with all countries that respect the independence and sovereignty of Vietnam.

9. We will re-establish normal relations between North and South as a first step toward peaceful reunification of the country.

10. We will oppose aggressive wars and actively defend world peace.

POSSIBLE PEACE NEGOTIATIONS IN VIETNAM[1]
Letter from President Johnson to Ho Chi Minh, President of the Democratic Republic of Vietnam, February 8, 1967

Dear Mr. President: I am writing to you in the hope that the conflict in Vietnam can be brought to an end. That conflict has already taken a heavy toll—in lives lost, in wounds inflicted, in property destroyed, and in simple human misery. If we fail to find a just and peaceful solution, history will judge us harshly.

Therefore, I believe that we both have a heavy obligation to seek earnestly the path to peace. It is in response to that obligation that I am writing directly to you.

We have tried over the past several years, in a variety of ways and through a number of channels, to convey to you and your colleagues our desire to achieve a peaceful settlement. For whatever reasons, these efforts have not achieved any results. . . .

In the past two weeks, I have noted public statements by representatives of your government suggesting that you would be prepared to enter into direct bilateral talks with representatives of the U.S. Government, provided that we ceased "unconditionally" and permanently our bombing operations against your country and all military actions against it. In the last day, serious and responsible parties have assured us indirectly that this is in fact your proposal.

---

[1] Reprinted from *The Department of State Bulletin*, LVI, No. 1450 (April 10, 1967), pp. 595–596.

Let me frankly state that I see two great difficulties with this proposal. In view of your public position, such action on our part would inevitably produce worldwide speculation that discussions were under way and would impair the privacy and secrecy of those discussions. Secondly, there would inevitably be grave concern on our part whether your government would make use of such action by us to improve its military position.

With these problems in mind, I am prepared to move even further towards an ending of hostilities than your Government has proposed in either public statements or through private diplomatic channels. I am prepared to order a cessation of bombing against your country and the stopping of further augmentation of U.S. forces in South Viet-Nam as soon as I am assured that infiltration into South Viet-Nam by land and by sea has stopped. These acts of restraint on both sides would, I believe, make it possible for us to conduct serious and private discussions leading toward an early peace.

I make this proposal to you now with a specific sense of urgency arising from the imminent New Year holidays in Viet-Nam. If you are able to accept this proposal I see no reason why it could not take effect at the end of the New Year, or Tet, holidays. The proposal I have made would be greatly strengthened if your military authorities and those of the Government of South Viet-Nam could promptly negotiate an extension of the Tet truce.

As to the site of the bilateral discussions I propose, there are several possibilities. We could, for example, have our representatives meet in Moscow where contacts have already occurred. They could meet in some other country such as Burma. You may have other arrangements or sites in mind, and I would try to meet your suggestions.

The important thing is to end a conflict that has brought burdens to both our peoples, and above all to the people of South Viet-Nam. If you have any thoughts about the actions I propose, it would be most important that I receive them as soon as possible.

Sincerely,

Lyndon B. Johnson

PRESIDENT HO CHI MINH'S REPLY TO PRESIDENT JOHNSON'S LETTER[1]
February 15, 1967

Excellency, on February 10, 1967, I received your message. Here is my response.

Viet-Nam is situated thousands of miles from the United States. The Vietnamese people have never done any harm to the United States. But, contrary to the commitments made by its representative at the Geneva

---

[1] Reprinted from *The Department of State Bulletin*, LVI, No. 1450 (April 10, 1967), pp. 596–597.

Conference of 1954, the United States Government has constantly intervened in Viet-Nam, it has launched and intensified the war of aggression in South Viet-Nam for the purpose of prolonging the division of Viet-Nam and of transforming South Viet-Nam into an American neo-colony and an American military base. For more than two years now, the American Government, with its military aviation and its navy, has been waging war against the Democratic Republic of Viet-Nam, an independent and sovereign country.

The United States Government has committed war crimes, crimes against peace and against humanity. In South Viet-Nam a half-million American soldiers and soldiers from the satellite countries have resorted to the most inhumane arms and the most barbarous methods of warfare, such as napalm, chemicals, and poison gases in order to massacre our fellow countrymen, destroy the crops, and wipe out the villages. In North Viet-Nam thousands of American planes have rained down hundreds of thousands of tons of bombs, destroying cities, villages, mills, roads, bridges, dikes, dams and even churches, pagodas, hospitals, and schools. In your message you appear to deplore the suffering and the destruction in Viet-Nam. Permit me to ask you: Who perpetrated these monstrous crimes? It was the American soldiers and the soldiers of the satellite countries. The United States Government is entirely responsible for the extremely grave situation in Viet-Nam. . . .

The Vietnamese people deeply love independence, liberty, and peace. But in the face of the American aggression they have risen up as one man, without fearing the sacrifices and the privations. They are determined to continue their resistance until they have won real independence and liberty and true peace. Our just cause enjoys the approval and the powerful support of peoples throughout the world and of large segments of the American people.

The United States Government provoked the war of aggression in Viet-Nam. It must cease that aggression, it is the only road leading to the re-establishment of peace. The United States Government must halt definitively and unconditionally the bombings and all other acts of war against the Democratic Republic of Viet-Nam, withdraw from South Viet-Nam all American troops and all troops from the satellite countries, recognize the National Front of the Liberation of South Viet-Nam and let the Vietnamese people settle their problems themselves. Such is the basic content of the four-point position of the Government of the Democratic Republic of Viet-Nam, such is the statement of the essential principles and essential arrangements of the Geneva agreements of 1954 on Viet-Nam. It is the basis for a correct political solution of the Vietnamese problem. In your message you suggested direct talks between the Democratic Republic of Viet-Nam and the United States. If the United States Government really wants talks, it must first halt unconditionally the bombings and all other acts of war against the Democratic Republic of Viet-Nam. It is only after the unconditional halting of the American bombings and of all other American acts of war against the Democratic Republic of Viet-Nam that the Democratic Republic of Viet-Nam and the United States could begin talks and discuss questions affecting the two parties.

The Vietnamese people will never give way to force, it will never accept conversation under the clear threat of bombs.

Our cause is absolutely just. It is desirable that the Government of the United States act in conformity to reason.

Sincerely,

Ho Chi Minh

PROPOSALS FOR ENDING THE VIETNAM CONFLICT[1]
Made by Secretary-General of the United Nations, U Thant, March 28, 1967

[ ]

Since my return to New York in the first week of March, a good deal of speculation has focused on my reported new proposals to end the Viet-Nam war. Some capitals have even come out with public reactions to those proposals. When this press conference was arranged for today, it was far from my intention to make those proposals public, but, in view of the widespread interest shown in those proposals, and in view of certain reactions which are likely to confuse the general public regarding my sincere desire for peace, I have now decided to make those proposals public. It is for the world community to judge and assess those proposals against the background of the growing fury of the war, with definite prospects of involving larger areas of Asia. I have already received in writing the reactions of the parties principally involved, which I must continue to regard as confidential, and therefore I cannot comment upon them. My purpose in presenting those proposals was only to try to find, if possible, a common ground among the participants in the conflict, in view of the known reactions to my earlier three-point proposals. However, I would emphasize that I continue to regard my three-point proposals as representing the most useful first steps in preventing further escalation and intensification of the war and in beginning the reverse process of de-escalation and negotiations. In particular, I have never ceased to consider that the bombing of North Viet-Nam constitutes an insurmountable obstacle to discussions. I also stand by my conviction that Viet-Nam is a political problem, which no amount of force will solve—and, after all, previous military measures have not succeeded in bringing about any talks. . . .

---

[1] United Nations, Office of Public Information, Press Release SG/SM/682, March 28, 1967, *Transcript of the Press Conference by Secretary-General U Thant Held on March 28, 1967*, pp. 2–5.

Now I shall read to you the proposals which, on 14 March, in the form of an *aide-mémoire* I presented to the parties directly involved in the Viet-Nam conflict. The text reads as follows:

On many occasions in the past, the Secretary-General of the United Nations has expressed his very great concern about the conflict in Viet-Nam. That concern is intensified by the growing fury of the war resulting in the increasing loss of lives, indescribable suffering and misery of the people, appalling devastation of the country, uprooting of society, astronomical sums spent on the war, and last, but not least, his deepening anxiety over the increasing threat to the peace of the world. For these reasons, in the past three years or so, he submitted ideas and proposals to the parties primarily involved in the war, with a view to creating conditions congenial to negotiations, which, unhappily, have not been accepted by the parties. The prospects for peace seem to be more distant today than ever before.

Nevertheless, the Secretary-General reasserts his conviction that a cessation of the bombing of North Viet-Nam continues to be a vital need, for moral and humanitarian reasons and, also, because it is the step which could lead the way to meaningful talks to end the war.

The situation being as it is today, the Secretary-General has now in mind proposals envisaging three steps:

(a) A general stand-still truce
(b) Preliminary talks
(c) Reconvening of the Geneva Conference.

In the view of the Secretary-General, a halt to all military activities by all sides is a practical necessity if useful negotiations are to be undertaken. Since the Secretary-General's three-point plan has not been accepted by the parties, he believes that a general stand-still truce by all parties to the conflict is now the only course which could lead to fruitful negotiations. It must be conceded that a truce without effective supervision is apt to be breached from time to time by one side or another, but an effective supervision of truce, at least for the moment, seems difficult to envisage as a practical possibility. If the parties directly involved in the conflict are genuinely motivated by considerations of peace and justice, it is only to be expected that earnest efforts will be exerted to enforce the truce to the best of their ability. Should a public appeal by the Secretary-General in his personal capacity facilitate the observance of such a truce, he would gladly be prepared to do so. Appeals to that effect by a group of countries would also be worthy of consideration.

Once the appeal has been made and a general stand-still truce comes into effect, the parties directly involved in the conflict should take the next step of entering into preliminary talks. While these talks are in progress, it is clearly desirable that the general stand-still truce should continue to be observed. In the view of the Secretary-General, these talks can take any of the following forms:

(1) Direct talks between the United States of America and the Democratic Republic of Viet-Nam.

(2) Direct talks between the two governments mentioned in (1) above, with the participation of the two Co-Chairmen of the Geneva Conference of 1954.

(3) Direct talks between the two governments mentioned in (1) above, with the participation of the members of the International Control Commission.

(4) Direct talks between the two governments mentioned in (1) above, with the participation of the two Co-Chairmen of the Geneva Conference of 1954 and of the members of the International Control Commission.

The Secretary-General believes that these preliminary talks should aim at reaching an agreement on the modalities for the reconvening of the Geneva Conference, with the sole purpose of returning to the essentials of that Agreement as repeatedly expressed by all parties to the conflict. These preliminary talks should seek to reach an agreement on the timing, place, agenda and participants in the subsequent formal meeting—the reconvening of the Geneva Conference. The Secretary-General deems it necessary to stress that the question of participants in the formal negotiations should not obstruct the way to a settlement. It is a question which could be solved only by agreeing that no fruitful discussions on ending the war in Viet-Nam could take place without involving all those who are actually fighting. Since the Government in Saigon, as well as the National Front of Liberation of South Viet-Nam, are actually engaged in military operations, it is the view of the Secretary-General that a future formal conference could not usefully discuss the effective termination of all military activities and the new political situation that would result in South Viet-Nam, without the participation of representatives of the Government in Saigon and representatives of the National Front of Liberation of South Viet-Nam.

Part VI

*

Bipolarization of Power in the Postwar World

··{*24*}·· *Unequal Giants— the United States and the Soviet Union*

**MEMORANDUM TO THE SUBCOMMITTEE OF
UNITED NATIONS DISARMAMENT COMMISSION[1]**
Submitted by France and the United Kingdom, June 11, 1954

The French and United Kingdom delegations submit the following proposals as a possible basis for compromise:

(1) The States members of the Sub-Committee regard themselves as prohibited in accordance with the terms of the Charter of the United Nations from the use of nuclear weapons except in defence against aggression. They recommend that the disarmament treaty should include an immediate and explicit acceptance of this prohibition by all signatory States, pending the total prohibition and elimination of nuclear weapons as proposed in the subsequent paragraphs of this memorandum. They further recommend that the obligations assumed by the Members of the United Nations to refrain in their international relations from the threat or use of force against the territorial integrity or political independence of any State should be accepted by all signatory States not members of the United Nations.

(2) The draft disarmament treaty prepared by the Disarmament Commission and submitted by it to the Security Council, to the General Assembly and to the World Disarmament Conference should include provisions covering the following:

(*a*) The total prohibition of the use and manufacture of nuclear weapons and weapons of mass destruction of every type, together with the conversion of existing stocks of nuclear weapons for peaceful purposes.

(*b*) Major reductions in all armed forces and conventional armaments.

(*c*) The establishment of a control organ with rights and powers and

---

[1] Disarmament Commission, The Security Council, 1/10, June 11, 1954, *Disarmament Commission, Supplement for April, May and June, 1954,* pp. 21–22.

functions adequate to guarantee the effective observance of the agreed prohibitions and reductions.

(3) After the approval of the draft treaty by the World Disarmament Conference this instrument would be open to signature and adherence by all States. The treaty would enter into force immediately [after] it had been ratified by those of the signatories who would be specified in the treaty.

(4) The treaty should provide that the disarmament programme should be carried out as described below.

(5) After the constitution and positioning of the control organ, which shall be carried out within a specified time, and as soon as the Control Organ reports that it is able effectively to enforce them, the following measures shall enter into effect:

(*a*) Overall military manpower shall be limited to 31 December 1953 levels.

(*b*) Overall military expenditure, both atomic and non-atomic, shall be limited to amounts spent in the year ending 31 December 1953.

(6) As soon as the control organ reports that it is able effectively to enforce them, the following measures shall enter into effect:

(*a*) One-half of the agreed reductions of conventional armaments and armed forces shall take effect.

(*b*) On completion of (*a*) the manufacture of all kinds of nuclear weapons and all other prohibited weapons shall cease.

(7) As soon as the control organ reports that it is able effectively to enforce them, the following measures shall enter into effect:

(*a*) The second half of the agreed reductions of conventional armaments and armed forces shall take effect;

(*b*) On completion of (*a*):
(i) The total prohibition and elimination of nuclear weapons and the conversion of existing stocks of nuclear materials for peaceful purposes shall be carried out;
(ii) The total prohibition and elimination of all other prohibited weapons shall be carried out.

(8) It is to be hoped that when all the measures enumerated above have been carried out the armaments and armed forces of the powers will be further reduced to the levels strictly necessary for the maintenance of internal security and the fulfilment of the obligations of signatory States under the terms of the United Nations Charter.

(9) The control organ shall remain in being to ensure that the reductions, prohibitions and eliminations are faithfully and permanently observed.

DYNAMIC PEACE[1]

*Address by United States Secretary of State, John Foster Dulles,
before the Associated Press in New York, April 22, 1957*

[ ]

A first requirement is that the door be firmly closed to change by violent aggression.

Of all the tasks of government the most basic is to protect its citizens against violence. Such protection can only be effective if provided by a collective effort. So in every civilized community the members contribute toward the maintenance of a police force as an arm of law and order.

Only the society of nations has failed to apply this rudimentary principle of civilized life.

An effort was made through the United Nations to create an armed force for use by the Security Council to maintain international order. But the Soviet Union vetoed that.

However, the member nations still had the possibility of cooperating against aggression. For the charter, with foresight, had proclaimed that all nations had the inherent right of collective self-defense.

The free nations have largely exercised that right. The United States has made collective defense treaties with 42 other nations. And the area of common defense may now be enlarged pursuant to the recent Middle East resolution. . . .

The Soviet rulers understandably prefer that the free nations should be weak and divided, as when the men in the Kremlin stole, one by one, the independence of a dozen nations. So, at each enlargement of the area of collective defense, the Soviet rulers pour out abuse against so-called "militaristic groupings." And as the free nations move to strengthen their common defense, the Soviet rulers emit threats. But we can, I think, be confident that such Soviet assaults will not disintegrate the free world. Collective measures are here to stay. . . .

It is also agreed that the principal deterrent to aggressive war is mobile retaliatory power. This retaliatory power must be vast in terms of its potential. But the extent to which it would be used would, of course, depend on circumstances. The essential is that a would-be aggressor should realize that he cannot make armed aggression a paying proposition. . . .

But we do not believe that the only way to security is through ever-mounting armaments. We consider that controls and reduction of arms are possible, desirable, and, in the last reckoning, indispensable. It is not essential that controls should encompass everything at once. In fact, progress is likely to come by steps carefully measured and carefully taken. Thus far it has not

---

[1] Reprinted from *The Department of State Bulletin* (May 6, 1957), pp. 715–719.

been possible to assure the inspection and other safeguards that would make it prudent for us to reduce our effective power. But we shall continue to seek that goal.

Armaments are nothing that we crave. Their possession is forced on us by the aggressive and devious designs of international communism. An arms race is costly, sterile, and dangerous. We shall not cease our striving to bring it to a dependable end.

Any police system is essentially negative. It is designed to repress violence and give a sense of security. But the sense of security is illusory unless, behind its shield, there is growth and development. Military collaboration to sustain peace will collapse unless we also collaborate to spread the blessings of liberty.

Trade, from the earliest days, has been one of the great upbuilders of economic well-being. Therefore, this Government advocates trade policies which promote the interchange of goods to mutual advantage.

Also, the United States, as the most productive and prosperous nation, assists other nations which are at an early stage of self-development. It is sobering to recall that about two-thirds of all the people who resist Communist rule exist in a condition of stagnant poverty. Communism boasts that it could change all that and points to industrial developments wrought in Russia at a cruel, but largely concealed, cost in terms of human slavery and human misery. The question is whether free but undeveloped countries can end stagnation for their people without paying such a dreadful price. Friendly nations expect that those who have abundantly found the blessings of liberty should help those who still await those blessings. . . .

Just as our policy concerns itself with economic development, so, too, our policy concerns itself with political change.

During the past decade, there have come into being, within the free world, 19 new nations with 700 million people. In addition, many nations whose sovereignty was incomplete have had that sovereignty fully completed. Within this brief span nearly one-third of the entire human race has had this exciting, and sometimes intoxicating, experience of gaining full independence. . . .

Today, nations born to independence are born into a world one part of which is ruled by despotism and the other part of which stays free by accepting the concept of interdependence. There is no safe middle ground.

International communism is on the prowl to capture those nations whose leaders feel that newly acquired sovereign rights have to be displayed by flouting other independent nations. That kind of sovereignty is suicidal sovereignty. . . .

Communism in practice has proved to be oppressive, reactionary, unimaginative. Its despotism, far from being revolutionary, is as old as history. Those subject to it, in vast majority, hate the system and yearn for a free society.

The question of how the United States should deal with this matter is not easily answered. Our history, however, offers us a guide. The United States came into being when much of the world was ruled by alien despots. That was a fact we hoped to change. We wanted our example to stimulate liberating forces throughout the world and create a climate in which despotism would shrink. In fact, we did just that.

I believe that that early conception can usefully guide us now. . . .

Let us also make apparent to the Soviet rulers our real purpose. We condemn and oppose their imperialism. We seek the liberation of the captive nations. We seek this, however, not in order to encircle Russia with hostile forces but because peace is in jeopardy and freedom a word of mockery until the divided nations are reunited and the captive nations are set free. . . .

Events of the past year indicate that the pressures of liberty are rising.

Within the Soviet Union there is increasing demand for greater personal security, for greater intellectual freedom, and for greater enjoyment of the fruits of labor.

International communism has become beset with doctrinal difficulties. And the cruel performance of Soviet communism in Hungary led many to desert Communist parties throughout the world.

The satellite countries no longer provide a submissive source of added Soviet strength. Indeed, Soviet strength, both military and economic, has now to be expanded to repress those who openly show their revulsion against Soviet rule.

And the Soviet Government pays a heavy price in terms of moral isolation.

Soviet rulers are supposed to be hardheaded. For how long, we may ask, will they expend their resources in combating historic forces for national unity and freedom which are bound ultimately to prevail? . . .

Surely the stakes justify that effort. As I am briefed on the capacity of modern weapons for destruction, I recognize the impossibility of grasping the full, and indeed awful, significance of the words and figures used. Yet we would be reckless not to recognize that this calamity is a possibility. Indeed history suggests that a conflict as basic as that dividing the world of freedom and the world of international communism ultimately erupts in war.

That suggestion we reject. But to reject in terms of words or of hopes is not enought. We must also exert ourselves to the full to prevent it. To this task, the American people must unswervingly dedicate their hearts and minds throughout the years ahead.

That is not too much to expect. Americans are a people of faith. They have always had a sense of mission and willingness to sacrifice to achieve great goals. Surely, our Nation did not reach a new peak of power and responsibility merely to partake of the greatest, and perhaps the last, of all human disasters.

[ ]

SUMMIT CONFERENCE STATEMENT BY N. S. KHRUSHCHEV[1]
May 16, 1960

As is generally known, a provocative act by the American air force against the Soviet Union has recently taken place. It consisted in the fact that on May 1 of this year a U.S. military reconnaissance plane intruded into the U.S.S.R. on a definite espionage mission of gathering intelligence about military and industrial installations on Soviet territory. After the aggressive purpose of the plane's flight became clear, it was shot down by a Soviet rocket unit. Unfortunately, this is not the only instance of aggressive and espionage actions by the U.S. air force against the Soviet Union.

Naturally, the Soviet government was obliged to describe these actions by their proper name and show their perfidious character, inconsistent with the elementary requirements of normal peacetime relations between states, to say nothing of their conflicting grossly with the aim of reducing international tension and creating the conditions needed for fruitful work at the Summit conference. This was done both in my speeches at the session of the U.S.S.R. Supreme Soviet and in a special protest note sent to the U.S. government.

At first the U.S. State Department gave out an absurd version to the effect that the American plane had violated the frontiers of the Soviet Union by accident and had not had any spying or subversive assignment. When this version was shown with incontrovertible facts to be manifest falsehood, the U.S. State Department on May 7, and then the Secretary of State on May 9, declared on behalf of the U.S. government that intrusions into the Soviet Union for purposes of military espionage were carried out by American aircraft in accordance with a programme approved by the U.S. government and by the President in person. Two days later President Eisenhower himself confirmed that flights by American planes over the territory of the Soviet Union were and remained a calculated policy of the United States. This was also stated by the U.S. government in its note to the Soviet government on May 12. Thereby the U.S. government has grossly flouted the generally accepted standards of international law and the lofty principles of the U.N. Charter, which bears the signature of the United States also. . . .

Now that the leaders of the governments of the Four Powers have come to Paris for their conference, the question arises: how is it possible to productively negotiate and examine the questions confronting the conference, when the U.S. government and personally the President have not only failed to condemn the provocative intrusion of an American military plane into the Soviet Union, but, on the contrary, have declared that such actions remain official U.S. policy towards the U.S.S.R? How can agreement be reached on this or that issue needing to be settled in order to lessen tension and remove suspicion and distrust between states, when the government of one of the

---

[1] Reprinted from *New Times*, No. 21 (May 1960), pp. 34–36.

Great Powers says outright that it is its policy to intrude into the confines of another Great Power for spying and subversive purposes, and consequently to heighten tension in the relations between the powers? Obviously, the proclamation of such a policy, which can only be adopted when nations are at war, dooms the Summit conference in advance to total failure. . . .

It follows from all this that for the conference to be successful, the governments of all the powers represented must adopt an honest and forthright policy and solemnly declare that they will not commit against each other any actions which constitute a violation of national sovereignty. That means that if the U.S. government is really prepared to co-operate with the governments of other powers in the interests of maintaining peace and strengthening confidence among the nations, it must, firstly, condemn the unpardonable provocative actions of the U.S. air force in regard to the Soviet Union and, secondly, renounce continuing such actions and such a policy against the U.S.S.R. in the future. It goes without saying that in that event the U.S. government cannot fail to call to stern account those immediately responsible for the deliberate violation of the Soviet Union's national frontiers by American planes. . . .

It is natural that under these conditions we are unable to work at the conference, unable to work at it because we see from what positions it is desired to talk to us—under threat of aggressive intelligence flights. Everyone knows that spying flights are undertaken for intelligence purposes with a view to starting war. Accordingly, we reject the conditions in which the United States is placing us. We cannot take part in any negotiations, not even in the settlement of questions which are already ripe, because we see that the U.S. has no desire to reach agreement. . . .

We wish to be rightly understood by the peoples of all countries of the globe, by public opinion. The Soviet Union is not abandoning its efforts for agreement, and we are sure that reasonable agreements are possible, but evidently at some other, not this particular time. . . .

The Soviet government is profoundly convinced that if not this U.S. government, then another, and if not another, then a third, will understand that there is no other solution than peaceful co-existence of the two systems, the capitalist and the socialist. It is either peaceful co-existence, or war, which would spell disaster for those now engaging in an aggressive policy.

We therefore consider that a certain amount of time should be allowed to elapse, so that the present issues may simmer down and those responsible for shaping the country's policies may analyze what a responsibility they have incurred in proclaiming an aggressive course in relation to the Soviet Union and the other socialist countries. Accordingly, we feel that the best thing will be to postpone the Heads of Government conference for some six or eight months.

The Soviet Union, for its part, will not relax its efforts to secure agreement. I think that public opinion will correctly understand our position, will understand that it was made impossible for us to participate in these negotiations.

However, we firmly believe in the necessity of peaceful co-existence, for to lose faith in peaceful co-existence would mean dooming humanity to war, it would mean accepting that war is inevitable—and everyone knows what calamities war today would spell for all the peoples of the globe. . . .

We regret that this meeting has been torpedoed by the reactionary element in the United States as the outcome of provocative flights by American military planes over the Soviet Union.

We regret that this meeting has not led to the results which all the peoples of the world expected to follow from it.

Let the shame and blame for it fall on those who have proclaimed a brigand policy in relation to the Soviet Union. . . .

I think that both Mr. Eisenhower and the American people will understand me rightly.

The Soviet government declares that it for its part will continue to do everything in its power to promote the relaxation of international tension and the solution of the problems which today still divide us; in this we shall be guided by the interests of furthering the great cause of peace on the basis of the peaceful co-existence of states with differing social systems.

SUMMIT CONFERENCE STATEMENT BY PRESIDENT EISENHOWER[1]
May 16, 1960

[ ]
Having in mind the great importance of this conference and the hopes that the peoples of all the world have reposed in this meeting, I concluded that in the circumstances it was best to see if at today's private meeting any possibility existed through the exercise of reason and restraint to dispose of this matter of the overflights, which would have permitted the conference to go forward. . . .

Accordingly, at this morning's private session, despite the violence and inaccuracy of Mr. Khrushchev's statements, I replied to him in the following terms:

In my statement of May 11th and in the statement of Secretary Herter of May 9th the position of the United States was made clear with respect to the distasteful necessity of espionage activities in a world where nations distrust each other's intentions. We pointed out that these activities had no aggressive intent but rather were to assure the safety of the United States and the free world against

---

[1] Reprinted from *The Department of State Bulletin*, XLII, No. 109 (June 6, 1960), pp. 904–905.

surprise attack by a power which boasts of its ability to devastate the United States and other countries by missiles armed with atomic warheads. . . .

There is in the Soviet statement an evident misapprehension on one key point. It alleges that the United States has, through official statements, threatened continued overflights. The importance of this alleged threat was emphasized and repeated by Mr. Khrushchev. The United States has made no such threat. Neither I nor my Government has intended any. The actual statements go no further than to say that the United States will not shirk its responsibility to safeguard against surprise attack.

In point of fact, these flights were suspended after the recent incident and are not to be resumed. Accordingly, this cannot be the issue.

I have come to Paris to seek agreements with the Soviet Union which would eliminate the necessity for all forms of espionage, including overflights. I see no reason to use this incident to disrupt the conference.

Should it prove impossible, because of the Soviet attitude, to come to grips here in Paris with this problem and the other vital issues threatening world peace, I am planning in the near future to submit to the United Nations a proposal for the creation of a United Nations aerial surveillance to detect preparations for attack. This plan I had intended to place before this conference. This surveillance system would operate in the territories of all nations prepared to accept such inspection. For its part, the United States is prepared not only to accept United Nations aerial surveillance but to do everything in its power to contribute to the rapid organization and successful operation of such international surveillance.

We of the United States are here to consider in good faith the important problems before this conference. We are prepared either to carry this point no further or to undertake bilateral conversations between the United States and the U.S.S.R. while the main conference proceeds.

[ ]

Mr. Khrushchev brushed aside all arguments of reason and not only insisted upon this ultimatum but also insisted that he was going to publish his statement in full at the time of his own choosing. It was thus made apparent that he was determined to wreck the Paris conference. . . .

In spite of this serious and adverse development I have no intention whatsoever to diminish my continuing efforts to promote progress toward a peace with justice. This applies to the remainder of my stay in Paris as well as thereafter.

PRESIDENT EISENHOWER'S FAREWELL TO THE NATION[1]
January 17, 1961

[ ]

We now stand 10 years past the midpoint of a century that has witnessed four major wars among great nations. Three of these involved our own

---

[1] Reprinted from *The Department of State Bulletin*, XLIV, No. 1128 (February 6, 1961), pp. 179–182.

country. Despite these holocausts, America is today the strongest, the most influential, and most productive nation in the world. Understandably proud of this preeminence, we yet realize that America's leadership and prestige depend not merely upon our unmatched material progress, riches, and military strength but on how we use our power in the interests of world peace and human betterment. . . .

A vital element in keeping the peace is our Military Establishment. Our arms must be mighty, ready for instant action, so that no potential aggressor may be tempted to risk his own destruction.

Our military organization today bears little relation to that known by any of my predecessors in peacetime, or indeed by the fighting men of World War II or Korea.

Until the latest of our world conflicts, the United States had no armaments industry. American makers of plowshares could, with time and as required, make swords as well. But now we can no longer risk emergency improvisation of national defense; we have been compelled to create a permanent armaments industry of vast proportions. Added to this, 3½ million men and women are directly engaged in the Defense Establishment. We annually spend on military security more than the net income of all United States corporations.

This conjunction of an immense Military Establishment and a large arms industry is new in the American experience. The total influence—economic, political, even spiritual—is felt in every city, every statehouse, every office of the Federal Government. We recognize the imperative need for this development. Yet we must not fail to comprehend its grave implications. Our toil, resources, and livelihood are all involved; so is the very structure of our society.

In the councils of government we must guard aginst the acquisition of unwarranted influence, whether sought or unsought, by the military-industrial complex. The potential for the disastrous rise of misplaced power exists and will persist.

We must never let the weight of this combination endanger our liberties or democratic processes. We should take nothing for granted. Only an alert and knowledgeable citizenry can compel the proper meshing of the huge industrial and military machinery of defense with our peaceful methods and goals so that security and liberty may prosper together.

Akin to and largely responsible for the sweeping changes in our industrial-military posture has been the technological revolution during recent decades. In this revolution research has become central; it also becomes more formalized, complex, and costly. A steadily increasing share is conducted for, by, or at the direction of the Federal Government.

Today the solitary inventor, tinkering in his shop, has been overshadowed by task forces of scientists in laboratories and testing fields. In the same fashion the free university, historically the fountainhead of free ideas and scientific discovery, has experienced a revolution in the conduct of research.

Partly because of the huge costs involved, a Government contract becomes virtually a substitute for intellectual curiosity. For every old blackboard there are now hundreds of new electronic computers.

The prospect of domination of the Nation's scholars by Federal employment, project allocations, and the power of money is ever present and is gravely to be regarded.

Yet, in holding scientific research and discovery in respect, as we should, we must also be alert to the equal and opposite danger that public policy could itself become the captive of a scientific-technological elite.

It is the task of statemanship to mold, to balance, and to integrate these and other forces, new and old, within the principles of our democratic system —ever aiming toward the supreme goals of our free society.   [ ]

TOWARD A STRATEGY OF PEACE[1]
Address by President Kennedy at The American University, Washington, D.C., June 10, 1963

[ ]
I have . . . chosen this time and this place to discuss a topic on which ignorance too often abounds and the truth is too rarely perceived—yet it is the most important topic on earth: world peace.

What kind of peace do I mean? What kind of peace do we seek? Not a *Pax Americana* enforced on the world by American weapons of war. Not the peace of the grave or the security of the slave. I am talking about genuine peace, the kind of peace that makes life on earth worth living, the kind that enables men and nations to grow and to hope and to build a better life for their children—not merely peace for Americans but peace for all men and women, not merely peace in our time but peace for all time. . . .

First: Let us examine our attitude toward peace itself. Too many of us think it is impossible. Too many think it unreal. But that is a dangerous, defeatist belief. It leads to the conclusion that war is inevitable, that mankind is doomed, that we are gripped by forces we cannot control.

We need not accept that view. Our problems are manmade; therefore they can be solved by man. And man can be as big as he wants. No problem of human destiny is beyond human beings. Man's reason and spirit have often solved the seemingly unsolvable, and we believe they can do it again.

I am not referring to the absolute, infinite concept of universal peace and good will of which some fantasies and fanatics dream. I do not deny the values of hopes and dreams, but we merely invite discouragement and incredulity by making that our only and immediate goal.

---

[1] Reprinted from *The Department of State Bulletin*, XLIX,. No. 1253 (July 1, 1963), pp. 2–6.

Let us focus instead on a more practical, more attainable peace, based not on a sudden revolution in human nature but on a gradual evolution in human institutions—on a series of concrete actions and effective agreements which are in the interest of all concerned. There is no single, simple key to this peace, no grand or magic formula to be adopted by one or two powers. Genuine peace must be the product of many nations, the sum of many acts. It must be dynamic, not static, changing to meet the challenge of each new generation. For peace is a process, a way of solving problems.

With such a peace there will still be quarrels and conflicting interests, as there are within families and nations. World peace, like community peace, does not require that each man love his neighbor; it requires only that they live together in mutual tolerance, submitting their disputes to a just and peaceful settlement. . . .

Second: Let us reexamine our attitude toward the Soviet Union. . . .

No government or social system is so evil that its people must be considered as lacking in virtue. As Americans we find communism profoundly repugnant as a negation of personal freedom and dignity. But we can still hail the Russian people for their many achievements—in science and space, in economic and industrial growth, in culture and in acts of courage.

Among the many traits the peoples of our two countries have in common, none is stronger than our mutual abhorrence of war. Almost unique among the major world powers, we have never been at war with each other. And no nation in the history of battle ever suffered more than the Soviet Union suffered in the course of the Second World War. . . .

Today, should total war ever break out again—no matter how—our two countries would become the primary targets. It is an ironical but accurate fact that the two strongest powers are the two in the most danger of devastation. All we have built, all we have worked for, would be destroyed in the first 24 hours. And even in the cold war, which brings burdens and dangers to so many countries—including this nation's closest allies—our two countries bear the heaviest burdens. For we are both devoting massive sums of money to weapons that could be better devoted to combating ignorance, poverty, and disease. We are both caught up in a vicious and dangerous cycle in which suspicion on one side breeds suspicion on the other and new weapons beget counterweapons.

In short, both the United States and its allies, and the Soviet Union and its allies, have a mutually deep interest in a just and genuine peace and in halting the arms race. Agreements to this end are in the interests of the Soviet Union as well as ours, and even the most hostile nations can be relied upon to accept and keep those treaty obligations, and only those treaty obligations, which are in their own interest. . . .

Third: Let us reexamine our attitude toward the cold war, remembering that we are not engaged in a debate, seeking to pile up debating points. We are not here distributing blame or pointing the finger of judgment. We must deal with the world as it is and not as it might have been had the history of the last 18 years been different. . . .

Speaking of other nations, I wish to make one point clear. We are bound to many nations by alliances. Those alliances exist because our concern and theirs substantially overlap. Our commitment to defend Western Europe and West Berlin, for example, stands undiminished because of the identity of our vital interests. The United States will make no deal with the Soviet Union at the expense of other nations and other peoples, not merely because they are our partners but also because their interests and ours converge.

Our interests converge, however, not only in defending the frontiers of freedom but in pursuing the paths of peace. It is our hope—and the purpose of Allied policies—to convince the Soviet Union that she, too, should let each nation choose its own future, so long as that choice does not interfere with the choices of others. The Communist drive to impose their political and economic system on others is the primary cause of world tension today. For there can be no doubt that, if all nations could refrain from interfering in the self-determination of others, the peace would be much more assured. . . .

I am taking this opportunity . . . to announce two important decisions . . .

First: Chairman Khrushchev, Prime Minister Macmillan, and I have agreed that high-level discussions will shortly begin in Moscow looking toward early agreement on a comprehensive test ban treaty. Our hopes must be tempered with the caution of history, but with our hopes go the hopes of all mankind.

Second: To make clear our good faith and solemn convictions on the matter, I now declare that the United States does not propose to conduct nuclear tests in the atmosphere so long as other states do not do so. We will not be the first to resume. Such a declaration is no substitute for a formal binding treaty, but I hope it will help us achieve one. Nor would such a treaty be a substitute for disarmament, but I hope it will help us achieve it.

Finally, my fellow Americans, let us examine our attitude toward peace and freedom here at home. The quality and spirit of our own society must justify and support our efforts abroad. . . .

It is the responsibility of the executive branch at all levels of government —local, State, and national—to provide and protect that freedom for all of our citizens by all means within their authority. It is the responsibility of the legislative branch at all levels, wherever that authority is not now adequate, to make it adequate. And it is the responsibility of all citizens in all sections of this country to respect the rights of all others and to respect the law of the land. . . .

While we proceed to safeguard our national interests, let us also safeguard human interests. And the elimination of war and arms is clearly in the interest of both. No treaty, however much it may be to the advantage of all, however tightly it may be worded, can provide absolute security against the risks of deception and evasion. But it can, if it is sufficiently effective in its enforcement and if it is sufficiently in the interests of its signers, offer far more security and far fewer risks than an unabated, uncontrolled, unpredictable arms race.

The United States, as the world knows, will never start a war. We do not want a war. We do not now expect a war. This generation of Americans has already had enough—more than enough—of war and hate and oppression. We shall be prepared if others wish it. We shall be alert to try to stop it. But we shall also do our part to build a world of peace where the weak are safe and the strong are just. We are not helpless before that task or hopeless of its success. Confident and unafraid, we labor on—not toward a strategy of annihilation but toward a strategy of peace.

UNITED STATES AID TO VIETNAM[1]
Letter from President Eisenhower to Ngo Dinh Diem, President of the Council of Ministers of Vietnam, October 23, 1954

DEAR MR. PRESIDENT: I have been following with great interest the course of developments in Viet-Nam, particularly since the conclusion of the conference at Geneva. The implications of the agreement concerning Viet-Nam have caused grave concern regarding the future of a country temporarily divided by an artificial military grouping, weakened by a long and exhausting war and faced with enemies without and by their subversive collaborators within.

Your recent requests for aid to assist in the formidable project of the movement of several hundred thousand loyal Vietnamese citizens away from areas which are passing under a *de facto* rule and political ideology which they abhor, are being fulfilled. I am glad that the United States is able to assist in this humanitarian effort.

We have been exploring ways and means to permit our aid to Viet-Nam to be more effective and to make a greater contribution to the welfare and stability of the Government of Viet-Nam. I am, accordingly, instructing the American Ambassador to Viet-Nam to examine with you in your capacity as Chief of Government, how an intelligent program of American aid given directly to your Government can serve to assist Viet-Nam in its present hour of trial, provided that your Government is prepared to give assurances as to the standards of performance it would be able to maintain in the event such aid were supplied.

The purpose of this offer is to assist the Government of Viet-Nam in developing and maintaining a strong, viable state, capable of resisting attempted subversion or aggression through military means. The Government

---

[1] Reprinted from *The Department of State Bulletin* (November 15, 1954), pp. 735–736.

of the United States expects that this aid will be met by performance on the part of the Government of Viet-Nam in undertaking needed reforms. It hopes that such aid, combined with your own continuing efforts, will contribute effectively toward an independent Viet-Nam endowed with a strong government. Such a government would, I hope, be so responsive to the nationalist aspirations of its people, so enlightened in purpose and effective in performance, that it will be respected both at home and abroad and discourage any who might wish to impose a foreign ideology on your free people.

Sincerely,

Dwight D. Eisenhower

THE ATTITUDE OF FRANCE TOWARD THE POLICY OF THE UNITED STATES IN VIETNAM[1]
Statement of President de Gaulle at His Tenth Press Conference in Paris, July 23, 1964

The Geneva Agreements concluded in 1954 put an end to the fighting in Indochina. At the time, everyone seemed to desire it sincerely. These agreements included provisions which varied according to the countries in question, but which had in common the absolute exclusion of all outside intervention. Cambodia pledged not to enter into any alliance and not to allow any base on its territory. Laos was to prohibit the presence of any foreign troops, with the exception of a French military mission and an airfield used by France in Seno. The two Vietnams could not ally themselves with anyone, or introduce on their soil any force from the outside, or receive armaments which would increase their potential. Moreover, general elections were scheduled to take place in Vietnam in 1956, so as to lead to the institution of a democratic Government and to reunification. The 1954 agreements were not applied for long. That is the least that can be said about them. Cambodia alone—thanks to its national unity and to the very skillful and determined way in which it is led by its Head of State—has known how and been able to remain intact, neutral and relatively peaceful until now. But in Vietnam everything conspired to bring that country back to the troubled situation from which it had just emerged, while Laos in its turn was caught up in domestic conflicts, aided from the outside.

Concerning Vietnam, it must be said that the existence of a communist State installed in Tonkin from where our troops withdrew in accordance with the agreements, and the shock caused in the south by the withdrawal of our administration and our forces, exposed the country to new perils. It was a matter of knowing whether it could find, in itself, a national cohesion and a

---

[1] The text of President de Gaulle's statement was made available through the courtesy of the French Press and Information Service, New York.

solid government. It was then that the Americans arrived, bringing their aid, their policy and their authority.

The United States, in fact, considered itself as being invested throughout the world with the burden of defense against communism. Since South Vietnam was running the risk of it, as the regime established in the north was aimed at imposing itself there, Washington wanted to put this State in a position to protect itself. It can be added, without any intention of being derogatory, that their conviction of fulfilling a sort of vocation, the aversion which they had to any colonial work which had not been theirs, and finally the natural desire in such a powerful people to ensure themselves of new positions, determined the Americans to take our place in Indochina.

We know that, back in 1954 they sponsored the Diem government, that Diem immediately and unfortunately assumed an unpleasant attitude toward us, that once Emperor Bao-Dai had left the country he replaced him, that he did not carry out the scheduled elections and lastly that in all fields, particularly those of defense, economy and administration, he placed himself in the orbit of Washington. But, as this policy was more and more unpopular, the day came when Diem tried to disentangle himself from it, while the Americans began to have doubts about him. Then a military putsch removed the President and gave him a successor. After that, a new putsch invested another one, the latter closely linked with the war action which the United States is supporting, staffing, financing and arming.

War action, indeed, for although the subversive elements of the Vietcong had disappeared from South Vietnam after the 1954 agreements, they reappeared there under pretext that the agreements were not being applied. Guerrilla fighting and some action carried out by constituted units are spreading more and more over the territory. At the same time, the populations, whatever their opinion of Communism, are less and less inclined to support a cause and an authority which in their view are intermingled with those of a foreign State. Thus it seems that, locally, a military solution cannot be expected. Some people imagine, it is true, that the Americans could seek it elsewhere by carrying the war to the north as far as it would be necessary. But, although they certainly dispose of all the desired means, it is difficult to assume that they wish to take the tremendous risk of a generalized conflict.

Lacking a decision by war, it is peace which thus must be made. Now, this implies returning to what was agreed upon ten years ago and, this time, complying with it, in other words, this implies that in North and South Vietnam, in Cambodia and in Laos, no foreign power any longer intervene in any way in the affairs of these unfortunate countries. A meeting of the same order and including, in principle, the same participants as the former Geneva conference would certainly be qualified to make a decision and to organize an impartial control. That is what France is proposing to all the States concerned, certain that, unless plunging Asia first and without doubt, at a later date, the entire world into very serious trials, this will have to be done, and the sooner, the better. This meeting, to which each must come without conditions or recriminations, would successively deal with the international aspects of the Laotian, Cambodian and Vietnamese situation and of which the essential is, in advance, their neutrality. No other road can be visualized which can lead to peace in Southeast Asia, provided that once the theoretical agreement is concluded, if it is to be, two practical conditions be realized. The first is that the powers, which directly or indirectly bear a responsibility in what was or is the fate of Indochina and which are France, China, the Soviet Union and America, be effectively resolved to be involved there no longer. The second is that massive economic and technical aid be furnished to all of Indochina by the States which have the means for it, in order that development replace cruel division. France, for her part, is ready to observe these two conditions.

THE TONKIN BAY RESOLUTION[1]
Joint Resolution of U.S. Congress: Public Law 88-408, August 7, 1964, Approved on August 10, 1964

To promote the maintenance of international peace and security in southeast Asia.

Whereas naval units of the Communist regime in Vietnam, in violation of the principles of the Charter of the United Nations and of international law, have deliberately and repeatedly attacked United States naval vessels lawfully present in international waters, and have thereby created a serious threat to international peace; and

Whereas these attacks are part of a deliberate and systematic campaign of aggression that the Communist regime in North Vietnam has been waging against its neighbors and the nations joined with them in the collective defense of their freedom; and

Whereas the United States is assisting the peoples of southeast Asia to protect their freedom and has no territorial, military or political ambitions in that area, but desires only that these peoples should be left in peace to work out their own destinies in their own way: Now, therefore, be it

Resolved by the Senate and House of Representatives of the United States of America in Congress assembled, That the Congress approves and supports the determination of the President, as Commander in Chief, to take all necessary measures to repel any armed attack against the forces of the United States and to prevent further aggression.

Sec. 2. The United States regards as vital to its national interest and to world peace the maintenance of international peace and security in southeast Asia. Consonant with the Constitution of the United States and the Charter

---

[1] Reprinted from *The Department of State Bulletin* (August 24, 1964), p. 268.

of the United Nations and in accordance with its obligations under the Southeast Asia Collective Defense Treaty, the United States is, therefore, prepared, as the President determines, to take all necessary steps, including the use of armed force, to assist any member or protocol state of the Southeast Asia Collective Defense Treaty requesting assistance in defense of its freedom.

Sec. 3. This resolution shall expire when the President shall determine that the peace and security of the area is reasonably assured by international conditions created by action of the United Nations or otherwise, except that it may be terminated earlier by concurrent resolution of the Congress.

AGGRESSION FROM THE NORTH[1]
The Record of North Vietnam's Campaign to Conquer South Vietnam

South Viet-Nam is fighting for its life against a brutal campaign of terror and armed attack inspired, directed, supplied, and controlled by the Communist regime in Hanoi. This flagrant aggression has been going on for years, but recently the pace has quickened and the threat has now become acute.

The war in Viet-Nam is a new kind of war, a fact as yet poorly understood in most parts of the world. Much of the confusion that prevails in the thinking of many people, and even many governments, stems from this basic misunderstanding. For in Viet-Nam a totally new brand of aggression has been loosed against an independent people who want to make their own way in peace and freedom.

Viet-Nam is *not* another Greece, where indigenous guerrilla forces used friendly neighboring territory as a sanctuary.

Viet-Nam is *not* another Malaya, where Communist guerrillas were, for the most part, physically distinguishable from the peaceful majority they sought to control.

Viet-Nam is *not* another Philippines, where Communist guerrillas were physically separated from the source of their moral and physical support.

Above all, the war in Viet-Nam is *not* a spontaneous and local rebellion against the established government.

There are elements in the Communist program of conquest directed against South Viet-Nam common to each of the previous areas of aggression and subversion. But there is one fundamental difference. In Viet-Nam a Communist government has set out deliberately to conquer a sovereign people in a neighboring state. And to achieve its end, it has used every resource of its own government to carry out its carefully planned program of concealed aggression. North Viet-Nam's commitment to seize control of the

---

[1] Reprinted from *The Department of State Bulletin*, LII, No. 1343 (March 22, 1965), pp. 404–406.

South is no less total than was the commitment of the regime in North Korea in 1950. But knowing the consequences of the latter's undisguised attack, the planners in Hanoi have tried desperately to conceal their hand. They have failed and their aggression is as real as that of an invading army. . . .

The evidence shows that the hard core of the Communist forces attacking South Viet-Nam were trained in the North and ordered into the South by Hanoi. It shows that the key leadership of the Viet Cong (VC), the officers and much of the cadre, many of the technicians, political organizers, and propagandists have come from the North and operate under Hanoi's direction. It shows that the training of essential military personnel and their infiltration into the South is directed by the Military High Command in Hanoi.

The evidence shows that many of the weapons and much of the ammunition and other supplies used by the Viet Cong have been sent into South Viet-Nam from Hanoi. In recent months new types of weapons have been introduced in the VC army, for which all ammunition must come from outside sources. Communist China and other Communist states have been the prime suppliers of these weapons and ammunition, and they have been channeled primarily through North Viet-Nam.

The directing force behind the effort to conquer South Viet-Nam is the Communist Party in the North, the Lao Dong (Workers) Party. As in every Communist state, the party is an integral part of the regime itself. North Vietnamese officials have expressed their firm determination to absorb South Viet-Nam into the Communist world.

Through its Central Committee, which controls the government of the North, the Lao Dong Party directs the total political and military effort of the Viet Cong. The Military High Command in the North trains the military men and sends them into South Viet-Nam. The Central Research Agency, North Viet-Nam's central intelligence organization, directs the elaborate espionage and subversion effort. . . .

Under Hanoi's overall direction the Communists have established an extensive machine for carrying on the war within South Viet-Nam. The focal point is the Central Office for South Viet-Nam with its political and military subsections and other specialized agencies. A subordinate part of this Central Office is the Liberation Front for South Viet-Nam. The front was formed at Hanoi's order in 1960. Its principal function is to influence opinion abroad and to create the false impression that the aggression in South Viet-Nam is an indigenous rebellion against the established government.

For more than 10 years the people and the Government of South Viet-Nam, exercising the inherent right of self-defense, have fought back against these efforts to extend Communist power south across the 17th parallel. The United States has responded to the appeals of the Government of the Republic of Viet-Nam for help in this defense of the freedom and independence of its land and its people.   [ ]

PATTERN FOR PEACE IN SOUTHEAST ASIA[1]
Speech Delivered by President Johnson at Johns Hopkins University, Baltimore, Maryland, April 7, 1965

[ ]

Tonight Americans and Asians are dying for a world where each people may choose its own path to change. This is the principle for which our ancestors fought in the valleys of Pennsylvania. It is a principle for which our sons fight tonight in the jungles of Viet-Nam.

Viet-Nam is far away from this quiet campus. We have no territory there, nor do we seek any. The war is dirty and brutal and difficult. And some 400 young men, born into an America that is bursting with opportunity and promise, have ended their lives on Viet-Nam's steaming soil.

Why must we take this painful road? Why must this nation hazard its ease, its interest, and its power for the sake of a people so far away?

We fight because we must fight if we are to live in a world where every country can shape its own destiny, and only in such a world will our own freedom be finally secure. . . .

The world as it is in Asia is not a serene or peaceful place.

The first reality is that North Viet-Nam has attacked the independent nation of South Viet-Nam. Its object is total conquest. Of course, some of the people of South Viet-Nam are participating in attack on their own government. But trained men and supplies, orders and arms, flow in a constant stream from North to South.

This support is the heartbeat of the war. . . .

Over this war—and all Asia—is another reality: the deepening shadow of Communist China. The rulers in Hanoi are urged on by Peiping. This is a regime which has destroyed freedom in Tibet, which has attacked India, and has been condemned by the United Nations for aggression in Korea. It is a nation which is helping the forces of violence in almost every continent. The contest in Viet-Nam is part of a wider pattern of aggressive purposes.

Why are these realities our concern? Why are we in South Viet-Nam?

We are there because we have a promise to keep. Since 1954 every American President has offered support to the people of South Viet-Nam. We have helped to build, and we have helped to defend. Thus, over many years, we have made a national pledge to help South Viet-Nam defend its independence.

And I intend to keep that promise.

To dishonor that pledge, to abandon this small and brave nation to its enemies, and to the terror that must follow, would be an unforgivable wrong.

We are also there to strengthen world order. Around the globe, from

---

[1] Reprinted from *The Department of State Bulletin*, LII, No. 1348 (April 26, 1965), pp. 606–612.

Berlin to Thailand, are people whose well-being rests in part on the belief that they can count on us if they are attacked. To leave Viet-Nam to its fate would shake the confidence of all these people in the value of an American commitment and in the value of America's word. The result would be increased unrest and instability, and even wider war.

We are also there because there are great stakes in the balance. Let no one think for a moment that retreat from Viet-Nam would bring an end to conflict. The battle would be renewed in one country and then another. The central lesson of our time is that the appetite of aggression is never satisfied. To withdraw from one battlefield means only to prepare for the next. . . .

Our objective is the independence of South Viet-Nam and its freedom from attack. We want nothing for ourselves—only that the people of South Viet-Nam be allowed to guide their own country in their own way. We will do everything necessary to reach that objective, and we will do only what is absolutely necessary.

In recent months attacks on South Viet-Nam were stepped up. Thus it became necessary for us to increase our response and to make attacks by air. This is not a change of purpose. It is a change in what we believe that purpose requires.

We do this in order to slow down aggression.

We do this to increase the confidence of the brave people of South Viet-Nam who have bravely borne this brutal battle for so many years with so many casualties.

And we do this to convince the leaders of North Viet-Nam—and all who seek to share their conquest—of a simple fact:

We will not be defeated.

We will not grow tired.

We will not withdraw, either openly or under the cloak of a meaningless agreement. . . .

We hope that peace will come swiftly. But that is in the hands of others besides ourselves. And we must be prepared for a long continued conflict. It will require patience as well as bravery—the will to endure as well as the will to resist. . . .

. . . peace demands an independent South Viet-Nam—securely guaranteed and able to shape its own relationships to all others—free from outside interference—tied to no alliance—a military base for no other country.

These are the essentials of any final settlement.

We will never be second in the search for such a peaceful settlement in Viet-Nam.

There may be many ways to this kind of peace: in discussion or negotiation with the governments concerned; in large groups or in small ones; in the reaffirmation of old agreements or their strengthening with new ones.

We have stated this position over and over again 50 times and more to friend and foe alike. And we remain ready with this purpose for unconditional discussions.

And until that bright and necessary day of peace we will try to keep conflict from spreading. We have no desire to see thousands die in battle—Asians or Americans. We have no desire to devastate that which the people of North Viet-Nam have built with toil and sacrifice. We will use our power with restraint and with all the wisdom that we can command.

But we will use it. . . .

Stability and peace do not come easily in such a land. Neither independence nor human dignity will ever be won, though, by arms alone. It also requires the works of peace. The American people have helped generously in times past in these works, and now there must be a much more massive effort to improve the life of man in that conflict-torn corner of our world.

The first step is for the countries of Southeast Asia to associate themselves in a greatly expanded cooperative effort for development. We would hope that North Viet-Nam would take its place in the common effort just as soon as peaceful cooperation is possible.

The United Nations is already actively engaged in development in this area, and as far back as 1961 I conferred with our authorities in Viet-Nam in connection with their work there. And I would hope tonight that the Secretary-General of the United Nations could use the prestige of his great office and his deep knowledge of Asia to initiate, as soon as possible, with the countries of that area, a plan for cooperation in increased development.

For our part I will ask the Congress to join in a billion-dollar American investment in this effort as soon as it is underway. And I would hope that all other industrialized countries, including the Soviet Union, will join in this effort to replace despair with hope and terror with progress.

The task is nothing less than to enrich the hopes and existence of more than a hundred million people. And there is much to be done.

The vast Mekong River can provide food and water and power on a scale to dwarf even our own TVA. The wonders of modern medicine can be spread through villages where thousands die every year from lack of care. Schools can be established to train people in the skills needed to manage the process of development. And these objectives, and more, are within the reach of a cooperative and determined effort.

I also intend to expand and speed up a program to make available our farm surpluses to assist in feeding and clothing the needy in Asia. We should not allow people to go hungry and wear rags while our own warehouses overflow with an abundance of wheat and corn and rice and cotton. . . .

We often say how impressive power is. But I do not find it impressive at all. The guns and the bombs, the rockets and the warships, are all symbols of human failure. They are necessary symbols. They protect what we cherish. But they are witness to human folly.

A dam built across a great river is impressive.

In the countryside where I was born, and where I live, I have seen the night illuminated, and the kitchen warmed, and the home heated, where once the cheerless night and the ceaseless cold held sway. And all this happened because electricity came to our area along the humming wires of the REA. Electrification of the countryside—yes, that, too, is impressive.

A rich harvest in a hungry land is impressive.

The sight of healthy children in a classroom is impressive.

These—not mighty arms—are the achievements which the American nation believes to be impressive. And if we are steadfast, the time may come when all other nations will also find it so. . . .

This generation of the world must choose: destroy or build, kill or aid, hate or understand. We can do all these things on a scale that has never been dreamed of before.

Well, we will choose life. And so doing, we will prevail over the enemies within man, and over the natural enemies of all mankind.

UNITED STATES POLICY IN THE DOMINICAN CRISIS[1]
Senator Fulbright's Appraisal, September 15, 1965

[ ]
I was in doubt about the advisability of making a statement on the Dominican affair until some of my colleagues made public statements on the floor. Their views on the way in which the committee proceedings were conducted and, indeed, on the Dominican crisis as a whole, are so diametrically opposed to my own that I now consider it my duty to express my personal conclusions drawn from the hearings held by the Committee on Foreign Relations. . . .

U.S. policy in the Dominican crisis was characterized initially by overtimidity and subsequently by overaction. Throughout the whole affair it has also been characterized by a lack of candor.

These are general conclusions I have reached from a painstaking review of the salient features of the extremely complex situation. These judgments are made, of course, with the benefit of hindsight and, in fairness, it must be conceded there were no easy choices available to the United States in the Dominican Republic. Nonetheless, it is the task of diplomacy to make wise decisions when they need to be made and U.S. diplomacy failed to do so in the Dominican crisis. . . .

. . . I am frankly puzzled as to the current attitude of the U.S. Govern-ment toward reformist movements in Latin America. On the one hand,

---

[1] Reprinted from the *Congressional Record: Proceedings and Debates of the 89th Congress, 1st Session*, Volume III, No. 170, Daily Edition (September 15, 1965), pp. 22998–23005.

President Johnson's deep personal commitment to the philosophy and aims of the Alliance for Progress is clear; it was convincingly expressed, for example, in his speech to the Latin American Ambassadors on the fourth anniversary of the Alliance for Progress—a statement in which the President compared the Alliance for Progress with his own enlightened program for a Great Society at home. On the other hand, one notes a general tendency on the part of our policy makers not to look beyond a Latin American politician's anticommunism. One also notes in certain Government agencies, particularly the Department of Defense, a preoccupation with counterinsurgency, which is to say, with the prospect of revolutions and means of suppressing them. . . .

It is of great importance that the uncertainty as to U.S. aims in Latin America be resolved. We cannot successfully advance the cause of popular democracy and at the same time aline ourselves with corrupt and reactionary oligarchies; yet that is what we seem to be trying to do. The direction of the Alliance for Progress is toward social revolution in Latin America; the direction of our Dominican intervention is toward the suppression of revolutionary movements which are supported by Communists or suspected of being influenced by Communists. The prospect of an election in 9 months which may conceivably produce a strong democratic government is certainly reassuring on this score, but the fact remains that the reaction of the United States at the time of acute crisis was to intervene forcibly and illegally against a revolution which, had we sought to influence it instead of suppressing it, might have produced a strong popular government without foreign military intervention. Since just about every revolutionary movement is likely to attract Communist support, at least in the beginning, the approach followed in the Dominican Republic, if consistently pursued, must inevitably make us the enemy of all revolutions and therefore the ally of all the unpopular and corrupt oligarchies of the hemisphere. . . .

It is not surprising that we Americans are not drawn toward the uncouth revolutionaries of the non-Communist left. We are not, as we like to claim in Fourth of July speeches, the most truly revolutionary nation on earth; we are, on the contrary, much closer to being the most unrevolutionary nation on earth. We are sober and satisfied and comfortable and rich; our institutions are stable and old and even venerable; and our Revolution of 1776, for that matter, was not much of an upheaval compared to the French and Russian revolutions and to current and impending revolutions in Latin America, Asia, and Africa. . . .

We must try to understand social revolution and the injustices that give it rise because they are the heart and core of the experience of the great majority of people now living in the world. . . .

It is the revolutionaries of the non-Communist left who have most of the popular support in Latin America. The Radical Party in Chile, for example, is full of 19th century libertarians whom many North Americans would find highly congenial, but it was recently crushed in national elections by a group of rambunctious, leftist Christian Democrats. It may be argued that the Christian Democrats are anti–United States, and to a considerable extent some of them are—more so now, it may be noted, than prior to the intervention of the United States in the Dominican Republic—but they are not Communists and they have popular support. . . .

The movement of the future in Latin American is social revolution. The question is whether it is to be Communist or democratic revolution and the choice which the Latin Americans make will depend in part on how the United States uses its great influence. It should be very clear that the choice is not between social revolution and conservative oligarchy but whether, by supporting reform, we bolster the popular non-Communist left or whether, by supporting unpopular oligarchies, we drive the rising generation of educated and patriotic young Latin Americans to an embittered and hostile form of communism like that of Fidel Castro in Chile [sic].

In my Senate speech of March 25, 1964, I commented as follows on the prospect of revolution:

I am not predicting violent revolutions in Latin America or elsewhere. Still less am I advocating them. I wish only to suggest that violent social revolutions are a possibility in countries where feudal oligarchies resist all meaningful change by peaceful means. We must not, in our preference for the democratic procedures envisioned by the Charter of Punta del Este, close our minds to the possibility that democratic procedures may fail in certain countries and that where democracy does fail violent social convulsions may occur.

I think that in the case of the Dominican Republic we did close our minds to the causes and to the essential legitimacy of revolution in a country in which democratic procedures had failed. That, I think, is the central fact concerning the participation of the United States in the Dominican revolution and, possibly as well, its major lesson for the future. . . .

The United States intervened in the Dominican Republic for the purpose of preventing the victory of a revolutionary force which was judged to be Communist dominated. On the basis of Ambassador Bennett's messages to Washington, there is no doubt that the threat of communism rather than danger to American lives was his primary reason for recommending military intervention. . . .

. . . The evidence does not establish that the Communists at any time actually had control of the revolution. There is little doubt that they had influence within the revolutionary movement, but the degree of that influence remains a matter of speculation.

The administration, however, assumed almost from the beginning that the revolution was Communist-dominated, or would certainly become so, and that nothing short of forcible opposition could prevent a Communist take-over. In their apprehension lest the Dominican Republic become another Cuba, some of our officials seem to have forgotten that virtually all reform movements attract some Communist support, that there is an important difference between Communist support and Communist control of a political movement, that it is quite possible to compete with the Communists for influence in a reform movement rather than abandon it to them, and, most important of all, that economic development and social justice are themselves the primary and most reliable security against Communist subversion. . . .

Intervention on the basis of Communist participation as distinguished from control of the Dominican revolution was a mistake in my opinion which also reflects a grievous misreading of the temper of contemporary Latin American politics. Communists are present in all Latin American countries, and they are going to inject themselves into almost any Latin American revolution and try to seize control of it. If any group or any movement with which the Communists associate themselves is going to be automatically condemned in the eyes of the United States, then we have indeed given up all hope of guiding or influencing even to a marginal degree the revolutionary movements and the demands for social change which are sweeping Latin America. Worse, if that is our view, then we have made ourselves the prisoners of the Latin American oligarchs who are engaged in a vain attempt to preserve the status quo—reactionaries who habitually use the term "Communist" very loosely, in part out of emotional predilection and in part in a calculated effort to scare the United States into supporting their selfish and discredited aims. . . .

In the eyes of educated, energetic and patriotic young Latin Americans —which is to say, the generation that will make or break the Alliance for Progress—the United States committed a worse offense in the Dominican Republic than just intervention; it intervened against social revolution and in support, at least temporarily, of a corrupt, reactionary military oligarchy.

It is not possible at present to assess the depth and extent of disillusion with the United States on the part of democrats and reformers in Latin America. I myself think that it is deep and widespread. . . .

The tragedy of Santo Domingo is that a policy that purported to defeat communism in the short run is more likely to have the effect of promoting it in the long run. Intervention in the Dominican Republic has alienated—temporarily or permanently, depending on our future policies—our real friends in Latin America. These, broadly, are the people of the democratic left. . . . By our intervention on the side of a corrupt military oligarchy in the Dominican Republic, we have embarrassed before their own people the democratic reformers who have counseled trust and partnership with the United States. We have lent credence to the idea that the United States is the enemy of social revolution in Latin America and that the only choice Latin Americans have is between communism and reaction.

If those are the available alternatives, if there is no democratic left as a third option, then there is no doubt of the choice that honest and patriotic Latin Americans will make: they will choose communism, not because they want it but because U.S. policy will have foreclosed all other avenues of social revolution and, indeed, all other possibilities except the perpetuation of rule by military juntas and economic oligarchies. . . .

The Foreign Relations Committee's study of the Dominican crisis leads me to draw certain specific conclusions regarding American policy in the Dominican Republic and also suggests some broader considerations regarding relations between the United States and Latin America. My specific conclusions regarding the crisis in Santo Domingo are as follows:

First. The United States intervened forcibly in the Dominican Republic in the last week of April 1965 not primarily to save American lives, as was then contended, but to prevent the victory of a revolutionary movement which was judged to be Communist-dominated. The decision to land thousands of marines on April 28 was based primarily on the fear of "another Cuba" in Santo Domingo.

Second. This fear was based on fragmentary and inadequate evidence. There is no doubt that Communists participated in the Dominican revolution on the rebel side, probably to a greater extent after than before the landing of U.S. marines on April 28, but just as it cannot be proved that the Communists would not have taken over the revolution neither can it be proved that they would have. There is little basis in the evidence offered the committee for the assertion that the rebels were Communist-dominated or certain to become so; on the contrary, the evidence suggests a chaotic situation in which no single faction was dominant at the outset and in which everybody, including the United States, had opportunities to influence the shape and course of the rebellion.

Third. The United States let pass its best opportunities to influence the course of events. The best opportunities were on April 25, when Juan Bosch's party, the PRD, requested a "United States presence," and on April 27, when the rebels, believing themselves defeated, requested United States mediation for a negotiated settlement. . . .

Fourth. U.S. policy toward the Dominican Republic shifted markedly to the right between September 1963 and April 1965. In 1963, the United States strongly supported Bosch and the PRD as enlightened reformers; in 1965 the United States opposed their return to power on the unsubstantiated ground that a Bosch or PRD government would certainly, or almost certainly, become Communist dominated. Thus the United States turned its back on social revolution in Santo Domingo and associated itself with a corrupt and reactionary military oligarchy.

Fifth. U.S. policy was marred by a lack of candor and by misinformation. The former is illustrated by official assertions that U.S. military intervention was primarily for the purpose of saving American lives; the latter is illustrated by exaggerated reports of massacres and atrocities by the rebels—reports which no one has been able to verify. It was officially asserted, for example— by the President in a press conference on June 17 according to an official State

Department bulletin—that "some 1,500 innocent people were murdered and shot, and their heads cut off." There is no evidence to support this statement. . . .

Sixth. Responsibility for the failure of American policy in Santo Domingo lies primarily with those who advised the president. In the critical days between April 25 and April 28, these officials sent the president exaggerated reports of the danger of a Communist takeover in Santo Domingo and, on the basis of these, recommended U.S. massive military intervention. . . .

Seventh. Underlying the bad advice and unwise actions of the United States was the fear of another Cuba. The specter of a second Communist state in the Western Hemisphere—and its probable repercussions within the United States and possible effects on the careers of those who might be held responsible—seems to have been the most important single factor in distorting the judgment of otherwise sensible and competent men.   [ ]

··{*25*}·· *The Role of the United Nations in Keeping International Peace*

CHARTER OF THE UNITED NATIONS[1]
June 6, 1945

We the peoples of the United Nations determined

to save succeeding generations from the scourge of war, which twice in our lifetime has brought untold sorrow to mankind, and

to reaffirm faith in fundamental human rights, in the dignity and worth of the human person, in the equal rights of men and women and of nations large and small, and

to establish conditions under which justice and respect for the obligations arising from treaties and other sources of international law can be maintained, and

to promote social progress and better standards of life in larger freedom, and for these ends

to practice tolerance and live together in peace with one another as good neighbours, and

to unite our strength to maintain international peace and security, and

to ensure, by the acceptance of principles and the institution of methods, that armed force shall not be used, save in the common interest, and

to employ international machinery for the promotion of the economic and social advancement of all peoples,

have resolved to combine our efforts to accomplish these aims.

Accordingly, our respective Governments, through representatives assembled in the city of San Francisco, who have exhibited their full powers found to be in good and due form, have agreed to the present Charter of the United Nations and do hereby establish an international organization to be known as the United Nations.

---

[1] Reprinted from the *Yearbook of the United Nations* (1946–1947), pp. 831–843.

CHAPTER I. PURPOSE AND PRINCIPLES

Article 1. The purposes of the United Nations are:

1. To maintain international peace and security, and to that end: to take effective collective measures for the prevention and removal of threats to the peace, and for the suppression of acts of aggression or other breaches of the peace, and to bring about by peaceful means, and in conformity with the principles of justice and international law, adjustment or settlement of international disputes or situations which might lead to a breach of the peace;

2. To develop friendly relations among nations based on respect for the principle of equal rights and self-determination of peoples, and to take other appropriate measures to strengthen universal peace;

3. To achieve international co-operation in solving international problems of an economic, social, cultural, or humanitarian character, and in promoting and encouraging respect for human rights and for fundamental freedoms for all without distinction as to race, sex, language, or religion; and

4. To be a centre for harmonizing the actions of nations in the attainment of these common ends.

Article 2. The Organization and its Members, in pursuit of the Purposes stated in Article 1, shall act in accordance with the following Principles.

1. The Organization is based on the principle of the sovereign equality of all its Members.

[ ]

7. Nothing contained in the present Charter shall authorize the United Nations to intervene in matters which are essentially within the domestic jurisdiction of any state or shall require the Members to submit such matters to settlement under the present Charter; but this principle shall not prejudice the application of enforcement measures under Chapter VII.

CHAPTER II. MEMBERSHIP

Article 3. The original Members of the United Nations shall be the states which, having participated in the United Nations Conference on International Organization at San Francisco, or having previously signed the Declaration by United Nations of 1 January 1942, sign the present Charter and ratify it in accordance with Article 110.

Article 4. 1. Membership in the United Nations is open to all other peace-loving states which accept the obligations contained in the present Charter and, in the judgment of the Organization, are able and willing to carry out these obligations.

2. The admission of any such State to membership in the United Nations will be effected by a decision of the General Assembly upon the recommendation of the Security Council.

[ ]

CHAPTER IV. THE GENERAL ASSEMBLY

Composition

Article 9. 1. The General Assembly shall consist of all the Members of the United Nations.

2. Each Member shall have not more than five representatives in the General Assembly.

Functions and Powers

Article 10. The General Assembly may discuss any questions or any matters within the scope of the present Charter or relating to the powers and functions of any organs provided for in the present Charter, and, except as provided in Article 12, may make recommendations to the Members of the United Nations or to the Security Council or to both on any such questions or matters.

Article 11. 1. The General Assembly may consider the general principles of co-operation in the maintenance of international peace and security, including the principles governing disarmament and the regulation of armaments, and may make recommendations with regard to such principles to the Members or to the Security Council or to both.

2. The General Assembly may discuss any questions relating to the maintenance of international peace and security brought before it by any Member of the United Nations, or by the Security Council, or by a state which is not a Member of the United Nations in accordance with Article 35, paragraph 2, and, except as provided in Article 12, may make recommendations with regard to any such questions to the state or states concerned or to the Security Council or to both. Any such question on which action is necessary shall be referred to the Security Council by the General Assembly either before or after discussion. . . .

Article 12. 1. While the Security Council is exercising in respect of any dispute or situation the functions assigned to it in the present Charter, the General Assembly shall not make any recommendation with regard to that dispute or situation unless the Security Council so requests.

[ ]

Article 19. A Member of the United Nations which is in arrears in the payment of its financial contributions to the Organization shall have no vote in the General Assembly if the amount of its arrears equals or exceeds the amount of the contributions due from it for the preceding two full years. The General Assembly may, nevertheless, permit such a Member to vote if it is satisfied that the failure to pay is due to conditions beyond the control of the Member.

[ ]

CHAPTER V. THE SECURITY COUNCIL

Composition

Article 23. 1. The Security Council shall consist of eleven Members of the United Nations. The Republic of China, France, the Union of Soviet Socialist Republics, the United Kingdom of Great Britain and Northern Ireland, and the United States of America shall be permanent members of the Security Council. The General Assembly shall elect six other Members of the United Nations to be non-permanent members of the Security Council, due regard being specially paid, in the first instance to the contribution of Members of the United Nations to the maintenance of international peace and security and to the other purposes of the Organization, and also to equitable geographical distribution. . . .

Functions and Powers

Article 24. 1. In order to ensure prompt and effective action by the United Nations, its Members confer on the Security Council primary responsibility for the maintenance of international peace and security, and agree that in carrying out its duties under this responsibility the Security Council acts on their behalf.
[ ]

Voting

Article 27. 1. Each member of the Security Council shall have one vote.

2. Decisions of the Security Council on procedural matters shall be made by an affirmative vote of seven members.

3. Decisions of the Security Council on all other matters shall be made by an affirmative vote of seven members including the concurring votes of the permanent members; provided that, in decisions under Chapter VI, and under paragraph 3 of Article 52, a party to a dispute shall abstain from voting.
[ ]

CHAPTER VI. PACIFIC SETTLEMENT OF DISPUTES

Article 33. 1. The parties to any dispute, the continuance of which is likely to endanger the maintenance of international peace and security, shall, first of all, seek a solution by negotiation, enquiry, mediation, conciliation, arbitration, judicial settlement, resort to regional agencies or arrangements, or other peaceful means of their own choice.
[ ]

Article 34. The Security Council may investigate any dispute, or any situation which might lead to international friction or give rise to a dispute, in order to determine whether the continuance of the dispute or situation is likely to endanger the maintenance of international peace and security.

Article 35. 1. Any Member of the United Nations may bring any dispute, or any situation of the nature referred to in Article 34, to the attention of the Security Council or of the General Assembly.

2. A state which is not a Member of the United Nations may bring to the attention of the Security Council or of the General Assembly any dispute to which it is a party if it accepts in advance, for the purposes of the dispute, the obligations of pacific settlement provided in the present Charter.

[ ]

CHAPTER VII. ACTION WITH RESPECT TO THREATS TO THE PEACE, BREACHES OF THE PEACE, AND ACTS OF AGRESSION

Article 39. The Security Council shall determine the existence of any threat to the peace, breach of the peace, or act of aggression and shall make recommendations, or decide what measure shall be taken in accordance with Articles 41 and 42, to maintain or restore international peace and security.

[ ]

Article 41. The Security Council may decide what measures not involving the use of armed force are to be employed to give effect to its decisions, and it may call upon the Members of the United Nations to apply such measures. These may include complete or partial interruption of economic relations and of rail, sea, air, postal, telegraphic, radio, and other means of communication, and the severance of diplomatic relations.

Article 42. Should the Security Council consider that measures provided for in Article 41 would be inadequate or have proved to be inadequate, it may take such action by air, sea, or land forces as may be necessary to maintain or restore international peace and security. Such action may include demonstrations, blockade, and other operations by air, sea, or land forces of Members of the United Nations.

Article 43. 1. All Members of the United Nations, in order to contribute to the maintenance of international peace and security, undertake to make available to the Security Council, on its call and in accordance with a special agreement or agreements, armed forces, assistance, and facilities, including rights of passage, necessary for the purpose of maintaining international peace and security.

[ ]

Article 51. Nothing in the present Charter shall impair the inherent right of individual or collective self-defense if an armed attack occurs against a Member of the United Nations, until the Security Council has taken the measures necessary to maintain international peace and security. Measures taken by Members in the exercise of this right of self-defense shall be immediately reported to the Security Council and shall not in any way affect the authority and responsibility of the Security Council under the present

Charter to take at any time such action as it deems necessary in order to maintain or restore international peace and security.

CHAPTER VIII. REGIONAL ARRANGEMENTS

Article 52. 1. Nothing in the present Charter precludes the existence of regional arrangements or agencies for dealing with such matters relating to the maintenance of international peace and security as are appropriate for regional action, provided that such arrangements or agencies and their activities are consistent with the Purposes and Principles of the United Nations. . . .

CHAPTER IX. INTERNATIONAL ECONOMIC AND SOCIAL COOPERATION

Article 55. With a view to the creation of conditions of stability and well-being which are necessary for peaceful and friendly relations among nations based on respect for the principle of equal rights and self-determination of peoples, the United Nations shall promote:

a. higher standards of living, full employment, and conditions of economic and social progress and development;

b. solutions of international economic, social, health, and related problems; and international cultural and educational cooperation; and

c. universal respect for, and observance of, human rights and fundamental freedoms for all without distinction as to race, sex, language, or religion.

[ ]

CHAPTER XI. DECLARATION REGARDING NON-SELF-GOVERNING TERRITORIES

Article 73. Members of the United Nations which have or assume responsibilities for the administration of territories whose peoples have not yet attained a full measure of self-government recognize the principle that the interests of the inhabitants of these territories are paramount, and accept as a sacred trust the obligation to promote to the utmost, within the system of international peace and security established by the present Charter, the well-being of the inhabitants of these territories, and, to this end:

a. to ensure, with due respect for the culture of the peoples concerned, their political, economic, social, and educational advancement, their just treatment, and their protection against abuses;

b. to develop self-government, to take due account of the political aspirations of the peoples, and to assist them in the progressive development of their free political institutions, according to the particular circumstances of each territory and its peoples and their varying stages of advancement;

c. to further international peace and security;

d. to promote constructive measures of development, to encourage research, and to cooperate with one another and, when and where appropriate, with specialized international bodies with a view to the practical achievement of the social, economic, and scientific purposes set forth in this Article. . . .

Chapter XII. International Trusteeship System

Article 75. The United Nations shall establish under its authority an international trusteeship system for the administration and supervision of such territories as may be placed thereunder by subsequent individual agreements. These territories are hereinafter referred to as trust territories.

Article 76. The basic objectives of the trusteeship system, in accordance with the Purposes of the United Nations laid down in Article 1 of the present Charter, shall be:

a. to further international peace and security;

b. to promote the political, economic, social, and educational advancement of the inhabitants of the trust territories, and their progressive development towards self-government or independence as may be appropriate to the particular circumstances of each territory and its peoples and the freely expressed wishes of the peoples concerned, and as may be provided by the terms of each trusteeship agreement;

c. to encourage respect for human rights and for fundamental freedoms for all without distinction as to race, sex, language, or religion, and to encourage recognition of the interdependence of the peoples of the world; and

d. to ensure equal treatment in social, economic, and commercial matters for all Members of the United Nations and their nationals, and also equal treatment for the latter in the administration of justice, without prejudice to the attainment of the foregoing objectives and subject to the provisions of Article 80.

Article 77. 1. The trusteeship system shall apply to such territories in the following categories as may be placed thereunder by means of trusteeship agreements:

a. territories now held under mandate;

b. territories which may be detached from enemy states as a result of the Second World War; and

c. territories voluntarily placed under the system by states responsible for their administration.

2. It will be a matter for subsequent agreement as to which territories in the foregoing categories will be brought under the trusteeship system and upon what terms.

Article 78. The trusteeship system shall not apply to territories which have become Members of the United Nations, relationship among which shall be based on respect for the principle of sovereign equality.

Article 79. The terms of trusteeship for each territory to be placed under the trusteeship system, including any alteration or amendment, shall be agreed upon by the states directly concerned, including the mandatory power in the case of territories held under mandate by a Member of the United Nations, and shall be approved as provided for in Articles 83 and 85.

Article 80. 1. Except as may be agreed upon in individual trusteeship agreements, made under Articles 77, 79, and 81, placing each territory under the trusteeship system, and until such agreements have been concluded, nothing in this Chapter shall be construed in or of itself to alter in any manner the rights whatsoever of any states or any peoples or the terms of existing international instruments to which Members of the United Nations may respectively be parties.

2. Paragraph 1 of this Article shall not be interpreted as giving grounds for delay or postponement of the negotiation and conclusion of agreements for placing mandated and other territories under the trusteeship system as provided for in Article 77.

[ ]

CHAPTER XV. THE SECRETARIAT

Article 97. The Secretariat shall comprise a Secretary-General and such staff as the Organization may require. The Secretary-General shall be appointed by the General Assembly upon the recommendation of the Security Council. He shall be the chief administrative officer of the Organization.

[ ]

Article 99. The Secretary-General may bring to the attention of the Security Council any matter which in his opinion may threaten the maintenance of international peace and security.

Article 100. 1. In the performance of their duties the Secretary-General and the staff shall not seek or receive instructions from any government or from any other authority external to the Organization. They shall refrain from any action which might reflect on their position as international officials responsible only to the Organization.

2. Each Member of the United Nations undertakes to respect the exclusively international character of the responsibilities of the Secretary-General and the staff and not to seek to influence them in the discharge of their responsibilities.   [ ]

UNITED NATIONS PEACE RESOLUTION[1]
November 3, 1950

The General Assembly,

Recognizing that the first two stated Purposes of the United Nations are:

To maintain international peace and security, and to that end: to take effective collective measures for the prevention and removal of threats to the

---

[1] Reprinted from United Nations, General Assembly, *Official Records, Fifth Session, Supplement No. 20, Resolutions,* pp. 10–11, 377(V)A.

peace, and for the suppression of acts of aggression or other breaches of the peace, and to bring about by peaceful means, and in conformity with the principles of justice and international law, adjustment or settlement of international disputes or situations which might lead to a breach of the peace, and

To develop friendly relations among nations based on respect for the principle of equal rights and self-determination of peoples, and to take other appropriate measures to strengthen universal peace,

Reaffirming that it remains the primary duty of all Members of the United Nations, when involved in an international dispute, to seek settlement of such a dispute by peaceful means through the procedures laid down in Chapter VI of the Charter, and recalling the successful achievements of the United Nations in this regard on a number of previous occasions,

Finding that international tension exists on a dangerous scale,

Recalling its resolution 290 (IV) entitled "Essentials of peace", which states that disregard of the Principles of the Charter of the United Nations is primarily responsible for the continuance of international tension, and desiring to contribute further to the objectives of that resolution,

Reaffirming the importance of the exercise by the Security Council of its primary responsibility for the maintenance of international peace and security, and the duty of the permanent members to seek unanimity and to exercise restraint in the use of the veto,

Reaffirming that the initiative in negotiating the agreements for armed forces provided for in Article 43 of the Charter belongs to the Security Council, and desiring to ensure that, pending the conclusion of such agreements, the United Nations has at its disposal means for maintaining international peace and security,

Conscious that failure of the Security Council to discharge its responsibilities on behalf of all the Member States, particularly those responsibilities referred to in the two preceding paragraphs, does not relieve Member States of their obligations or the United Nations of its responsibility under the Charter to maintain international peace and security.

Recognizing in particular that such failure does not deprive the General Assembly of its rights or relieve it of its responsibilities under the Charter in regard to the maintenance of international peace and security,

Recognizing that discharge by the General Assembly of its responsibilities in these respects calls for possibilities of observation which would ascertain the facts and expose aggressors; for the existence of armed forces which could be used collectively; and for the possibility of timely recommendation by the General Assembly to Members of the United Nations for collective action which, to be effective, should be prompt,

A

1. *Resolves* that if the Security Council, because of lack of unanimity of the permanent members, fails to exercise its primary responsibility for the

maintenance of international peace and security in any case where there appears to be a threat to the peace, breach of the peace, or act of aggression, the General Assembly shall consider the matter immediately with a view to making appropriate recommendations to Members for collective measures, including in the case of a breach of the peace or act of aggression the use of armed force when necessary, to maintain or restore international peace and security. If not in session at the time, the General Assembly may meet in emergency special session within twenty-four hours of the request therefor. Such emergency special session shall be called if requested by the Security Council on the vote of any seven members, or by a majority of the Members of the United Nations;

2. *Adopts* for this purpose the amendments to its rules of procedure set forth in the annex to the present resolution;

B

3. *Establishes* a Peace Observation Commission which, for the calendar years 1951 and 1952, shall be composed of fourteen Members, namely: China, Colombia, Czechoslovakia, France, India, Iraq, Israel, New Zealand, Pakistan, Sweden, the Union of Soviet Socialist Republics, the United Kingdom of Great Britain and Northern Ireland, the United States of America and Uruguay, and which could observe and report on the situation in any area where there exists international tension the continuance of which is likely to endanger the maintenance of international peace and security. Upon the invitation or with the consent of the State into whose territory the Commission would go, the General Assembly, or the Interim Committee when the Assembly is not in session, may utilize the Commission if the Security Council is not exercising the functions assigned to it by the Charter with respect to the matter in question. Decisions to utilize the Commission shall be made on the affirmative vote of two-thirds of the members present and voting. The Security Council may also utilize the Commission in accordance with its authority under the Charter;

4. *Decides* that the Commission shall have authority in its discretion to appoint sub-commissions and to utilize the services of observers to assist it in the performance of its functions;

5. *Recommends* to all governments and authorities that they co-operate with the Commission and assist it in the performance of its functions;

6. *Requests* the Secretary-General to provide the necessary staff and facilities, utilizing, where directed by the Commission, the United Nations Panel of Field Observers envisaged in General Assembly resolution 297 B (IV);

C

7. *Invites* each Member of the United Nations to survey its resources in order to determine the nature and scope of the assistance it may be in a

position to render in support of any recommendations of the Security Council or of the General Assembly for the restoration of international peace and security;

8. *Recommends* to the States Members of the United Nations that each Member maintain within its national armed forces elements so trained, organized and equipped that they could promptly be made available, in accordance with its constitutional processes, for service as a United Nations unit or units, upon recommendation by the Security Council or the General Assembly, without prejudice to the use of such elements in exercise of the right of individual or collective self-defence recognized in Article 51 of the Charter;

9. *Invites* the Members of the United Nations to inform the Collective Measures Committee provided for in paragraph 11 as soon as possible of the measures taken in implementation of the preceding paragraph;

10. *Requests* the Secretary-General to appoint, with the approval of the Committee provided for in paragraph 11, a panel of military experts who could be made available, on request, to Member States wishing to obtain technical advice regarding the organization, training, and equipment for prompt service as United Nations units of the elements referred to in paragraph 8;

D

11. *Establishes* a Collective Measures Committee consisting of fourteen Members, namely: Australia, Belgium, Brazil, Burma, Canada, Egypt, France, Mexico, Philippines, Turkey, the United Kingdom of Great Britain and Northern Ireland, the United States of America, Venezuela and Yugoslavia, and directs the Committee, in consultation with the Secretary-General and with such Member States as the Committee finds appropriate, to study and make a report to the Security Council and the General Assembly, not later than 1 September 1951, on methods, including those in section C of the present resolution, which might be used to maintain and strengthen international peace and security in accordance with the Purposes and Principles of the Charter, taking account of collective self-defence and regional arrangements (Articles 51 and 52 of the Charter);

12. *Recommends* to all Member States that they cooperate with the Committee and assist it in the performance of its functions;

13. *Requests* the Secretary-General to furnish the staff and facilities necessary for the effective accomplishment of the purposes set forth in sections C and D of the present resolution;

E

14. *Is fully conscious* that, in adopting the proposals set forth above, enduring peace will not be secured solely by collective security arrangements against breaches of international peace and acts of aggression, but that a

genuine and lasting peace depends also upon the observance of all the Principles and Purposes established in the Charter of the United Nations, upon the implementation of the resolutions of the Security Council, the General Assembly and other principal organs of the United Nations intended to achieve the maintenance of international peace and security, and especially upon respect for and observance of human rights and fundamental freedoms for all and on the establishment and maintenance of conditions of economic and social well-being in all countries; and accordingly

15. *Urges* Member States to respect fully, and to intensify, joint action, in co-operation with the United Nations, to develop and stimulate universal respect for and observance of human rights and fundamental freedoms, and to intensify individual and collective efforts to achieve conditions of economic stability and social progress, particularly through the development of under-developed countries and areas.

N. S. KHRUSHCHEV'S ADDRESS TO THE UNITED NATIONS GENERAL ASSEMBLY[1]
September 23, 1960

[ ]
Our century is the century of the struggle for freedom, the century in which nations are liberating themselves from foreign domination. The peoples desire a worthwhile life and are fighting to secure it.

Victory has already been won in many countries and lands. But we cannot rest on our laurels, for we know that tens of millions of human beings are still languishing in colonial slavery and are suffering grave hardships. . . .

Every intelligent individual gives some thought to what scientific progress, what this great twentieth century, is bringing mankind. Some rightly say that the world has been given new horizons, unlimited opportunities for the creation of abundant material wealth and for the ample satisfaction of human needs. With no less justification, others point to the great danger of scientific and technical achievements being used, not for these beneficial purposes, but primarily for the production of appalling means of destruction. These means of destruction are not being used at the present time. But, in the last analysis, they are produced to be used.

This argument between optimists and pessimists reflects the facts of our times. The most important of these facts is the conflict between two trends or lines of policy in international relations. I am not, of course, referring here to differences in social systems, since this is a domestic issue, which can and must be settled only by nations and States themselves. . . .

---

[1] Reprinted from United Nations, General Assembly, *Official Records, Fifteenth Session*, pp. 68–84.

These two lines of policy in international relations have long been in opposition. Although parallel lines never meet in elementary geometry they may come into collision in international affairs. That would be a fearful moment indeed. Only ten or fifteen years ago, few could predict the outcome of the struggle between these two lines of international policy. In the year 1960, however, only the blind can fail to see how the majority of peoples are becoming more and more positively and plainly convinced of the need to maintain peace.

The peoples of all countries—workers, peasants, intellectuals and the bourgeoisie, excluding a small handful of militarists and monopolists—want not war but peace, and peace alone. And if, therefore, the peoples actively fight to tie the hands of the militarist and monopolist circles, peace can be ensured. . . .

No one can dispute the fact that the Soviet Union has been unsparing in its efforts to ensure the continuation of this welcome trend in the development of international relations. But the sinister forces which profit from the maintenance of international tension are clinging tenaciously to their positions. Though only a handful of individuals is involved, they are quite powerful and exert a strong influence on the policy of their respective States. A major effort is therefore required to break their resistance. As soon as the policy of easing international tension begins to yield tangible results, they immediately resort to extreme measures in order to ensure that the people should feel no relief; they strain every nerve to plunge the world back again and again into an atmosphere of gloom and to exacerbate international tension.

We saw a dangerous manifestation of the work of these forces last spring when the aircraft of one of the largest States Members of the United Nations, the United States of America, treacherously invaded the air space of the Soviet Union and that of other States. What is more, the United States has elevated such violations of international law into a principle of deliberate State policy.

The aggressive intrusion into our country by a United States aircraft and the whole course of the United States Government's subsequent behaviour showed the peoples that they were dealing with a calculated policy on the part of the United States Government, which was trying to substitute brigandage for international law and treachery for honest negotiations between sovereign and equal States. . . .

The flights by the United States spy aircraft are also instructive in another respect. They have shown up the danger to peace presented by the network of United States bases in which dozens of States in Europe, Asia, Africa and Latin America are enmeshed.

Like a deep-seated form of acute infection in a living organism, these bases disrupt the normal political and economic life of the States upon which they have been foisted. They hinder the establishment of normal relations between those States and their neighbours. How, indeed, can there be any question of normal relations if the people of these neighbouring countries cannot sleep peacefully, if they have to live with the threat of being subjected to an annihilating blow whenever the United States militarists take it into their heads to embark on fresh acts of provocation? . . .

United States relations with Cuba are illuminating. As you know, before the victory of the popular revolution, all branches of the Cuban· economy were wholly dominated by United States monopolies which earned vast profits from exploiting the working people of Cuba and the wealth of their fertile soil.

Some people in the United States occasionally like to boast that the standard of living in their country is higher than that in other countries. There is no gainsaying the fact that the standard of living in the United States is now higher than in Cuba, but why is that so? Is it because the Cuban people are less industrious or because the Cuban soil is less fertile? No, this of course is not the reason. The Cuban people are well known for their industry and for their attachment to their country and to their soil. The explanation is entirely different. For many years the fruits of the Cuban people's toil were enjoyed not by the Cuban people but by United States monopolies. Is it therefore surprising that in 1958, for example, the *per caput* income in Cuba was 6.5 times lower than in the United States? This telling fact speaks for itself. . . .

We are all witnesses to the fact that many peoples are being continually subjected to hostile acts and crude pressure by a certain group of States which seek to set at naught the legitimate interests and rights of other countries. This is why the international situation is fraught with acute conflicts, the danger of which is intensified by the mounting arms race.

It is quite evident that international relations cannot continue on such a basis, as that would mean a headlong descent to the abyss. It is the sacred duty of the United Nations to uphold the sovereign rights of States, and to press for the re-establishment of international relations on a sound legal basis and for the ending of the arms race.

Unfortunately, the policy of violating the inalienable rights of peoples is still in evidence in the United Nations itself.

Take, for instance, the question of the representation in the United Nations of the Chinese people. To impede the reinstatement of the People's Republic of China in its legitimate rights in the United Nations, simply because the socialist régime of that State is not to the taste of the leading circles of certain Western countries, and in particular of the United States, is to disregard the facts; it betokens the absence of any desire for a relaxation of international tension; it means that the interests of strengthening world peace and of developing international cooperation are being sacrificed to the narrow political calculations of a small group of States. This situation is inimical to peace and is degrading to the United Nations. . . .

Is the solution of major international problems really conceivable today without the participation of the People's Republic of China? Is it possible to solve these problems without the participation of India, Indonesia, Burma, Ceylon, the United Arab Republic, Iraq, Ghana, Guinea and the other States? If anyone has this idea, let him try to disregard the opinion and the votes of the representatives of the Asian, African and Latin American States here in the United Nations. It is true that the appearance of the new Asian and African States in the United Nations is giving rise to apprehension in certain Western countries. More than that, people are beginning to discuss ways of limiting the further influx of newly-emerging States into the United Nations.

As regards the Soviet Union, I can say frankly that we are glad to see a great number of new States making their appearance in the United Nations. We have always opposed and we shall continue to oppose any curtailment of the rights of peoples who have won their national independence. We share with these States the desire to preserve and strengthen peace, to create on our planet conditions for the peaceful coexistence and co-operation of countries regardless of their political and social structure, in accordance with the peaceful principles proclaimed at the Conference of African and Asia States at Bandung. The facts show that the liberation of nations and peoples under colonial domination leads to an improvement in international relations, an increase in international co-operation and the reinforcement of world peace. . . .

It would be difficult to exaggerate the vast significance which the abolition of the colonial system would have for the entire world. Everyone knows that the economies of the colonies and the Trust Territories are at present subordinated to the mercenary interests of foreign monopolies, and the industrialization of these countries is being deliberately impeded. Imagine that the situation has changed and that these countries and territories, having become independent, are in a position to make ample use of their rich natural resources and to proceed with their industrialization, and that a better life has begun for their peoples. This would lead to a tremendous growth in the capacity of the world market, which would no doubt have a beneficial effect, not only on the economic development of the countries of the East but also on the economies of the industrially-developed countries of the West. . . .

A year has elapsed since the General Assembly adopted the resolution on general and complete disarmament. Having regard to the present pace of life, that is a comparatively long period of time and we need have no doubt that those engaged in the production of weapons and in the perfection and invention of new lethal means have not let it go to waste.

But in the sphere of disarmament not the slightest progress has been made in the past year. What are the reasons for this state of affairs to which we are forced to refer with great regret and serious concern? Who is preventing the implementation of the General Assembly resolution on general and complete disarmament, perhaps the most important and outstanding decision in the history of the United Nations? Who is making it impossible to break the deadlock on the problem of disarmament?

The facts show that the absence of any progress towards the solution of the disarmament problem is the consequence of the position taken by the United States and by certain other States linked with it through NATO.

Throughout the work of the Ten-Nation Committee on Disarmament, the Western Powers refused to start working out a treaty on general and complete disarmament and in every way avoided discussion of the substance of the Soviet programme of general and complete disarmament [A/4219] which the General Assembly had referred to the Committee for detailed consideration. For their part, they made proposals which provided for neither general nor complete disarmament, nor any disarmament at all, but only for measures of control over armaments, i.e. control without disarmament. However, one cannot but see that the establishment of control without disarmament would be tantamount to setting up an international espionage system which, far from contributing to the consolidation of peace, could, on the contrary, make it easier for a potential aggressor to realize his plans which pose a threat to the peoples. . . .

The Soviet Government, together with the Governments of a number of other States, was compelled to suspend its participation in the work of the Ten-Nation Committee which the Western Powers had turned into a screen for concealing the arms race. It was not easy for the Soviet Government to take this decision, because it was precisely our country that had first raised the issue of general and complete disarmament, and had been doing its utmost to achieve in the Committee a constructive solution to the problem, in strict conformity with the General Assembly resolution. In the circumstances, however, staying on in the Committee would only have meant helping the opponents of disarmament. It was impossible to tolerate attempts to make the great cause of disarmament an object of speculation for purposes inimical to the interests of universal peace.

That is why the Soviet Government has placed the question of disarmament before the United Nations General Assembly, a considerable majority of whose members have no interest whatever in the arms race and sincerely wish to see it brought to an end. . . .

The new Soviet proposal on the question of general and complete disarmament, which is based on the provisions of the proposal dated 2 June 1960 [A/4374], submitted by the Soviet Government to all the Governments of the world for consideration, has been drafted with due regard for all the useful ideas expressed in the past year in the course of the discussions on this question in political and public circles in various countries. This proposal goes a long way towards meeting the position of the Western Powers and this we hope will make for early agreement on disarmament.

We now provide, in particular, that all means of delivering nuclear weapons to their targets should be eliminated in the very first stage of general and complete disarmament; we have worked out detailed measures for effective international control at all stages; and we have taken into account the wish of certain Western Powers that, from the outset, there should be provision for reduction in the strength of armed forces and in conventional armaments. We have also introduced quite a number of other amendments to and modifications of our programme. In our view all these amendments render the programme of general and complete disarmament more concrete and even more realistic and practicable. . . .

The Soviet Government is deeply convinced that only a radical solution of the problem of disarmament, providing for the complete prohibition of nuclear weapons together with the cessation of their manufacture and testing and the destruction of all accumulated stockpiles of these weapons, can accomplish the task of delivering mankind from the threat of nuclear war which hangs over it. This is precisely the aim which the Soviet Union is pursuing in consistently and resolutely advocating general and complete disarmament.

All this, in our view, leads to one important conclusion. In order finally to break the deadlock on the disarmament problem, the General Assembly should call to order those who are hindering its solution and are trying to replace business-like negotiations on disarmament by empty beating about the bush. . . .

The peoples of the Soviet Union and the Soviet Government are striving unremittingly to have the principles of peaceful coexistence firmly established in relations between States, and to ensure that these principles become the fundamental law of life for the whole of modern society. There is no communist-devised "trick" behind these principles, but simple truths dictated by life itself, such as that relations between all States should develop peacefully, without the use of force, without war and without interference in each other's internal affairs.

I am revealing no secret when I say that we have no liking for capitalism. But we do not want to impose our system on other peoples by force. Let those, then, who determine the policy of States with a different social system from ours, renounce their fruitless and dangerous attempts to dictate their will. It is time they also recognized that the choice of a particular way of life is the domestic concern of every people. Let us build up our relations having regard to actual realities. That is true peaceful coexistence. . . .

The policy of peaceful coexistence assumes a readiness to solve all outstanding issues without resort to force, by means of negotiations and reasonable compromises. We all know that during the cold war years such questions for the most part did not find a solution, and that led to the creation of dangerous foci of tension in Europe, Asia and other parts of the world.

The Soviet Union considers that, in order to strengthen peace in the Far

East and throughout the world, it is most essential to settle the Korean question.

Only madmen could think of settling the Korean question by armed force. The only correct proposal, namely to leave the solution of the question of the peaceful reunification of Korea to the Koreans themselves with no interference from outside, is finding ever wider acceptance. An essential condition for this is the immediate and complete withdrawal of all United States troops from South Korea, for their presence poisons the atmosphere not only in Korea but throughout the Far East and has made possible such shameful facts as the rigging of elections in South Korea. The proposal of the Government of the Democratic People's Republic of Korea to establish a confederation of North and South Korea is just as reasonable as the proposal of the Government of the German Democratic Republic to set up a confederation of the two German States. It is the only way to lay a sound foundation for the reunification of these States. . . .

We are now firmly convinced that the time has come to take steps to create conditions for an improved functioning both of the United Nations as a whole and of the Organization's executive, working organ. I repeat, the matter relates primarily to the Secretary-General and his staff. We must particularly bear in mind the necessity for certain changes and improvements, with a view to the immediate future. . . .

We consider it reasonable and just for the executive organ of the United Nations to consist not of a single person—the Secretary-General—but of three persons invested with the highest trust of the United Nations, persons representing the States belonging to the three basic groups I have mentioned. The point at issue is not the title of the organ but that this executive organ should represent the States belonging to the military block of the Western Powers, the socialist States and the neutralist States. This composition of the United Nations executive organ would create conditions for a more correct implementation of the decisions taken. . . .

The Soviet Government hopes that the proposals it has raised for questions to be considered at the present session of the General Assembly will meet with support and understanding, since they are prompted by a sincere desire to secure a better life and tranquillity on our planet. . . .

The Soviet Government is ready to do its utmost in order that colonial servitude may be destroyed here and now, that here and now the problems of disarmament may find their concrete and effective solution.

The Soviet Government is ready to do its utmost in order that the testing of nuclear weapons may be prohibited here and now, that this means of mass destruction may be prohibited and destroyed.

It could be said that these are complicated problems and that they cannot be solved at one stroke. But these are problems posed by life itself and they must be solved before it is too late. Their solution cannot be evaded.

In concluding my statement I wish to emphasize once again that the

Soviet Government, guided by the interests of the Soviet people, by the interests of the citizens of a free socialist State, once again proposes to all: let us talk, let us argue, but let us settle the questions of general and complete disarmament and let us bury colonialism that is accursed of all mankind.

[ ]

UNITED NATIONS DECLARATION ON GRANTING INDEPENDENCE TO COLONIAL COUNTRIES AND PEOPLES[1]
General Assembly Resolution 1514 (XV), December 14, 1960

The General Assembly,

Mindful of the determination proclaimed by the peoples of the world in the Charter of the United Nations to reaffirm faith in fundamental human rights, in the dignity and worth of the human person, in the equal rights of men and women and of nations large and small and to promote social progress and better standards of life in larger freedom,

Conscious of the need for the creation of conditions of stability and well-being and peaceful and friendly relations based on respect for the principles of equal rights and self-determination of all peoples, and of universal respect for, and observance of, human rights and fundamental freedoms for all without distinction as to race, sex, language or religion,

Recognizing the passionate yearning for freedom in all dependent peoples and the decisive role of such peoples in the attainment of their independence,

Aware of the increasing conflicts resulting from the denial of or impediments in the way of freedom of such peoples, which constitute a serious threat to world peace,

Considering the important role of the United Nations in assisting the movement for independence in Trust and Non-Self-Governing Territories,

Recognizing that the peoples of the world ardently desire the end of colonialism in all its manifestations,

Convinced that the continued existence of colonialism prevents the development of international economic co-operation, impedes the social, cultural and economic development of dependent peoples and militates against the United Nations ideal of universal peace,

Affirming that peoples may, for their own ends, freely dispose of their natural wealth and resources without prejudice to any obligations arising out of international economic co-operation, based upon the principle of mutual benefit, and international law,

Believing that the process of liberation is irresistible and irreversible and

---

[1] Reprinted from United Nations, General Assembly, *Official Records, Fifteenth Session, Supplement No. 16,* pp. 66–67.

that, in order to avoid serious crises, an end must be put to colonialism and all practices of segregation and discrimination associated therewith,

Welcoming the emergence in recent years of a large number of dependent territories into freedom and independence, and recognizing the increasingly powerful trends towards freedom in such territories which have not yet attained independence,

Convinced that all peoples have an inalienable right to complete freedom, the exercise of their sovereignty and the integrity of their national territory,

Solemnly proclaims the necessity of bringing to a speedy and unconditional end colonialism in all its forms and manifestations;

And to this end
Declares that:

1. The subjection of peoples to alien subjugation, domination and exploitation constitutes a denial of fundamental human rights, is contrary to the Charter of the United Nations and is an impediment to the promotion of world peace and co-operation.

2. All peoples have the right to self-determination; by virtue of that right they freely determine their political status and freely pursue their economic, social and cultural development.

3. Inadequacy of political, economic, social or educational preparedness should never serve as a pretext for delaying independence.

4. All armed action or repressive measures of all kinds directed against dependent peoples shall cease in order to enable them to exercise peacefully and freely their right to complete independence, and the integrity of their national territory shall be respected.

5. Immediate steps shall be taken, in Trust and Non-Self-Governing Territories or all other territories which have not yet attained independence, to transfer all powers to the peoples of those territories, without any conditions or reservations, in accordance with their freely expressed will and desire, without any distinction as to race, creed or colour, in order to enable them to enjoy complete independence and freedom.

6. Any attempt aimed at the partial or total disruption of the national unity and the territorial integrity of a country is incompatible with the purposes and principles of the Charter of the United Nations.

7. All States shall observe faithfully and strictly the provisions of the Charter of the United Nations, the Universal Declaration of Human Rights and the present Declaration on the basis of equality, non-interference in the internal affairs of all States, and respect for the sovereign rights of all peoples and their territorial integrity.

UNITED NATIONS RESOLUTION ON RACE CONFLICT IN SOUTH AFRICA[1]
Resulting from the Policy of Apartheid in the Union of South Africa, April 13, 1961

The General Assembly,

Recalling its previous resolutions on the question of race conflict in South Africa resulting from the policies of *apartheid* of the Government of the Union of South Africa, . . .

Recalling also that the Government of the Union of South Africa has failed to comply with the repeated requests and demands of the United Nations and world public opinion and to reconsider or revise its racial policies or to observe its obligations under the Charter,

1. *Deplores* such continued and total disregard by the Government of the Union of South Africa and furthermore its determined aggravation of racial issues by more discriminatory laws and measures and their enforcement, accompanied by violence and bloodshed;

2. *Deprecates* policies based on racial discrimination as reprehensible and repugnant to human dignity;

3. *Requests* all States to consider taking such separate and collective action as is open to them, in conformity with the Charter of the United Nations, to bring about the abandonment of these policies;

4. *Affirms* that the racial policies being pursued by the Government of the Union of South Africa are a flagrant violation of the Charter of the United Nations and the Universal Declaration of Human Rights and are inconsistent with the obligations of a Member State;

5. *Notes with grave concern* that these policies have led to international friction and that their continuance endangers international peace and security;

6. *Reminds* the Government of the Union of South Africa of the requirement in Article 2, paragraph 2, of the Charter that all Members shall fulfil in good faith the obligations assumed by them under the Charter;

7. *Calls upon* the Government of the Union of South Africa once again to bring its policies and conduct into conformity with its obligations under the Charter.

---

[1] Reprinted from United Nations, General Assembly, *Official Records, Fifteenth Session, Supplement No. 16A, Resolution No. 1598* (XV), pp. 5–56.

THE UNITED NATIONS FINANCIAL CRISIS[1]
Memorandum Submitted by the United States to United Nations Secretary-General U Thant, October 8, 1964

The United States is vitally interested in the survival of the United Nations as an effective institution, and is deeply troubled by the financial crisis facing the Organization.

The crisis is painfully clear. The UN has a net deficit of $134 million.

On June 30 the UN had on its books unpaid obligations owed to governments and other outsiders totaling some $117 million. In addition, it owed to its own Working Capital Fund—which it is supposed to have on hand in order to keep afloat and solvent pending the receipt of assessments—$40 million. Other internal accounts were owed $27 million. Against this total of $183 million of obligations it had $49 million in cash resources, or a net deficit of $134 million.

What does this mean?

It means that the UN does not have the money to pay its debts, and that it would be bankrupt today if it were not for the forbearance of the Member Governments to which it owes those debts.

It means that, unless something is done, the United Nations will have to default on its obligations to Member Governments which, in good faith and in reliance on the UN's promises and good faith, have furnished troops and supplies and services to the UN, at its request, for the safeguarding of the peace. In so doing, these Governments incurred substantial additional and extraordinary expenditures which the UN agreed to reimburse—an agreement which the Secretary General referred to in his statement at the opening session of the Working Group of 21 on September 9 as "the commitment which the Organization has accepted, in its collective capacity, towards those of its Members who have furnished the men and material for its successive peace-keeping operations."

Which are those Governments?

The UN owes significant amounts to Argentina, Austria, Brazil, Canada, Denmark, Ethiopia, Ghana, Indonesia, India, Iran, Ireland, Italy, Liberia, Malaysia, Mali, Morocco, Netherlands, Nigeria, Norway, Pakistan, Philippines, Sierra Leone, Sudan, Sweden, Tunisia, UAR, the United Kingdom, Yugoslavia, and the United States. It is to be noted that 19 of these 29 countries are developing countries.

As the Secretary General said at the opening session of the Working Group of 21 on September 9th, these 29 Members "are surely entitled to expect the United Nations to keep faith with them." For the United Nations

---

[1] Reprinted from *The Department of State Bulletin*, LI, No. 1324 (November 9, 1964), pp. 681–690.

to keep that faith, it must get the money from its Members, for it has no other practicable source.

These 29 countries will suffer if the UN is forced, by the default of the Members which owe it, into defaulting to those which it owes; the entire organization will suffer if it does not honor its just obligations and becomes morally bankrupt.

The 29 Members would suffer by a default, but the real sufferer would be the UN itself. How could an enfeebled and creditless defaulter maintain peace and security? Indeed, how could any institution that had committed such a breach of faith hope long to survive as a credit-worthy and effective organization?

As the Secretary General said at the opening session of the Working Group of 21, "failure to take care of the past may not leave us with much of a future."

What has caused this crisis?

The crisis has been thrust upon the United Nations by those Members which have refused to pay the assessments for the Middle East (UNEF) and Congo (ONUC) operations as voted by the General Assembly in accordance with the Charter. . . .

The United Nations' financial crisis is not an adversary issue between individual Members; it is an issue between those who refuse to pay and the Organization itself, the Organization as a whole. It is an issue which involves the future capacity of the United Nations as an effective institution. If the United Nations cannot collect what is due from its Members, it cannot pay what it owes; if it cannot collect what is due from its Members, it will have no means of effectively carrying on its peacekeeping functions and its economic and social programs will be jeopardized.

The issue is one which vitally affects *all* Members of the United Nations. . . .

The sincere and earnest desire of the United States to find a way out of the United Nations' financial crisis, and to avoid confrontation under Article 19, is evidenced by the repeated attempts it has made to reach common ground.

On March 6 of this year the United States proposed to the Soviet Delegation certain ideas as to the initiation, conduct and financing of future peacekeeping operations which it was hoped—without sacrificing the rights of the General Assembly—would emphasize the *primary* role of the Security Council in peacekeeping and the desirability of according full weight to the views and positions of the Permanent Members of the Security Council and other major contributors to peacekeeping expenses. The United States hope was that agreement as to *future* peacekeeping operations would facilitate the solution of the present problem.

However, despite frequent inquiries as to when a reply to the United States suggestions could be expected, four months went by without any answer. Then in early July, the Soviet Union circulated a memorandum, dated July 10, 1964, which merely repeated the familiar Soviet thesis that only the Security Council has any rights under the Charter with respect to peace-keeping operations, and that the General Assembly and the Secretary General have none. There was no mention of the arrears problem or of any of the ideas the United States had suggested for discussion. . . .

It is recognized that the Soviet Union and certain other States in arrears for UNEF and ONUC have strongly-held views against paying these arrears. However, the example of what other States have done when in a similar position indicates that loyalty to the Organization, respect for the International Court of Justice and the rule of law, and consideration for the overwhelming views of Members, should be overriding. . . .

In 1954 the United States itself faced a somewhat similar predicament in connection with an issue on which it had very strong convictions. This was a matter involving awards made by the United Nations Administrative Tribunal to certain former officials of the United Nations Secretariat. The United States and a number of other countries objected strongly on legal grounds to the payment of such awards by the General Assembly. To settle the matter, the General Assembly decided to seek an advisory opinion from the International Court of Justice. The United States vigorously argued its position before the Court. Nevertheless, the Court handed down an advisory opinion contrary to that sought by the United States.

Despite its strongly-held views on the issue, the United States voted with the majority to act in accordance with the opinion of the International Court of Justice. It was not easy for the United States to accept the majority view as to the issue, but it saw no real alternative if the rule of law and the Charter, as interpreted by the Court, were to be maintained. . . .

The United Nations is faced with a financial and constitutional crisis which must be solved if the Organization is to continue as an effective instrument. The Charter cannot be ignored. Faith cannot be broken. Commitments must be met. Bills must be paid.

The problem is one which is of crucial importance to *all* Members, and a solution can be found only if *all* Members work together in a search for common ground.

The issue is one between (a) the countries that have brought on the crisis by their refusals to pay and (b) the other Members of the Organization. It is now the task of *all* those other Members to get the help of those who have thus far refused to pay in solving the crisis that faces the entire Organization.

[ ]